THE AGE OF ROCK

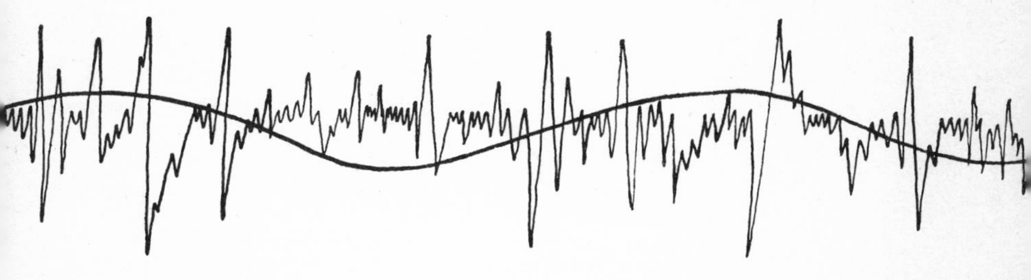

A Reader, Edited by JONATHAN EISEN

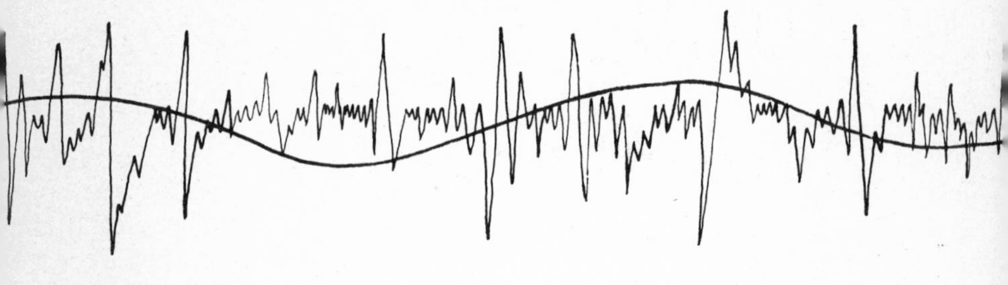

THE AGE OF ROCK

SOUNDS OF THE AMERICAN CULTURAL REVOLUTION

RANDOM HOUSE / NEW YORK

9 8 7 6 5 4 3 2

 Published in the United States by Random House, Inc., New York, and simultaneously in Canada by Random House of Canada Limited, Toronto.

Acknowledgment is hereby made to the following for permission to reprint:

American Quarterly—"Popular Music Since the 1920s: The Significance of Shifting Taste," by H. F. Mooney. Copyright © 1968 by Trustees of the University of Pennsylvania Published by the University of Pennsylvania.

New American Library—"The New Music and the New Scene" from *The Hippies* by Burton H. Wolfe.

Esquire Magazine—"A Hound Dog, to the Manor Born," by Stanley Booth. Copyright © 1968 by Esquire, Inc.

Jazz and Pop—"The Scene" and "Frank Zappa Interview," by Frank Kofsky.

The American Scholar—"Like a Rolling Stone," by Ralph J. Gleason. Copyright © 1967 by Ralph J. Gleason.

Cheetah—"Groupies: A Story of Our Times," and "Underground Radio," by Tom Nolan. "Captain Pimple Cream's Fiendish Plot," by Harry Shearer, "In Person: The Mothers of Invention," by Doon Arbus.

Nova—"I Used to Think I Was Really Ugly," by Fred Newman.

New Left Review—"Stones/Comment," by Alan Beckett and Richard Merton. "Rolling Stones," by Michael Parsons.

New Society: The Weekly Review of the Social Sciences, London—"Arts in Society: John Lennon's School Days," by Michael Wood. Used by permission of the copyright holder, *New Society*.

Columbia University *Forum*, fall, 1967, Vol. X, No. 3—"The Music of Sound or, the Beatles and the Beatless," by Joan Peyser. Copyright © 1967 by The Trustees of Columbia University in the City of New York.

Washington Post—"Beatles Not All that Turned On," by Alan Aldridge.

New York Post: "The Beatles," by Murray Kempton. Reprinted by permission of the *New York Post*. © 1966 by New York Post Corporation.

The New York Review of Books—"The Music of the Beatles," by Ned Rorem. Copyright © 1968 by Ned Rorem.

Partisan Review—"Learning from the Beatles," by Richard Poirier. Copyright © 1967 by Partisan Review.

Harper & Row, Publishers—"New Music in a New World," by Wilfrid Mellers. Abridged from pp. 140–150, "The New Music in

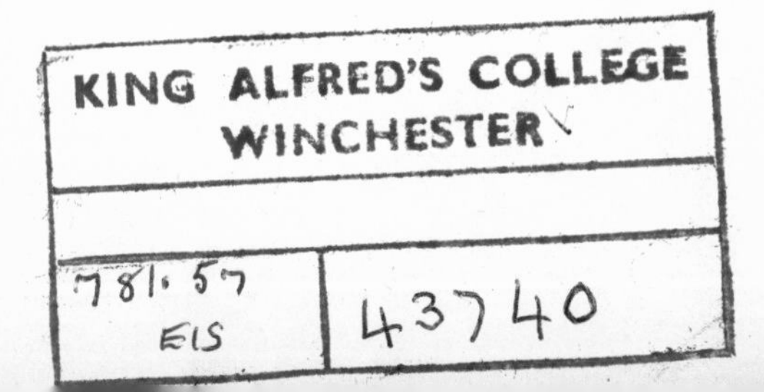

Manufactured in the United States of America
by The Colonial Press, Clinton, Massachusetts

In memory of Richard Fariña

To all the rock groups, the sine qua non *of this anthology, but especially to the Grateful Dead, Simon and Garfunkel, the Beatles, the Pink Floyd. Not to omit Frank Zappa, the King of Hair, the anti-guru of all time. Also, to Alice Mayhew, my editor, who has patience and a well-honed sense of the extraneous; to Pat Finlay, for love and support and criticism; to Jean Strouse, for her help and commiseration; to Margaret Wolf, for all sorts of assistance above and beyond. Lastly, thanks to Jahn Sanders, for her capable editing and general acuity.*

CONTENTS

INTRODUCTION

● In the 1940s rock didn't exist. There was Ellington, the big apple, Glen Miller and the Dorsey Brothers, jitterbugging and Benny Goodman. In the 1950s when people stifled under the dead weight of Joseph McCarthy and went into fits over the benign smile of Ike, they were listening to the stirrings of cool jazz, bebop, crooners in the Crosby tradition, Rosemary Clooney. Rock-and-roll was still inchoate, a faint stirring on the musical scene, struggling to be born. Elvis Presley, Chuck Berry and Bill Haley were setting about to change the world, and radios were playing songs like "Rock-and-Roll Will Never Die," but everyone believed that it probably would. After all, it was the province of the pre-teens, and they would grow up to be like everyone else.

In those days, though, rock-and-roll was easily identifiable. A four-four beat, predictable melodies (with an occasional falsetto thrown in for laughs) and uniformly banal lyrics. A little humor occasionally sneaked into the interstices of moon/June/spoon, as in "Poison Ivy" (which came a creepin' when you were sleepin'). But by and large the fifties were musically Neanderthal. You listened to the music; you were not "turned on" to it. It wasn't a "total" experience; it was diversion, or dance music; you studied to it, perhaps, while parents railed at the imminent possibility of failing grades at school.

The pre-teens didn't grow up just like everybody else. Marshall McLuhan has shown why, and today rock music is as varied—perhaps more so—as any other. There are even several journals such as *Crawdaddy!* which devote full time to exploring the nuances of the music, while nobody even attempts to define it any more. Definitions went out almost simultaneously with rock's coming in; and the kids who are now turned on to it range from ten to past forty, while nobody seems very interested any more in putting labels on what it has become. Born a hybrid of blues and country-western, it is now a full-throated school that incorporates everything from blues to Indian classical raga, from Bach to Stockhausen and Cage. Rock music is now much more than music for its devotees, it is a subculture in the strictest sense of the word—and the term "pop" must be redefined radically.

Richard Fariña, Bob Dylan, the Beatles and drugs are testimony to the fact that rock now must be seen as an art form like any other that arises from and talks to the people in direct, charged and organic ways. The fifties marked the end of the divorce between "art" for those at the top and "circuses" for those at the bottom. Today there is a sense of participation in the air, a sense of involvement with society and with everyone else in one's generation—among the young. This is also true in the musical world where, as Frank Kofsky has shown, there is a less distinct line between the audience and the performer, where there is less and less a tangible effort on the part of a musical-taste elite to impose standards on its listeners, more of a feeling that the music is what the people themselves want to hear—in fact, have themselves created. Nowhere is this more evident than in San Francisco, but it can be felt anywhere. Folk music dispersed guitars as widely as Castro distributed rifles; everybody became a musician. Rock music hastened the process along, while what is fondly called the "new leisure" gave time enough for the new musicians to develop their art, and for the new audience to groove to what was being written. Out of the banality of the fifties emerged the poetry of the sixties, a poetry that, at least until Dylan, was the preserve mostly of English majors, and certainly very few of those outside the university. Now we seem to be back in the days of Chaucer—in a more verbal era when poetry and music are back in the hands of the people.

Nevertheless, it took quite a while for the critics to catch on to what was happening. As recently as 1964, Paul Johnson, editor of the *New Statesman,* was writing that rock music was a plot by the System to exploit the gullible young and to keep them subservient, indolent and stupid. Describing the shape of youth, he wrote that they were a "bottomless chasm of vacuity."

> Their huge faces, bloated with cheap confectionery and smeared with chainstore make-up, the open sagging mouths and glazed eyes, the hands mindlessly drumming in time to the music, the broken stiletto heels, the shoddy stereotyped "with-it" clothes: here, apparently, is a collective portrait of a generation enslaved by a commercial machine.
>
> (*New Statesman,* February 28, 1964)

For Johnson, this was what had become of the socialist hope, the agent for positive social change: mesmerized by a music that left them comatose, content and forever ignorant—the future mainstay of a rapacious, rancid culture.

In several ways the argument is valid: the entertainment industry and its satellites exist not to further the revolution, but to make money, and they exist largely through cultural debasement and the crassest form of exploitation. A billion-dollar-a-year industry, it lives through the propagation of transient tastes and meaningless crazes. But in point of fact there is no consensus in the industry other than to sell, and they will sell antiwar songs and good poetry just as eagerly as they will sell the schlock; they will respond to new popular desires as much as they create them. They can awaken as much as they can mesmerize, enliven as much as they deaden. And there is no denying that the music has been getting better, and is likely to get better still, and in this process may create avenues for the teenagers of modern England to liberate a part of themselves. Johnson himself came close to getting that point when he wrote in the same article that "the teenager comes not to hear but to participate in a ritual, a collective groveling to gods who are themselves blind and empty." The tone is denunciatory, but the implication is otherwise: unwittingly he hit on the central motif of the rock movement—participation. One of the benchmarks of the ascendency of youth in the present decade has been the demand for greater participation in the decisions that affect them personally. This has been a consistent theme in the protest movements, as well as in the protest songs. A kind of visceral anarchism, an antiauthoritarianism has been the result, and its catch phrase has been "doing your own thing." The ritual that Mr. Johnson speaks of is part of the whole thing of being together, enjoying, or in the contemporary argot, grooving to the same music. No music has been able to inspire a greater degree of participation than has rock, except perhaps tribal music, with which rock shares many analogies. To see the ritual as implying a "groveling to gods who are themselves blind and empty" is to miss the point.

Part of the rebellion of youth in the 1960s has involved the attempt to move away from hero worship. One need only look at those who *are* the "heroes" of contemporary youth to see the point. Certainly the teenagers thrill, overtly and sexually, to their demigods, their heroes. But as they move away from the passion of the dance hall and the rock concert, they seem to be moving into greater independence, not greater dependence on charismatic figures. The people they venerate are those like Bob Dylan, who is liked less for his pelvic contortions than for the poignancy and poetry of his songs, and for what is seen as his genuine ability to speak to the needs of a generation alienated from technological, manipulative society. All too often people like Mr. Johnson have sanctioned only the dispassionate; passion was something reserved for the more animal side of human nature, a side which they saw as breeding fascism, nativism and a host of destructive political and social impulses. Freedom in their lexicon depended on rational man entering into a common discourse uninvolved with the coarser, baser instincts. Indeed, the whole framework of Western political thought since the Enlightenment has rested on a repressive theory, one that did not allow for the expression of that which was or could be potentially disruptive. And the experience of the Second World War did not serve to reinforce common trust in the instinctual.

For a generation and indeed a civilization premised on such assumptions, Bob Dylan's statement that he has accepted chaos must seem threatening and portentous of a moral breakdown. Indeed, some exponents of a right-wing point of view have chosen to portray the Beatles as agents of the communist conspiracy. The rock movement in general has taken on that aspect to many who tend to fear the libidinal. The whole movement *is* most involved with the idea that freedom is *not* that which lies in such codes as equal protection of the laws, but in liberating that which has been repressed, even if it means the disruption of the on-going processes of our social institutions.

The communal emphasis must also be reckoned with. Like the search for new forms and definitions of freedom, the rock people—even Mr. Johnson's writhing pre-teenagers—have groped for ways to reconstitute the sense of community. Rock music must not be seen apart from the movement among young people to reshape their lives in ways reflecting their intense disenchantment with societies that seem to thrive on driving people apart from each other and from all but the most vapid, romantic notions of love. As such it is a profoundly *political* form of music, one that opts for a different form of social organization, one that lets people love rather than makes them go to war, lets them accept the chaos and see uncertainty as a legitimate and understandable part of life.

Mr. Johnson is right in his implied feeling that rock is

basically antiliberal. But it does not necessarily follow that rock is therefore authoritarian and destructive of Western values. Young people have, as we learn from observers like Kenneth Kenniston, an intense awareness and respect for the best that is handed down to them: they have an honesty and a respect for the most fundamental meaning of democracy. And these qualities are reflected in their music, which does not rail against everything traditionally cherished, but more often speaks to the hypocrisy by which these values are traduced, and to the ways in which the person is denied in favor of the machine or some other extrapersonal goal. For young people liberalism has become a discredited ideology, interested more in propping up an illegitimate state that reigns terror on innocent hamlets in Vietnam than in making life better, more tolerable and more beautiful at home. Rock music was born of a revolt against the sham of Western culture: it was direct and gutsy and spoke to the senses. As such it was profoundly subversive. It still is.

This book, then, is an attempt to explore some of the ramifications of the movement and its music. Rock is definitely a music of revolt, even if that revolt is frequently patternless and inchoate. It is profoundly involved with the search for new categories of thought and action. It does not suffice to say that the old standards are coming down; that is evident. What is important is that new standards are coming up, and that Paul Johnson in 1964, and many others in 1968, were not really aware of their implications or their meaning. Perhaps this book will help explain what's happening, if you don't know what it is . . . There will be no attempt to explain it away: the forces are too diverse for anyone to handle that.

I have not placed as much emphasis on the music of the black community as I have on that of the white. The reasons, I trust, are evident. In recent years young black musicians on the whole have been involved within an entirely different milieu, both social and musical, most of them concentrating on developing greater nationalistic self-consciousness. The electronic music "bag" has been primarily confined to white musicians, with most of the blacks working in the area of jazz and soul. Some of them have become generally known to the rock community and have influenced white musicians: Otis Redding and Aretha Franklin are the most outstanding. Others, like Sun Ra, have evolved new musical forms about which entire volumes like this one could written (see *Black Music* and *Blues Peo-*

ple, by LeRoi Jones; *Urban Blues* by Charles Keil—among others). While by late 1968 there were signs that rock and jazz forms were merging and that soul groups were turning on to electronic music, the two movements were still speaking to different constituencies in different idioms and with different meaning—though with equal infectiousness and intensity.

J. E.

THE AGE OF ROCK

SOMETHING'S HAPPENING AND YOU DON'T KNOW WHAT IT IS, DO YOU, MR. JONES?

●

NAT HENTOFF

"The medium is the message," Marshall McLuhan keeps insisting. Grownups hear fragments of the pounding beat and the electronically raw sound making it in pop music and they don't get the message. The words, it's hard to hear the words. And when they do come through, what are they *saying?* The young talk of Bob Dylan. "What do *you* think of Bob Dylan?" a reporter asks Howard Nemerov, poet and professor to the young. "Mr. Dylan is not known to me. Regrets."

There's no one to tell the adults in the language of the adults what's happening. The only writer who comes close is Ralph Gleason in the *San Francisco Chronicle.* He's been in the territory long enough so that he never says "pop culture." You won't find any maps to that land in *The New York Review of Books* or *Kenyon Review* or *Partisan Review.* (Well, Leslie Fiedler has acted as a guide partway for the readers of PR—"The New Mutants," *Partisan Review,* fall, 1965. But he's telling it from a distance. And so am I. Besides, nobody can go that route for you. You have to listen for yourself. Dig for yourself. Dig yourself.)

But from a distance, you can hear some of the language, musical and others. And while you won't get to think in it if you're the wrong age, you may absorb part of its outer texture. Remember, the printed language can only travel a little way inside. You might try reading this with a transistor radio on. Almost any disc jockey will do, except, of course, those on the "good music" stations.

"The sound," says Gleason, "is the sound of the electronic age, a dissent from older forms. The costumes are a dissent from The Ed Sullivan slick . . . These performers *never* have a nose-bob or cap their teeth. Instead of hiding a so-called bad feature, they accentuate it, like a living caricature." And what of the words, which have to be heard inside the sound, not in books? A songwriter, Malvina Reynolds "Little Boxes," talks of the "flexible, new, lively, American language" in them. British too. It takes listening, she, an adult, adds. "I am a prisoner of logic myself, but logic, like a neat appearance, has been used against the world."

It also takes at least a temporary suspension of the delusion that age makes for knowing, that only an adult's way of seeing, hearing and feeling is where things and people and death are really at. Like Pablo Casals, who called rock-and-roll "poison put to sound," he isn't going to get there. But he doesn't want to go. And Sinatra, who, when rock began to break through, called it a "rancid-smelling aphrodisiac." He stopped being able to go to new places a long time ago.

Even a younger, a little too consciously hip observer like Pete Hamill of the magazines and the *New York Post* looks out of too-old eyes: "There is something elegantly sinister about the Rolling Stones. They sit before you at a press conference like five unfolding switchblades, their faces set in rehearsed snarls, their hair studiously unkempt and matted, their clothes part of some private conceit, and the way they walk and they talk and the songs they sing all become part of some long mean reach for the jugular."

They don't want your jugular, man. Even if you offered it. And who's rehearsed, them or you?

But a look at the Stones as the Stones, not as five unfolding switchblades, may be of some aid on the journey. They started from a distance. Not in age, but in the music. Growing up in London, they found a sound on American records that made visceral sense to them. Records by Negro blues singers. Muddy Waters, Jimmy Reed, Howlin' Wolf. Names still unknown to nearly all the white, and many of the black, American teen-agers who find the Stones' sound makes visceral sense to *them.* It also happened to the Beatles, the Animals, and the other British rock groups who invaded our young, bearing what our young already had but didn't know they had. The Animals picked up on records by Tampa Red and John Lee Hooker. And they were ahead of the white American teen-agers in plunging into the rhythm-and-blues-based pop music of city Negroes their own age—Martha and the Vandellas, and that scene. And gospel singers.

"The real artists," Ringo Starr of the Beatles says like he

oughtn't have to say it, it's so clear to him, "are mainly colored artists. I never did like the Perry Comos or the Sinatras. I don't buy that kind of art. If whites sang like the coloreds did, I'd buy their records." Simultaneously the British groups and Bob Dylan and the Lovin' Spoonful here were growing up, absorbing, so far as they could, black ways of reacting against and into the world. Being young, they were on the outside. Being bright and untied, they could see the naked lunch on the end of the white grownups' forks. Sure, it wasn't the same as living black, but the sound and the feeling in the sound were real, palpable. Not like Sinatra or Como and what they sang about and how they sang it.

It wasn't only black. Since the Second World War and since the end of the ASCAP monopoly (ASCAP writers had the melody, the white, big-city-with-a-doorman melody), other outsiders were coming into the across-the-board pop music scene. Country and western singers. Bluegrass banjo pickers. And more recently, a Johnny Cash, part Cherokee. Out of Memphis into big hits and big money, swapping songs with Bob Dylan as both were making it, and recording an album, *Bitter Tears*, about how few have ever said anything about the civil rights bill applying to Indians. And going to the state of Washington for a march on the state Capitol by the Puyallup Indians who were bugged at a broken agreement by the state concerning their reservation. And the chief, in his speech, using some of the words from Cash's songs.

So for a long time now, the pop charts have been democratized, miscegenated, deregionalized, unclassed. For the first time, without having to search, without having to be a "collector," a buff, all kinds of kids—including the white, middle-class kids in their little boxes—were hearing black and country. They were hearing all kinds of people who couldn't come to dinner or be elected to the school board where they were at physically. Where they were at inside their heads and with each other was their own business. Their parents didn't know anything about that, as *their* parents in turn hadn't. But these kids had different kinds of allies in their music than their parents ever had.

A shame, some of the parents said, and nearly all the old ASCAP songwriters said. A shame, middle-aged hacks in the Brill Building manufacturing this noise and bribing disc jockeys and force-feeding it into our young. But it wasn't like that. The parents didn't even know *that*. The songwriters making it now are young and often are themselves performers in one of the bags we're talking about. The a&r men are getting younger and younger. Sure, bread was passed in different ways, and still is, but no radio station makes it by trying to manipulate today's listeners. The bribery bit is a cultural lag. Old shortcuts die hardest even when they don't lead anywhere any more. You want to connect into what's happening these days, says Dylan, you turn on the radio. You don't go to plays or concerts. That's all dead, or for somebody else who uses old-time language, who didn't grow up with a transistor in his ear. And if the radio station isn't with it, you know that instantly. The radio station can't tell you what to want. You tell them. Except you don't bother. If one station switches to "good music," there are plenty of others that have learned where you are.

But what are they *saying?* "Do you plan to record any antiwar songs?" a reporter asks the Beatles. "All our songs," John Lennon looks at this museumed man, "are antiwar." But do those kids really understand that jumble of surrealism (isn't it surrealism?) in Dylan's *Subterranean Homesick Blues?* "Don't follow leaders," a line in the song says. They understand that.

And Joan Baez, no longer lost back in her vibrato with those distantly tragic British ballads, announces the next number for an audience of the young. "This one is dedicated to President Johnson and his marvelous foreign policy," she smiles. And she sings part of a rock-and-roll hit by the Supremes, "Stop! In the Name of Love."

No, they're not all pacifists. Maybe none is. No, they don't read Martin Buber. And only a very few of them read I. F. Stone or *Studies on the Left*. The thing is, they are, to begin with. And they want to stay that way. You'll get them in the army, but more and more have had it with the abstractions and the abstract emotions. Free World? Christ, they've seen their parents up close. So far as the young know, existentially know, who could be less free? Let me not con you. Most of them will go that way too, later or sooner. And they know it. And the ones who haven't yet been entirely society-broken by school are putting that off for a while. But when they do go that way, they won't be as surprised later as their parents were by how bad it really is. In the decades ahead, look for sales of pills to go UP.

They know where the quicksand is. Beatle Paul McCartney, aren't you at least a little disturbed at the heroes who sent back their Orders of the British Empire because the Queen gave you an M.B.E.? "We think," says new statesman McCartney (party affiliation vague), "it's much better to entertain people and get medals than to kill them and get medals for that." But respect, respect. Where is respect? What of Hector Dupuis, a former Liberal member of the Canadian Parliament, who returned his M.B.E.? "I don't care if Mr. Dupuis eats his medal," says Ringo Starr in self-respect. "For once, young people get an award. What's wrong with that?"

The singers and their listeners still have an illusion of mobility, not having yet been locked in place in the rationalized, the Great Society. We gotta get out of this place, say the Animals. "See my daddy in bed a-dyin', see his hair turnin' gray, he's been workin' and slavin' his life away. He's been workin', workin', work—work."

But they don't have any illusions about peace through strength, the nuclear balance of terror. Can you imagine Dean Rusk moving to a Rolling Stones' record? Or consider the smile with which Robert McNamara would listen to "The Universal Soldier" who "really is to blame" because "his orders come from faraway no more, they come from him and you and me and brother can't you see, this is not the way we put an end to war." McNamara knows better. But those are two different ways of knowing. One with power and one without. What if Bob Dylan ran for office in five years? He won't. He's cut out from politics and protest. He doesn't think anything out there can be really changed. But what if he did? And others with charisma who know the way to put an end to war? Bring the vote down to sixteen. Or to fourteen. But that's an old-time fantasy.

And what is Dylan saying now? In his liner notes for *Highway 61 Revisited,* he's telling about how "when the Cream met Savage Rose & Fixable, he was introduced to them by none other than Lifelessness—Lifelessness is the Great Enemy & always wears a hip guard—he is very hipguard . . . Lifelessness said when introducing everybody 'go save the world' & 'involvement! that's the issue' & things like that & Savage Rose winked at Fixable & the Cream went off with his arm in a sling singing 'summertime & the Livin is easy.' "

And inside the album, in "Ballad of a Thin Man," he's talking to you: "You hand in your ticket and you go watch the geek who immediately walks up to you when he hears you speak and says, 'How does it feel to be such a freak?' and you say, 'Impossible!' as he hands you a bone. Something is happening, but you don't know what it is, do you, Mr. Jones?"

But what is he *saying?* What are all of them *saying?* Ask a psychiatrist, of course. Like Dr. James F. Masterson, head of the Adolescent Out-Patient Clinic at the Payne-Whitney Psychiatric Clinic: "These songs reflect the mood of depression many teen-agers experience, the feeling of loss of old things, of childhood. Children mind losing their childhood."

Why is that, Dr. Jones? What are *you* saying, Dr. Jones?

Try just listening, Dr. Jones. Forget the words. Just move. Come into the beat, like it says in *Time,* the weekly newspeak: ". . . where the sound is so loud that conversation is impossible, the hynotic beat works a strange magic. Many dancers become literally transported. They drift away from their partners; inhibitions flake away, eyes glaze over, until suddenly they are seemingly swimming alone in a sea of sound. Says Sheila Wilson, eighteen, a student at Vassar: 'I give everything that is in me. And when I get going, I'm gone. It's the only time I feel whole.' "

Is that what they're saying? Something about being whole?

"Oh, my God," says Mr. Jones in "Ballad of a Thin Man," "am I here all alone?"

Is it only your childhood you've lost, Mr. Jones?

POPULAR MUSIC SINCE THE 1920s: THE SIGNIFICANCE OF SHIFTING TASTE

●

H. F. MOONEY

In the fall 1954 *American Quarterly*, this writer discussed the significance of shifting tastes in American popular music since 1890. In retrospect it appears that the major trends established over or during the previous seventy years continued into the 1960s. First, the long-range trend away from the blandness, urbanity or introspection of the 1920s and 1930s persisted. Second, the Negroid tone of popular music as well as of jazz was increasingly prominent in "roots" jazz and in rock-and-roll dance music. Third, related to the Negroid tendency, a further plebeianization—to the point of crudeness—undermined older middle-class decorum. Fourth, along with this was a diminution of romantic love, amatory frustration and sentimental brooding or nostalgia. Fifth, the folk-protest vogue paralleled the aggressive "roots" movement in jazz and the general attack on what was called the "middle-class Establishment." Sixth, orchestration of popular songs rejected older standards almost as much as did jazz technique. Seventh, there was a reaction from the sort of music once produced copiously by the nostalgic or melancholy—and often quite sophisticated—urban Jew or Irishman so prominent for several decades among songwriters in New York. Into the vacuum created by what David Ewen calls the "death of Tin Pan Alley" after the 1930s exploded the rock-folks and soul shouts from a score of urban slums throughout the country. The public was predisposed to accept this vulgarization, the latest expression of eight decades of rebellious sensationalism in American popular music beginning with ragtime "coon songs." Thus, popular music after 1930 continued to express long-range tendencies evident by the 1920s or even before. Even so, however, the tastes of the mid-1960s were sufficiently different from those of the 1920s and 1930s to necessitate retrospection.

People in the 1920s and 1930s, as before then, were rebellious in certain ways—rebellious sexually and artistically; and economically as well in the 1930s. Their rebellion was evidenced in a greater infusion of jazz into popular music, and in the growing popularity of colored vocalists and instrumentalists; but it was limited by compromises with middle-class conventions. Most Negroes were little short of outcasts, too poor and too segregated from the mainstream of life to maximally influence taste. Colored musicians were discriminated against in commercial dance orchestras, in radio and, at least until the 1930s, in recording sessions.[1] The prevailing taste in popular music was shaped by a white middle class, self-consciously hedonistic, relatively prosperous at a time when—particularly during the depression of the 1930s—income was so narrowly distributed as to prevent many people from acquiring even necessities. By 1932, the sale of phonograph records had dropped to 6 per cent of the volume of 1927, a year which was itself somewhat below the sales of the postwar months of 1919–20. Small record companies which had catered to the Negro market in the 1920s were wiped out, and the larger companies curtailed or eliminated their "race" (i.e., Negro performers') catalogues as the marginal Negro market was, as usual, the first to dip in any recession.[2] Consequently, the influence of Negro jazz was further minimized. Middle-class Negroes who desired to "come up," as they put it, during the 1930s and the 1940s responded to the smoothly harmonized arrangements of a white Jimmy Dorsey's watered-down jazz. Duke Ellington himself was influenced by Guy Lombardo's "sweetest music this side of heaven," and brought something of the sound of the Roosevelt Hotel ballroom to Harlem. Commercial orchestras of the period around 1920–50 followed more or less the "safe bet"—the aesthetic aspirations of the middle-class market—as did, indeed, most of the big Negro bands. They presented a music which, despite solo variations, emphasized precise, lush, ensemble harmony.[3] The highest compliment most of the public

[1] Neil Leonard, *Jazz and the White Americans* (Chicago, 1962), p. 146.

[2] Roland Gelatt, *The Fabulous Phonograph* (New York, 1955), pp. 191, 208, 246, 255; Leonard, p. 91.

[3] Chadwick Hansen, "Social Influences on Jazz Style," *American Quarterly*, XII (Winter 1960), 501–3; N. Ertegun, "A Style and a Memory," *Record Changer*, VI (July 1947), 7; Leonard, pp. 124 ff. For Ellington's absorption of Lombardo's style, listen to "Creole Rhapsody" (1931), reprocessed in RCA Camden Album CAL 459, *Duke Ellington at the Cotton Club*.

could pay to big-band jazz between 1928 and 1950 was "symphonic" or "advanced." Orchestrations of bands like Boyd Raeburn's, Stan Kenton's, Claude Thornhill's or Elliot Lawrence's (out of which came some of the "cool" musicians of the 1950s) reflected the influence of Debussy, Ravel and the post-Impressionists.

Who were the middle class whose buying tastes thus helped create this trend? One hazards a reasonable guess that they were older than today's record buyers and on the whole higher on the socioeconomic scale. A sale of less than 20,000 records and a sheet music sale of 100,000 characterized a "hit" in the mid-1930s, as contrasted with a record sales of at least 500,000 and perhaps a million twenty years later.[4] Buyers would have belonged largely among the fortunate minority with steady income. In days when one was lucky to have a job even at less than one hundred dollars a month, expenditure of seventy-five cents or even thirty-five cents for a record or a piece of sheet music was limited. Very few, apparently, of the people who bought records desired truly Negro jazz—since, for one thing, even during past "prosperity" they had had so little opportunity to hear it. Radio networks, apprehensive over the reactions of sponsors and public, had exercised a ruthless veto over this "immoral" music. Although the censorship was aimed more at lyrics than orchestrations, it resulted in smoothing out roughness in both. The situation changed somewhat toward the end of the 1930s, when Benny Goodman, after having used the Negro Fletcher Henderson's arrangements for several years, took advantage of increasing liberalism to hire such colored artists as Teddy Wilson. But the times had not changed radically, Henderson was a middle-class Negro with remarkably sophisticated arrangements for that time; and even at that, Goodman carefully "polished" them so as to conform to the standards of European rendition.[5] Teddy Wilson's piano was urbane, light, deftly polished, as was that of the increasingly popular Count Basie. Soon Goodman hired the white Eddie

[4] Gelatt, p. 272; David Ewen, *Life and Death of Tin Pan Alley* (New York, 1964), p. 300; George Marek, "Oh, Dem Golden Records," and Jim Walsh, "Crobsy's . . . Disk Sales," *Variety*, CCV (Jan. 9, 1957), 237, 239. Frank Sinatra recalls that Bing Crosby's popularity in the 1930s was centered among post-adolescents and even older adults. "My Life and My Music," *Life*, LVIII (Apr. 23, 1965), 99.

[5] Marshall Stearns, *The Story of Jazz* (New York, 1956), p. 144; Leonard, pp. 98–100, 122. Leonard's second chapter brilliantly analyzes the tastes of the older middle class and the reasons for its opposition to jazz.

Sauter to develop a rich, very "white" symphonic sound which caught public fancy so well that Sauter developed it further into the "progressive" sound of the highly acclaimed Sauter-Finnegan band of the early 1950s. Seen in retrospect, the very popular orchestral tendencies of the entire period between 1920 and 1950, from Paul Whiteman down to the progressive and "West Coast" movements which looked back at him with scorn, reflected the demand of the urban middle class for a highly refined, quasi-"classical" jazz.

Lyrics no less than orchestrations and vocal style reveal much about the music patrons of the 1930s. Songs like

I get along without you very well—
Of course I do
—except perhaps in spring,
or when somebody laughs like you.[6]

or

Thanks for the memory
Of your lips next to mine
Castles on the Rhine
The Parthenon, and moonlight on
The Hudson river line . . .
Remember the night that we parted
When I got as high as a steeple
But we were intelligent people
—No tears, no fuss, Hooray for Us! [7]

or (from George and Ira Gershwin's "But Not for Me"):

With love to lead the way
I've found more skies of gray
Than any Russian play could guarantee.[8]

were subtle and understated, aimed at an audience of some maturity and education—of at least a smattering of and respect for art history and Maxim Gorky. They were very popular before the lifting of the depression by 1941 and the deepening of

[6] By Hoagy Carmichael. Copyright 1938, 1939 and renewed 1965, 1966 by Famous Music Corp. Lyrics reprinted by special permission of the copyright holder. A typical rendition was by Charlie Barnet's orchestra on Bluebird 10119.

[7] By Leo Robin and Ralph Rainger. Copyright 1937, renewed 1964, by Paramount Music Corp. Lyrics reprinted by special permission of the copyright holder. An original recording has been reprocessed on RCA Camden CA (S) 872e, *Memorable Vocal Performances With the Benny Goodman Orchestra.*

[8] Copyright 1930 by New World Music Corp. Used by permission.

the market in the war and postwar years modified the prevailing taste.

The intense, lovelorn ballad, while it lasted, reflected taste and life in the 1920s and especially the 1930s, when the purchasers of records were older and more middle class—or middle-class aspiring—than those of the 1960s. As such they wanted more adult themes and an often tim-idly "respectable" jazz infused by a "sweet," "harmonious" (or sometimes even "advanced," dissonant), but always *European* tone. Teen-agers made up a relatively smaller segment of the population, and were not as affluent as later. Naturally, best-selling music dealt more fully with the problems of the post-adolescent consumer, as in "Mad About the Boy":

> *Lord knows I'm not a schoolgirl in the*
> *flurry of her first affair . . .*
> *I'm hardly sentimental . . .*
> *I've got to pay my rental and I can't afford*
> *To waste much time.*[9]

Thoroughly middle-class sentiments! Also in deference to middle-class ideas of "taste," the best-selling records of the 1930s were frequently orchestrated like symphonic tone poems. Duke Ellington, and even a highly successful middle-of-the-road white band like Hal Kemp's, attempted to infuse Delius into ballad fox trots.[10] The popular tastemakers of the 1930s appear as somewhat cautious, compromising, middle-class young adults experimenting gingerly with jazz but tempering it with "highbrow" innovations or just sweetly pretty styling.

[9] Copyright 1935, 1962, by Chappell, Inc. Lyrics quoted by special permission of the copyright holder. One of the top eighty or so best sellers in the United States in 1935. See Sigmund Spaeth, *History of Popular Music in America* (New York, 1948), p. 648.

[10] See liner notes on RCA Camden Album 811, *Great Bands of Our Times.* The 1930s emerge as the most "intellectual" period in American popular music. The sales appeal of such songs as "Tender is the Night" and "Moon and Sixpence" was evidently to be enhanced by the titles of Fitzgerald's and Maugham's then new novels. In the late 1930s and early 1940s were concentrated many such adaptations of highbrow music as "Reverie," from Debussy; "Pavanne," from Ravel; "June on the Isle of May," from Tschaikowsky's *Andante Cantabile;* and Victor Herbert's "Yesterthoughts" and "Indian Summer." Tschaikowsky's *Piano Concerto No. 1 in B Flat* furnished "Tonite We Love," and his waltz theme from the *Pathetique* emerged as "The Night is Filled With Music," recorded like the others, as a slow, dreamy fox trot ballad with only the slightest pulsation of the bass fiddle and a light tapping of the cymbal or wire brushing of the drum to accent the rhythm.

This ambivalent generation of 1920–50, which supported ambivalent orchestras like that of Glenn Miller, would have its cake and eat it too. A generation of transition, facing both ways, it compromised between the gentility of the Victorian parlor and the libidinism of the beatnik's pad. If the popular music of its time appealed strongly to young women, then the personality of the girl who bought the music is well expressed therein. The middle-class young woman of the 1920s and the 1930s who had broken her home ties to take a job and an apartment in the city lived in the hothouse of a pseudo-Freudian romanticism. The theme song of the day was, "Love, Your Magic Spell Is Everywhere." And, said the pseudo-Freudian (perhaps sincerely, perhaps just to give the girl the latest "line"), "Love is not love, is not truly, healthily, wholly a giving and receiving, without Sexual Expression." So the girls in their little apartments, with their radios and record players, pulsed with desire unrecognized, unacknowledgeable or unfelt by the sheltered girls of the 1880s. Susceptible and vulnerable, increasingly without real religious convictions, they awaited the Great Experience and Fulfillment of Love (or Sex), listened in glaze-eyed anticipation to songs like "I Surrender, Dear." Singers, catering to the mood, moaned with frustration, "Blue Evening (After a Lonely Day)." There was the frustration of balked expectations; there was also the painful anxiety, the fear of losing love—("How Long Will It Last?" "Why Can't This Night Go On Forever, Why Must the Morning Find You Gone?"); [11] and finally, the denouement, the last bitter dregs of what had turned out to be mere sex without love—the brush-off, the awakening, the sobbing; but still so often the assertion that love had redeemed the whole sordid affair, as in Libby Holman's number, "I'm Doing What I'm Doing for Love," [12] and in Grace Hayes's 1930 recording of "My Lover."

And while I live, I'll want him madly;
I'm not ashamed to admit it.
All I could give I gave him gladly;
And I'm not sorry I did it.[13]

[11] An elegant 1932 recording of the latter is reprocessed on RCA Vintage LPV 504, *The Great Isham Jones.*

[12] Recorded on Brunswick 4459. An original pressing is in the Archives, Stanford University Music Library.

[13] Copyright 1930 by Advanced Music Corp. Used by permission. Recorded on Victor 22381.

Such ballads reveal the interwar mood. In the 1920s and 1930s middle-class girls were not prone to "play around" for the fleshly joy of it. Despite an increasingly rebellious promiscuity, the code was still tinged with the ideals of monogamous love—that is, sex could be truly good and beautiful, truly redeemed, only if part of a romantic love affair. If not chastity, if not marriage, there must be Love. And this love must be, as in a marriage, monogamous, exclusive, rather than "cheap," promiscuous. In the words of the song from Sigmund Romberg's operetta *Desert Song* (1926): "One Alone." In short, something of Victorian sentiments remained. Love was not to be treated casually. One might defy the Victorian double standard, but must uphold Victorian courtly fidelity. Such songs compromised in lyrics, orchestration and vocal rendition between the sacred and the profane, the "high class" and the low-down, the refined and the sensual. They approached Sex obliquely—"Tonight is Mine," "One Night of Love." The raw blues feeling underlying a ballad like Ruth Etting's "What Wouldn't I Do for That Man?" was refined by a soft vocal, a limp saxophone, violin and piano accompaniment.[14] Apparently girls who wanted love, both sacred and profane, were attracted toward a music appropriately ambivalent.

By 1960 the climate had changed. One reason for the shifting taste was a change in the music business. By 1941, the virtual monopoly of the ASCAP (American Society of Composers, Authors, and Publishers, organized in 1914), which had practically protected New York's ascendancy in the music market, was broken by legal judgment. The consequent opening of broadcasting and recording channels to non-ASCAP composers and publishers, many of them unknowns outside the conventional music establishment of Tin Pan Alley and catering to a wider public of newly affluent people—Negroes, workers who had migrated from rural areas, especially in the Southeast and Midwest to urban war jobs—marked the end of an era of increasingly urbane New York composers. These had been heavily Jewish. In 1930, for example, out of the forty-one hits listed in Sigmund Spaeth's *History of Popular Music in America,* seventeen were written by composers and/or lyricists with names *recognizably* Jewish.[15] Especially after 1945, how-

[14] The original recording, along with others of the period and genre, is reprocessed in Columbia Album C3 L35, *The Original Sound of the Twenties.*

[15] Pp. 641–42.

ever, the dispersal of composing and publishing throughout the nation tended to diminish their influence at a time when middle-class values had been weakened by war. Such New York Jews as Harold Arlen, George and Ira Gershwin, Jerome Kern, Vernon Duke (né Dukelsky), Herman Hupfeld and Vincent Youmans had produced a pensive music of finesse and polish, often using minor strains in the cantorial tradition. Their melodic concepts influenced "white" jazz instrumentalists—themselves frequently Jewish—flowing with increasing facility through plaintive but delicately restrained saxophones from Benny Kreuger in the early 1920s through Frank Trumbauer to Stan Getz; and through the arabesque clarinets of Benny Goodman and Artie Shaw. Until midcentury, immigrant and other minority groups, particularly in New York City, who as they rose became so influential in popular music, embraced standards still admired by many of the American middle class and by a more middle-class-aspiring lower class. The years 1920–50 were still much closer than our own to traditional WASP values. This is one reason why it was so difficult for Negro jazz to make greater headway. Aspiring Negro artists, jazz as well as nonjazz—Marian Anderson, Paul Robeson, Ellington, Henderson—themselves rejected much of the raw, gutty blues of an embarrassing past in favor of a concert style. The New York Jew and Negro, raised in the early years of the century—especially before Harlem became so largely a slum for ex-field hands from the South—were still awfully respectful of what some of their grandchildren would later call the "square" or "ofay" world of the symphony, of refinement and gentility. Indeed, there is evidence that even the more contemptuous Negroes of the 1920s adopted the "sweet" tones of pseudo-"classical" middle-class music because they were determined to beat the white man on his own grounds as a performer.[16] Regardless of their motives and outlooks, songwriters and orchestrators, white and colored, adapted the Negro idiom to the gentility of their aspirations and/or to the tastes of the white middle class, who after all purchased so many leisure-time products, including music. It may have been true that both Negro and Jew had a certain common sense of alienation, a common bitterness or sadness, and a mutual empathy; but since they also both admired the culture of the Establishment whose doors they were forcing, their music, however, sad, alienated

[16] Hansen, pp. 496, 500.

or bitter, had nevertheless passed through a "refining" process. Excellent examples of this are, again, Benny Goodman's music; and such performances as Duke Ellington's 1940 recording of Harold Arlen's "Stormy Weather," with Ivy Anderson's subdued (by 1960 standards) vocal.[17] But, encouraged by the breakdown of ASCAP's hegemony and by prosperous new markets among formerly depressed and minority groups, rival publishing and recording companies had arisen by 1950 in many other, frequently less sophisticated localities—the Negro slums of Chicago, Los Angeles, Philadelphia and Oakland and the rural-music center at Nashville, Tennessee, where Negroid and country music fused into Roy Orbison's "rockabilly" or "folk-rock." Many of the typical million-plus sellers in the 1950s and early 1960s were written, published and/or recorded in such new centers. From Louisville, Kentucky, came "Slow Poke." From Nashville, Patti Page and "Tennessee Waltz"; Jimmy Dean's "Big Bad John"; Hank Williams' "Cold Cold Heart" and "Jumbalaya"; "Your Cheatin' Heart"; "Half as Much"; and the Everly Brothers' "Bird Dog." "Rose and a Baby Ruth" came from Chapel Hill, North Carolina; "This Old House" from Arcadia, California. Such early rock numbers as "Rock Around the Clock" and "A Whole Lot of Shakin' Goin' On," originated in Philadelphia,[18] later, from the Portland, Oregon, area came "Looie, Looie, Looie, Ya, Ya, Ya."

These titles amply suggest a trend. There were no references to the Russian drama, to Penthouse Serenades, to Park Avenue Fantasies, Stairways to the Stars or to the Parthenon. The nation was apparently too prosperous to glamorize wealth and highlife, and too juvenile, too aggressively lowbrow or pseudo-lowbrow to admire "polished" or high-flown songs: many lower-class and minority-group high school students now *hated* the middle-class culture which they felt was being forced on them. Then too, cold war nationalism may have stimulated a marked taste for tunes with a folksy, grass-roots flavor. True, middlebrow holdouts for the old "culture" might in the early 1950s cling to Mantovani's "Shimmering Strings," but a decade later, even the worst "squares" had shifted to the Tijuana Brass, which in its own banal way leaned more to the Big Beat of the 1960s than toward the pseudo-"classic" modulations of the early 1940s. If any doubt remains about a change in mood between 1941 and 1966, the contrast between Herb Alpert and Gene

[17] Columbia 35556.
[18] Ewen, pp. 328–29.

Krupa's recordings of "Flamingo" tells the story.[19] During the period 1940–60, not only had many of the urban middle class become antibourgeois themselves, but also many buyers now came from newly prosperous segments of the population less influenced by WASP standards to begin with. Minority groups who shared in rising affluence and leisure were able in larger numbers to demand *their* kind of music. Negroes in particular, thronging from the rural South into Northern cities, intensified a demand for the gospel shouts and rough-edged blues which helped change the tone of urban popular music. Even the poorer among them, filled with a new sense of pride, were aware of grievances, bitter against whites, anxious to support Negro artists and Negro music. By 1960 they were at least prosperous enough, and sufficiently concentrated in cities, to nourish a demand for a self-consciously "black" music performed by black entertainers. Negroes had become purveyors of and consumers of a musical product which aggressively emphasized their "roots." An active and even violent black protest supported within and outside the Negro minority was reflected in the scorching heat, the volume, the drive, the guttiness, the slurred tones of "soul" or "roots" or "funky" jazz, as well as in rock-and-roll and in gospel shouts.[20]

Such music, which blacks in particular created, appealed to youth generally by 1960. Protest, rebellion, the muscular-visceral approach to music, the dance, to life itself, is of course typical of the adolescent and the very young adult at any time. By the later 1950s, youngsters were a relatively larger segment of the population than ever before in the twentieth century. They were also more prosperous than before as their parents' earnings and their own job opportunities increased. They were now catered to as consumers. Although relatively prosperous, they appeared to lack a sense of identification with the adult world. They were restlessly seeking status, pleasure, self-expression, sometimes an answer to the problems of the world. Such seeking brought them into conflict with the adult world. They were almost a minority group of their own. In 1959, Arnold

[19] Krupa's 1941 record is Okeh 6120. An original pressing is in the Rodgers and Hammerstein Archives of Recorded Sound of the New York City Public Library.

[20] Archie Shepp, tenor saxophonist with the late John Coltrane's 1963–66 group, tended to identify his music with the struggles of his black people, in particular with Black Nationalism, according to Martin Williams, "The Problematic Mr. Shepp," *Saturday Review*, XLIX (Nov. 12, 1966), 90.

Shaw found the major market for popular music to lie between the ages of nine or ten and seventeen or eighteen, among youngsters who were much less demanding of intricacy, restraint, nuance or polish than were a previous generation of older buyers.[21] These were the youth who "bopped" to the Big Beat of rock-and-roll, and who sang "Yakety Yak," a flippant take-off on parental discipline. Such lyrics as could be heard in the gregarious din of vocal groups of the late 1950s and early 1960s were often mindlessly extroverted expressions of the gang—"Yeah, yeah, yeah"—the lyrical equivalent of the teenagers' private street corner or drive-in banter. Nobody who bought "Rose and a Baby Ruth," one of the more tender and romantic songs of 1957, seemed to laugh at its bathos, so appropriate was it to a pre-adolescent taste—the same taste which brought out the little sensation seekers to gape at *Teen-Agers From Outer Space.* The somber, heavily orchestrated, introspective ballads of the young adults of the 1930s were passing out of the major trend.

So much for the obvious. The trend was away from suavity, however, not only in this music for children, but also to an extent in the jazz which had become a cult of many intellectuals. To a certain degree, jazz is always visceral; and to a certain degree, the popularity of visceral music among both adolescents and rebellious intellectuals is nothing new in the twentieth century—it has been, in fact, a long-range trend since the ragtime of the 1890s. But modifications in jazz as well as popular music after around 1954 appear significant, coming as they did at the height of the extremely irrationalist "white Negro" or "beatnik" movement among young writers. The anti-intellectual intellectuals followed Norman Mailer and Jack Kerouac, and then Norman Brown and Timothy Leary, into the outer reaches of thrill or even violence. By 1960, a searingly intense "hard bop" or "soul music" was crowding the chamber-music sound of the post-progressive cool or West Coast jazz. To be truly arty in the early 1960s, one had to be glandular.[22]

[21] "Mr. Harper's After Hours," *Harper's,* CCXVIII (May, 1959), 82.

[22] Thus, tenor saxophonist Stan Getz, once acclaimed in 1955 as "subtle" (liner notes of NorGran Album NGN 1032, *West Coast Jazz*) was acclaimed in liner notes of 1963 as "having a more mature emotionalism . . . a gutsy maleness" (Verve Album V/V6-8545, *Getz-Gilberto*). In the early 1960s it was indeed impossible to be *subtly* male—one must wear horsehide boots—or *subtly* feminine—one must wear barbaric globs of eye make-up and great varnished swirls and swatches of hair.

Taste ran to a big, honking, stomping, earsplitting saxophone, heavier beat, shrieking revival shouts, recordings bursting with the din of screaming teen-age togetherness. The unobtrusive Maxine Sullivan and Connie Boswell of the 1930s; the Modernaires, Pied Pipers, Jo Stafford, Margaret Whiting, Mel Torme and June Christy of the "slick" 1940s; the husky-dreamy Julie London and Johnny Mathis, the Hilos and the Honey Dreamers and the Four Freshmen and other richly-chorded precision groups who held their popularity well into the 1950s despite a reversal in taste—all these were by 1960 paled by the church revival mood of the Clara Ward singers, Mahalia Jackson, Timi Yuro; or by the often inarticulate shouts of the transistor-set favorites—the Supremes, the Orlons. Popular music, often used as a psychedelic experience, became a "happening," a numbing bombardment of the auditory nerves. On whatever cultural level one might look, to Rojack of the *American Dream* or to James Bond, there must be rawness, constant stimulation. A primitive emotionalism (nonsentimental) must make no compromises with WASPishness in life, literature, music. The "well-adjusted," modal personality, the middle-class "average guy," was Out. Bing Crosby or Perry Como's accommodating, casual pleasantness was anathema: sweat and suffering made an artist popular in the early 1960s. He must, it would appear from the record jackets and liner notes, bear the stigma—or the stigmata, really, in the new religion of the Holy Barbarians—of Alienation from a crucificial Society—a Society composed of Crosbys and Comos with their casual tweeds and pipes and not-so-casual homes in Belair, their golf matches and stables of horses. Crosby and Como were passé in a period which sang, "Here's to the Losers." Perhaps the first indication of the change had been Johnny Ray's "Cry" in 1951. At any rate, music of the sort young people felt WASP over thirty would sing, compose or listen to, went into a decline. The liner blurbs, intended to sell records at first sight, spoke less of the home and family of the performer than of his "searchings," his bitterness, his inability or refusal to accommodate to the Establishment, his mental and/or physical handicaps or deviations, his daemonic immersion in environment-obliterating alcohol, sex or drugs. Such a recitation might in whole or in part apply to many of the folk heroes, or antiheroes (musical and nonmusical) of the 1960s—Ray Charles, Billie Holiday, Parker, Mailer and his Rojack, Brendan Behan, Bob Dylan, Thomas (did the identification of the folksinger's family name with the given name of the early-deceased alcoholic poet stimulate his popularity?). The stale remnants of the placid "boy-and-girl-next-door" singers of the 1930s could hardly compete with the lacerated, gorgeously uninhibited wailing of Ray Charles—blind, drug addicted, low class, black, and—needless to say, to the old middle class, thoroughly disreputable—with his "Get Your Buddy, and Go Get Stoned." A period in which the three leading playwrights were said to be militantly if obliquely homosexual in their work and, partly because of this, were extremely popular; a period, in short, of rising nonconformity, deviation and some sympathy for minorities, would find in Charles a welcome personification of the Outcast. The years of James Baldwin and LeRoi (*The Toilet*) Jones heard the violently surging saxophonic "sheets of sound" of John Coltrane, the explosive reed of Ornette Coleman. The suave colored singers of the 1940s and earlier 1950s who had accommodated to the white hotel-and-club world—Billy Eckstine, Sarah Vaughan, Lena Horne, Ella Fitzgerald (now much too poised and benignly self-possessed) were not much imitated among younger singers—a sure sign of obsolescence. Instead, Dinah Washington, Della Reese, Roy Hamilton, Brook Benton and Hank Ballard set the trend for the Chubby Checkers, Don Covays, Dee Dee Sharps and Sugar Pie Depintos who sang ever more intensely "black." All were Negro. In quantity as well as in vocal quality, singers were now substantially—and proudly—black. Into the 1950s most singers had been white, and on the whole, rather tepid crooners. By the mid-1960s Petula Clark, one of the few top white singers, sang "soul" like blacks, which meant a full-throated openly emotional delivery such as few white or black singers had demonstrated in the past. Indeed, it had not been as greatly demanded in the past. But by 1960 the old stiff-upper-lip Calvinist distrust of emotional expression had softened more than ever before. The grim lips relaxed and opened. Songs were shouted. The older ideal of the clean-cut crew-cut Nordic hero, silently self-controlled, was shrinking, along with the phase of conformity expressed in 1954's "Counting My Blessings." Music, like the film, documents a resurgent rebellion in the mid-1950s. James Dean, Elvis Presley, Sal Mineo—all were white, to be sure, but, like Mailer's "white Negro," dropouts from the WASP world who foreshadowed the popularity of Ray Charles's "Crying Time." Here was a *man* sobbing, and he was a glamorous youth hero on account of it. And unlike his less evocative predecessor, Johnny Ray, he was black.

By the 1960s, then, the bland "white" vocal was passé. And so was the polished "white" orchestration. The typical rock group of the late 1950s and early 1960s—amplified guitars, percussion, saxophone—was designed for rhythm and individual variations rather than for tone color. It dispensed with *fortissimo-pianissimo* modulations and played one way—loud. Never had such primitive jazz been exploited with such wide success among whites as well as Negroes. Even the more advanced jazz of the 1960s, which utilized the intricate techniques and rhythmic complexities of the bop revolution, also emphasized beat, solo variations and rhythmic experiment more than harmonics and modulation. Such a trend reflected the Negro's pride in his own roots, his "funky" contempt for white aesthetic standards; and also appeared to indicate that many whites as well, ashamed of or resentful of WASPishness, were seeking in music what some of them sought in LSD, a piling up of new sensation upon sensation to smash their Square prison.[23]

It would of course be naïve to call all this "new." Change, rebellion, the distortion or smashing of old forms, has long been a part of American culture. Change is the rule. Much of the change of 1960 was really a continuation of trends begun at least by the 1890s—the elevation of the once-degraded, the degradation of the once-elevated, the rebellion against older values. *Plus ça change, plus le même chose.* The intellectual and plebeian revolt against the middle class had by 1960 turned full blast against the generation of 1920–50, themselves once rebels of a sort now passé. The rejection of the big, white-stylized, highly arranged "swing" orchestra (once thought to be so untrammeled!) in favor of smaller, cruder groups; indeed, in favor of one singer and his guitar—the epitome of individualism—came when youth was attracted by the anarchism of Paul Goodman. Joan Baez's folksinging could be seen as a rebellion against the kind of society which had produced the Big Bands of the previous generation, where musicians had been straight jacketed into an Organization formula aimed at

[23] From liner notes by LeRoi Jones for Impulse Album A50, *Coltrane Live at Birdland* (1963): "The long tag of 'Afro-Blue,' with Elvin [Jones, drummer] thrashing and cursing beneath Trane's line, is unbelievable. Beautiful has nothing to do with it, but it is (I got up and danced while writing these notes, screaming at Elvin to cool it). . . . The crashing cymbals, bombarded tom-toms . . . [are] like the wild pulse of all living." Regarding another selection in the album, called "Alabama," he wrote: "If that real Alabama was the catalyst, more power to it, and may it be this beautiful, even in its destruction." Sorel had Arrived.

profits more than freedom, improvization, "soul." [24] If youth in the 1960s often tended to reject large organizations, the depersonalized, self-effacing vocalists who in the 1930s and 1940s had been merely components of the big orchestras were now scarcely heard among the folk and church-revival singers.

The immense popularity of the church-revival mood also suggested a return to or reformulation of "religion." Youth, never more millenarian than in the early 1960s, had rediscovered mysticism, the shared but intensely individual purification of the psyche through hallucinogenic "trips," which somehow suggested the transports of the old tent meeting. To those who, like Dr. Timothy Leary, searched for a transcendental "spiritual discovery," the soul singing of Sister Odetta could fill a need unsatisfied by delicate secular love ballads. Young people bored by what one critic called the "dessicated" cool jazz of the 1950s bought John Coltrane's best-selling album, *A Love Supreme* (Impulse A/AS 77), whose liner notes consisted of Coltrane's devotional poetry.[25]

The love music of the 1960s, sacred or profane, was not much like that of a previous generation. Of course, in all ages men sing of love, and so they did in the 1960s, sometimes with a lachrymose sentimentality which in itself catered to a different level of taste than did many of the brittle ballads of the 1930s. Nevertheless, sentimental love songs, lachrymose or otherwise, declined in popularity. Love lyrics were often so hopelessly submerged in and mangled by arrangements aimed primarily at rhythmic effect that observers could easily conclude that the love song as they remembered it had all but disappeared.[26] Certainly boys didn't worship girls in such 1942-style effusions as "You Are a Poem Set to Music." Nor did girls much attempt to promote this sort of veneration. If one heard fewer "pretty songs" one saw fewer girls in "pretty dresses,"

[24] According to Miss Baez, her simple vocal-with-guitar rejected the "commercial." "The Folk Girls," *Time,* LXXIX (June 1, 1962), 40.

[25] A college student editor, Peter B. Riley, notes that the "tough" sound of such groups as the Butterfield Blues Band (called the "Marat/Sade of Blues") "seems to act on some people in the manner of an aural LSD." *Recorder* (Central Connecticut State College), Feb. 28, 1967, 3:2. Similarly, a review of another John Coltrane devotional album, *Meditations,* says "I *feel* this. . . . It opens up a part of myself that is tightly closed. Seldom recognized emotions well up and sear my consciousness." Don DeMicheal in *Downbeat,* XXXIII (Dec. 1, 1966), 28.

[26] See for example, Tom Prideaux, "Whatever Happened to Love Songs?" *Life,* LXI (Sept. 16, 1966), 61–62.

even on Sundays. A sexually more casual generation appeared to reject the tradition of chivalric *amour*. They might be aggressively sensuous and sensual, but casually so, and not with the great daintiness or delicacy which had once characterized days of a stronger double standard and sense of sin. They were more direct and companionate in the minidress, car-coat-and-Levis era. God's death, or at least the weakening of Pauline concepts of deity, evidently meant you could junk much of your Platonism and let yourself go.

The noticeable dip in the popularity of the exclusive type of love song among many younger buyers cannot be traced to any one simple cause. A decline in traditional religion probably played a part. If God were not dead, He was, at least to the "hip" culture, a God created in man's image, a "swinger" to be found in "gay" bars and in jazz-happening services. As such, He did not demand chaste refinement in music. His demands of human nature were few, but He did demand of his flower children a communal love rather than middle-class monogamy. At any rate, many youths, whether "hip" or not, and particularly among the middle class, caught the spirit. They desired greater sexual freedom. They rejected the (to them) hypocritical compromises, the puritanical indirection, and often the exclusiveness as well, of many of the older ballads. For them, the egocentric, monogamous lyrics, the bourgeois-plushy orchestrations of even the passionate "Body and Soul" sort of thing was, as they would put it, "beside the point." The older love song, even the more sensual, no longer caught on. After all, among many students, particularly in the first half of the 1960s, sexual revolt was but part of a much wider rejection of middle-class mores and prejudices. It was part of a fervent attempt to regenerate man. Youthful energies flowed out toward social reconstruction—"We Shall Overcome"—or into the purification of or expansion of the individual psyche through hallucinogens —"Puff, the Magic Dragon," "The Trip." Such youth stressed the one-ness of mankind, the overcoming of the crippling guilt feelings imposed by an artificial Establishment. They opposed the middle-class mores of their parents, often attributing these to the egocentricity of Western civilization; and some turned to their version of a pantheistic Buddhism as a cure for the ills of the West. (Thus the "acid rock" emanating from San Francisco's Hashbury was infused with the raga of an oriental culture considered beatific by the hippies.) The more activistic youth in the 1960s, puritanical hedonists or hedonistic Puritans who equated sensual pleasure (widely diffused) and self-expression with cosmic betterment, saw in love not a misty-eyed, pallid, etherealized retreat from the world but a means of social regeneration. (At least so went the gospel of Lawrence Lipton's *Erotic Revolution.*) These outlooks hardly promoted the popularity of such old musical standards as "When Your Lover Has Gone." All compromise with artificial bourgeois social and sexual barriers must go—among these compromises, the romantic ballad of the past. If the middle-class record purchasers of the previous generation had stressed monogamy within or without marriage, the new, young communalists rejected songs which sentimentally glorified one girl. A new world could not be built upon middle-class hypocrisy, possessiveness, exclusiveness. This dislike of the middle class by the self-styled "neo-Marxists" contributed to the decline of the old-style love song.[27]

The youth culture we have been describing, though it did help shape a trend away from the old ballads, was only a minority of the market. However noisily influential, it is doubtful that its outlook totally determined popular trends. It just so happened that other, larger segments of the market were also not enthusiastic middle-class devotees of the old monogamous love ballad. Perhaps one of the most potent changers of taste was the horde of highly permissive and hedonistic lower classes entering the record market. These buyers, along with the less numerous upper-middle-class young rebels, weakened the hold of the romantic, oblique, sublimated "If I Loved You" approach toward love, taking it out of the sphere of the angels and pulling it down toward earth. (1955's "Earth Angel" was a step along the way.) Trends in music since around 1955 espe-

[27] Richard Goldstein's article on the "Flower Children" among the middle class, in the Denver *Post Contemporary* section, June 18, 1967, 12, 21, points up the generalized ideal of love. Such youth of course could have plenty of fun shocking the oldsters with their Four Letter Word Movement, all for a good cause. Two of the "frank" folksongs popular in the early 1960s were at least straightforward enough to ruffle the remaining hairs on a middle-class pate—especially if sung by girls of the rising generation: i.e., "Keep Her Good and Drunk and Goozy" and "Sally Let Your Bangs Hang Down," sung respectively by Gibson and Camp and by Dian and the Greenbrier Boys:

Now we know what Sally's got
Makes a man think she's so hot
Sally let your bangs hang down.

(from Crestview Album CRS 7807, *The Original Hootenanny*). This was hardly Norman Burroughs, but neither was it Irving Berlin or Cole Porter.

cially have appeared to bear out the assumptions of sociologists, and of Professor Hayakawa's invaluable work on jazz,[28] that the working class generally, and especially the colored lower class, lack the WASPish inhibitions which are apt to generate genteelly romantic, melancholy, frustrated songs. In short, they gratify themselves without making a cosmic issue out of it. By 1955 a best-selling rock number, "Honey Love," reduced the description of desire to three little words—not "I Love You," but "I Want It." In contrast, fifteen years previously, Ray Eberle had softly vocalized, over Glenn Miller's Debussyesque background, this Lawrence-Shapiro ballad:

I recall a story of love in all its glory
A night that left my heart romantic scars
When I reached up to heaven . . .
And gathered you a handful of stars.[29]

Boys and girls who take sexual freedom for granted would hardly be as captivated by such songs as would be the more frustrated. They would be just as interested in motorcycling and, the boys at least, in hot-rodding; finding in these activities something of the same muscular enthusiasm and visceral excitement involved in their sexual relations. Indeed, an infusion of prosperous, rather unsentimental lower-class leather boys into the record market—the kind who like to be out with their buddies Sunday afternoons—may have helped create the hot-rod music craze of the early 1960s.

Thus, lower-class youth unassimilated by middle-class culture joined with middle-class rebels against middle-class culture to alter the tone of American popular music. To the lower class, sex was nothing to moan over or sing pretty little sad poems about. To the crusading middle-class student rebels it was something which must be handled robustly, erotically, "honestly," rather than euphemized or sublimated out of all recognition as their parents had frequently done. Middle-class rebel and lower-class "swinger"; hippy and minority groups had a common distaste for pretty songs. The folk music of youth in the 1960s could hardly follow schoolmarmish rules of rhyme or the meter of Victorian poetry. Rejecting the formulae of the

[28] For example, "Popular Songs versus the Facts of Life," *ETC: A General Review of Semantics,* XII (Winter 1955), 83–95.

[29] Copyright 1939, 1940 by Leo Feist, Inc. Recorded on Bluebird 10893. Original pressings are in Rodgers and Hammerstein Archives, New York City Public Library; and Archives, Stanford University Music Library.

classroom, more and more lyrics were sung—or spoken—free style, like streetcorner or coffee-house conversation.

If monogamous romantic love was out in the music of the young and many of the would-be-young, *Agapé* was in. By 1964, the tone of Erich Fromm, Martin Buber and Paul Goodman pervaded even a Broadway hit musical, *Funny Girl*. Barbra Streisand (first name unconventionally spelled, last name obviously minority group; exotic-ugly non-Anglo face; muscular voice throbbing with all the subtlety of a sledge hammer; personality problems [30]—how could she have failed?) sang "People Who Need People Are the Luckiest People in the World." Two years later, in similar Tennessee Williams spirit, Simon and Garfunkel (names which would have been anglicized by any sane public-relations man in 1930, but only by an insane one in 1966) popularized their ironic, "I Am a Rock, I Am an Island":

> *And a rock can feel no pain,*
> *And an island never cries.*[31]

The neo-proletarian Togetherness, like the rough-edged songs and singers, was appropriate to the jeans and horsehide boots of the young "neo-Marxists." This was still romanticism, of course, but it was not "bourgeois" prettiness. The point is that the "tastefully" orchestrated romantic love ballad had such severe competition that it was much less in evidence.[32] As middle-class youth conceived of the one-ness mankind and refurbished the vision of the noble savage, they gravitated toward the music of people considered inferior by their parents, by all who still aspired to older middle-class standards. Thus, the tastes of the young did not run heavily to "pretty" love ballads. With their fondness for the old films of James Dean and Marlon Brando and Humphrey ("gentle-tough guy") Bogart, they liked Roger Miller's "King of the Road."

This brings us back to a basic generalization. Despite eddies and cross currents always present in the streams of taste, the outstanding trend in American popular music in the 1950s and the earlier 1960s was a rejection of prettiness, overrefinement, academic orchestration and lyrics, smoothness, even

[30] See Shana Alexander, "Barbra," *Life*, LVI (May 22, 1964), 52.

[31] Copyright © 1965, Charing Cross Music. Lyrics quoted with permission of the copyright holder.

[32] But not dead. Songs by Andy Williams, Jerry Vale, Al Martino and Tony Bennett (albeit more exuberantly and "cornilly" rendered than songs in the 1930s and 1940s) were still heard on TV and especially on jukeboxes in restaurants and bars catering to people around thirty or older.

subtlety. Although by 1965 a few of the lyrics written for the recently expanded college market, like "I Am a Rock," sensitively articulated the preoccupations of young adults, many lyrics, as well as most orchestrations, of the late 1950s and early 1960s were crude. Classicism, polish, formal discipline, carefully contrived arrangements, adherence to accepted rules in music, as in literature and art—these were likely to be anathematized even by many intellectuals for coldness, lack of spontaneity or "hypocrisy." In short, there was an attack on middle-class standards, on that residue of puritanism which distrusted the "natural." It would be a mistake, however, to assert that since music contained much protest against all aspects of the Establishment, from war to "Ticky Tacky Houses" and conformity, a thorough-going iconoclasm was the order of the day. Even though the folk song might so often protest, it could also reaffirm for large audiences a traditional patriotism—"This Land Is Our Land," "Ballad of the Green Beret." Musical trends can hardly be made any more coherent or consistent than the society which produces them. Two hundred million Americans living in the same years could among them find room for Barry Sadler's "Green Beret" and Bob Dylan's "World War III Blues." And yet, there was a similarity between the performers. Both were leather-booted, wild-animal-type young men (one a disheveled gazelle, the other a wild boar). Both were typical of years in which some of the most popular vocal and instrumental groups were called the "Animals," the "Monkees," the "Critters." Both these men were as far removed as could be from the Regional Accounting Office, the classroom or "Cocktails for Two" in the sleek white-on-whiteness of an *art moderne* penthouse in Gotham.[33] They would, both of them, be classified at any employment agency as Non-U. To this extent they perhaps validate the one generalization we can make about the musical temper of the later 1950s and the earlier 1960s: It was one of those times when the perennial reaction of youth against the norms of older people is accelerated, heightened, intensified. Youth boldly threw in the faces of its elders its own musical description of love: "Gimme Gravy for My Mashed Potatoes." The very appearance of Cass of the Mamas and the Pappas—lazy-fat, slovenly,

[33] "Cocktails for Two" was introduced by Duke Ellington in a 1934 musical film. He played in full dress, and on a white piano. The song mentioned two hands slyly meeting beneath a serviette while an orchestra played "an exquisite *chansonette.*"

serenely sensual, affronted the middle-class ideal of refined womanhood as a trimly neat, highly disciplined, meticulous housewife, teacher or stenographer.

Again, lest we interpret such a generalization to mean that all middle-class restraints, social and musical, were on the junk heap, Jeremy Larner reminds us that the popular songs of the early 1960s, if less than those of the 1930s, still paid some lip service to older values. Some sentimental lyrics continued to be written and sung even in rock-and-roll numbers, if only, as Mr. Larner explains, to sublimate the orgasm of the music. True, these lyrics were often not clearly articulated; engulfed in a pounding, shrieking sound, they were rarely audible. But they were there. The new generation of rebels still hedged a bit.[34] The Critters occasionally would sing soft, subtly blended arrangements of lovelorn ballads like "Mr. Die-ingly Sad"; and if you listened carefully enough to the young black voices of the Orlons shouting "The Rules of Love," you could hear the old plea for bourgeois fidelity.

[34] Jeremy Larner, "What do They Get from Rock-'n'-Roll?" *Atlantic*, CCXIV (Aug. 1964), 48.

THE NEW MUSIC AND THE NEW SCENE

●

BURTON H. WOLFE

While Kesey had been holding his Acid Tests, another thing was happening to bring about the 1966 explosion on Haight Street that Jay Thelin described: the creation of a new style of rock-and-roll.

In the day of the North Beach beatnik, music was jazz and folk singing with soft guitar accompaniment, to be enjoyed with poetry reading, wine, and beer in coffee houses or with a pipeful of marijuana while supine in somebody's pad. Dancing was not the "in" thing to do, especially in public. Like the most sophisticated members of the bygone Edwardian set, who looked upon it as an attempt at something best accomplished in a boudoir, the North Beach beatniks eschewed dancing because they considered it "dry fucking."

With the advent of the Beatles—a second, third, and fourth coming of Christ to the young generation—the "in" music even for most beatniks became electrified, amplified, bouncy rock-and-roll that was definitely meant for motion. This was the kind of music that acid heads like Kesey and the Merry Pranksters were digging the most, and it was dance music. That meant a significant change for the beatnik scene that was becoming reincarnated in the Hashberry.

In communal houses and pads around the Hashberry, combinations of folk, pop, jazz, and blues musicians gathered to talk, smoke pot, and experiment with the basic patterns produced by the Beatles and Rolling Stones rock-and-roll bands. Somewhere along their rock-on-drug trips, they created a form of electric music that became known as "folk rock," or more esoterically, "San Francisco rock" and "Western rock." It was amplified as loudly as the human ear could tolerate—louder than some human ears could tolerate. It blasted, it socked you in the head, and it mimicked, poked fun, antagonized. The names of the folk rock bands were adapted from the mood: the Great Society, Big Brother & the Holding Company, the Grateful Dead.

Few music or social critics would deny that the hippie bands created a new sound. It is an amalgam of other musical forms, but the totality of it is different from the rock-and-roll that Elvis Presley, Fabian, the Beatles, and the Rolling Stones used to play. In fact, the Beatles and the Rolling Stones had to alter their old styles and imitate it in order to keep up with the change.

The primordial quality of the hippies' folk rock music, like their intellectuals' vision of the new society, is primitive. Melodies are simple, harmony consists of a few basic chords, drum beats are narrow throbs, and everything together is repetitious and hypnotic. Around the primitive quality, however, the amplifiers, loudspeakers, tape recorders, electronic machines, and electrified musical instruments from guitars to oboes—yes, oboes, electric oboes—have woven a variety of effects.

The music is an outgrowth of Negro blues, rock-and-roll, country-western, and finally, ragas from India. Ragas are thematic note groupings with seventy-two parent scales, known as melas. Each raga is supposed to have its own character, color, and mood, according to the time of day, the season, or the occasion. It is then up to the musicians to improvise within these given forms. The main instruments used are: for melody, the sitar—a guitar-like instrument with twenty strings; the tamboura—a four- or five-stringed instrument that is used to maintain a continuous hypnotic drone; and the tabla—a pair of drums serving as tenor and bass. Sometime in 1966, the folk rock bands began using ragas and these three Indian instruments in their amalgamated music forms or else imitated them with guitars, oboes, and other Western instruments. This development has led to the suggestion that hippie music be identified as raga rock.

Despite the primitive quality in most of the rock music, it is wrong to use the term "simple" as a generalization for all of the compositions and all of the hippie musicians. Several of the numbers that the Jefferson Airplane recorded on the RCA Victor album, *Surrealistic Pillow,* require close listening for an appreciation of all their effect. For example, take "Coming Back to Me," a sweet, lolling song somewhat in the style of seventeenth-century English folk music. After getting that much out of it, a repetition may produce the sensation of drifting into a dreamy meadowland. A third repetition, paying attention to the Baroque touch added by Grace Slick on recorder, can produce the image of a shepherd grazing his flocks.

You can also pick up the delineation of the hippie life style in the words of the songs, if you can hear them. For example, take "The Golden Road," on Warner Brothers' Grateful Dead album, celebrating the girls on Haight Street in the following paeon:

> *See that girl, barefoot (doeeyoumoo)/ Whistlin' and a-singin'/ She's a-carryin' on/ Laughin' in her eyes, dancin' in her feet/ She's a (neonwhirrwhirrmoo)/ And she can live on the street.*

The strange words in parentheses are the nearest approximation I can make to what I hear coming from the Dead, even with my ear smack against the phonograph speaker. For the other way they delineate the hippie style is to blast everything at top volume with amplifiers so that all other sounds of the world are wiped out.

The next generalization about the hippie music that's safe to make is that it depicts the philosophy of the New Community. Most of the philosophizing is taken up with odes to love, a reflection of alienated youth's desperate desire to gain affection from parents and tenderness from a dog-eat-dog, violent society. When Grace Slick of the Airplane sings "don't you need somebody to love," she also means: *I* need somebody to love; *we* need somebody to love.

Of course, the love gives way in the rock groups' songs, even as it does in their lives, to blatant sex—e.g., the Fugs' "Wet Dream Over You." But this again is part of the philosophy, to challenge the old order's moral structure in a loud, aggressive, blunt manner. No subjects, no words must be banned. Drugs, death, violence, war, race prejudice, sex, religion, and the President of the United States must all be discussed, challenged, pranked, and satirized with complete openness. Hence, Country Joe and the Fish use the word "fuck" on television and describe President Johnson as "a man insane" in the song "Superbird." The Fugs sing "kill, kill for peace" as part of what their leader, Ed Sanders, calls their "total assault on the culture."

Any critic who calls this a put-on does not know the hippie musicians, only their imitators. The members of the hippie folk-rock groups not only sing and play their philosophy, but they also live it.

In the first place, they all take drugs, as announced in some of their names—the Mind Benders, the Loading Zone, the Induction Center, the Weeds. In the second place, the musicians, like all other hippies, are dropouts. Almost every one of them has given up school or profession to become a folk-rock musician and live the life of a hippie.

The Grateful Dead, the original associates of Ken Kesey in producing the Acid Tests, are all high school and college dropouts living in a tribal setup like the Merry Pranksters. At the time that I met them, their house on Ashbury Street was shared with them by their girl friends, managers Danny Rifkind and Rock Scully, and several teen-age school dropouts using the place as a crash pad. The earth mother was Mountain Girl, now Jerry Garcia's mistress, but still bearing testimony to her former relationship with Ken Kesey with a blond-haired baby that he sired.

The Dead's music, when all other analyses are thrown in as qualifications, is primarily an imitation of Negro blues. The style of singing is guttural, down, and dirty; and the diction is that of Negro slang: "Ah luhv you, babuh." That, plus the fact that the music drowns out the words, is why middle-class white people have such a difficult time understanding what the Dead are singing. You have to be a hippie, Negro, or drug addict. And even that is no guarantee that you can pick up the words. The Dead's music is the very heart of acid rock—guitar, organ, and bass intertwined in a whirling, blurring, mind-shattering mass of Negro, hillbilly, and Indian music. Its basic purposes are to blow the mind and provide action sound for dancing, although sometimes Jerry Garcia's rapid runs on the guitar can be interesting as music.

"Captain Trips" he is called, a play on both his guitar runs and mind journeys on LSD. Dressed in a white-and-red striped high hat, he reminds you of Ken Kesey, "Mr. Stars and Stripes." Both are pranksters. Both like to live in a tribal setup. Both have given funny nicknames to their people—bassist Phil Lesh is "Reddy Kilowatt," organist Ron McKernan "Pig Pen," and drummer Bill Sommers "Bill the Drummer." Both are basically scholarly men who have deliberately adopted the loose Negro style of life and slang. Both have taken their minds apart with drugs.

"I didn't need Timothy Leary or LSD to do it, either," Garcia told me. "Back in high school I was high on bennies, things like that. I never heard of Leary. Nobody in the Haight-Ashbury follows Leary. The people here would have done this thing without acid, without Leary. I would have been a member of some weird society wherever I went. Don't ask why. Don't try to analyze it, man. It just is, that's all. This is where we're at. This is our trip. We just don't dig that other way."

Garcia is one of the impossible people in the New Community for a writer to talk to, even one who is living with it. Because of his massive mop of curly black hair, he has been described in print as a "troll" and "a cross between Wanda Landowska and the Three Stooges." He and the Dead have been ridden by critics as musical illiterates and drug addicts leading flower children down the path of sin. So, he has taken to pure pranking when a journalist questions him. No writer is closer to the folk-rock bands than Ralph Gleason of the *Chronicle*. Yet, this is how Garcia described his music to Ralph:

"We're working with dynamics now. We've spent two years with loud, and we've spent six months with deafening." And so on.

It gets no better in the hippie press. Here is the way the Grateful Dead summed up their philosophy for the Underground Press:

> *Garcia:* I wake up automatically at 9 EVERY morning (except for sometimes when I wake up later or earlier), and gaze out the window at the flocks of geese flying north/south for the winter/summer and ask myself what does it all mean? I drink as much orange juice as I can get my dirty hands on because I know that it's gonna taste good. My boots don't fit me perfectly, so my little toe hurts. Sometimes I see someone that I think I recognize, and I say hello or smile or something like that. It's fun to shoot at strangers, while they're innocently passing the house, with the sonic blaster. Especially if they're pretty, heh. Philosophically, I have nothing to say. . . . I like to play loud. . . . If I had a rocket ship or some extraterrestrial friends, you'd never see me. I hope that humanity survives the incredibly stupid hassles that we've gotten ourselves into.

Last I saw of the Dead, officially, they were on television explaining their philosophy to dazed newsmen. Unofficially, they were going about their usual business of planning free benefits in which the toilets would be stopped up with money. For further analysis, await the new philosophical tome in the music sections of the national magazines.

The most well-remembered communal pad where the new sound was created was at 1090 Page Street in the Hashberry. Oftentimes, the New Community's budding musicians would find food and shelter there when they were broke, and they would join a gathering clan playing and taking drugs in the garage below the house. Friends and neighbors began dropping in to listen to the sound—might as well, couldn't concentrate on anything else if you lived anywhere within a block of it—and the Hashberry had its first free rock concerts.

One of the familiar figures on the Page Street garage scene was Chet Helms, a twenty-two-year-old dropout from Baptist theological school. Like many of the musicians' and beatniks' connections in the Haight-Ashbury, Helms lived the beat life style. Long before most of them let their hair grow out, he had long blond Jesus tresses flowing down his shoulders and a scraggly beard and moustache.

But Helms was not so doggedly noncommercial as the new breed of beat, making music and fun. He suggested that the folk-rock bands charge admission to the garage. (His version of the story is that he it to discourage more people from coming because the place was getting too crowded.) When even larger crowds came to the garage, Helms organized a folk-rock concert and dance at the Longshoremen's Hall in October of 1965. Several hundred youngsters came to the hall, some with long hair and dressed in beatnik garb, others straight. Obviously, money was to be made from the new folk-rock scene. All that Helms needed was an organization with some capital and a dance hall.

With an engineer from New York, Bob Cohen, Helms put together the Family Dog, named after a tiny spaniel pooch that lived with him and his friends in one of the communal pads. Then, he approached another New Yorker, Bill Graham, owner of the Fillmore Auditorium and producer-director of the San Francisco Mime Troupe, about working together to make folk-rock dance concerts a big happening on the neobeatnik scene. Graham had already put on his own folk-rock concerts in November and December of 1965, using the Fugs, the Great Society, and the Jefferson Airplane to do several benefit performances for the Mime Troupe. Its actors and actresses had been busted for "obscene performances in public places" under a recently enacted California antipornography law. Around four thousand people showed up for the second benefit performance in the Fillmore Auditorium, waiting in a long line around the block outside or finally being turned away because the capacity of the place is only fifteen hundred at a time. Then, in the first month of 1966, Graham collaborated with Kesey for the Trips Festival in creating a "total environment" performance. This meant that movie projectors, strobes, tape recorders, and amplifiers were used to bombard every creaky floorboard and every cobwebbed corner of the old Fillmore Auditorium with music, electronic blips and bleeps, flashing lights, and moving pictures of amoebas, holy men, Indians, and other symbols of the acid head's world.

When Helms told Graham about the success of the Family Dog and suggested a sort of merger of these New World business ventures, Graham was indifferent. He was on the verge of resigning from the Mime Troupe over "political differences," and he was not sold on the future of folk rock (it killed him at first to admit it after he made a million dollars from it, but then he started taking a Socratic irony in recalling his original mood). So, Helms asked if the Family Dog could rent the hall, and Graham agreed.

Later, Helms and Graham parted company, and Helms opened up his own business in the Avalon Ballroom at Sutter and Van Ness streets, staffed entirely by people with long hair and beards.

"The Family Dog is the largest brain trust in the world," Helms likes to say in interviews. "We are roughly arranged around a sort of organic tribal structure in the sense that people who are natural organizers are generally the leaders" and since he and Bob Cohen did the organizing, there is no doubt left about who he means.

"Helms is definitely an organizer," I was told by Grace Slick, who knew him in the formative rock days when he was peddling dope. "Instead of running a bank, he runs the Avalon and the Family Dog, that's all."

Helms drifted into the Hashberry from Texas when he was twenty-one, leaving behind him a broken future that was supposed to have led to the Baptist ministry. He wound up on drugs instead of religion, but he kept on wearing a deacon's frock coat. Neither that nor his long blond Jesus tresses had anything to do with hippies; there was no such thing as hippies then. Helms, like so many hippie men, was obsessed with a Jesus self-image. When he picked the motto for the Family Dog, it was the following graffito that he took from the wall of a men's room:

May the Baby Jesus Shut Your Mouth and Open Your Mind

Later, he became enraged over *Ramparts* cover story on the hippies, in which the motto was deliberately reversed to: open your mouth and shut your mind.

Evening at the Avalon provides plenty of the ear-splitting sound characteristic of the hippie band. Continuously changing light projections of liquid colors and protoplastic forms bathe the dancers. Their luminescent, striped, and dotted clothes glow eerily amid the flashing lights. Symbols, concentric circles, and pictures of Indians and Oriental priests are beamed onto the walls.

Suddenly, the fast, screaming music dies down to a soft love song and then gives way to a mournful Indian dirge. The light show changes. On one wall there is a picture of Buddha and on another a picture of Christ on the cross. Several hundred of the youngsters on the dance floor join hands. They sway back and forth in a trancelike state. They keep it up until the musicians come on again with another fast, loud set and the lights begin blipping all over the cavernous dance hall. Once more, the Avalon is a sea of maddening motion and deafening sound.

Bill Graham at the Fillmore kept on with the Jefferson Airplane and other folk rock groups and made his million with them. The Fillmore remained the same place and Graham remained the same man: blunt, unpretentious, obsessed with man's need for hard work and honesty. The Fillmore is as dingy as it has always been. The floor is still dirty and creaky, and the plaster on the walls is still cracking. One of the cracks is covered with a blown-up photo of Ronald Reagan dressed in a cowboy suit, looking tough as he points a gun in his left hand; under the photo is the caption: "Thanks for the votes, suckers." There are also anti-Vietnam posters, an anti-LBJ cartoon, and a picture of Graham, wearing a suit and tie, in a cage held by a female labeled "S.F. Society," with the serpent of Eden for her headband and dollar-signs for her earrings; the caption is: "So, I sold out, so what?"

At the Fillmore's nighttime rock-dance concerts, where Graham still insists on supervising everything personally, the confrontations between him and the hippies who come into the place have become legend. Knowing that he is wealthy, some of the school dropouts ask him: "Hey, man, got a dime? Got a quarter? I wanna get into the dance."

Graham turns on them: "Do *you* have a penny?"

"Well, I asked you first."

"I know you asked me first, but do you have a penny?"

"Well, hell, man . . ."

But Graham is gone to raise hell with four young hippies breaking up the line formation at the window. "Get in line!" he yells at them. "All these other people are in line. You think you're any better? Get in the line. You like to touch people. Here's your chance. Stay in line, like good flower children."

"Hey, Mr. Graham," they say. "Come on now, where's your love?"

"Fuck love," Graham says. "Get in line!"

I interviewed Graham in his cubbyhole office amid the usual chaos—secretary beside him clacking away on her typewriter, messages strewn all over his desk, telephone ringing continuously with calls from *Time, Newsweek,* and promoters from New York to Brazil. Posters announcing various folk-rock dance concerts covered almost every inch of the wall. His skinny legs bounced nervously, and his lips worked up and down as he tried to answer phones, direct his staff, make new appointments, read messages, and talk to me all at once.

"The first folk-rock dance concerts were held *right here,* before Kesey or Helms came in this place," he said. "I mean, you want to talk about Acid Tests, Trips Festivals, hippies, dates, purposes—it's all a crock of shit. The dance concerts were put on as benefits, and then they were put on for people to have fun. What is Trips Festivals? People dancing and having fun, that's all. These things were never exclusively for people with long hair or beards freaking out on the floor. They were for anybody. A guy with a tuxedo could come in here with a half-naked blonde bitch, and they could wiggle their butts all over the floor and do their thing, and nobody would give a damn. Let 'em groove.

"Now, of course, there are certain laws we have to abide

by or we're out of business. I mean, I had this thing going with the cops: you let us be loose, don't be too uptight about the way people dress or act, let 'em do their thing, and I'll make sure nothing happens here to make trouble for you."

Out of the Fillmore and the Avalon came vibrations shooting across the country, drawing school and job dropouts to San Francisco. Hitchhiking or driving in imitations of Ken Kesey's psychedelic bus, they headed for where the action was—the Avalon and Fillmore like two giant magnets, with LSD and folk rock their energy fields.

By March of 1966, the *San Francisco Chronicle,* the daily newspaper that had done more than any other in the country to publicize the beatnik scene, was finally paying front-page attention to the new arrivals in the Haight-Ashbury. On the front page of March 15, 1966, the *Chronicle* carried a big, banner headline:

Inside S.F. Pad
THE NEW BEATNIK LIFE

Underneath it were two stories about the new happening in the Haight-Ashbury. The first introduced a foil reminiscent of the North Beach police-beatnik warfare—Officer Gerrans:

> A barefoot blonde led police early yesterday to a rambling Ashbury Street pad bursting with beatniks and heavy with the sweet smell of freshly smoked marijuana.
>
> The fuzz walked into the flat at 408 Ashbury behind 18-year-old Kathryn Shirley—and walked out with 24 partygoers destined for City Prison or the Youth Guidance Center.
>
> Their blonde guide, a San Leandro high school dropout, agreed to show them where she was staying with a 17-year-old girl friend, police said, after they stopped her in the Panhandle about 12:30 A.M.—strolling barefoot with a young artist.
>
> Officers Fred Mott and Arthur Gerrans, reinforced by four more Park Station officers, then began a search of the flat's ten rooms.
>
> The walls were covered with crayoned and painted "art" work, they said and the floors with straw sleeping mats and mattresses.
>
> Although there was little furniture, the flat was populated by 15 men, nine girls, three cats, two dogs, and two hamsters.
>
> When the raiders had completed their search of the warren, they turned up two more unlit reefers found on a window sill, an attaché case containing four syringes and three hypodermic

needles, plus four packets of suspected heroin, and another needle and syringe found in a rear bedroom.

In the second story, the beatniks were given a chance to talk back to the fuzz:

> The heat is on in the Haight-Ashbury District, and beatniks living there say police harassment is running the fun.
>
> Bohemians (or beatniks or beats) complain of police bullying, of being pestered at their "pads" by plainclothesmen seeking narcotics and stopped and searched on the streets "just for wearing sandals and long hair."
>
> Several residents of the low-rent, mixed-race district between the Panhandle and Twin Peaks spoke to the *Chronicle* outside 408 Ashbury Street, where 24 party-goers were arrested early yesterday.
>
> One long-haired writer from Massachusetts who was loud in his complaints was Michael van Nuis, 22, of 1900 Page Street.
>
> "This used to be easy living around here, a real good neighborhood," he said, "but lately the cops have really gotten nasty, taking you into the park to search you, bugging you all the time. If you've got long hair, you're bothered."
>
> A friend of some of the people who were arrested was Harriet Forrest, 19, a sometime office worker who lives on Stanyan Street and who said she just got back from a Mexico trip two days ago.
>
> Had she ever been questioned by police?
>
> "Wow! All you have to do is walk down Haight Street. The police stop and hassle you. They just bug you."

It was the late 1950s and early 1960s all over again, with Officer Gerrans substituted for Officer Bigarani. Long-haired boys and barefoot girls were arrested for curfew violations or loitering in front of stores on Haight Street. They were tailed into the pads of friends, and whenever Gerrans sniffed the scent of marijuana, there was a bust. The police were determined to ride the neobeatnik scene out of existence before it could be built up into another North Beach. They did not realize that by March 1966 it was already too late. The new music had magnetized far too many people for any police squad to deter, and at the center of the energy field, with information to help the New Community's arrivals survive and stay in the Hashberry, was the Psychedelic Shop on Haight Street.

"Like, wow! There was an explosion," Jay Thelin recalled.

"People began coming in from all over and our little information shop became a sort of clubhouse for dropouts, and, well, we just let it happen, that's all. We let people sit around on our floor because they had no place else to go. It was the only place on the street where they could get good vibrations. Some were on trips, and we made it possible for them to get through more easily without having to worry about where to go."

A HOUND DOG, TO THE MANOR BORN

●

STANLEY BOOTH

Between Memphis and Walls (you turn right a bit past a big sign saying *Church of God, Pastor C. B. Brantley,* DRINK DR. PEPPER), there is a small ranch, a hundred and sixty green and gently rolling acres, a prettier spread than you'd expect to see in the poor, bleak land of North Mississippi. The owner, at thirty-three, has been a millionaire for more than a decade. He has other, more elegant homesteads, but these days he prefers the ranch. Behind the formidable chain-link fence and the eight-foot picket walls that hide his neat red-brick house, he finds a degree of privacy to share with his pretty new wife. The privacy is also shared by twenty-two purebred horses, counting colts, and nine hired hands, counting guards. (There were twelve hands, but the number was reduced recently, so the story goes around the ranch, at the request of the owner's wife.) Then, too, there are the continual visitors—the ones who are allowed inside (some driving Cadillacs given them by the owner as Christmas or birthday presents) and the ones who must stay outside, peering over or through the fences. At times, such as when the owner is out riding, the roadside is solidly lined with sight-seeing cars. Privacy—the privacy in which to enjoy his leisure time—is extremely valuable to the ranch's young owner, especially since he works less than half the year. Taxes would make more work pointless; his annual income is about five million dollars.

And yet, not too many years ago, he was living in a Federal low-rent housing project, working as a truckdriver, movie usher, sometimes forced to sell his blood at ten dollars a pint. Elvis Presley, a Great American Success Story.

By the ranch's main gate, in an air-conditioned hut, sits Elvis' Uncle Travis, a small, grinning man, with hair as black and skin as dark as an Indian's. A straw cowboy hat rests on his knee. He wears black Western pants and a white shirt with *E.P.* monogrammed in black Gothic script across the front. Travis likes to reminisce about the girls he has captured and ejected from his nephew's premises. "I dragged one out from under that old pink Cadillac. She must of heard me comin' and hid under there, and all I saw was her feet stickin' out. I said, 'Come on out of there,' and she didn't move, so I reached down, took ahold of her feet, and pulled. She had a coat of motor oil a inch thick." Travis belches.

"How do they get in?"

"Slip in. Jump a fence just like a billygoat. If they can't climb over, they'll crawl under. If the gate ain't locked they'll drive right through. I had a carload slip past me up at Graceland. Hell, I didn't even go after them, I just locked the damn gate. They made the circle in front of the house, come back down the drive, and when they seen they couldn't get out, the one drivin' says, 'Please op'n the gate.' I told her 'Yes, ma'am, soon's the sheriff got there.' Made out like I was real hot, you know. She says, 'Please don't call the sherriff, my mama will kill me.' I said, 'Not till you get out of jail, I don't reckon.' She like to died. Then I started laughin', and they seen it was all right, and asked me if they could come back after while and talk. So I told them yeah, but while they was gone I got to thinkin', Why'd they have to leave, why couldn't they just stay and talk? But one of they mamas came back with them, and she told on them. I'd scared her daughter so bad she'd peed her pants."

Travis pitches his head back and laughs, displaying a strong white set of uppers. Parked in the drive is a shiny red Ford Ranchero with his name, T.J. Smith, on one door under the ranch's Circle G brand, actually a flying Circle G. I ask what the "G" stands for.

"Could be Graceland," Travis says, "or it could be his mother's name. He meant it to stand for her name." Travis' expression becomes serious when he speaks of Elvis' dead mother, his own sister. "He still keeps that old pink Cadillac he bought for her. Don't never drive it, just keeps it as a keepsake. He's got all the cars he needs. Had a Rolls-Royce up on blocks four or five years. Bought a hundred thousand dollars' worth of trucks and trailers right after he got this place. Money ain't nothing to him. Ole boy from Hernando was down here the other evenin', workin' on the fence, and Elvis drove down in one of his new pickups to take a look. Feller says, 'Shore do like that truck. Always wanted me one of them.' So Elvis says, 'You got a dollar?' Feller says, 'Yeah, I got one,' and gives it to Elvis. 'It's your truck,' Elvis says."

Next Travis tells how Priscilla, the new wife, likes Elvis to take her for rides in one of his souped-up go-karts (top speed, more than a hundred miles an hour) around the driveway at Graceland, tantalizing the squealing girls outside the fence.

Then he spits. "I sit down here, keepin' people out, seven in the mornin' till six in the evenin', five days a week, and I'm about wore out. I think I'll go in the hospital for two or three weeks, take me a rest."

"Maybe you could get a television set to watch while you're working," I suggest.

"Yeah, I believe I will get me one. Either that, or some funny books."

Just outside the gate, in a rented green Impala, are two girls who have come, so they tell me, all the way from New Zealand. "Is he home?" they ask.

"Who?"

One sneers, one ignores. "Did you talk to him? What did he say?"

I look away, trying to select a representative quote. On the roof of the house across the road a man is kneeling behind a camera, snapping pictures of the Circle G. "Let's ride up to Rosemark tomorrow and look at that mare," I tell the girls.

"Pardon?"

"That's what he said."

"What, is *that* all?"

"You should have been here yesterday. He said, 'Would somebody please bring me a Pepsi?' " Pepsi-Cola, I would have explained to the girls, is Elvis' favorite drink, just as his favorite snack is peanut-butter-and-mashed-banana sandwiches; but the Impala roars away, leaving a cloud of dust to settle on my shoes.

Sometime ago, before I saw for myself what Elvis is like, I asked a mutual acquaintance about him. "He's all right," I was told. "Pretty interesting guy to talk to."

"Really. What's the most interesting thing he's ever said to you?"

My friend sat and thought, pulling the hair on his chin. Finally he said, "Well, once he told me, 'Like your beard. How long'd it take you to grow it?' I said it took about three months, and he said, 'I'd like to grow me one sometime, but I don't think I could get away with it. Y'know?' And he sort of winked."

Another friend, whose relation to the Presley household was for a time unique, told me that Elvis is a very straight guy, who uses neither grass nor acid. In Hollywood, Elvis never goes to nightclubs or premieres. Except for work, he hardly leaves his Bel-Air mansion. "He's afraid he wouldn't know how to act," says one of his oldest friends. "And he wouldn't."

Even in Memphis, his recreational activities have been, for a millionaire, unpretentious. In the early days at Graceland (the large, white-columned estate, rather like an antebellum funeral parlor, which Elvis bought in 1957), the big kick was roller skating. After a local rink closed for the evening, Presley and his entourage would come in, skate, eat hot dogs and drink Pepsi-Cola till dawn. When skating palled, Elvis started renting the entire Fairgrounds amusement park, where he and his friends could ride the Tilt-a-Whirl, Ferris wheel, roller coaster, Dodgem cars (Elvis' favorite), and eat hot dogs and drink Pepsis till dawn. Until quite recently, Presley has been in the habit of hiring a local movie theater (the Memphian) and showing rented movies, emphasizing the films of actresses he has dated. The Memphian has no hot-dog facilities, but provides plenty of popcorn and, of course, Pepsis. Now that he is married and an expectant father, he does not get out so much at night, but the daytime is as glamorous, as exciting as ever.

On a day not long ago, when Presley happened to be staying at Graceland, the house was crowded with friends and friends of friends, all waiting for old El to wake up, come downstairs, and turn them on with his presence. People were wandering from room to room, looking for action, and there was little to be found. In the basement, a large, divided room with gold records hung in frames around the walls, creating a sort of halo effect, they were shooting pool or lounging under the Pepsi-Cola signs at the soda fountain. (When Elvis likes something, he *really* likes it.) In the living room boys and girls were sprawled, nearly unconscious with boredom, over the long white couches, among the deep snowy drifts of rug. One girl was standing by the enormous picture window, absently pushing one button, then another, activating an electrical traverse rod, opening and closing the red velvet drapes. On a table beside the fireplace of smoky molded glass, a pink ceramic elephant was sniffing the artificial roses. Nearby, in the music room, a thin, dark-haired boy who had been lying on the cloth-of-gold couch, watching Joel McCrea on the early movie, snapped the remote-control switch, turning off the ivory television set. He yawned, stretched, went to the white, gilt-trimmed piano, sat down on the matching stool and began to play. He was not bad, playing a kind of limp, melancholy boogie, and soon there was an audience facing him, their backs to the door.

Then, all at once, through the use of perceptions which could only be described as extrasensory, everyone in the room knew that Elvis was there. And, stranger still, nobody moved. Everyone kept his cool. Out of the corner of one's eye Presley could be seen, leaning against the doorway, looking like Lash La Rue in boots, black Levis and a black silk shirt.

The piano player's back stiffens, but he is into the bag and has to boogie his way out. "What is this, amateur night?" someone mutters. Finally—it cannot have been more than a minute—the music stops. Everyone turns toward the door. Well I'll be damn. It's Elvis. What say, boy? Elvis smiles, but does not speak. In his arms he is cradling a big blue model airplane.

A few minutes later, the word—the sensation—having passed through the house, the entire company is out on the lawn, where Presley is trying to start the plane. About half the group has graduated into the currently fashionable Western clothing, and the rest are wearing the traditional pool-hustler's silks. They all watch intently as Elvis, kneeling over the plane, tries for the tenth time to make the tiny engine turn over; when it sputters and dies a groan, as of one voice, rises from the crowd.

Elvis stands, mops his brow (though of course he is not perspiring), takes a thin cigar from his shirt pocket and peels away the cellophane wrapping. When he puts the cigar between his teeth a wall of flame erupts before him. Momentarily startled, he peers into the blaze of matches and lighters offered by willing hands. With a nod he designates one of the crowd, who steps forward, shaking, ignites the cigar, and then, his moment of glory, of service to the King at an end, he retires into anonymity. "Thank ya very much," says Elvis.

They begin to seem quite insane, the meek circle proffering worship and lights, the young ladies trembling under Cadillacs, the tourists outside, standing on the roofs of cars, waiting to be blessed by even a glimpse of this young god, this slightly plump idol, whose face grows more babyish with each passing year.

But one exaggerates. They are not insane, only mistaken, believing their dumpling god to be Elvis Presley. He is not. One remembers—indeed, one could hardly forget—Elvis Presley.

The time is the early fifties, and the scene is dull. Dwight Eisenhower is President, Perry Como is the leading pop singer. The world has changed (it changed in 1945), but the change is not yet evident. Allen Ginsberg is a market researcher for a San Francisco securities company. William Burroughs is in New Orleans, cooking down codeine cough syrup. Malcolm X, paroled from Massachusetts' Charlestown Prison, is working in a Detroit furniture store. Stokely Carmichael is skinny, insolent, and eleven years old.

It is, let us say, 1953. Fred Zinnemann rehashes the past with *From Here to Eternity,* and Laslo Benedek gives us, in *The Wild One,* a taste of the future. This is a movie with good guys and bad guys, and the good guys are the ones who roar on motorcycles into a town which is small, quiet, typically American and proceed to take it apart. Their leader, Marlon Brando, will be called an anti-hero. But there is no need for the prefix. He is a new, really contemporary hero: the outcast.

Soon James Dean repeats the theme with even greater success. But Dean's career was absurdly short. "You know he was dead before you knew who he was," someone said. The outcasts of America were left without a leader.

Then, one Saturday night early in 1956 on a television variety program, a white singer drawls at the camera: "Ladies and gentlemen, I'd like to do a song now, that tells a little story, that really makes a lot of sense—'Awopbopaloobop—alopbamboom! Tutti-frutti! All rootie! Tutti-frutti! All rootie!' "

Though nearly all significant popular music was produced by Negroes, a white rhythm-and-blues singer was not an entirely new phenomenon. Bill Haley and the Comets had succeeded with such songs as "Shake, Rattle and Roll," and "Rock Around the Clock." But the pudgy Haley, in his red-plaid dinner jacket, did not project much personal appeal. This other fellow was something else.

He was not quite a hillbilly, nor yet a drugstore cowboy. He was a Southern—in that word's meaning of the combination of rebellion and slow, sweet charm—version of the character Brando created in *The Wild One*. Southern high-school girls, the "nice" ones, called these boys hoods. You saw them lounging on the hot concrete of a gas station on a Saturday afternoon, or coming out of a poolroom at three o'clock of a Monday afternoon, stopping for a second on the sidewalk as if they were looking for someone who was looking for a fight. You even see their sullen faces, with a toughness lanky enough to just miss being delicate, looking back at you out of old photographs of the Confederate Army. They were not named Tab or Rock, nor even Jim, Bill, Bob. They all had names like Leroy, Floyd, Elvis. All outcasts, with their contemporary costumes of duck-ass haircuts, greasy Levis, motorcycle boots, T-shirts for day and black leather jackets for evening wear. Even their unfashionably long sideburns (Elvis' were *furry*) expressed contempt for the American dream they were too poor to be part of.

No one writing about Presley should forget the daring it took to be one of these boys, and to sing. A "hood" might become a mechanic or a house painter or a busdriver or even a cop, but nobody would expect him to be a singer. If he tried it at all, he would have to have some of his own crowd playing with him; he'd have to sing some old songs his own people had sung before him; and he would have to sing them in his own way, regardless of what people might say about him.

"Mama, do you think I'm vulgar on the stage?"

"Son, you're not vulgar, but you're puttin' too much into your singin'. Keep that up and you won't live to be thirty."

"I can't help it, Mama. I just have to jump around when I sing. But it ain't vulgar. It's just the way I feel. I don't feel sexy when I'm singin'. If that was true, I'd be in some kinda institution as some kinda sex maniac."

These days, when asked about the development of his career, Elvis either ignores the question or refers it to "my manager." Generally speaking his manager is the person standing closest to him at the time. This is often Alan Fortas, officially the ranch foreman, a young man only slightly less stocky than a bull, with a history of hostility to reporters. When The Beatles visited Elvis in Hollywood, Fortas, not troubling to remember their names, addressed each of them as, "Hey, Beatle!" They always answered, too; nobody wants to displease Alan.

A more voluble source of information is Dewey Phillips. During Elvis' early career Phillips was probably as close to him as anyone except his mother, Gladys. Now retired, Phillips was then one of the most popular and influential disc jockeys in the nation. He still speaks the same hillbilly jive he used as a broadcaster.

"Nobody was picking up on the ole boy back then. He was a real bashful kid, but he liked to hang around music. They'd chased him away from the switchboard at WMPS, and he'd come hang around Q. That's WHBG, where I was doing my show, *Red Hot and Blue,* every night. Weekends, he'd come down to Sun Records—he'd cut that record, 'My Happiness,' for his mother, paid four dollars for it himself—and Sam Phillips, president of Sun, finally gave him a session. Tried to record a ballad, but he couldn't cut it. Sam got Bill Black, the piano player, and Scotty Moore, the guitarist, to see if they could work anything out with him.

"After a lot of tries, Elvis, Bill and Scotty fixed up a couple of old songs, 'That's All Right, Mama,' and 'Blue of Kentucky' so they sounded a little different. When Elvis began to cut loose with 'That's All Right,' Sam came down and recorded these sonofaguns. One night I played the record thirty times. Fifteen times each side. When the phone calls and telegrams started to come in, I got hold of Elvis' daddy, Vernon. He said Elvis was at a movie, down at Suzore's number-two theater. 'Get him over here,' I said. And before long Elvis came running in. 'Sit down, I'm gone interview you,' I said. He said, 'Mr. Phillips, I don't know nothing about being interviewed.' 'Just don't say nothing dirty,' I told him.

"He sat down, and I said I'd let him know when we were ready to start. I had a couple of records cued up, and while they played we talked. I asked him where he went to high school, and he said 'Humes.' I wanted to get that out, because a lot of people listening had thought he was colored. Finally I said, 'All right, Elvis, thank you very much.' 'Aren't you gone interview me?' he asked. 'I already have,' I said. 'The mike's been open the whole time.' He broke out in a cold sweat."

According to Phillips, Elvis at this time considered himself a country singer. "Sam used to get him, Roy Orbison, Jerry

Lee Lewis and Johnny Cash down at Sun and play Big Bill Broonzy and Arthur Crudup records for them, trying to get them on the blues thing, because he felt like that was going to be hot. One of Elvis' first public appearances was at a hillbilly jamboree at the downtown auditorium. Webb Pierce was there, and Carl Smith, Minnie Pearl, a whole houseful of hillbillies. Elvis was nervous, said he wanted me with him. But Sam and I were out at my house, drinking beer, or we had something going, and I missed the afternoon show. Elvis came looking for me, mad as hell. I asked him what he'd sung and he said, ' "Old Shep" and "That's How My Heartaches Begin." ' What happened? 'Nothing.'

"So that night I went along with him and told him to open with 'Good Rockin' Tonight' and not to sing any hillbilly songs. I introduced him and stayed onstage while he sang. He went into 'Good Rockin',' started to shake, and the place just blew apart. He was nobody, didn't even have his name on the posters, but the people wouldn't let him leave. When we finally went off we walked past Webb Pierce, who had been waiting in the wings to go on. I smiled at him and he said, 'You son of a bitch.' "

The sales of Elvis' records enabled him to get more bookings, and Dewey Phillips bought him an old Lincoln sedan for $450 so he could play out-of-town jobs. Appearing in Nashville at a convention of the Country and Western Disc Jockeys' Association, he was seen, "discovered," by talent scouts for RCA Victor. In a moviehouse matinee in Texarkana, he was discovered by Thomas Andrew Parker, a latter-day Barnum out of W. C. Fields by William Burroughs. A carnival orphan, he had worked in his uncle's "Great Parker Pony Circus," dipped candied apples, shaved ice for snow cones, operated merry-go-rounds, even put in a stretch as dog-catcher in Tampa, Florida.

Astute techniques in these businesses had enabled Parker to rise in the world to a position of some prestige. The title "Colonel" had been conferred upon him by, as he put it, "a few governors." He was managing the careers of such big-name country entertainers as Hank Snow and Eddy Arnold. But in all his years as a promoter, he had never found so promotable a commodity as Presley.

He had seen Elvis at, for his purposes, just the right time. The demand for Elvis' records prompted RCA to offer $35,000 for Presley, lock, stock, and tapes. Sam Phillips accepted.

"Elvis knew he was going big time," Dewey Phillips remembers, "and he needed a manager. That was late spring of fifty-five. He was the hottest thing in show business, and still just a scared kid. He had got his mother and daddy a nice house, they had three Cadillacs, and no phone. He asked me to be his manager. I told him I didn't know anything about managing. Then Colonel Parker came to town. He knew what he was doing. He didn't talk to Elvis. He went out to the house and told Gladys what he could do for the boy. That Parker is a shrewd moo-foo, man."

Elvis' first appearances on network television, on the Tommy and Jimmy Dorsey show in January and February 1956, changed him from a regional phenomenon into a national sensation. This might not have happened, the American public might simply have shuddered and turned away, had there not been a new group among them: teen-agers, the enemy within. When the older generation, repelled by Presley's lean, mean, sexy image, attacked him from pulpits and editorial columns, banned him from radio stations, the teen-agers liked him more than ever, and went out and bought his records. Entrepreneurs could not afford to ignore Presley. As one radio producer asked, How can you argue with the country's number-one recording star? Reluctantly, almost unwillingly, show business accepted Elvis. Ed Sullivan, who only a couple of months before had condemned Presley as being "unfit for a family audience," now was obliged to pay him $50,000 for three brief appearances. However, Elvis was photographed only from the waist up, and his material was diluted by the addition of a ballad, "Love Me Tender," which oozed syrup.

Such attempts to make Elvis appear respectable were very offensive to the good ole boys back in Memphis. Steve Allen, involved in a ratings battle with Sullivan, booked Presley, but assured the audience that they would see only "clean family entertainment." Elvis appeared and sang, standing still, wearing white tie and tails, with top hat and cane, but without a guitar. Just after the show went off the air, Dewey Phillips' telephone rang. "Hello, you bastard," Dewey said.

"How'd you know it was me?" asked Elvis.

"You better call home and get straight, boy. What you doing in that monkey suit? Where's your guitar?"

So when Elvis made his next hometown appearance (it was on July 4, 1956) he reassured his people. The occasion was a charity benefit and Colonel Parker had turned down paying engagements so that Elvis could be part of the show. His was the closing spot, and he was preceded by more than a hundred performers, including the orchestras of Bob Morris and Aaron Bluestein, the Admiral's Band of Navy Memphis, a barbershop quartette called the Confederates, Charlotte Morgan's dancing Dixie Dolls, and innumerable singers, by no means the least of which was one Helen Putnam, founder of Fat Girls Anonymous, who dedicated *A Good Man Is Hard to Find* to Elvis.

After nearly three hours, with the audience so bored that it was on the point of having a religious experience, Dewey Phillips, who was master of ceremonies, said, "All right. Here he is," and there he was, his hair hanging over his forehead, a wad of gum in his jaw. He wore a black suit, black shoes, black shirt, red tie, and red socks, clothes with so much drape and flash that they created a new sartorial category, somewhere on the other side of corny. He sang all the old songs in the old way, from "That's All Right" to "Blue Suede Shoes" to "Heartbreak Hotel." He sang until he was dripping with sweat, and when at last he spoke, his words were a promise to his friends, a gift of defiance to his enemies: "I just want to tell y'awl not to worry—them people in New York and Hollywood are not gone change me none."

Then his voice became a growl, an act of rebellion: "You ain't nothin' but a houn'dog," he sang, and proceeded to have sexual intercourse with the microphone.

They told me you was high class
Well, that was just a lie—

If the police had not been there, forming a blue wall around the stage, the audience might have eaten Elvis' body in a Eucharistic frenzy. They were his and he was theirs, their leader: it was an incandescent moment.

And at the same time it was a climactic one. For as he stood there singing defiance at his natural enemies, those with power, prestige, money, the Humes High hood, the motorcycle jockey, was gone, and in his place there was a star, with power, prestige, money. A few months from now at about three o'clock one morning, he would be standing with one of his hired companions outside the Strand Theatre on Main Street in Memphis when a couple of his high-school classmates would drive past, not going much of anywhere, just dragging Main. They would slow their car as they came alongside the Strand; they would see it was Elvis; and then, without a word, they would drive on. "A few years ago," Elvis said, "they would have spoken to me."

Elvis had tried to go on being himself. When Paramount offered him a movie contract with a clause forbidding him to ride motorcycles, he said, "I'd rather not make movies." They let him keep his motorcycles. All that was really necessary was that he stop doing his thing and start doing theirs. His thing was "Mystery Train," "Milkcow Blues Boogie." Theirs was "Love Me Tender," "Loving You," "Jailhouse Rock," "King Creole."

Then he was drafted. The Army cut his hair, took away his fancy clothes, and Elvis let them. His country had served him well and he was willing to serve his country. He is nothing if not fair-minded.

While he was stationed in Fort Hood, Texas, Elvis moved his parents to a rented house in the nearbly town of Killeen. His mother, who had been doing poorly for more than a year, worsened, and on August 8, 1958, Elvis put her on a train to Methodist Hospital in Memphis. The prognosis was grave and Elvis requested the customary special leave.

It was refused. When the doctors, at Elvis' request, advised his command of the seriousness of his mother's illness, they were told in effect, "If it were anybody else, there'd be no problem. It's standard procedure. But if we let Presley go everybody will yell special privilege."

Days passed while Gladys Presley sank lower and lower. In spite of constant urging from Elvis and his doctors, the leave still was not granted. Finally, on the morning of August 12, Elvis decided that he had had enough. "If I don't get a pass by two o'clock this afternoon," he told the doctors, "I'll be home tonight."

The doctors reasoned with him, urged him to remember that he set an example for millions of others boys. But Elvis had made up his mind. A Humes High boy can be pushed only so far. The doctors could only advise the command of Elvis' plans.

So naturally, the pass came through. The Army is not that dumb. Elvis had the same rights as any other American boy.

Back in Memphis Elvis fought his way through the crowds of newsmen outside the hospital. He was in his mother's room for only a few minutes; then he came out, walked down the hall to an empty waiting room, sank into a chair and cried.

His mother had been the one, perhaps the only one, who had told him throughout his life that even though he came from poor country people, he was just as good as anyone. His success had not surprised her, nor had it changed her. Shortly after Gladys Presley was buried, her husband and son were standing on the magnificent front steps at Graceland. "Look, Daddy," Elvis sobbed, pointing to the chickens his mother had kept on the lawn of the hundred-thousand-dollar mansion. "Mama won't never feed them chickens no more."

He has never really gotten over his mother's death. He treasured for many years and may still have, in his office at Graceland, a lighted, fully decorated, artificial Christmas tree, souvenir of the last Christmas the family spent together. He had the tree cared for all the time he was in Germany, where the Army had put him safely away.

Elvis liked Germany and both he and his father found wives there. When his tour of duty was ended, he came out with sergeant's stripes. The whole thing was fictionally celebrated in *G.I. Blues,* a happy movie with a multi-million-dollar gross. One Elvis Presley film followed another: *Flaming Star, Wild in the Country, Blue Hawaii, Girls! Girls! Girls!, Kid Galahad, Follow that Dream, It Happened at the World's Fair, Fun in Acapulco, Viva Las Vegas, Kissin' Cousins, Roustabout, Girl Happy, Tickle Me, Harem Scarem, Frankie and Johnny, Paradise Hawaiian Style, Spinout; Easy Come, Easy Go; Double Trouble, Speedway, Clambake.* They all have two things in common: none lost money, none is contingent at any point upon reality.

But this is not quite true; there is one reality which they reflect. In *Fun in Acapulco,* which played on television recently, Elvis walks into a bar which is full of Mexicans, all of whom have good teeth. A mariachi band is playing. Elvis comes in on the chorus, and carries away the verse. Everyone applauds. The men smile and the girls turn on to him. They all think he's a hell of a fellow. One expects that at any moment he may produce a model plane and lead them out onto the lawn.

Elvis has fulfilled the American dream: he is young, rich, famous, adored. Hardly a day passes in Memphis without a politician wanting to name something after him. So far nothing has been found worthy of the honor. Presley has become a young man of whom his city and his country can be truly proud.

And he may not even know whether he misses the old days, the old Elvis. At Graceland, through the powder-white living room, past the gilded piano, there is a door that looks out onto the swimming pool. If you had been standing there on a recent afternoon, you would have seen Elvis, all alone for a change, riding his motorcycle around the pool, around and around and around.

THE SCENE

•

FRANK KOFSKY

Speaking quite generally, it seems to me that the major *innovations* of rock—aside from the considerable achievement of having thoroughly revolutionized the popular song lyric—lie in the areas of what I shall broadly call presentation and the use of electronics; at least it is in these areas that rock has the most to offer jazz.

By *presentation* I mean not only the way in which rock music is performed in front of a "live" audience, but also the way in which the audience feels itself able to respond to the performance. It is true that rock bands are more intimate with their audiences—whether in the mock-insulting manner of Frank Zappa or the casual friendliness of the Jefferson Airplane and especially the Grateful Dead—than are most jazz bands. In the 1940s, the most advanced jazz musicians decided that their music was art rather than entertainment; and accordingly, they adopted a performing stance that they felt was more appropriate to that of an artist. Ultimately, however, this stance has served to enhance the isolation of performer from audience—an isolation that, owing to variables of age, race, and class, are already large enough to comprise a serious barrier. Thus the jazz musician of today does not feel comfortable in the role of entertainer; to him, this smacks of Tomming. On the other hand, by the very nature of the music and the physical exertions inherently involved in playing it, it is impossible for him to preserve the glacial aloofness of the concert or conservatory ("classical") performer. As a result, many jaz performances suffer from an air of stiffness, artificiality: the artists would perhaps like to communicate with their audience; but at this advanced date they hardly know how to begin.

The jazz audience, for its part, is equally hung-up. Time and again I have attended concerts of the new music in New York's Village Theatre (now called Fillmore East) and wondered how on earth the overwhelming majority of the audience could possibly be content to sit perfectly still during such exciting fare, without uttering a sound or giving forth with a single kinetic response. If the music affects them so little, I asked myself, why do they even bother attending? Not that the disease of unresponsiveness is confined to concerts; I have observed the same phenomenon at most jazz clubs on either coast and at points between (though there are some very prominent exceptions, such as San Francisco's Jazz Workshop).

But to fault the audience, or the artists, I have concluded, is mistaken. For we are all, artists and audience alike, victims of a stereotyped idea of what constitutes the "proper" artistic stance and audience response. Prior to the Renaissance (or to McLuhan's Gutenberg Age, or to Marx's period of Original Accumulation—they are synonymous), art was integrated into the everyday activities of most people. But with the rise of the new commercial wealth in Italy, the Germanies, the Low Countries, and later England and France, *parvenu* bourgeois families who had made their fortune through commercial and/or mercantile activities (the Medici in Machiavelli's Florence are a good case in point) began using art as a weapon in the campaign to establish themselves as the social equals of the hereditary landed aristocracy, winning the artists over to their side in the process. Such behavior appears to be characteristic of all *nouveau-riche* business classes, as you can readily demonstrate from the history of this country by counting up the number of museums, hospitals, art galleries, public parks, observatories, universities, opera houses, and the like, that bear the name of Rockefeller, Carnegie, Frick, Guggenheim, Mellon, Morgan, Yerkes, and the other celebrated Robber Barons of the last third of the nineteenth century.

In any event, as the arts in Europe increasingly came to be subsidized by wealthy lay patrons, the artists themselves began to develop elitist ideas. In music, such ideas took the form of separating music from its hitherto ever-present partner, the dance. Since dancing was a form of entertainment for the vulgar (notwithstanding the existence of certain aristocratic dances such as the minuet), the "serious" composer, if he had his choice, found it more in accord with his longing for elite status to write for listening only. For an audience which listened without dancing could hardly be taken for anything but an audience of gentle birth. After all, from the time of Plato on, passive contemplation (of which listening is one form) had been identified with the aristocratic life; whereas active physical exertion was, quite clearly, characteristic of those base-born plebians who were born to toil.

In the evolution of the composer as an artist one also notes the increasing development of the division of labor, which, as Hegel and Marx so trenchantly observed, had the effect of alienating from man the product of his own hands. Previous to the time of the Renaissance, there had not been any such specialized vocation as that of *composer*. The *de facto* composer was a performer first—an *improvising* performer at that—and a composer of written music a far-distant second. The period of the rise of Commercial Capitalism put an end to all that quickly enough. The composer, now an *artist* and no longer merely an artisan, lost his function as a performing musician and instead specialized in the production of musical scores. These, in turn, were performed not by himself but by others—the first professional concert musicians, who were trained to play nothing that was not written; and to play what was written with total uniformity, regardless of whether the musician received his training in Leipzig or Potsdam, Vienna or Budapest, Bologna or Florence, Paris or London. There was the burgeoning factory system of early capitalism translated into musical terms.

It is this whole cultural "apparatus" of composer-aloof performer-passive audience that we have inherited *en toto* from the halcyon days of Western capitalism's youth. And alas, such was the only model available to the innovators of the bebop era when they decided that their music was to be regarded as art rather than entertainment. To be sure, jazz musicians have clearly put a dent into this stereotyped notion of "the artist" even as they appropriated it: one thinks of Miles Davis turning his back on his listeners, Thelonious Monk doing his eccentric but functional dances around the piano. But Miles and Monk are the exceptions. In the main, jazz musicians (for reasons which ought to be obvious to any socially perceptive reader, but which will not be gone into here in any event) have tended to take over the European model of the concert artist and leave it relatively intact, right down to the jacket, white shirt, and tie that is standard performing garb for all save the new musicians.

SMASHING THE IKONS

It has remained for the new rock musicians to demolish this model altogether, by the simple expedient of restoring dance to its rightful place alongside music. Of course, jazz was also once a music for dancing. But the jazz writers of that generation and the following ones, hypnotized (as are all good middlebrows) by the European idea of what constitutes "culture," were indecently eager to repudiate dancing so as to demonstrate that jazz was as "refined" (i.e., white and European) as "serious" or "classical" music. How ironic! A music potentially so rebellious and anti-European forced to fit into a Procrustean bed of European "good manners." Even now, one of the things that most horrifies many jazz critics when first confronted with the new rock is that people actually do *dance* to it. "Reeeealy, my deah. Dawncing. How dreadfully vulgah. *We* outgrew that *ages* ago." Just so must the first *parvenu* capitalist have sneered for the benefit of his newly acquired aristocratic peers at the habits of the plebian mass from which he had so recently sprung.

One of the great joys of the new rock is not just that it has reinstituted dancing to music, but that it has legitimized the visceral response to art: the bands *want* you to enjoy the music, to be swept away by it, to show them your pleasure—in short, to freak out. That is why Frank Zappa allows (actually encourages) anyone who wishes, to roam around on stage during performances. (In Los Angeles, his concerts usually feature the freaky Fraternity of Man dancers on stage as part of the "act"; this is Zappa's way of loosening up the listeners.) That is why the Jefferson Airplane and the Grateful Dead continually entreat their audiences to get up and dance. For when you dance—or scream, or jump up and down, or roll around on the floor, or leap up on stage and kiss Gracie Slick or Jerry Garcia —you are showing that you have been *moved* by the music; and this in turn spurs on the entire band to play harder and heavier. (How often while listening to jazz have I wished that I could feel free to express my feelings, without being afraid of calling attention to myself as some kind of weirdo! But can you imagine anyone freaking out in the Village Theatre or the Village Gate?)

On this point, jazz fans certainly ought to be willing to accept the testimony of no one less than John Coltrane (*Jazz & Pop*, September 1967):

Kofsky: If people do enjoy the music, how would you like them to demonstrate it? Do you like an audience that's perfectly still and unresponsive, or do you like an audience that reacts more visibly to the music?

Coltrane: Well, I guess I like an audience that does show what they feel; to respond.

Kofsky: I remember when you played the Jazz Workshop in San Francisco, you sometimes got that kind of an audience, which you didn't get when you played at Shelly's Manne-hole in Los Angeles; and it seemed to me that that had some effect on the music.

Coltrane: Yes, because it seems to me that the audience, in listening, is in an act of participation, you know. And when you know that somebody is maybe moved the same way you are, to such a degree or approaching the degree, it's just like having another member of the group.

I am not sure just how jazz groups could go about creating the easy rapport and the sense of interaction between musicians and audience that can be felt at the best rock performances. Verbal encouragement to the listeners to respond to the music, including dancing free-form to it if they are so inclined, would seem the place at which to begin. But just calling upon your listeners to dance is not going to provide any instant panacea. At base, the reason dancing in a rock context works to produce a positive feedback from audience to band is because the musicians do not feel estranged from the people for whom they are playing. On the contrary, in San Francisco especially, there is usually enough of a shared ethos present to bind artist and audience together in a common endeavor. Or so I have been told by many of the San Francisco rock performers I have interviewed.

It doesn't seem likely that this particular aspect of rock can be totally duplicated in a jazz setting. There is, to begin with, the racial barrier to contend with: black performers, white or integrated audience. Beyond that, there may be other obstacles of class, age, and so on. But for all of that, even if we grant that jazz musicians and their following cannot achieve the same emotional cohesiveness as a San Francisco rock band and its local entourage, it does not follow that it is completely futile to try. There is much to be gained and nothing to be lost in the attempt.

LIKE A ROLLING STONE

●

RALPH J. GLEASON

> Forms and rhythms in music are never changed without producing changes in the most important political forms and ways.

Plato said that.

> There's something happenin' here. What it is ain't exactly clear. There's a man with a gun over there tellin' me I've got to beware. I think it's time we STOP, children, what's that sound? Everybody look what's goin' down.

The Buffalo Springfield said that.

> For the reality of politics, we must go to the poets, not the politicians.

Norman O. Brown said that.

> For the reality of what's happening today in America, we must go to rock-'n'-roll, to popular music.

I said that.

For almost forty years in this country, which has prided itself on individualism, freedom and nonconformity, all popular songs were written alike. They had an eight-bar opening statement, an eight-bar repeat, an eight-bar middle section or bridge, and an eight-bar reprise. Anything that did not fit into that framework was, appropriately enough, called a novelty.

Clothes were basically the same whether a suit was double-breasted or single-breasted, and the only people who wore beards were absent-minded professors and Bolshevik bomb-throwers. Long hair, which was equated with lack of masculinity—in some sort of subconscious reference to Samson, I suspect—was restricted to painters and poets and classical musicians, hence the the term "long-hair music" to mean classical.

Four years ago a specter was haunting Europe, one whose fundamental influence, my intuition tells me, may be just as important, if in another way, as the original of that line. The Beatles, four long-haired Liverpool teen-agers, were busy changing the image of popular music. In less than a year, they invaded the United States and almost totally wiped out the standard Broadway show/ Ed Sullivan-TV-program popular song. No more were we "flying to the moon on gossamer wings," we were now articulating such interesting and, in this mechanistic society, unusual concepts as "Money Can't Buy Me Love" and "I Want to Hold Your Hand."

"Societies, like individuals, have their moral crises and their spiritual revolutions," R. H. Tawney says in *Religion and the Rise of Capitalism.* And the Beatles appeared ("a great figure rose up from the sea and pointed at me and said 'you're a Beatle with an "a"' "—Genesis, according to John Lennon). They came at the proper moment of a spiritual cusp—as the martian in Robert Heinlein's *Stranger in a Strange Land* calls a crisis.

Instantly, on those small and sometimes doll-like figures was focused all the rebellion against hypocrisy, all the impudence and irreverence that the youth of that moment was feeling vis-à-vis his elders.

Automation, affluence, the totality of instant communication, the technology of the phonograph record, the transistor radio, had revolutionized life for youth in this society. The population age was lowering. Popular music, the jukebox and the radio were becoming the means of communication. Huntley and Brinkley were for Mom and Dad. People now sang songs they wrote themselves, not songs written *for* them by hacks in grimy Tin Pan Alley offices.

The folk-music boom paved the way. Bob Dylan's poetic polemics, "Blowin' in the Wind" and "The Times They Are A-Changin'," had helped the breakthrough. "Top-40" radio made Negro music available everywhere to a greater degree than ever before in our history.

This was, truly, a new generation—the first in America raised with music constantly in its ear, weaned on a transistor radio, involved with songs from its earliest moment of memory.

Music means more to this generation than it did even to its dancing parents in the big-band swing era of Benny Goodman. It's natural, then, that self-expression should find popular music so attractive.

The dance of the swing era, of the big bands, was the fox trot. It was really a formal dance extended in variation only by experts. The swing era's parents had danced the waltz. The fox trot was a ritual with only a little more room for self-expression. Rock-'n'-roll brought with it not only the voices of youth singing their protests, their hopes and their expectations (along with their pathos and their sentimentality and their personal affairs from drag racing to romance), it brought their dances.

"Every period which abounded in folk songs has, by the same token, been deeply stirred by Dionysiac currents," Nietzsche points out in *The Birth of Tragedy*. And Dionysiac is the word to describe the dances of the past ten years, call them by whatever name from bop to the twist to the frug, from the hully gully to the Philly dog.

In general, adult society left the youth alone, prey to the corruption the adults suspected was forthcoming from the song lyrics ("All of me, why not take all of me," from that hit of the thirties, of course, didn't mean *all* of me, it meant, well . . . er . . .) or from the payola-influenced disc jockeys. (Who ever remembers about the General Electric scandals of the fifties, in which over a dozen officials went to jail for industrial illegalities?)

The TV shows were in the afternoon anyway and nobody could stand to watch those rock-'n'-roll singers; they were worse than Elvis Presley.

But all of a sudden the *New Yorker* joke about the married couple dreamily remarking, when a disc jockey played "Hound Dog" by Elvis, "they're playing our song," wasn't a joke any longer. It was real. That generation had suddenly grown up and married and Elvis was real memories of real romance and not just kid stuff.

All of a sudden, the world of music, which is big business in a very real way, took another look at the music of the pony-tail and chewing-gum set, as Mitch Miller once called the teen-age market, and realized that there was one helluva lot of bread to be made there.

In a short few years, Columbia and R.C.A. Victor and the other companies that dominated the recording market, the huge publishing houses that copyrighted the music and collected the royalties, discovered that they no longer were "kings of the hill." Instead, a lot of small companies, like Atlantic and Chess and Imperial and others, had hits by people the major record companies didn't even know, singing songs written in Nashville and Detroit and Los Angeles and Chicago and sometimes, but no longer almost always, New York.

It's taken the big ones a few years to recoup from that. First they called the music trash and the lyrics dirty. When that didn't work, as the attempt more recently to inhibit songs with supposed psychedelic or marijuana references has failed, they capitulated. They joined up. R.C.A. Victor bought Elvis from the original company he recorded for—Sun Records ("Yaller Sun records from Nashville" as John Sebastian sings it in "Nashville Cats")—and then bought Sam Cooke, and A.B.C. Paramount bought Ray Charles and then Fats Domino. And Columbia, thinking it had a baby folk singer capable of some more sales of "San Francisco Bay," turned out to have a tiny demon of a poet named Bob Dylan.

So the stage was set for the Beatles to take over—"with this ring I can—dare I say it?—rule the world!" And they did take over so thoroughly that they have become the biggest success in the history of show business, the first attraction ever to have a coast-to-coast tour in this country sold out before the first show even opened.

With the Beatles and Dylan running tandem, two things seem to me to have been happening. The early Beatles were at one and the same time a declaration in favor of love and of life, an exuberant paean to the sheer joy of living, and a validation of the importance of American Negro music.

Dylan, by his political, issue-oriented broadsides first and then by his Rimbaudish nightmare visions of the real state of the nation, his bittersweet love songs and his pure imagery, did what the jazz and poetry people of the fifties had wanted to do—he took poetry out of the classroom and out of the hands of the professors and put it right out there in the streets for everyone.

I dare say that with the inspiration of the Beatles and Dylan we have more poetry being produced and more poets being made than ever before in the history of the world. Dr. Malvina Reynolds—the composer of "Little Boxes"—thinks nothing like this has happened since Elizabethan times. I suspect even that is too timid an assessment.

Let's go back to Plato again. Speaking of the importance of new styles of music, he said, "The new style quietly insinuates itself into manners and customs and from there it issues a greater force . . . goes on to attack laws and constitutions, displaying the utmost impudence, until it ends by overthrowing everything, both in public and in private."

That seems to me to be a pretty good summation of the answer to the British rock-singer Donovan's question, "What goes on? I really want to know."

The most immediate apparent change instituted by the new music is a new way of looking at things. We see it evidenced all around us. The old ways are going and a new set of assumptions is beginning to be worked out. I cannot even begin to codify them. Perhaps it's much too soon to do so. But I think there are some clues—the sacred importance of love and truth and beauty and interpersonal relationships.

When Bob Dylan sang recently at the Masonic Memorial Auditorium in San Francisco, at intermission there were a few very young people in the corridor backstage. One of them was a long-haired, poncho-wearing girl of about thirteen. Dylan's road manager, a slender, long-haired, "Bonnie Prince Charlie" youth, wearing black jeans and Beatle boots, came out of the dressing room and said, "You kids have to leave! You can't be backstage here!"

"Who are you?" the long-haired girl asked.

"I'm a cop," Dylan's road manager said aggressively.

The girl looked at him for a long moment and then drawled, "Whaaaat? With those boots?"

Clothes really do *not* make the man. But sometimes . . .

I submit that was an important incident, something that could never have happened a year before, something that implies a very great deal about the effect of the new style, which has quietly (or not so quietly, depending on your view of electric guitars) insinuated itself into manners and customs.

Among the effects of "what's goin' on" is the relinquishing of belief in the sacredness of logic. "I was a prisoner of logic and I still am," Malvina Reynolds admits, but then goes on to praise the new music. And the prisoners of logic are the ones who are really suffering most—unless they have Mrs. Reynolds' glorious gift of youthful vision.

The first manifestation of the importance of this outside the music—I think—came in the works of Ken Kesey and Joseph Heller. *One Flew Over the Cuckoo's Nest*, with its delightful utilization of crackpot realism (to use C. Wright Mills's phrase) as an explanation of how things are, were work of seminal importance.

No one any longer really believes that the processes of

international relations and world economics are rationally explicable. Absolutely the very best and clearest discussion of the entire thing is wrapped up in Milo Minderbinder's explanation, in *Catch-22*, of how you can buy eggs for seven cents apiece in Malta and sell them for five cents in Pianosa and make a profit. Youth understands the truth of this immediately, and no economics textbook is going to change it.

Just as—implying the importance of interpersonal relation and the beauty of being true to oneself—the under-thirty youth immediately understands the creed patiently explained by Yossarian in *Catch-22* that everybody's your enemy who's trying to get you killed, even if he's your own commanding officer.

This is an irrational world, despite the brilliant efforts of Walter Lippmann to make it rational, and we are living in a continuation of the formalized lunacy (Nelson Algren's phrase) of war, any war.

At this point in history, most of the organs of opinion, from the *New York Review of Books* through the *New Republic* to *Encounter* (whether or not they are subsidized by the C.I.A.), are in the control of the prisoners of logic. They take a flick like *Morgan* and grapple with it. They take *Help!* and *A Hard Day's Night* and grapple with those two beautiful creations, and they fail utterly to understand what is going on because they try to deal with them logically. They complain because art doesn't make sense! Life on this planet in this time of history doesn't make sense either—as an end result of immutable laws of economics and logic and philosophy.

Dylan sang, "You raise up your head and you ask 'is this where it is?' And somebody points to you and says 'it's his' and you say 'what's mine' and somebody else says 'well, what is' and you say 'oh my god am i here all alone?' "

Dylan wasn't the first. Orwell saw some of it, Heller saw more, and in a different way so did I. F. Stone, that remarkable journalist, who is really a poet, when he described a *Herald Tribune* reporter extracting from the Pentagon the admission that, once the first steps for the Santo Domingo episode were mounted, it was impossible to stop the machine.

Catch-22 said that in order to be sent home from flying missions you had to be crazy, and obviously anybody who wanted to be sent home was sane.

Kesey and Heller and Terry Southern, to a lesser degree

in his novels but certainly in *Dr. Strangelove*, have hold of it. I suspect that they are not really a *new wave* of writers but only a *last* wave of the past, just as is Norman Mailer, who said in his Berkeley Vietnam Day speech that "rational discussion of the United States involvement in Vietnam is illogical in the way surrealism is illogical and rational political discussion of Adolf Hitler's motives was illogical and then obscene." This is the end of the formal literature we have known and the beginning, possibly, of something else.

In almost every aspect of what is happening today, this turning away from the old patterns is making itself manifest. As the formal structure of the show-business world of popular music and television has brought out into the open the Negro performer—whose incredibly beautiful folk poetry and music for decades has been the prime mover in American song—we find a curious thing happening.

The Negro performers, from James Brown to Aaron Neville to the Supremes and the Four Tops, are on an Ed Sullivan trip, striving as hard as they can to get on that stage and become part of the American success story, while the white rock performers are motivated to escape from that stereotype. Whereas in years past the Negro performer offered style in performance and content in song—the messages from Leadbelly to Percy Mayfield to Ray Charles were important messages—today he is almost totally style with very little content. And when James Brown sings, "It's a Man's World," or Aaron Neville sings, "Tell It Like It Is," he takes a phrase and only a phrase with which to work, and the Supremes and the Tops are choreographed more and more like the Four Lads and the Ames Brothers and the McGuire Sisters.

I suggest that this bears a strong relationship to the condition of the civil right movement today in which the only truly black position is that of Stokely Carmichael, and in which the N.A.A.C.P. and most of the other formal groups are, like the Four Tops and the Supremes, on an Ed Sullivan/TV-trip to middle-class America. And the only true American Negro music is that which abandons the concepts of European musical thought, abandons the systems of scales and keys and notes, for a music whose roots are in the culture of the colored peoples of the world.

The drive behind all American popular music performers, to a greater or lesser extent, from Sophie Tucker and Al Jolson, on down through Pat Boone and as recently as Roy Head and Charlie Rich, has been to sound like a Negro. The white jazz musician was the epitome of this.

Yet an outstanding characteristic of the new music of rock, certainly in its best artists, is something else altogether. This new generation of musicians is not interested in being Negro, since that is an absurdity.

The clarinetist Milton Mezzrow, who grew up with the Negro Chicago jazzmen in the twenties and thirties, even put "Negro" on his prison record and claimed to be more at home with his Negro friends than with his Jewish family and neighbors.

Today's new youth, beginning with the rock-band musician but spreading out into the entire movement, into the Haight-Ashbury hippies, is not ashamed of being white.

He is remarkably free from prejudice, but he is not attempting to join the Negro culture or to become part of it, like his musical predecessor, the jazzman, or like his social predecessor, the beatnik. I find this of considerable significance. For the very first time in decades, as far as I know, something important and new is happening artistically and musically in this society that is distinct from the Negro and to which the Negro will have to come, if he is interested in it at all, as in the past the white youth went uptown to Harlem or downtown or crosstown or to wherever the Negro community was centered because there was the locus of artistic creativity.

Today the new electronic music by the Beatles and others (and the Beatles' "Strawberry Fields" is, I suggest, a three-minute masterpiece, an electronic miniature symphony) exists somewhere else from and independent of the Negro. This is only one of the more easily observed manifestations of this movement.

The professional craft union, the American Federation of Musicians, is now faced with something absolutely unforeseen—the cooperative band. Briefly—in the thirties—there were co-op bands. The original Casa Loma band was one and the original Wood Herman band was another. But the whole attitude of the musicians themselves worked against the idea, and co-op bands were discouraged. They were almost unknown until recently.

Today almost all the rock groups are cooperative. Many live together, in tribal style, in houses or camps or sometimes in traveling tepees, but always, *together* as a *group;* and the young girls who follow them are called "groupies," just as the girls who in the thirties and forties followed the bands (music does more than soothe the savage breast!) were called "band chicks."

The basic creed of the American Federation of Musicians is that musicians must not play unless paid. The new generation wants money, of course, but its basic motivation is to play anytime, anywhere, anyhow. Art is first, then finance, most of the time. And at least one rock band, the Loading Zone in Berkeley, has stepped outside the American Federation of of Musicians entirely and does not play for money. You may give them money, but they won't set a price or solicit it.

This seems to me to extend the attitude that gave Pete Seeger, Joan Baez and Bob Dylan such status. They are not and never have been for sale in the sense that you can hire Sammy Davis to appear, as you can hire Dean Martin to appear, any time he's free, as long as you pay his price. You have not been able to do this with Seeger, Baez and Dylan any more than Allen Ginsberg has been for sale either to *Ramparts* or the C.I.A.

Naturally, this revolt against the assumptions of the adult world runs smack dab into the sanctimonious puritan morality of America, the schizophrenia that insists that money is serious business and the acquisition of wealth is a blessing in the eyes of the Lord, that what we do in private we must preach against in public. Don't do what I do, do what I say.

Implicit in the very names of the business organizations that these youths form is an attack on the traditional, serious attitude toward money. It is not only that the groups themselves are named with beautiful imagery: the Grateful Dead, Loading Zone, Blue Cheer or the Jefferson Airplane—all dating back to the Beatles with an A—it is the names of the non-musical organizations: Frontage Road Productions (the music company of the Grateful Dead), Faithful Virtue Music (the Lovin' Spoonful's publishing company), Ashes and Sand (Bob Dylan's production firm—his music publishing company is Dwarf Music). A group who give light shows is know as the Love Conspiracy Commune, and there was a dance recently in Marin County, California, sponsored by the Northern California Psychedelic Cattlemen's Association, Ltd. And, of course, there is the Family Dog, which, despite *Ramparts,* was never a rock group, only a name under which four people who wanted to present rock 'n roll dances worked.

Attacking the conventional attitude toward money is considered immoral in the society of our fathers, because money is sacred. The reality of what Bob Dylan says—"money doesn't talk, it swears"—has yet to seep through.

A corollary of the money attack is the whole thing about long hair, bare feet and beards. "Nothing makes me sadder," a woman wrote me objecting to the Haight-Ashbury scene, "than to see beautiful young girls walking along the street in bare feet." My own daughter pointed out that your feet couldn't get any dirtier than your shoes.

Recently I spent an evening with a lawyer, a brilliant man who is engaged in a lifelong crusade to educate and reform lawyers. He is interested in the civil liberties issue of police harassment of hippies. But, he said, they wear those uniforms of buckskin and fringe and beads. Why don't they dress naturally? So I asked him if he was born in his three-button Dacron suit. It's like the newspaper descriptions of Joan Baez's "long stringy hair." It may be long, but *stringy?* Come on!

To the eyes of many of the elder generation, all visible aspects of the new generation, its music, its lights, its clothes, are immoral. The City of San Francisco Commission on Juvenile Delinquency reported adversely on the sound level and the lights at the Fillmore Auditorium, as if those things of and by themselves were threats (they may be, but not in the way the Commission saw them). A young girl might have trouble maintaining her judgment in that environment, the Commission chairman said.

Now this all implies that dancing is the road to moral ruin, that young girls on the dance floor are mesmerized by talent scouts for South American brothels and enticed away from their happy (not hippie) homes to live a life of slavery and moral degradation. It ought to be noted, parenthetically, that a British writer, discussing the Beatles, claims that "the Cycladic fertility goddess from Amorgos dates the guitar as a sex symbol to 4800 years B.C."

During the twenties and the thirties and the forties—in other words, during the prime years of the Old Ones of today—dancing, in the immortal words of Bob Scobey, the Dixieland trumpet player, "was an excuse to get next to a broad." The very least effect of the pill on American youth is that this is no longer true.

The assault on hypocrisy works on many levels. The adult society attempted to chastise Bob Dylan by economic sanction, calling the line in "Rainy Day Woman," "everybody must get stoned" (although there is a purely religious, even biblical, meaning to it, if you wish), an enticement to teen-agers to smoke marijuana. But no one has objected to Ray Charles's "Let's Go Get Stoned," which is about gin, or to any number of other songs, from the Kingston Trio's "Scotch and Soda" on through "One for My Baby and One More [ONE MORE!] for the Road." Those are about alcohol and alcohol is socially acceptable, as well as big business, even though I believe that everyone under thirty now knows that alcohol is worse for you than marijuana, that, in fact, the only thing wrong about marijuana is that it is illegal.

Cut to the California State Narcotics Bureau's chief enforcement officer, Matt O'Connor, in a TV interview recently insisting, à la Parkinson's Law, that he must have more agents to control the drug-abuse problem. He appeared with a representative of the state attorney general's office, who predicted that the problem would continue "as long as these people believe they are not doing anything wrong."

And that's exactly it. They do not think they are doing anything wrong, any more than their grandparents were when they broke the prohibition laws. They do not want to go to jail, but a jail sentence or a bust no longer carries the social stigma it once did. The civil rights movement has made a jailing a badge of honor, if you go there for principle, and to a great many people today, the right to smoke marijuana is a principle worth risking jail for.

"Make Love, Not War" is one of the most important slogans of modern times, a statement of life against death, as the Beatles have said over and over—"say the word and be like me, say the word and you'll be free."

I don't think that wearing that slogan on a bumper or on the back of a windbreaker is going to end the bombing tomorrow at noon, but it implies something. It is not conceivable that it could have existed in such proliferation thirty years ago, and in 1937 *we* were pacifists, too. It simply could not have happened.

There's another side to it, of course, or at least another aspect of it. The Rolling Stones, who came into existence really to fight jazz in the clubs of London, were against the jazz of the integrated world, the integrated world arrived at by rational processes. Their songs, from "Satisfaction" and "19th Nervous Breakdown" to "Get Off of My Cloud" and "Mother's Little

Helper," were antiestablishment songs in a nonpolitical sort of way, just as Dylan's first period was antiestablishment in a political way. The Stones are now moving, with "Ruby Tuesday" and "Let's Spend the Night Together," into a social radicalism of sorts; but in the beginning, and for their basic first-thrust appeal, they hit out in rage, almost in blind anger and certainly with overtones of destructiveness, against the adult world. It's no wonder the novel they were attracted to was David Wallis' *Only Lovers Left Alive,* that Hell's Angels story of a teen-age, future jungle. And it is further interesting that their manager, Andrew Loog Oldham, writes the essays on their albums in the style of Anthony Burgess' violent *A Clockwork Orange.*

Nor is it any wonder that this attitude appealed to that section of the youth whose basic position was still in politics and economics (remember that the Rolling Stone Mick Jagger was a London School of Economics student, whereas Lennon and McCartney were artists and writers). When the Stones first came to the West Coast, a group of young radicals issued the following proclamation of welcome:

> Greetings and welcome Rolling Stones, our comrades in the desperate battle against the maniacs who hold power. The revolutionary youth of the world hears your music and is inspired to even more deadly acts. We fight in guerrilla bands against the invading imperialists in Asia and South America, we riot at rock-'n'-roll concerts everywhere: We burned and pillaged in Los Angeles and the cops know our snipers will return.
>
> They call us dropouts and delinquents and draftdodgers and punks and hopheads and heap tons of shit on our heads. In Viet Nam they drop bombs on us and in America they try to make us make war on our own comrades but the bastards hear us playing you on our little transistor radios and know that they will not escape the blood and fire of the anarchist revolution.
>
> We will play your music in rock-'n'-roll marching bands as we tear down the jails and free the prisoners, as we tear down the State schools and free the students, as we tear down the military bases and arm the poor, as we tattoo BURN BABY BURN! on the bellies of the wardens and generals and create a new society from the ashes of our fires.
>
> Comrades, you will return to this country when it is free from the tyranny of the State and you will play your splendid music in factories run by the workers, in the domes of emptied

city halls, on the rubble of police stations, under the hanging corpses of priests, under a million red flags waving over a million anarchist communities. In the words of Breton, THE ROLLING STONES ARE THAT WHICH SHALL BE! LYNDON JOHNSON–THE YOUTH OF CALIFORNIA DEDICATES ITSELF TO YOUR DESTRUCTION! ROLLING STONES–THE YOUTH OF CALIFORNIA HEARS YOUR MESSAGE! LONG LIVE THE REVOLUTION! ! !

But rhetoric like that did not bring out last January to a Human Be-In on the polo grounds of San Francisco's Golden Gate Park twenty thousand people who were there, fundamentally, just to see the other members of the tribe, not to hear speeches—the speeches were all a drag from Leary to Rubin to Buddah *—but just to *Be*.

In the Haight-Ashbury district the Love Generation organizes itself into Job Co-ops and committees to clean the streets, and the monks of the neighborhood, the Diggers, talk about free dances in the park to put the Avalon Ballroom and the Fillmore out of business and about communizing the incomes of Bob Dylan and the Beatles.

The Diggers trace back spiritually to those British millenarians who took over land in 1649, just before Cromwell, and after the Civil War freed it, under the assumption that the land was for the people. They tilled it and gave the food away.

The Diggers gave food away. Everything is Free. So is it with the Berkeley Provos and the new group in Cleveland —the Prunes—and the Provos in Los Angeles. More, if an extreme, assault against the money culture. Are they driving the money changers out of the temple? Perhaps. The Diggers say they believe it is just as futile to fight the system as to join it and they are dropping out in a way that differs from Leary's.

The Square Left wrestles with the problem. They want a Yellow Submarine community because that is where the strength so obviously is. But even *Ramparts,* which is the white hope of the Square Left, if you follow me, misunderstands. They think that the Family Dog is a rock group and that political activity is the only hope, and Bob Dylan says,

*The Be-In heard speeches by Timothy Leary, the psychedelic guru, Jerry Rubin, the leader of the Berkeley Vietnam Day movement, and Buddah, a bartender and minor figure in the San Francisco hippie movement who acted as master of ceremonies.

"There's no left wing and no right wing, only up wing and down wing," and also, "I tell you there are no politics."

But the banding together to form job Co-ops, to publish newspapers, to talk to the police (even to bring them flowers), aren't these political acts? I suppose so, but I think they are political acts of a different kind, a kind that results in the Hell's Angels being the guardians of the lost children at the Be-In and the guarantors of peace at dances.

The New Youth is finding its prophets in strange places—in dance hall and on the jukebox. It is on, perhaps, a frontier buckskin trip after a decade of Matt Dillon and *Bonanza* and the other TV folk myths, in which the values are clear (as opposed to those in the world around us) and right is right and wrong is wrong. The Negro singers have brought the style and the manner of the Negro gospel preacher to popular music, just as they brought the rhythms and the feeling of the gospel music, and now the radio is the church and Everyman carries his own walkie-talkie to God in his transistor.

Examine the outcry against the Beatles for John Lennon's remark about being more popular than Jesus. No radio station that depended on rock-'n'-roll music for its audience banned Beatles records, and in the only instance where we had a precise measuring rod for the contest—the Beatles concert in Memphis where a revival meeting ran day and date with them—the Beatles won overwhelmingly. Something like eight to five over Jesus in attendance, even though the Beatles charged a stiff price and the Gospel according to the revival preacher was free. Was my friend so wrong who said that if Hitler were alive today, the German girls wouldn't allow him to bomb London if the Beatles were there?

"Nobody ever taught you how to live out in the street," Bob Dylan sings in "Like a Rolling Stone." You may consider that directed at a specific person, or you may, as I do, consider it poetically aimed at plastic uptight America, to use a phrase from one of the Family Dog founders.

"Nowhere to run, nowhere to hide," Martha and the Vandellas sing, and Simon and Garfunkel say, "The words of the prophets are written on the subway walls, in tenement halls." And the Byrds sing, "A time for peace, I swear it's not too late," just as the Beatles sing, "Say the word." What has formal religion done in this century to get the youth of the world so well acquainted with a verse from the Bible?

Even in those artists of the second echelon who are not,

like Dylan and the Beatles and the Stones, worldwide in their influence, we find it. "Don't You Want Somebody to Love," the Jefferson Airplane sings, and Bob Lind speaks of "the bright elusive butterfly of love."

These songs speak to us in our condition, just as Dylan did with "lookout kid, it's somethin' you did, god knows what, but you're doin' it again." And Dylan sings again a concept that finds immediate response in the tolerance and the anti-judgment stance of the new generation, when he says, "There are no trials inside the Gates of Eden."

Youth is wise today. Lenny Bruce claimed that TV made even eight-year-old girls sophisticated. When Bob Dylan in "Desolation Row" sings, "At midnight all the agents and the superhuman crew come out and round up everyone that knows more than they do," he speaks true, as he did with "don't follow leaders." But sometimes it is, as John Sebastian of the Lovin' Spoonful says, "like trying to tell a stranger 'bout a rock-'n'-roll."

Let's go back again to Nietzsche.

> Orgiastic movements of a society leave their traces in music [he wrote]. Dionysiac stirrings arise either through the influence of those narcotic potions of which all primitive races speak in their hymns [—dig that!—] or through the powerful approach of spring, which penetrates with joy the whole frame of nature. So stirred, the individual forgets himself completely. It is the same Dionysiac power which in medieval Germany drove ever-increasing crowds of people singing and dancing from place to place; we recognize in these St. John's and St. Vitus' dancers the bacchic choruses of the Greeks, who had their precursors in Asia Minor and as far back as Babylon and the orgiastic Sacea. There are people who, either from lack of experience or out of sheer stupidity, turn away from such phenomena, and strong, in the sense of their own sanity, label them either mockingly or pityingly "endemic diseases." These benighted souls have no idea how cadaverous and ghostly their "sanity" appears as the intense throng of Dionysiac revelers sweeps past them.

And Nietzsche never heard of the San Francisco Commission on Juvenile Delinquency or the Fillmore and the Avalon ballrooms.

"Believe in the magic, it will set you free," the Lovin' Spoonful sing. "This is an invitation across the nation," sing Martha and the Vandellas, and the Mamas and the Papas, "a chance for folks to meet, there'll be laughin', singin' and music swingin', and dancin' in the street!"

Do I project too much? Again, to Nietzsche. "Man now expresses himself through song and dance as the member of a higher community; he has forgotten how to walk, how to speak and is on the brink of taking wing as he dances . . . no longer the *artist*, he has himself become *a work of art*."

"Hail hail rock-'n'-roll," as Chuck Berry sings. "Deliver me from the days of old!"

I think he's about to be granted his wish.

GROUPIES: A STORY OF OUR TIMES

TOM NOLAN

The March of Time's issue about teen-age girls is worth seeing in the sense that one might examine with interest a slide of cancer tissue. These girls may be no worse than the teen-age girls of any other country, class, or generation, but I would be sorry really to believe that, and am sorrier still to imagine their children.

—JAMES AGEE, 1945

It was the warm Saturday afternoon blues concert at the Monterey Pop Festival, and Brian Jones of the Rolling Stones was sitting in the second row of wooden chairs in the press section sipping on a Budweiser, dressed in a tattered-looking nineteenth-century gown of lace-and-fur-and-Tudor-ragged-cloth, an Iron Cross dangling from his neck. He looked, with his pallid face, like an attenuated, dissipated little man: lines about his eyes, bleached and wrinkled and wrapped in lace and fur—the washed-out face of a randy Pan, Harpo touched with the acerbic leer of the sixties.

Sitting next to him was Nico, regal, untouchable, a slender reed in a velvet gown, sipping on a Lucky Lager.

The beer made everything hazily pleasant, even Monkee Peter Tork conspicuously walking up, conspicuously presenting his conspicuous hand. "It's a great honor, sir, it's a great *honour,*" he beams, shaking, Monkee-bashful. Then, Monkee-cute, "You know . . . there's about a hundred photographers just *dying* to get that shot; would you mind, again?"

"Oh," says Brian, taken aback. "Oh, well . . . if you really *want* to."

They shake again, and Monkee Peter beams, golliwogs down the aisle, clowning for the cameras, a puppet on a string.

"Eeeea*aah,*" says Brian softly. "How . . . *embarrassing.*"

Then someone asks Brian what he things about groupies;

and he looks narrowly at the questioner. And thinks. And says carefully, noncommittally, "Well . . . sort of depends. Depends on your definition of *groupie*. All sorts of definitions, you know. Ah dunno, they're easily avoidable."

But later the question gets more specific. Brian is walking with Nico in the artist-and-press area, and someone comes up to him and asks what does he think of Sherry Sklar. Brian tosses his hair. "Uhmmmm, well . . . it's hard to say, actually. Oh, hallo!" and takes the opportunity to wave to someone he has just seen, and walkoffveryquickly because even though he doesn't like to talk about it, Brian Jones of the Rolling Stones knows Sherry Sklar.

Knows Sherry Sklar. *Knows* Sherry Sklar. Now Sherry Sklar isn't walking beside him; no, of course not—Nico is: Nico, silver-haired moon goddess in a velvet gown; Nico, the solitary queen in her midnight castle; Nico, the poets' lady. Dylan "discovered" her in Europe and he and Grossman, his manager, urged her to come to New York, where she soon became Andy Warhol's Chelsea Girl-of-the-Year; and French movie stars were known to call that summer, and then Eric Anderson and Timmy Hardin and Leonard Cohen and Jackson Browne and all the fine young men began writing songs *for* her, *about* her: Nico, the poets' lady—because Nico is, after all, the most awe-inspiring, lonely, ghostly-death's-head-of-a-god-awful-gorgeous-girl in the whole round world.

But Sherry Sklar is no Nico—not by a long long long long shot. Though she tries very hard; and she *has* attained a certain position.

At about this time Sherry is wandering around the same backstage area, looking as she does, pale, blond, reasonably attractive, in orange-tinted shades (which, if she removes them, reveal the faintly predatory look most often seen in Hollywood starlets-on-the-make, a look that always sadly surprises when found in one so young—Sherry is nineteen). But Sherry is not speaking to Brian, or to the ex-Raiders, or to any of the others she knows who are there; perhaps because of a certain propriety observed in such matters (after all, they are with other people, after *all*), or just because right now she is so very *involved*—as Sherry is always involved, *busy*, so many places to go, people to see. . . .

But right now she is busy because the most wonderful thing may be happening, all the incredible rumors are spreading like mad locusts: the Beatles are here, the Beatles are here, McCartney has checked into the Motor Inn and all their equipment stashed in the back (which is cordoned off); George is backstage with no beard or mustache; McCartney is traveling under the name of Mr. Webb; no the Beatles are all together and yes have registered under the name "Sgt. Pepper's Band;" yes they're going to close the show Sunday night; singing, no they're not going to sing but they will talk; yes it's decided; no nothing's decided until they see how the crowd is acting. . . .

And through all of this Sherry is going absolutely mad—she cannot pay attention to Monkee Micky Dolenz wandering around dressed as an American Indian, sitting down on the ground to lecture a group of twelve-year-olds on philosophy. She has enough problems trying to convince her friends to come back with her to the Motor Inn—they've *got* to get to him if he's there. And meanwhile the two girls she is with, the sister of the drummer-singer of America's No. 1 Clean-Cut-Wholesome-Group (whose group co-member is paying for Sherry's motel room—are you catching this?—even though she's driven up there with the drummer from yet *another* group, an Englishman) and *her* friend, and the other two girls don't like the coat she's wearing; it's a pink imitation-leather carcoat-jacket-thing and she *likes* it you see but the other girls want her to take it off (they are, all three of them, up on acid) and getting involved in their thing, she figures why should she take the coat off because the coat is *her* isn't it? and if they don't like her and want to accept her as she is, well that's just too bad isn't it and they know what they can do then, on the other hand, I mean, after all, if it's *bringing them down*—oh, what to *do!*

2

The excitement is everywhere. . . .

The two girls live together in a Hollywood apartment where the walls are covered with collages, more ambitious than accomplished, of rock-group members cut from teen magazines. They are finishing off a joint, and one girl is cocktailing the roach, placing it in the end of a Tareyton with the last inch of tobacco removed; the end is twisted and lit for a few drags: no tobacco, very stony.

"I heard Arthur Lee is leaving Love," she says.

"Oh no, *not* Arthur! They'll be *nothing* without him."

"Somebody on KFWB said it; BMR, or maybe it was Gene Weed, I forget which."

"Well, he'll be on the album at least, because he's in the picture on the billboard on Sunset."

She means the billboard on the Sunset Strip heralding their next record, captioned: "Watch for the Third Coming of Love." The Nitty Gritty Dirt Band has a billboard, too, as does Jim Kweskin's Jug Band and the Doors. The excitement is everywhere. The rock poets are today's Hemingways and Fitzgeralds; work-in-progress is eagerly awaited; its appearance causing critical discussion. Group members are watched closely: Zally's left the Spoonful to go it on his own, just like Harry James left Benny Goodman; three of the Stones got busted for drugs, just like Gene Krupa—pop fans being as interested today as in the days of swing. With an added interest.

The excitement is everywhere.

At the newsstands they cluster (the younger ones: thirteen, fourteen) on alternate Wednesdays, glomming through the new issues of *Tiget Beat, Teenset, Go!*—Look, Denny's back with the Springfield! And isn't McGuinn's beard *bitchen!* And all the Raiders are gone—what a bummer! And look, Brian Jones shaking hands with Peter!

They wait outside the RCA Hollywood Studios when word gets out that the Monkees or Stones are recording, and standing outside, hoping to catch a glimpse next to the Magic-marker autographs of Monkees Micky and Davy, they hesitantly leave scrawls of affection:

Peter	Mike	
o	is a	Mick Rules
R	Doll	
K		

"Micky rules all, especially me!" and others—nasties—which will eventually be obliterated by spray paint.

They go into the girls' room of the Hullabaloo (a club on Sunset for mostly pre-teenyboppers) and (along with general information like "Bullwinkle lives on in acid" and "A friend with weed is a friend indeed") leave anonymous judgments: "Larry of the Knack is bitchen," "Doors are outasite," "Lovin' Spoonful rule over all and everyone," and—hopefully —"Steve Boone and me."

They went to the Beatles' movies over and over and over and screamed and sighed and melted and Ringo is so sad—oh!—and laughed when he said, "I've 'ad a lotta *fun* with this finguh"—they knew what *that* meant! And they go to the Stones concerts—"O, God if he sings 'Lady Jane' I'll die! O, God if he sings 'Under My Thumb'! Or God if he sings 'Lady Jane' or 'Under My Thumb' I'll die!"—screaming and writhing and moaning, their apple asses a-tremble in flowered bell-bottoms while old Mick bumps and grinds and prances in the evening air, his tight white pants showing the lumpy shadow of his—*you* know—"*Oh, MICK, oh, MICK! UP HERE! Oh, that dancing* turns me on more than his *singing! OOAAWWHH!* Oh mister mister *please* mister *please please* mister let me use your binoculars please I'll do anything please I'll do anything if you let me use 'em, please mister please I'll do *anything!*"

But while all those legions of wistful bell-bottomed girls are dreaming about Paulie and screaming for Mick to come up here where I can get my *fingernails* into you! there are an ambitious few who are doing something about it. While all the nubile fans dream and wish and hope—well, maybe someday I could-might-would . . . *meet,* maybe, someday, maybe—and write pointless fan letters with flowers drawn on the envelopes (well, he *might* read it)—there are girls who are making the dream reality, the unattainable available . . .

In the girls' room of the Hullabaloo, a graffito proclaims: "I was screwed by Joe Naples and *wow!*"

Outside the RCA Studios the security guard says: "Yeah, I put twelve extra men out when the Stones are here, but a few girls still get in. They break locks; they bust doors. They get in."

Some don't even have to bust locks.

Baby baby baby you're
Out of time . . .

There are two session men on guitar recording a rock album, seasoned pros, and every time the tuba plays this part, the one on bass guitar, behind the rock leader's back, goes into his silly routine of an arm-flopping prancing elephantine fairy-child (all the while still seated in his metal folding chair), and this pretty much breaks up the other guitarist just about every time. The next coffee break the second guitarist starts building a riff off an old song (he used to be one of the most famous jazz guitarists in the country)—"Do you know what that is? 'Sweet Georgia Brown.'" No-gal-made-has-scadoobetyoopn-scoobedybleeopmbliblip— "That's the trouble with these songs today, you just can't *jam* on 'em"—Guys-she-can't-get-scoody-lyoopmatwidbbidybopmbleopblipblop-bli-blop—and then they get started talking about the kids today, and the fellow who's jamming away on Georgia is saying how the thing that really worries him, the thing that has *him* scared, is what happens when these kids today, who have no responsibility at *all* of *any* kind (just can't fathom the kind of things that can *happen* to them), is what happens to them when they have to face some kind of *stark reality,* like being confronted with the fact that *they're pregnant*. . . .

And then for some reason that reminds him of something he heard the other day, Jerry told him, you know Jerry? Well he was over at some studios, and he says *no*body could get in, but he was there on a session the other night, and those guys, the *Mmm*-mm-mmm, they were in there in Studio B, and they had two chicks from somewhere, and they were down there on the floor, two of the *Mmm*-mm mmm, just . . . *doing* it . . . and everybody else was just standing around watching; I guess they were *producing* the session, right? Oh, *wow*. . . .

3

Have you seen your mother, baby,
Standing in the shadow?

Sherry's parents are sitting quietly in the living room of the closest-thing-residential-Bel Air-can-come-to-a-minor-modern-palace. Her mother, a now mostly quiet woman exuding the somewhat sad air of one who has paid the dues of her husband's long ascent up the pyramid of corporate corridors, is sitting under the tasteful Tiffany lamp, braving her way through Chapter 18 of Elia Kazan's *The Arrangement.* Mr. Sklar, sitting in a somewhat garish orange armchair (the sole concession to *his* decorating taste), is watching the third night of ABC's Very Special Season in color (tomorrow he will watch the fourth night of NBC Week). The phone rings, it is for Sherry; even though Sherry has had her own phone disconnected, an incredible number of people manage to get the family number; and Mrs. Sklar smiles sweetly, gently, primly, and explains that Sherry is not at home this evening, she has gone to the library to return a book, no, she doesn't know when. . . .

At about this time Sherry, overdue library book in hand, is parked in her pink Mustang high in the Hollywood Hills, the city all a-twinkle below her, below her, and she watches the house she is about to enter, the house of the drummer of America's Number One Money-Making Group. She watches through the window of his den as he, unawares, flails away at his drums. His group is often accused of being blatant bogus-Beatles, and so it is somewhat ironic (and Sherry, cynical-sharp, is not unaware of this) that the record he is practicing to is the Beatles' "Lucy in the Sky with Diamonds"; and even though it is a fairly slow song, he can't . . . quite . . . keep the beat . . . and just before going in, she smiles slightly around the corners of her mouth and mind; she keeps her sense of perspective.

It all began for Sherry, all of it, when she formed the Boss Beatle Booster Fan Club in 1964, when she was fifteen and innocent. This was the year of the English Invasion: the Beatles, Stones, Gerry and the Pacemakers, Billy Jay Kramer and the Dakotas, the Dave Clark Five, the Searchers, Herman's Hermits, Peter and Gordon, Chad and Jeremy, Manfred Mann, Zombies, Kinks—and it was all so exciting and fun, and anyway it was something to *do.*

Because you must understand Sherry was really *innocent;* not that she had any particular scruples then, just a vague sort of sense of respectability, due mainly to her not yet being exposed to any intrusion (in the form of some randy back-seat young hard-breathing son of a golfing tycoon) that would break the vacuum of and expose the half-ridden hypocrisy behind her parents' country-club world of what proper young girls did and did not do—Sherry, then, was Innocent.

The idea of her Boss Beatle Booster Fan Club was that everyone who showed their Sincere Affection and joined could get a Boss Beatle Booster Fan Club Card, each of which is probably worth a small fortune now, expressions of Sincere Affection coming at a premium price these days; but still, Sherry was not content with what was, after all, really a minor sort of gesture. It was all somehow not quite right, there seemed to be something missing here; perhaps Sherry was slightly out-of-place.

At the giant Beatle Rally at the Coliseum, for instance,

when all of L.A.'s pretty young things turned out merely to stand up and be counted; they came from Glendale and Pasadena and Pacoima for the Fab Four, Tarzana and Orange and Encino for the Lovely Liverpool Lads, Long Beach and Lakewood and Burbank for the Bashful Bragging Beautiful Boys—and—they wore almost-bursting bell-bottoms, the thin-tight cloth flower-painting their bods, they had just learned to love their mod-bods, tanned and lean and budding, and they shook their hair in the open air with just the touch of a frosted-pink slicker lipstick mist-kiss on their lips—and then—there was Sherry, a bit demure (as was only proper), blond of course but wearing the prim white dress-suit she and Mother had picked out because it was Her.

Well, she had to do something; something had to be done. Something large, and really *major.* She decided on a scroll, a really *major* scroll, with hundreds of names giving testimony to Great Affection and Sincere Loyalty (with each signer getting a Boss Beatle Booster Fan Club Card); she began collecting the signatures.

And yet—it somehow still didn't seem quite enough, and she noticed the beginnings of what she could only think of as . . . strange . . . *stirrings,* which began about the time she went to see the Rolling Stones on the Hollywood Palace TV Show, where Dean Martin kept cracking all his silly "jokes" about the Stones and all the old people in the audience, of course, they all *laughed;* and near the end of the show Sherry had run down from the balcony outside to the stage door to see the Stones, but really, it was something *else,* she couldn't say quite what, she'd never dreamed aloud, but it was . . . *strange;* and the handful of girls there seemed (she sensed) to be driven by the same strange Muse—and nothing happened, the Stones didn't show. But—

Somethin' happened to me yesterday
Somethin' I can't speak of right away

The oddness continued, through the next week and up to the Wednesday morning when she heard the one and only radio announcement that A—— and W—— were arriving at the airport, and naturally she hurried on down to welcome them and, as it turned out, was the only one there. Which was nice, because they talked to her. Alone. On and on they talked, and she welcomed them to California, and the one who had taken an especial interest in her, he smiled with his tired eyes, and leaned over; she was wearing a darling little A-line dress with rather large buttons over the, uh, breasts, and he just pressed the buttons; firmly. And this pretty little innocent little blond girl just didn't know what to *do,* she just didn't know *what* to do; so she went home. . . .

Give it to me now,
I've no objec-tion . . .

But it was a brush with fame, and Sherry had liked the hint of the something she had sniffed, and somehow couldn't just stop now. And so, to put it briefly, decided to take the Ultimate Step—not so hard as some might imagine, in fact ridiculously easy to arrange, and though details are boring, it was with a fairly popular English group that has since faded into obscurity, but they weren't a bad beginning, pretty auspicious in those days; and she would eventually make it with much much bigger groups. And once she got over her initial shyness, why, you'd think she had been doing it all her life! Rolling around in a giant bed, the four of them, she and her newfound friend Karen, and two members of a Philly White-Soul group, trading, switching, tumbling around—those guys, Sherry concedes, when she starts remembering the good old times in a misty-wistful kind of way, those guys, re*mem*ber? those guys were . . . *probably* . . . the best.

No one knows;
She comes, and goes . . .

She usually got in on the action by finding out when groups were in town and cruising the hotels on the Strip, looking up at balconies, and sooner or later—sure enough! there they'd be, shaggy-haired, lonely-looking, raunchy-looking . . . randy-looking. . . . She'd shout up and ask them their room numbers; and just in case the guys hadn't gotten the idea by then—and also for general use (she was going into this in a really big way), she had all these engraved cards printed up, plain little white cards that simply say I WANT YOU—though lately she has been having variations made up, like LET'S GET IT ON. And after a while she began collecting souvenirs, and now has a giant jingling chain full of keys from hotel rooms, the rooms of all the famous boys she has "been with."

We love they
We hope you love they too . . .

But of course the very best of boys were still the Beatles, and Sherry had by now, on the side, gathered hundreds of signatures for her major scroll which she planned to present to the Beatles, whose arrival was imminent. Finding them, though, was something else. She found out approximately where they'd be by going into a closet with a rock DJ and working on him for three hours—his stupid velour and his shades and Jay Sebring razorcut—boy was *he* terrible!

She had camped there then, up in Bel Air, at a strategic point; the Beatles could not leave without passing her, there being only one way down the hill; and even if the guard wouldn't let her in, why, she'd get a chance at them on their way to the airport. And sure enough, they finally came down, and saw her following them, and probably thought she'd stop once they got on the San Diego freeway to the airport, but they were wrong because Sherry kept up with them, pulled alongside, in fact (no small thing, as they were going about 85 mph). Sherry leaned out the window and there were the Beatles, dreamlike, in the next lane, rocketing down the freeway with the Beatles' driver trying to lose her or something. Sherry was just trying to throw her goddam scroll through their window but Brian Epstein (who was in the Beatle car too) thought she was trying to *hurl* herself from her car to theirs or something, and he started yelling "DON'T—JUMP! DON'T BE—ALITTLE—FOOL! YOU—WILL—ONLY—INJURE—YOURSELF!" And by this time they were going about 95 mph, and finally she pulled back to the car behind, where one of the Beatles' staff was fondling some chick in his lap, and Sherry threw the goddam scroll through the window and he dumped the girl off his lap and started *reading* it! Wow! How funny! But then a cop pulled her over and she gets tagged for —tailgating! and that was that.

Not that she always goes to such extremes, because compared to some people she knows, that's a relatively primitive ploy. There was one girl, for instance, who along with her friends decided to find where the Beatles were staying one time by hiring a helicopter and flying all over Bel Air so she and her friends could wave to the Guys at poolside; she didn't get *in,* but they waved a lot. And the next day the Beatles held a press conference to which this girl managed to get herself invited through persuading some DJ—all these girls know *all* the DJ's—to let her in, providing she didn't cause a fuss.

So the girl hangs around for an hour or so, and then leaves just before it ends, hoping to beat the Beatles' cars to the Bowl; and just at that point some DJ is talking to Paul and saying there were these girls, you know, Paul, who rented a copter; you know, Paul, a *helicopter,* and flew over your house, did you know that Paul? And Paul says, oh yes, we'd like to meet them, are they here? Girls? Girls? and eager to please Paul, the murmur starts growing louder and louder, filling the room, girls? girls? GIRLS? That moment, when that girl remembers it, the moment she will never forget as long as she lives, that moment, drives her to moaning and turning green and writhing in agony and everything just short of pulling out all her lovely California-chic hair—she came—*so close!*

No, Sherry usually sticks to relatively less imaginative ways of finding groups, like the habit she developed of hiring limousines to cruise the streets in, up and down Sunset, that sort of thing. After a while the drivers got to know her, and what she was up to, and they'd point to likely-looking long-hairs at bus stops: How 'bout him? Ya wanna pick him up? And now it's not too cool to take the limousines because all the drivers know about her and have started making big old hints like, *weeeeee!* now, wouldn't mind *havin'* some a' that there stuff yer givin' away there, nosirnosirnosirnosir. . . .

Of course Sherry has her memories, fond ones, many of them funny, like the time she and Karen decided to take their friend Linda to see her fave-rave English group leader at his hotel at some ungodly hour, and the girls drag her out of the shower, clinging wet, all this is sort of a joke anyway, because this girl is seventeen and *incredibly* pure, never been with *any*one, and they drag her into the poor guy's room, and he offers her his bathrobe, which she goes into the bathroom to put on. Meanwhile there is a knock on the door and in burst her parents, with the hotel manager, and Linda emerges from the bathroom in this star's dressing gown, with her father yelling about aliens! coming over here! and—oh! and everybody is shouting and explanations are demanded and papers are seized and—finally, this nice guy with his faggoty glasses and his beard is deported, and can never come back to America again, and—because record-plugging tours are often essential—will never have a hit here *ever again.* Wow, remembers Sherry, it's all too funny! And she wouldn't have even let him do anything with her! Oh *wow!*

Or the time she had lassoed two entire groups at the airport, and they were waiting for her by her car and she couldn't find the car keys! Here she is at the airport and they're standing around, about eight guys, shuffling their feet, and she's pouring out her handbag, shaking it out on the hood, just can't find them! Well! And she was laughing so hard she pissed in her pants! . . .

Of course a lot of things have happened since then; a lot of things have changed. And you must not get the idea that Sherry has no standards; some people, after all, are really just out-of-the-question; for instance, *Ne*-groes, well, that's really perverted, isn't it? and she doesn't go in for any of those *kinky* practices. And one group she wouldn't "be with" because when they switched from good-time music to intellectual-rock, well, they just went way out of their league, she wouldn't have a thing to do with them.

Following these somewhat strange standards, Sherry has attained a certain status. She is not your run-of-the-mill groupie: when she goes somewhere it is because she has been invited. At Monterey she travels with a member of one of the most famous groups: she is his guest, having all the privileges of same; she is part of pop society, even if only the fringes, but retrenching all the time; and even though she may not absolutely be *the numero uno* (there is a girl in New York rumored to have had *both* Jagger and McCartney, and another girl who has only had Keith Richard, which is, after all, not the same as having had Jagger, but this is made up for by her having had Lennon, who counts for two times with McCartney), nonetheless she is *known*, a person in her own right, and whenever major crises come up she is there to help. Like when a famous teenybopper idol raided one group to refill his own depleted ranks, causing a certain amount of bad feeling, why, Sherry was right in there, acting the intermediary, hopping in her car, let's find out what all this is all about! Let's settle this!

Meanwhile her old friend and sometime-companion Karen is beginning to wonder about it all, or at least certain parts of it, like the way she will ask strangers do they think she looks—well, *used* . . .

Who wants yesterday's papers
Who wants yesterday's girl . . .

and it is true that her fragile blonde prettiness is beginning to harden around the edges, and though she isn't quite as hard-looking as Sherry, maybe she has gotten to the point where the faces are all beginning to blur together in a hazy kind of fog. . . .

4

Dying all the time;
Lose your dreams and you will lose your mind—

I saw her first at my high school, where I would return melancholic to the scene of my past and most recent triumphs—she was awfully unquestionably pretty in a way that brought back the unbearable loneliness of a summer afternoon—in a pretty calendar-day-sort-of-way; some must have called her beautiful, but just as surely it was a sad beauty; for she was the girl who seemed somehow sadly older, this coming with the territory, and boys (and some girls too) would whisper jokes about her behind their hands. And she smiled often (though wistfully) and was touched deeply by any small act of kindness, that commodity being more precious to her, perhaps, and less given, than for the rest of us.

And she wanted to be a model, of course, like every other halfway decent-looking girl in town, and even some who weren't but made the trek anyhow from Racine, Wisconsin, with money for pictures and The School. But she didn't have to worry, she was beautiful; life for her was different, I thought—the candy apple of the month.

I had hardly spoken to her at all, only briefly, passing in a corridor—could she sense my clumsy, well-meaning feelings? But we saw her, my older cousin and I, he on a visit from Cleveland, Ohio, with his fine Marine sensibilities honed on a life of drive-in-theater passion with the rest of his buddies looking on from their own back seats—"Sure, they knew what we were doin' back there; after that I left her. She wanted me, but I left her, an' now you can see her at the dances up at Broadview Heights. Waitin' round. Tryin' to pick up somebody; anybody"—he shakes his head at her stupidity, the awful and comical depth of her fall.

And then we saw my friend on TV, some teen-age show; she was taking telephone votes for the dance contest and I said, "I *know* that girl; isn't she great looking?" and because (I knew) he didn't believe me (I had been making these claims through three days of watching television), I phoned her on the show, at which point my now-convinced cousin started whispering hoarsely, "Can-she-fix-me-up? Ask-her-can-she-fix-me-up!" and a double-date was arranged; and even though my cousin, an unbearable clod, had been just that—on our way to pick them up, for instance, I had asked why the blanket folded neatly on the back seat? "Oh, leave it, that's to show we're . . . *studs*"—and when we had gone (of all places) bowling, and he leaned over suavely with the ball poised suavely studying the length of the alley, his shirt pulled up to reveal his underwear—bad enough, but he had also comically managed to put his shorts on inside-out, so that in the small of his back is the little square cloth proclaiming "Fruit of the Loom"—and she looks at her friend—and s-i-l-e-n-t-l-y l-a-u-g-h-s . . . but in spite of my cousin, she is nice to me, and on the way back she allows me to kiss her and then, tentatively, fondle her breast, enough to impress my cousin, his eyes glued constantly to the rear-view mirror, she and I wrapped under his precious flannel stud-blanket.

I never saw her too often after that, either, but I kept in touch; she had fallen into a certain circle, calculated to enlarge her somewhat hazy plans of a singing-dancing-modeling career, and soon she was dancing on a go-go show, jerking swaying moaning bumping hips glistening with the best long-haired blond-haired Strip-chicks of all, while the director who by-god knew his trade jockeyed the cameras for the up-the-skirt shot; and the groups who guested stared and licked their lips and smiled. (Oh the first one, yes, the first one: California Good-Time Music he made, he told her, in the back seat of his car.)

Connections of sorts developed—here and there; this and that. Plans to be made, something brewing all the time. This and that, here and there; a trip to Brazil for that TV show that never quite came off, but then again . . . maybe she would go on a tour, she and three other girls, they'd sing and dance, a little go-go revue; like, this guy was fixing it up, their manager, maybe next month. Things are coming, you know, okay, not bad, you know, pretty good, oh except for this and that—some dyke keeps phoning, says she's going to kill her—but then—acid is new and very large and there are always lots of famous people around, she is getting known in a small way, she's had some of the best of the less-known groups, this bass player, that lead singer, and one night Dylan even came over, a bunch of people brought him by, she could show the pictures to you. . . . And everything seemed to be fine, the world it seemed was turning ever-sweetly in a funny kind of way, if a bit slanted on its axis, but just . . . certain things . . .

Where she lived, the way she lived; the hint of something else (a plea perhaps) on the edge of a question. She stayed with a friend, another dancer, having moved out from her mother's some time ago. They had fixed the place up, she and her friend, with a lot of painfully artsy pop collages and the like, and there were always a lot of books lying around but she never quite got around to finishing any of them, and she and her friend would put on some campy little record, "Snow White and the Seven Dwarfs," and put on big floppy hats and jump all over and dance through the kitchen and into the living room and it was strangely sad; and upsetting.

Or the way you'd be talking and for no reason at all she'd say something like "Well, after all, who's to say what's Good and what's Bad?" and I didn't realize she might after all desperately want some kind of an answer.

After a while I fell out of touch and didn't see her for many months. When I did it was about one in the morning in front of a bittersweet coffeehouse in Hollywood, and any trace of that special spring-freshness she had once had seemed irretrievably lost; her face was drawn, dissipated, almost haggard; perhaps she ran through a Garbo beauty before her eyes turned harsh. Maybe it was the gonorrhea; she joked about being cured three different times, but most likely she had never lost it the first time. Surely it was one thing or another.

While her girl friend—the latest in a long succession of friends, boy and girl, none of whom stayed for much of the trip—was inside having her foot read by a kindly melancholy old German in spectacles, she told me about the spacemen. They had contacted her one night, now they wanted her to spy on the world for them, to spy on earth, and they would pay her very well, don't you know, very well indeed, and give her all the clothes she could ever imagine, and take her places, far away, but she didn't *know,* she just didn't know what to *do,* you see; she just didn't know what to do. . . .

5

By the time you're thirty gonna look
sixty-five
You won't look purty and your
friends will have kissed you good-bye . . .

Sherry is looking out the window of the Laurel Canyon house where she lives with Danny, a computer programmer in his twenties. (Karen cuts his hair.) Covering one window is a giant poster of James Dean. Sherry sits down on the floor, barefoot in white capris and sweater, starts playing with Pepper, their white kitten named after the Beatles' *Sgt. Pepper.* She grabs the rubber ball he is pawing, holding it just out of reach. "Hey, you're a sadist, you know, that's what you are. A sadist," Danny says. He grabs Kitten by the scruff of the neck, holds it up, drops it. Sherry goes to the window again to look out into the street. "Hey, here comes one of those freaky-looking guys," she says. "Wow! What a freaky-looking guy. Maybe he's in a group."

Sherry doesn't see too much of her old friends any more. There's really not that much to do, now that she's sort of settled down. Karen comes over about once a week, of course; but they don't . . . *go out.* And once in a while some of Danny's friends come over, and they'll all sing old Beatle songs, or the Mamas and Papas—she has a guitar and a big stack of songbooks—and Sherry sings in her strident slightly flat way and maybe Danny will make a joke, you know, just a little *remark* or something, and she'll flash her eyes at him, a trifle harsh, a trifle mean, and—"Well, mister, if it's so easy why don't *you* sing it!"—and it's just not the same; not like when she and Karen and who knows, maybe a guy or two, would go out *cruising,* looking for guys in rock groups, and maybe end up bribing the guard at the Hollywood Bowl with a cup of coffee and a doughnut (they'd cruised there so many times they knew to get him coffee. With cream. And now the guard—it was *too funny!*—he'd been starting to act a little randy, just a *l-e-e-t-l-e* bit, don't-you-know, looking at them, smiling, lips dry), and getting up on the stage at one in the morning, whatever and singing "If I Fell [for You]"; those were good times. Sherry doesn't see her friends any more.

Sherry stares out the window and the Stones are on the phonograph, and Sherry starts to chant along off-key:

All of my friends from school grew
and they mortgaged off their lives.
up and settled down

Karen has enrolled in Ravi Shankar's Indian music school, hoping one day to get at George Harrison.

THE DECLINE AND FALL OF BRITISH RHYTHM AND BLUES

●

IAN BIRCHALL

Is it possible to make a serious social analysis of popular music, and relate stylistic developments within it to the context in which they occur? The contention of this article is that it is possible to see a correspondence between the content of popular songs and the ideas and attitudes of the social groups among which they are popular. It will therefore be as well to begin by looking at some of the common objections to the validity of such an approach.

First, it is commonly argued that popular music is a purely commercial art form, and that changes of taste result from blatant manipulation of the market by commercial interests. In reply, three points can be made. One, that all art, since the decline of patronage in the eighteenth century, has been commercial art, produced for the market. Though this may exercise a distorting influence, it would be hard to claim that no novel, no symphony, produced for the market has any intrinsic value. Second, as any close study of "plugging" will reveal, the manufacturer is not always able to enforce new fashions onto the audience. On the contrary, many of the most significant developments in popular music have come from fields like jazz and rhythm and blues which were commercially neglected until they achieved chart success. And third, if popular music is compared with the most blatant form of commercial manipulation, advertising, a clear distinction will be seen; advertising appeals to the arrogance, confidence and virility of the consumer; popular music comes much closer to reflecting his real feelings and insecurities.

Then it is often claimed that popular music is too trivial to require serious analysis. The question of ultimate aesthetic values may safely be left to posterity. It needs only to be pointed out that if a significant number of people devote a considerable amount of time and money to an art form, then a study of that art form will reveal something of their attitudes and preoccupations. For example, popular music is quite clearly at least as "serious" as comic picture postcards. And, as George Orwell demonstrated in *The Art of Donald McGill,* a study of such postcards reveals a great deal of the basic attitudes of the British working class.

The method of analysis remains a problem. In particular, there is the question as to how much importance can be attached to the words of popular songs. Mick Jagger has gone on record as saying of some lyrics: "a lot of it is very good verse, and is easily as good as popular verse in the last century." (*International Times,* May 17, 1968.) Providing one is not pedantic in interpretation, and providing also that words are not taken in abstraction from the music which sets the mood to a whole song, a study of lyrics may be of value.

At the same time, it is dubious to what extent one can rely on the published charts as an indication of popularity—especially when increased radio time and tape recorders may be altering the whole pattern of record-buying. Certainly changes of fashion are not clear cut—one can hope only to identify general trends.

What follows is an attempt, *on an impressionistic level only,* to relate some recent trends over the period 1966–1968 in British popular music to some of the changes in British society over that same period.

On May 1, 1968, half the records in the *New Musical Express* Top Thirty were by American artists. This represents a dramatic shift back to the situation before 1963, when the Beatles, Rolling Stones, etc., established an authentic British style of rhythm and blues which excluded all but a few American artists from the British charts, and created a worldwide audience for British rock music.

The return to American hegemony of the British charts only confirms a fact that has been obvious for some time—the disintegration of the particular school of British rhythm and blues that grew up in the wake of the Beatles. Many of the best groups, like the Searchers or Gerry and the Pacemakers, have disbanded or sunk into oblivion; others have changed their whole style. The Beatles have completely renounced the style of their early hits and embarked on a series of formal experiments, some of which have been audacious successes, while others have verged dangerously on the esoteric, and have, one suspects, been successful only on the basis of the group's previous reputation. This group, whose early records owed their success to the concreteness of the lyrics and the situations they evoked, have had a long flirtation with mysticism and meditation.

The Rolling Stones have suffered badly from misfortunes having nothing to do with music as such, but have also been seduced by formal experiment. They are far from being the automatic chart-toppers they were in 1965 and 1966. Eric Burdon, who in his early work with the Animals gave an authentic feel of Newcastle even when using American material, has fallen prey to the cult of San Francisco. The Hollies, who with "Just Like Me," "Searchin' " and "Stay" produced some of the best and hardest rock sounds of 1963, are now allowing a strong element of sentimentality into their work. Songs like "Carrie Anne" and "Jennifer Eccles" appear to be primarily aimed at a junior high school market.

In short, the basic trend that can be observed in the development of British music in the period 1966 to 1968 is a move away from rhythm and blues as a basic style. A look at the history of rhythm and blues will show the importance of this. As its very name suggests, rhythm and blues contains a fundamental antinomy. The "blues" element reflects its origin among the American Negroes as the art form of an oppressed social group. It evokes melancholy and frustration, whether sexual or social in origin. Added to this, is, however, the element of "rhythm," the driving aggressive beat of rock music. Rhythm and blues therefore combines an awareness of frustration and oppression with a vigorous rejection of it. With only minor modifications, this style, originating among American Negroes, could be transferred to reflect the attitudes and preoccupations of British working-class youth in the early sixties.

The tension inherent in rhythm and blues is apparent in all the early classics of British beat music. All the first Beatles' hits combine a feeling of buoyant optimism and a wistful melancholy—to which they added an earthy realism provided by their effective use of phrases from everyday language—"Please Please Me"; "From Me to You"; "Thank-you, Girl." For the first time rhythm and blues was speaking English rather than American.

In a more aggressive key is the mood of injured frustration

and individualistic resentment in such Stones' classics as "Satisfaction" and "Get Off of My Cloud."

The first emergence of rock-and-roll in the mid-fifties represented a particular historical conjuncture. The first cracks were appearing in the structure of the cold war, with the end of the Korean war and the Hungarian revolution. The world situation was no longer totally polarized—one could be a rebel without being guilty of treason. Added to this was the arrival at adolescence of a new generation with no memory of the suffering and demoralization of the Second World War.

Britain in the late fifties and early sixties saw an unprecedented degree of political stability and general prosperity. The Conservative Government survived for thirteen years on the slogan of "You've never had it so good." The Labor Government took power in 1964, not so much because of anger and discontent as on a wave of rising expectations—there was a general feeling that outstanding problems could be solved within the framework of consensus politics.

But above all society was fragmented and individualistic. Improvements in living standards in a boom situation came from local bargaining and direct action—politics or identification with a social class seemed increasingly irrelevant to the real concerns of life. More and more working-class people, especially the young, told social scientists and opinion pollsters that they were not working class. Political apathy was defined, in the phrase of the distinguished historian E. P. Thompson, as "private solutions to public problems." For youth above all frustration and satisfaction were defined, not in social terms, but in relation to personal, and particularly sexual relations. It was this pattern of life that found its cultural reflection in the rock music of the years 1963 to 1966.

And it is precisely this individualism and privatization which characterizes the whole of popular music as a genre, and defines its limitations. The dominant theme of almost all popular music has been love in one form or another. There is an almost complete absence of both work songs and political songs, which in other periods have had wide popular currency. This seems to reflect the close on total sense of alienation in modern British society. A man's work is no longer a part of his real existence in any sense—it is not an experience which deserves a place in his culture (what sort of a song does one sing about an assembly line anyhow?). Similarly, politics in the conventional sense is so remote from everyday reality that it earns no place in a popular culture.

And so the vacuum created by this sense of alienation from social life is filled by personal relations. The cliché title of Engelbert Humperdinck's *There Goes My Everything* might sum this up—in a world where all else is meaningless, the love affair becomes everything.

But from 1966 onward the whole political climate was sharply transformed. The continuing economic crisis began to break down the feeling of security. Unemployment began to creep higher, affecting particularly the youth just leaving school. Wage restraint, price and rent increases, cuts in social services, all meant a steady erosion of living standards. A search for scapegoats for this decline led to an ugly upsurge of racist feeling directed against colored immigrants. The Vietnam war, although Britain was only indirectly involved, projected violence onto television screens; one consequence was the emergence of a much more violent approach by both police and demonstrators in political demonstrations.

Without further development of this sketched social analysis, it is obvious that British society, and British record-buying youth, is a good deal less secure than it was two or three years ago. Rhythm and blues offered a "controlled revolt"—an attitude of rebellion within a framework of acceptance; a position akin to the gradualistic reformism of consensus politics. Such a position no longer seemed tenable. The only attitudes that seemed meaningful were a complete acceptance of the status quo and an effort to hang onto the established patterns; or a total revolt against all established values in the name of a purely individualistic vision. Such a choice, of total inclusion or total exclusion, seems likely to remain the choice for British youth until some radical and plausible political alternative, of the left or right, emerges.

The result, as I have suggested, has been the decline of rhythm and blues as the dominant mode. Certainly there has been the much prophesied and much heralded "rock-'n'-roll revival." But this has been almost completely derivative. Bill Haley's old records are reentering the lower reaches of the charts—but very little music of a similar kind, though drawing on the developments of the last ten years, is being newly created. A great deal of recent rock music could be best described as "rhythm *without* blues"—a drearily insistent and repetitive beat with no authentic feeling in it.

The two most significant trends have reflected the choice of total inclusion or total exclusion—on the one hand the revival of the old-style ballad; on the other the various branches of so-called "psychedelic" music.

One of the most surprising features of recent British pop music, though explicable in terms of the above analysis, has been the outstanding success of Engelbert Humperdinck in singing a string of melodious, sentimental ballads with a faint touch of tame country and western about them. Tom Jones, forsaking the petulant eroticism of "It's Not Unusual" and "What's New, Pussycat?," and confining his attempts at rock to LPs, cashed in on this vogue, as have a number of other ballad singers. It would appear that the audience for this style is the older age range of the record-buyers—but many of them are the same generation who slashed cinema seats in honor of early Presley and Haley, or even screamed for the emergence of Lennon and Jagger.

In melody such songs are backward-looking; they reawake memories of the sort of music that was dominant before rock-and-roll emerged—and with it the more secure world that seemed to exist then; nostalgia for childhood is combined with a sense of increasing social crisis. The easily captured melody reinforces this sense of security.

In theme, too, the songs are essentially conservative; they are dominated by two basic myths: one, that love is the supreme consolation for all the other ills of life; secondly, that sorrow and suffering is inevitable, and must be stoically borne. The line "Tears have been my only consolation," from Ken Dodd's "Tears," sums up this stoicism neatly.

One need only compare the pleading tone of lines like:

> *Please release me, let me go,*
> *Release me and let me love again.*

with the aggressive anguish of the Stones "I can't get no satisfaction" to see a juxtaposition of two completely different approaches to life.

The opposite tendency may also be characterized as escapist, but in a very different way. Melody has been totally abandoned—it is rare to hear anyone with the skill to whistle a Pink Floyd or Procol Harum tune in the streets. Whereas traditionally pop music has evoked common situations—primarily, as I have suggested, of love lost or found—which finds a ready echo in the audience's experience, the new style concentrates on insistence on unique and individual experience.

Often, as in the Move's "I Can Hear the Grass Grow," there is a quite obvious claim to a private vision—and here the association with drug-induced fantasy is scarcely concealed. The necessity for a song to tell a story is abandoned completely—all that is required from the words is the creation of a striking and haunting image—thus the "sixteen vestal virgins leaving for the coast" of the Procol Harum's "A Whiter Shade of Pale."

A more complex effect is achieved by the juxtaposition of the unreal world of fantasy and the banality of everyday existence. This is a common theme of nineteenth-century poetry, but has only now reached popular music lyrics. Thus:

I walked thru' a field
That just wasn't real
One hundred tin soldiers
Which stood at my shoulder, and
All that I knew
Was the hole in my shoe
*Which was letting in water.**

The ultimate debt of such fantasy and irrationalism is to surrealism. How exactly such an influence percolated into popular music is not clear—if indeed it is an influence, and not just an apprehension of the irrational nature of the modern world. John Lennon, one of the best-read and most articulate of modern lyric writers, who has published two volumes of surrealistic writings, promptly denied firsthand knowledge of literary influences which were attributed to him. One source may be the radio comedy program of the fifties, *The Goon Show*, which showed a brilliant range of experiment in sound and linguistic effects. Another obvious influence is Bob Dylan,

* From "Hole in My Shoe," words and music by Davis Mason. Copyright © 1967 by Island Music Ltd., London, England. All Publication Rights controlled by Tro-Essex Music, Inc., New York, for the U.S.A., Canada, Central and South America. Used by permission.

whose sources would require a work of scholarship all to themselves.

But the source is not so important as the attempt to open up new ranges of experience. André Breton, the founder of surrealism as a literary movement, defined it thus:

> Surrealism is based on the belief in the superior reality of certain forms of association hitherto neglected, on the supremacy of dream, and the disinterested play of thought. It tends to definitively destroy all other physical mechanisms and substitute itself for them in the resolution of the principal problems of life.

Breton himself soon came to see that this revolt was not to be confined in purely escapist channels. It led him to a lifelong association with the political ideas of Leon Trotsky. Similarly, as the social crisis of modern Britain accelerates (and people seriously ask how soon it will be before the French crisis of May, 1968, is reenacted in Britain), it will be seen whether popular music continues to act merely as a form of escapism, or whether it will come to embody a more positive response to life.

There is some evidence that this may be happening. The earlier vogue for "protest songs" seems to have passed—Donovan, whose "Universal Soldier" made him a central figure of the "protest" school, has publicly renounced his belief in political commitment in pop music. But in any case these often seemed to be a manifestation of some kind of moralizing external to the real concerns of the people listening to them—as in antiwar songs when Britain was not at war. Now a significant number of songs are beginning to challenge the very bases of social alienation in modern Britain. Thus Manfred Mann sneers effectively at the patterns of middle-class complacency:

Do you think you will be happy
Taking doggy for a walk
With your semidetached suburban Mr. James

Cat Stevens, in "Matthew and Son," paints a picture of the demoralization and boredom of a group of employees of Matthew and Son where

No one asks for more money
'Cause nobody dares.

The Kinks, in "Dead End Street," present a picture of working-class life far removed from the cosy security traditionally ascribed to it in popular song.

Whether this trend will grow, and perhaps establish a new school of "anti-alienation blues," one hesitates to forecast. But then, one hesitates to forecast the political future of Britain.

"I USED TO THINK I WAS REALLY UGLY"

●

FRED NEWMAN

Michael Philip Jagger, at the relatively tender age of twenty-four, is idolized, abused, envied and abhorred by millions throughout an allegedly civilized world. Polls show he is better known than De Gaulle, U Thant, Olivier or Einstein. His every move is dutifully recorded. To-hell-with-protocol Jagger arrived at Covent Garden with girl friend Marianne Faithfull five minutes after Princess Margaret. To-hell-with-the-Palladium Jagger refused to go on their revolving stage. To-hell-with-everyone Jagger is constantly reported as not believing in God, society, hairdressers or going to bed before four in the morning.

Jagger is the high-priest of beat. The ecstasy he arouses is a curious and disturbing amalgam of desire, fear and aggression. The fans want him. They are repelled by him. At one emotional stroke they would like to tear him apart, give themselves to him and run from the horror he somehow represents. His monstrous image has a nightmarish fascination that haunts and torments those who fall under its spell.

At close quarters and in the relative sanity of the Rolling Stones' London office on the third floor of a decidedly unhypnotic building behind Bond Street, Jagger's monster bit is temporarily switched off. Indeed he is inclined to play down this particular role as if the hysteria he arouses were some disembodied manifestation for which he has only incidental responsibility.

As he talks it is not the hair reaching hopefully for the dark blue shirt which one notices, but the mouth and lips. The lips are thick and sensuous and seem too large for the mouth between them. As Jagger pauses to think, he strums them like loose elastic. The effect is innocent and friendly rather than sinister, particularly when the lips stretch even further in a little-boy smile.

"Of course I do occasionally arouse primaeval instincts," he concedes, "but I mean, most men can do that. They can't do it to so many. I just happen to be able to do it to several thousand people. It's fun to do that. It's really just a game, isn't it? I mean these girls do it to themselves. They're all charged up. It's a dialogue of energy. They give you a lot of energy and take a lot away. Maybe they want something from life, from me. Maybe they think I can give it to them. I don't know."

The evidence suggests that Jagger is wanted and demanded because he satisfies a compelling need felt by his millions of fans. Whether he cares to acknowledge it or not, he is the catalyst by which an unmanageable flood of excitement is released. His expertise at pelvic gyration and rhythmic movement—he has been referred to as the Rhythm and Blues Nureyev—provides the visually suggestive symbolism that sparks the mass orgy.

Psychiatrists have long known that the source of mass hysteria springs from repressed sexual urges, composed of both sadistic and aggressive elements. The number of occasions on which pop singers are physically assaulted by their fans—Jagger himself was recently pulled off a twenty-foot platform in a Zurich stadium and almost torn to pieces—confirms the nature of the emotions involved. Essentially therefore the concert-hall hysteria represents a sudden escape of the kind of emotions which the forces of puritanism, morality and authority—both social and parental—normally seek to contain. When a pop audience blows its top it is, in fact, indulging in a communal act of defiance against a set of values which it feels to be unnecessarily and intolerably restrictive. It is a group protest against a society which it regards as impersonal, mechanistic and money-bound. Undoubtedly Mick Jagger, purveying as he does his own brand of untamed rebelliousness, is at once a symbol and focal point of this seething insurrection.

The role becomes him. There exists, between him and his screaming fans, a wave length of mutual understanding. Jagger both receives and transmits their feelings, defending them and himself from the common enemies of established order and convention. Like them, he wants out. Normal codes of behavior are derided and publicly flouted in a bleak philosophy where compromise and concession are regarded as weakness.

The rules are: no rules. Everything goes but nothing

matters. The Lord Chief Justice, Lord Parker, when he granted Jagger a conditional discharge in the drugs case, suggested he had a responsibility to his fans. Jagger brushes this notion aside.

"I don't really quite know what he meant. I'd really like to talk to him about that but I suppose he's pretty busy. If he meant that I have a responsibility to set an example to young people I don't agree with him. I think over the drugs thing we did set a good example. The fact is I had three pep pills which I bought legally. As far as I am concerned we did pretty well because we never said everyone should take this and that. We never said you shouldn't. We just left it up to everyone else which is the way it should be. Which is my version of responsibility. It's not up to me to make the fans be like at school where they have to do everything. Everyone has to be responsible to themselves. It's not my job to uphold standards which other people consider to be the only ones in existence."

All the same Jagger himself moves in a circle which, despite its disdain for convention, conforms to its own unspoken codes. Marriage is tolerated as a side-effect of love. Money is tolerated as a side-effect of success. Success is tolerated as a side-effect of life.

If Jagger really believes all the things he says—and he is a smoothly articulate talker—his scene is one of casual unconcern. His pessimistic fatalism is brutal, too brutal. One begins to suspect he scorns the ideals and illusions that keep most of humanity ticking over not from a fear of holding them but rather of losing them. Beneath the protective shell of his shining pop-suited armor he may be much more sensitive than he cares publicly to admit.

"There's no point in caring," he outwardly insists. "I'd rather not know what I was like. I mean I am what I am and everything just happens, doesn't it. So I let things happen to me. I wanted to be a singer but not a pop singer. I wanted to be in a group but I didn't particularly want to make money. I can't really remember ever thinking it would be nice to be rich. When I was at school I would vaguely think things like I would like to have a nice car. I used to think what a drag I couldn't borrow my father's. My pipe dreams weren't really very large. I keep reading in the papers that I spend £150 a month on clothes. Sometimes it's more, sometimes it's less. The trouble is I lose half the clothes I buy. I leave them around. I can't keep them together. But I don't seem to spend as much as I used to."

If he excuses himself all the way to the bank it is because money represents a bastion of the very society to which he and his followers are implacably opposed. He is not exactly embarrassed by his wealth but treats it with studied carelessness. He tells you that he doesn't want to be a tycoon; that he hates businessmen. Nevertheless the Rolling Stones' empire is a temple of finance of which mammon himself would approve. So the atmosphere in their London headquarters is as unbusiness-orientated as possible; carefully informal and deliberately friendly. Two unopened bottles of Coca-Cola on the reception desk. A board-room table decorated with empty coffee cups and two green telephones. A rocking chair. All the same Mick Jagger's personal fortune cannot be gain-said. He owns a dark blue Aston Martin, £25,000 eleven-bedroomed house in Hampshire with butler's cottage and artifical lake, a £45,000 town house in Chelsea and has an ecstatic bank manager.

Since he gave up his studies at the London School of Economics five years ago to form the Stones, record sales have topped £30 million. Discs like "Satisfaction," "Let's Spend the Night Together," and "Have You Seen Your Mother, Baby?" have hit the headlines and thumped the cash-tills. In one year alone their fans have bought ten million singles, five million LPs and paid more than £2 million to watch the group jigging and jerking in the concert hall.

Today the Jagger features are as internationally known as the Empire State building and about as forbidding. He confesses that at one time he thought he was "really ugly," but now he's not so sure.

Certainly women find him physically fascinating in the way that Beauty always has been compulsively attracted to the Beast. They are drawn to him like loving-lemmings, courting the thrill of their own possible destruction. His romance with Chrissie Shrimpton, a fragile good-looker and the younger sister of model Jean Shrimpton, broke up early last year. Their relationship endured for four years and was, by all accounts, tempestuous. She says, "He was constantly arguing. I suppose we had a sort of love-hate relationship." Ultimately the hate bit seems to have won. She decided she would "rather get old with someone else" and found the prospect of marriage altogether "too frightening." Jagger looks back at this episode with no detectable rancor. "Four years is a pretty long time for an adolescent. Anyway we tried."

His current girl friend, singer Marianne Faithfull, was educated at a convent and married briefly to a Cambridge student. She has been painted in the nude by Dali, admonished for appearing in a West End restaurant without a bra, and nurtures an ambition "to be killed by some man in a fit of passionate jealousy." She shares completely Jagger's rebelliousness and attitude to marriage. "Marriage spoils the whole game. It's just not the scene. It's disillusioning."

The intellectual trade-unionism that welds the Jagger-style Establishment together views marriage as a kind of restrictive practice, now unnecessary and outdated. Jagger himself argues the case against persuasively.

"In London we don't live in that kind of society any more. There are no pressures to get married, not even from your own family. In a small village you're under great stress if you're going out with a girl, but not here. I mean, I've been going out with women for years—very happily, a beautiful edification of the spirit"—he throws back his head and grins—"but I've never considered marriage. I mean, I can't quite see the point in getting married. Not even if you want to produce children, not even then. Of course you have a responsibility to the children—but what matters to the child is not whether they're illegitimate or not, but whether they've had a happy home life. I was a happy child but I don't think it would have made any difference really if my parents hadn't been married.

"As far as I can see the marriage thing is security not so much for the children as for the woman, because she hasn't reached the stage of economic independence in our society. They have to make a law that a man should provide for his own woman and children."

Twanging his lips a little he ponders the question of whether a woman, too, might not need the security of legalized marriage? If he were in love with a woman who wanted to marry him, what would he do?

"If she wanted it, yes, I'd give it to her if that's what she really needed, but I don't think that would ever arise. It wouldn't be my kind of woman who needed that kind of security. But if I did meet one who really wanted to get married and who I wanted to have children by and spend the rest of my life with and she couldn't make it unless she was married—I'd marry her." He describes his relationship with

Marianne Faithfull as "very nice at the moment," but is not prepared to speculate on whether it will last. "I don't think about things like that," he says.

Always one comes up against this prohibited area in Jagger's mind which he is reluctant to enter even himself. He genuinely dislikes talking about himself—"I don't think about myself unless people like you ask me." Even on stage before his screaming audiences, he experiences a need to hang on to Michael Philip Jagger. He says that unleashing your ego at the audience is permissible, but that you should remain calm yourself. It's all right letting yourself go as long as you can get yourself back.

Behind the outward self-assurance he nurses this basic uncertainty about his own identity. In a way Jagger-the-public-monster haunts him as much as his fans. He seems to sense that his efficiently promulgated image is somehow a threat to his own reality. He is a rebel for what he is, rather than for what he believes. His scene is a mutual-protection society where marriage and responsibility with all their demands are conveniently dismissed and therefore need not be faced.

The protest he leads appeals to the young because it is a protest against growing up into a world seen as cynical, uncaring and unaffectionate. He offers, to an army of emotional children, the unlimited excitement and license that adulthood invariably curtails. He can continue to ride this tide only as long as he remains young himself.

STONES / COMMENT

ALAN BECKETT / RICHARD MERTON

The group takes its name from Muddy Waters' *Rolling Stone Blues* (NLP28040). Their initial direction is taken from a broad spectrum of American Negro popular music, including both rhythm-and-blues, from Muddy Waters and Howling Wolf to Chuck Berry, Bo Diddley and Rufus Thomas, and soul music from Ray Charles to Tamla Motown. The only white group included in their initial influences was the Crickets, a group that was closer to rhythm-and-blues than most other white groups in the fifties. Thus, though they arose on the crest of the r&b boom of the early sixties, they were never completely identified with blues purism. Mick Jagger did not try to introduce Negro mannerisms into his singing, nor did the group as a whole ever attempt an exact reproduction of the classical rhythm-and-blues sound. Instead they relied on simplifications, sometimes obviously because of technical inadequacies.

Some of their earlier work—the Chuck Berry numbers, for instance—is pleasant, but unremarkable. Some is downright bad when looked at in relation to the original. Thus, "I Just Want to Make Love to You" is frantic and has none of the power and dignity of the original, while the Bo Diddley-style number on the same record is overadorned and generally in complete contradiction to the simplicity and relaxation of the latter artist's music. Other early pieces, however, are perhaps the most important work in this idiom ever recorded in Britain; good examples are their versions of Howling Wolf's "Little Red Rooster" and Slim Harpo's "King Bee." Because no attempt is made to reproduce the specific mannerisms, these works are effective translations rather than replications of something essentially foreign. In these pieces the erotic narcissism becomes a possibility in English life, rather than remaining something that one reads about in Paul Oliver or listens to on Chess Records. Other attempts at this kind of music have failed precisely because they have stuck too close to the letter of the original. On The Who's "I'm a Man," for example, though the instrumental work with its use of electronic effects is far ahead of any of The Stones', Roger Daltrey's vocal is tense, lifeless and ultimately rather juvenile, so that "When I get you in bed, darling, gonna make love all the time" becomes one of the most ridiculous lines in pop music.

The Stones' greatest early achievements occurred when they moved close to soul music, where the singer's role is a more dynamic one of improvising so as to increase and decrease the level of excitement by means of dynamic variation, fragmenting and rebuilding the vocal line, and other means. (Of course, this process is spontaneous, depending largely upon momentary response to the audience, and the rest of the group, and any analysis of it sounds stilted.) Very early on, Mick Jagger developed this style to a degree of excellence which is rarely found, so that he has become the greatest artist ever to come out of British popular music. His style is rhythmically fluid and graceful as well as forceful—natural and neither histrionic nor mannered. The best recorded examples of Jagger's talent displayed to the full are "Everybody Needs Somebody to Love" and "Going Home." On the last-named track he constructs some particularly striking melodic and rhythmic shapes; listen, for instance, to "it won't be long . . . it won't be a long long time till I see my baby." Even in less discursive numbers it is Jagger's performance that is responsible for most of the impact. In this respect Jagger's music is better than that of many of the Negro artists The Stones have admired. The late Otis Redding's version of "Satisfaction" is frantic and very stylized compared with The Stones' original. Wilson Pickett, whose "Midnight Hour" Jagger claimed as the best record of 1965, is a far more limited and mechanical performer. In fact The Stones have become something of an influence on the traditions that first influenced them. American soul groups play and record Stones' compositions, and though there is no recorded evidence of this, it is probable that their influence extends down into the American rhythm-and-blues circuits. More recently they have moved away from these sources towards the center of contemporary pop. Here they have never been major innovators on a technical level, even in the restricted sense of the term that is applicable in this kind of music. They have moved forward at least one

LP behind The Beatles, incorporating their influence and others, such as the Dixieland and vaudeville elements discernible in "Between the Buttons," into a style that has remained basically simple. Their instrumental resources are being continually widened, but though they have dropped most of the specific trappings of soul and rhythm-and-blues, they retain the essential spirit of these influences by relying on strong, simple rhythms and conventional chord patterns and meter. Thus they also preserve the most basic function of popular music—to provide music for dancing—and there is probably no other contemporary group that does this so well. These features of their style do not limit their musical impact in any way. The simple instrumental approach provides exactly the right backing for the lyric. (Occasionally the "backing" is so loud that it obscures the lyric, but this is no more a fault than it is when Art Blakey occasionally obscures his front line with his drumming.)

As they have developed they have included more original material in their recordings, and the last three albums have been made up exclusively of their own work. Compositions are usually credited to both Jagger and Richard, and there seems to be no way of finding out who has the major responsibility in this area; however, they are certainly lyrics of considerable force and originality. Their first function is to increase the realism of the music. The Stones' music is now very much related to social life in the 1960s, and even specifically to London life. Though their music certainly has general reference, it seems probable that their full impact can only be realized by someone who has experience of the metropolitan environment. For instance, consider the archetypal girl who is described first in "Playing with Fire," and subsequently in "19th Nervous Breakdown" and elsewhere—rich, spoiled, confused, weak, using drugs, etc. Anyone who has been around Chelsea and Kensington can put at least one name to this character; probably she does not mean so much to anyone else. Jagger's voice as well betrays London and Home Counties origins, so that sometimes the music seems to relate to London Music Hall, with its jeering and derisive overtones, as well as to the sources previously discussed. Where, for instance, does the exclamation "oi" at the end of "Mother's Little Helper" come from?

Narcissism and arrogance, concisely set out in "Get Off My Cloud," are the keynotes of most of The Stones' lyrics.

Mostly the songs are concerned with narcissism and arrogance in heterosexual relationships. We have, for instance, "Cool, Calm and Collected," ultimately a very aggressive and intrusive attempt as seduction. In "Under My Thumb," we have the expression of unmitigated triumph and control over the loved one. This lyric is particularly well set off by the music. The rhythm suggests trampling down; the use of the marimba, however, makes it more delicate, suggesting that altogether different things may happen in the forecourt of the relationship, and that the jubilation is really furtive.

Then there are songs expressing rejection. "Yesterday's Papers" is certainly one of The Stones' most arresting lyrics: Who wants yesterday's papers, who wants yesterday's girl?

"Lady Jane" is concerned with the same topic. Here, however, the method is different. While in most of their songs no attempt is made to disguise the general ferocity, the presentation here is that of a gentle ballad. Nonetheless the theme is still "I'm going to make it with someone else." The only other song of this type is "Backstreet Girl," where another phase of narcissism, that of turning the other into an object, something to be used, is described: Don't want you part of my world, just you be my backstreet girl. In some ways, these two songs are the most sophisticated music The Stones have ever made, because of the relationship between content and presentation, and because some self-criticism is implied. One cannot present such material so simply without transcending it to some extent. However, they do not have the simple impact of the more straightforward material.

The paranoia and persecution that must be part of this narcissistic attitude comes over clearly in "Please Go Home." In "2000 Light Years From Home" there is some awareness of the loneliness and exclusion that is attendant upon narcissism, but the isolation is tremendously idealized—this is perhaps the most *beautiful* of The Stones' pieces—and made to seem seductive. Songs dealing with negative self-feeling are comparatively rare in The Stones' work; however, one of their finest songs is "Paint It Black," which deals with depression mixed with jealousy and rage resulting from a rejection.

Most of The Stones' material partakes of these general characteristics. In intellectual circles it is fashionable at present to dismiss this group as being, albeit rather colorful, unoriginal, hedonistic, and basically reactionary—in contrast to other groups, particularly The Beatles, whose music is seen as original, mature, serious and thoughtful. It is quite impossible to accept this evaluation. Concerning the question of originality, one should note that, though The Stones are not major innovators, their music is a constructive development of the tradition from which they emerged. There is a clear relationship between the honesty and directness of their music and the supposed honesty of their sources, and The Stones' music should by no means be seen as a dilution of these sources, but as a superior realization of all that is good in them. The accusations of juvenility and thoughtless hedonism also have no foundation, and they completely miss the point of The Stones' music. The arrogance and brutality of the content constitute a completely justifiable and welcome attack on the amorous clichés of popular music, and on the clichés that fill many people's minds, irrespective of any music. What is more important it is clear that the isolation of these moments and the momentary complete identification with them that comes in The Stones' music can have a very constructive, liberating effect on the individual. It is only when such feelings have been isolated, recognized and incorporated into the self that they can be transmuted. And these feelings most often contain the individual's most potent parts.

However, comparison of The Rolling Stones with The Beatles is appropriate, although it would be wrong to make any polarization of the Stravinsky-Schoenberg type. One might argue that The Beatles' work contains a more mature and intelligent appreciation of the other person, and that it has more reparative intent behind it. One could cite such pieces as "She's Leaving Home" and "We Can Work It Out" in this context, and claim that in general many more of The Beatles' pieces celebrate the bliss of being together. This is true to some extent. The nearest The Stones come to this theme is "Let's Spend the Night Together." In "She's A Rainbow," which seems to contain considerable awareness of the other person, she is idealized so much as to be unreal, and The Beatles' "Lovely Rita," for example, does contain a much more realistic and adult awareness. However, the danger in work like much of The Beatles' is the tendency towards manic denial that there is anything difficult in relationships—anything that cannot be achieved immediately and magically. In their typically arrogant and narcissistic themes, The Stones are providing criticism of this kind of facile intimacy which The Beatles have never really advanced. For this reason The Stones annoy many people. It is probably because of this that they have got into so much trouble recently, while some of their adorned contemporaries can admit in the mass media to using drugs, and carry on their lives unimpeded.

The style and content of The Stones' music has been relatively unchanged for some time. *Between the Button* is certainly their best album, because, with the effective incorporation of diverse influences, the music avoids the monotony which is perhaps The Stones' worst fault. (This comes out most clearly on the *High Tide and Green Grass* album.) *Their Satanic Majesties Request,* their latest record, is an ambivalent production. It reflects all the major developments of 1967—The Mothers of Invention ("On with the Show"); The Byrds' science-fiction themes ("2000 Light Years from Home"); and The Human Host and The Heavy Metal Kids (in the long instrumental passages). Particularly, of course, it reflects the influence of *Sgt. Pepper.* In some ways the record constitutes an advance for The Stones. It is more sophisticated than their previous work in terms of orchestration, and there is some development of the composing style (using two tempi within the same piece, etc). Some of the songs are effective continuations of typical themes; notable are "On with the Show," a very arrogant degradation of parental enjoyment, and "2000 Man," a portrayal of alienation from psychobiological reality. The latter can be compared with The Beatles' "Nowhere Man," and the comparison clearly demonstrates the greater critical force of The Stones' work. In other ways, however, particularly when this record is compared with The Beatles' most recent work, it seems to be a failure. The attempts at complex soundmixes, such as the one which concludes the album, are confused compared with The Beatles' best work in this area. Also it seems that the lyrics are more frequently obscured on this record than ever before, so that some of the music ("The Citadel" and "The Lantern" in particular) is hard to evaluate. Previously The Stones had never equalled the hi-fi achievements of The Beatles, but this had not mattered so much because the general intention was simpler. A considerable amount of space on this record is wasted. The long instrumental passages are nice to dance to, but there is nothing remarkable in them, and they do not have the same force as the songs. Also, because they are obviously orchestrated, the shamanistic intention behind them is rendered ineffectual. Nigel Weymouth and Mick Farren do this kind of thing much more effectively simply by banging and scraping everything they can find in the recording studio. Lastly, there is the question of the ventures into psychedelicism, which had never previously played any part in The Stones' program. Without trying to dismiss psychedelicism from a vulgar materialist/behaviorist position, one can still criticize songs such as "In Another Land" and "Gomper" on the grounds that the imagery is hackneyed, and because in general the attempt to evoke a climate of mystery, "hallucination" and dream is not nearly so successful as The Beatles' "Strawberry Fields" or "I Am The Walrus." On the present evidence, The Stones are at their best when they keep away from this kind of material. However one cannot conclude after listening to this album that The Rolling Stones have sold out and lost their potency. Obviously they are floundering in unfamiliar territory, but we can expect recovery and reassertion in their subsequent music.

COMMENT

Alan Beckett's assessment of The Stones must be unequivocally welcomed. It represents the first serious critical account of the group to be written. The current maudlin patronage of pop music by Sunday newspapers and literary weeklies makes it all the more important to establish a genuine canon and the concepts necessary to underpin it. A *politique des auteurs* is required. Alan Beckett's critique of The Stones, following his prolegomenon to pop music (NLR 39), is a pioneering start.

His analysis, however, calls for some comment. He unerringly isolates the distinctive circle of themes which form the effective ambit of The Stones' music. The account of the key songs which enact them is in many respects a model. It is this approach which may, however, be questioned. Beckett's method is to align The Stones' music on an evolutionary axis borrowed from psychoanalysis. The perspective is a basically psychological one. Thus the music expresses "narcissism" and "arrogance," which may have a liberating effect on "the individual," but invariably leads to "paranoia" and "persecution," unless transcended towards a more "reparative" attitude. The Kleinian connotations of this line of argument are evident.

My own view is that this terminology contradicts to some

extent the intention of Beckett's analysis, and involuntarily buffers the explosive potential of The Stones' music. Some retranslation of the concepts used by Beckett may be necessary to capture the exact nature of their achievement. Let us take "narcissism and arrogance" first. Beckett uses the odd phrase "in heterosexual relationships" to complete this. The implication seems to be that it might equally well be in a homosexual relationship, but contingently is not. But this confuses the essential issue. "Under My Thumb," "Stupid Girl," "Back Street Girl" or "Yesterday's Papers" are about sexual exploitation, not narcissism. The one is a permanent, structural feature of our society, the other a random psychological stance of the individual. The enormous merit—and audacity—of The Stones is to have repeatedly and consistently defied what is a central taboo of the social system: mention of sexual inequality. They have done so in the most radical and unacceptable way possible: by *celebrating* it. The light this black beam throws on the society is too bright for it. Nakedly proclaimed, inequality is *de facto* denounced. The "unmitigated triumph" of these records is their rejection of the spurious world of monadic personal relationships. They are concerned with the oppressive matrix that is their general truth.

The same is true of the second main theme articulated by The Stones—mental illness. Again this is a tabooed topic as a *normal* social experience. Elementary reflection confirms that it is so, yet polite convention relegates it to the realm of the particular and abnormal. Beckett surely misrepresents the insistence on this by identifying it merely with the image of an "archetypal girl—rich, spoiled, confused, weak, using drugs" from Chelsea or Kensington. Not only is the moralism of these epithets dubious; The Stones' subject matter is clearly far wider. "Mother's Little Helper," for example, is not about a rich girl, but an average housewife of middle age. "Paint It Black," another of this cycle, is about the confident male himself. Mental collapse is not an exceptional breakdown: it is a prevalent condition, part of the ordinary routine of living under advanced capitalism. The third important theme, this time not emphasized by Beckett, is eroticism. Once again this is tabooed territory. The two antipodal classics here are, of course, "Satisfaction" and "Going Home"—precise musical notations of grinding physical blockage and jubilant physical release. The unity of lyric, melody and instrumentation has never been surpassed. These songs are uniquely brutal and truthful, broaching realities which are constantly denied or diluted in the enervating mists of traditional pop music.

If this account is reliable, it is incorrect to say that The Stones are "not major innovators." Perhaps a polarization Stones-Beatles such as Adorno constructed between Schoenberg and Stravinsky (evoked by Beckett) might actually be a fruitful exercise. Suffice it to say here that, for all their intelligence and refinement, The Beatles have never strayed much beyond the strict limits of romantic convention: central moments of their *oeuvre* are nostalgia and whimsy, both eminently consecrated traditions of middle-class England. Lukàcs's pejorative category of the *Angenehme*—the "pleasant" which dulls and pacifies—fits much of their work with deadly accuracy. By contrast, The Stones have refused the given orthodoxy of pop music; their work is a dark and veridical negation of it. It is an astonishing fact that there is virtually not one Jagger-Richards composition which is conventionally about a "happy" or "unhappy" personal relationship. Love, jealousy and lament—the substance of 85 per cent of traditional pop music—are missing. Sexual exploitation, mental disintegration and physical immersion are their substitutes.

A final comment. The reason why an appraisal of the group has some importance is this. Britain today is a society stifling for lack of any art that expresses the experience of living in it. Our theatre is a quaint anachronism, our novel is dead, and our cinema a mere obituary of it. Perhaps the only art form which has an authentic expressive vitality in England is pop music. It at least reflects back to us the immediate constituents of experience, even when it does not illuminate them. It is no accident that it is the one product of contemporary British culture which has any international currency. For how long?

ROLLING STONES

•

MICHAEL PARSONS

Both accounts of the music of the Rolling Stones offered in NLR 47 seem to evade the question of how good the songs are as music, by evaluating them according to external, non-musical values. Both adopt different kinds of moralistic approach towards them. Beckett's a psychological one, Merton's a political one. Speaking, for instance, of the Stones' "celebration" of sexual exploitation, Merton writes: "Nakedly proclaimed (sexual), inequality is *de facto* denounced." What can *de facto* mean here, and who does the denouncing? Merton seems to mean that by presenting us with a blatant and undisguised statement of male domination and exploitation, which is usually expressed only in confused or concealed ways, the Stones give it to us in a form in which we can recognize it clearly for what it is, and so denounce it. There does not seem to be any grounds for assuming the Stones themselves, in their performance, adopt a critical attitude towards it. Merton's interpretation of his experience of listening to the music according to his own perspective—in terms of a critique of the values of advanced industrial capitalist society—is quite extraneous to the music itself.

Beckett falls into another kind of moralism when he assesses the music in terms of its effect on the listener: he speaks of the "momentary, complete identification" of aggressive feeling which "can have a constructive, liberating effect on the individual." His account of how, through fulfillment in fantasy, feelings of arrogance and narcissism can be "incorporated" and "transmuted" by the listener may be accurate psychologically, but he also fails to deal with the songs as music. To talk about feeling as such, instead of about the way it is presented and realized in music, is again to adopt an external standpoint.

Both of thesse accounts concentrate on the words, with only an occasional reference to the way the music presents or underlines them. To speak as if the words were the primary element and the music subsidiary to them is to reduce the impact and oversimplify the complexity of feeling of which words and music together are capable. It is true that in much pop music, the music is not closely interrelated with the words, but is a mechanical and standardized vehicle for them. But there are cases, in the Stones' work, in which this standardization of form is itself exploited. In "Paint It Black" for example, the relentlessly unvarying four-line verse reinforces the feeling of oppressed, suicidal depression in the words, and at the one point where the words seem to suggest a possibility of recovery, the music does not let up. It is by putting the repetitive and mechanical features of pop music to such use that the Stones occasionally raise them to a new level of expressiveness. Elsewhere--as in "Satisfaction"—there is a real fusion of words and music. This song acquires its particular force from the slow triplet rhythm of the opening words, which goes against and *frustrates* the flow of the four-time beat; a straightforward-enough procedure, but in the context of the predominantly uncomplicated beat of pop music, a graphic dislocation. This is the specific means which make it, as Merton rightly says, a "precise musical notation of grinding physical blockage." Here are examples of words and music reinforcing each other. But there are other examples in which the interaction of several dimensions, and the tension generated between them when the music contradicts the surface meaning of the words, are essential to the total experience. In "Backstreet Girl" the complexity of feeling is the result of the contradiction between the overtly arrogant and patronizing words and the gentle tenderness of the melody. Brecht wrote somewhere that what was needed, in the theatre, was music which would call forth a feeling so precisely that actors could play *against* it: here is a simple case of exactly that. By going against the overt meaning of the words the music here offsets them and transforms their impact into something quite different. Alone, the words would be merely patronizing. It is the musical setting—an amplification and articulation of the way feeling can be expressed to some extent in gesture or tone of voice—which makes this song a confrontation between tenderness and arrogance towards the girl. Its success lies in capturing and realizing this opposition of feelings with such accuracy and subtlety of nuance, and fusing them into a musical whole.

A critical account of pop music must be based not on judgments of the feelings and attitudes expressed (in this respect, to applaud the Stones for their attitude is just as irrelevant to their music as to berate them for their clothes or their behavior), but on an assessment of how these feelings are embodied in musical forms—i.e., how coherently the musical material is presented and articulated. If the material of pop music is restricted, in comparison with other forms of music, that doesn't necessarily mean the possibilities for coherence and articulation within its own limits are less. Any attempt to talk about it as music—and to treat it any other way is, finally, to devalue it—must begin with the specific materials and conventions it employs, and discuss how its use of these is able to provide convincing *symbolic*, not literal presentations of experience.

ARTS IN SOCIETY: JOHN LENNON'S SCHOOL DAYS

●

MICHAEL WOOD

A heavy man with glasses sits on a chair looking at a green monster with four legs. Caption? "An adult looks at a Beatle." The caption is mine, but the drawing is John Lennon's. It appears in his second book, *A Spaniard in the Works.*

There are four-legged things everywhere in Lennon's drawings: sheep, cats, cows, Sherlock Holmes on his knees. The first book, *In his own Write,* has a huge Wrestling Dog ("But who would fight this wondrous beast? I wouldn't for a kick off"), and a piece called "Liddypool" is accompanied by a sketch of chatting quadropuses.

It is a child's world, or a world that Thurber might have drawn for a child. Animals and freaks have comic dignity while adults look silly and too big, bending over and crawling. A double suggestion runs through the writing in both books: adults *are* silly, they give children rubbish to read and expect them to like it; and left to themselves, adults are worse than children—they talk jabberwocky about politics and color and religion, and they believe what they say.

So we get Enig Blyter's famous five—ten of them taking off for Woenow Abbey—" 'Gruddly Pod, Gruddly Pod,' the train seemed to say, 'Gruddly Pod, we're on our hollidays'." There is a trip to Treasure Ivan with Large John Saliver, Small Jack Hawkins, Cpt Smellit and Squire Trelorgy. But Prevelant ze Gaute also appears, and Docker Adenoid along with Harrassed MacMillion and the late Cassandle of the Mirror on the Wall. The Bible, hymns, newspapers, the telly, bad films: the world shrinks to the nonsense of a book for small children.

The trick is simple, a standard schoolboy game. You retreat to baby talk, to mock-childishness, to the linguistic pranks of Lewis Carroll and Edward Lear. This is your revenge on all the language, life and literature that people are asking you to take seriously. You bend and break what they teach you; you make their world sound like Wonderland. Vile ruperts spread through a village, an old man leaves his last will and testicle, there is dirty weather off Rockall and Fredastaire. A day is a red lettuce day.

The jokes are John Lennon's, but they have already seen good service in most grammar schools in this country. The grammar school is the place for this intelligent, informed and infantile humor, I think; and school may have been more important for Lennon and McCartney than either home or Liverpool, whatever sociologists and trendmen say. Grammar school pupils are alert, disciplined and frightened. Their pleasures are psychological—torturing a nervous teacher—and fairly secret.

I remember a joke that ran for months when I was at school. Whenever a teacher left the room, someone would draw a head, side view, on the blackboard. It would be a policeman in a huge helmet or a guardsman in a vast busby. At the side of this would appear a drawing of the policeman or guardsman without his helmet or busby. His head would be exactly the same shape as his hat. Another version showed a grotesque clubfoot—with or without a shoe, it looked the same.

Thinking back, I can see two things in our enjoyment of those gruesome gags. First, a hope that the world would stay simple, that our fears of mess and complication might prove to be unfounded. Just think. If the mask should fall to reveal a face just like the mask, if the truth about life, which parents and teachers hinted at so darkly, should turn out to be exactly like the façade, then they would be the fools with their conspiracy theories, and we would be right in our scared simplicity. And, secondly, I think we were fascinated by disease and deformity, which represented the future ugliness of life itself. If we could keep that at the level of a joke, if we could tame it in the safeness of school, everything would be all right.

All this is in Lennon. The adult world makes him larf, and his books are a vengeance. He has verbal forms of the clubfoot joke—Mr. Borris Morris, in the story of that name, has a happy knack of being in the right place at the right place—and a splendid visual version. Two beggars stand side by side, each complete with stick, trumpet, dog and begging tin. One of them has dark glasses, and his dog has dark glasses too. The man carries a placard on his chest saying: I am blind. The other man also has a placard. It says: I can see quite clearly. Thus does the world shed its secrets for the innocent. Although for the person who can make such a joke, as for the boys who could laugh at our drawings, innocence is already a fantasy, an incipient nostalgia, no longer a state of mind.

But most strikingly Lennon sets up a gallery of deformed and violent people, a literal menagerie of creatures born on the blackboard during a break. A man clubs his wife to death. A friendly little dog ("Arf, Arf, he goes, a merry sight") is put to sleep. Eric Hearble, who has a growth on his head, loses his job teaching spastics to dance (" 'We're not having a cripple teaching our lads,' said Headmaster"). Randolph is killed at Christmas by his pals ("At least he didn't *die* alone did he?") and a girl wonders about flowers for her wheelchair at her wedding—luckily her father comes home and cancels the husband. Little Bobby, thirty-nine years old, gets a hook for his missing hand as a birthday present. Only the hook is for the wrong hand, his good left hand, and they have to chop that off to fit the hook.

It is absurd to compare Lennon to Joyce. Lennon's puns are piecemeal, scattered and unequal. Joyce's punning in *Finnegans Wake* is a system, a metaphysic for melding worlds. When Joyce writes of the flushpots of Euston and the hanging garments of Marylebone, the Bible and London really collide. But Lennon has some fine effects. A pun is what Durkheim in another context called a logical scandal, it is an escape from linear meaning. It is language on holiday, and Lennon occasionally gets the authentic glee of this.

"Anything you say may be used in Everton against you." "Father Cradock turns round slowly from the book he is eating and explains that it is just a face she is going through." People dance with wild abdomen, and send stabbed, undressed envelopes.

Why is there so little of all this in the songs Lennon writes with Paul McCartney? McCartney's sobering influence? Hardly. More likely both are being tactful towards their public. They know that people are offended by nonsense, by things they can't understand; they know that people tend to take jokes that baffle them as a personal insult, a calculated exclusion. And their songs after all are a commercial enterprise —Lennon and McCartney have written well over one hundred songs since 1962, and their work has been recorded by almost everyone you can think of.

Certainly there are occasional puns—"It won't be long/Till I belong to you." "A Hard Day's Night," the nonsense title of a film and a song, comes from a Lennon story called "Sad Michael." There are all the double meanings concerning pot and LSD on the *Sergeant Pepper* album, there is the sound play of by, buy, bye-bye in the song "She's Leaving Home." And the songs have developed towards complexity.

Lennon and McCartney's early lyrics were thin and conventional. There was rain in the heart, there were stars in the sky, birds were always threatening not to sing. The tunes were good, some of them as good as those of Rodgers or Leonard Bernstein. But the gap between words and music in pieces like "If I Fell," "And I Love Her," "Ask Me Why," "Not a Second Time," was embarrassing for anyone who wanted to take the songs seriously. The best lyrics, which went with up-tempo numbers like "I Feel Fine," "All My Lovin'," "Can't Buy Me Love," were the ones which said the least. They said yeh, approximately. I'm not suggesting that Lennon and McCartney didn't know how conventional they were being, or that they couldn't have done better. But they didn't do better, presumably because they weren't interested.

Now they are interested. We get the sharpness of "Your day breaks/Your mind aches," where the rhyme really does something. People, characters, begin to take the place of the anonymous lover of the early songs, shouting, sobbing, missing, losing, promising his standardized love. We get Rita the meter maid, and the man who wants to be a paperback writer. We get Eleanor Rigby and all the lonely people, and the sights and sounds of Penny Lane. To say nothing of Billy Shearer, Sgt. Pepper and Mr. Kite. And we get the complex compassion of songs like "Wait" ("If your hearts breaks/Don't wait") and "She's Leaving Home," where the girl going off writes a note "that she hoped would say more," and her parents moan their incomprehension: "We gave her most of our lives . . ." The whole work develops a sense of waste, of "tears cried for no one," as one song has it.

But still, the music has developed more than the language, and the language is not a main attraction in these songs. Lennon and McCartney's words are still less important than those of Bob Dylan, or Lorenz Hart, or Cole Porter, or Ira Gershwin. We have to look elsewhere for the link between the songs and Lennon's stories.

The link is not hard to find. It takes us back to school, and Lennon and McCartney's repeated flights into the past. Think of the titles: "Yesterday," "The Night Before." Think of the nostalgia in songs like "Things We Said Today," or "In My

Life": "There are places I'll remember all my life." Think of the echoes of melodrama and music hall in the *Sergeant Pepper* album, the jaunty George Formby tone of "When I'm Sixty-four." In "Good Morning, Good Morning" we take a walk past the old school—"Nothing has changed, it's still the same"—and "She Said She Said" flings a bewildered boy out of the class-room on to a hard life. The girl tells him that she knows what it's like to be dead, and he can only reply, "No no you're wrong when I was a boy everything was right . . ." Lennon and McCartney in their songs do indeed "live the past in the present," as Richard Poirier wrote about them in *Partisan Review* last year. But it is a personal and sentimental past, not a historical one—it is the specific past of good school days, when the world was simpler and adults looked like fools. Lennon and McCartney are not naïvely nostalgic, but they are nostalgic. Their songs and Lennon's stories express the *good child's* hostility to grown-ups. That is what we mean by the youth of the Beatles, an attitude, not an age—after all, they were in their twenties when they began to make it around 1962. The attitude is not dangerous, at worst it deserves a detention, and this is why adults have been so keen to endorse the Beatles. This is safe play for children, mild naughtiness, and much better than breaking up Margate or digging up Paris.

The Beatles are a middle generation between the old conformers and the new rebels, between those who find it hard to believe that the world will change and those who know it's got to. Lennon and McCartney protest against the world adults have made, of course. They hate its pain and loneliness. But their protests are quiet, and their only answer so far has been escape into dope or India.

But the question remains. The Beatles have by-passed adulthood, and this links them with the revolutionary students who are asking why they should grow up when growing up means napalm, treachery, compromise and Porton Down. For years we have sold maturity as a virtue, we have preached the careful ethic of the status quo. But the Beatles are nearly thirty and wildly successful on anyone's terms. If they haven't grown up yet, why should they now?

THE MUSIC OF SOUND OR, THE BEATLES AND THE BEATLESS

●

JOAN PEYSER

Many people ask what are Beatles? Why Beatles? Ugh, Beatles? How did the name arrive? So we will tell you. It came in a vision—a man appeared on a flaming pie and said unto them, "From this day on you are Beatles with an 'A'." Thank you, Mister Man, they said, thanking him.
And so they were Beatles.

JOHN LENNON, 1960

A thousand years ago small groups of uncultivated, bizarrely dressed, oddly named musicians traveled from town to town, singing and accompanying themselves on the vielle. The most famous of these—Jumping Hare, Little String, Ladies Praiser and Rainbow—were rewarded with such fame and luxury that they were imitated by hordes of less gifted, envious men. During the late Middle Ages chronicles refer to "large armies of minstrels," the better ones playing for nobility while lesser troupes entertained at peasant celebrations. Despite the demand for their performances at all levels of society, these itinerant poet-musicians were held in contempt throughout the era. The animus stemmed principally from the Church, which held that their obvious secular *joie de vivre* posed a threat to the spiritual welfare of its people.

Once again, to a degree unparalleled since the fourteenth century, Western society loves and rewards its itinerant minstrels. The Beatles, royalty of rock-and-roll, were received by the Queen of England ("She was like a mum to us"), have appeared on satellite television with Alexander Calder, Van Cliburn, and Joan Miro ("We would rather be rich than famous—that is—more rich and slightly less famous"), and live in a state of growing luxury ("We're not rich by rich standards. I could not afford to run four Rolls Royces like people do"). John Lennon, author of the last statement and the first of the Beatles, owns one Rolls Royce equipped with folding bed, television set, writing desk and telephone. He also owns a mini-Cooper, a Ferrari, five stationary television sets, innumerable tape recorders and telephones and an 1874 carriage, yellow with wild flowers, drawn by two white horses in front with two more trotting at the rear—a $10,000 toy purchased for his four-year-old son. Like their medieval predecessors, the Beatles are considered subversive by respectable society. Lennon's flip comment about contemporary Christianity ("We're more popular than Jesus now") prompted an Alabama disk jockey to instruct his listeners to burn Beatle records. Mayors across the continent picked up the disk jockey's lead and at the beginning of the group's last American tour, in August, 1966, protected citizens by banning Beatles from their cities.

Who would have thought that the pop music of the 1960s would develop into a force as vital as that of the jongleur of old? Starting simply as a vehicle for solo performers, rock-and-roll didn't differ radically from some of the popular music that had preceded it. Out of Negro rhythm and blues and country and western came Elvis Presley. The tunes were predictable, the twelve-bar phrases symmetrical, and the lyric content primitive —"You ain't nothin' but a hound dog." When Presley was drafted, relieved adults predicted the end of an unattractive fad. They were wrong. Rock-and-roll did not die; it only changed. Presley, with his long sideburns, tights pants and suggestive gyrations, reached only one segment of the population, although a large one. The Beatles, bursting onto the scene in the early sixties with Edwardian clothes and English schoolboy haircuts, transformed the original primitive Negro sound, making it acceptable to the mass of young white people all over the world. They brought to prominence Group Rock, one of the most attractive symbols of our nonprivate, corporate, thoroughly electronic age. Now literally "armies of minstrels" —the Beach Boys, the Jefferson Airplane, the Grateful Dead, the Who, the Bee Gees, the Doors, the Mothers of Invention, the Buffalo Springfield, and so on—indicate the awesome potential of electronic sound. Even Bob Dylan, who provoked shouts of "traitor" when he plugged his guitar into an electronic amplifier at the Newport Jazz Festival several years ago, committed himself to the medium in which his generation is making its messages.

Meanwhile, although little noticed by the general public, similar developments have been taking place in the serious music of our time. The explosive electronics of the pop field has diverted attention from the fact that technology came to art music well before it came to rock. As early as 1922 the French-American composer, Edgard Varèse, declared that composer and electrician would have to labor together to produce new media of expression. Rejected by musicians and critics alike during the thirties and forties, when accessibility of music was the keynote, Varèse's views began to gain recognition in the 1950s, and American universities and European radio stations built well-equipped laboratories to experiment with electronic techniques in sound. This gave rise in Europe to the works of Pierre Boulez and Karlheinz Stockhausen and in this country to the construction of machines such as the RCA Synthesizer, a complex, costly apparatus which generates its own sounds, and the Syn-Ket, an instrument which performs "live" electronic music. Columbia University has been in the forefront of the development of the electronic medium. Professors Otto Luening and Vladimir Ussachevsky of the Music Department deposited one of their electronic compositions in the Westinghouse Time Capsule, scheduled to be opened in the seventieth century, and the RCA Synthesizer is housed at the Columbia-Princeton Electronic Music Center on 125th Street in Manhattan.

Despite the prestige and backing electronic art music has been given since the end of World War II, its audience has remained sharply limited. In contrast, electronic rock, within a few years, has attracted an audience of staggering size. Contemporary art and rock music share a medium; the crucial differences are stylistic. Art music has abandoned beat; rock has revived it. Art music is essentially nonvocal and abstract—a feature it has in common with cool contemporary jazz—whereas rock has become increasingly verbal and concrete. Finally, electronic art music aimed at total control of its materials, is at least partly motivated by the desire to eliminate the performer; he is frequently seen as the potential distorter of the composer's idea. Electronic rock propels the performer into the spotlight; he is singer and instrumentalist and recently poet and composer as well. Art music has not yet sought inspiration from rock. Rock, as many writers have pointed out, has drawn upon everything from Gregorian chant to the most far-out techniques of the avant-garde.

Consider the history of the archetype of Group Rock. John Lennon, Paul McCartney and George Harrison met in 1956 when they were in their midteens and, although none of them could read or write music, they began to play guitar together. Drummer Richard Starkey, now Ringo Starr, joined in 1962. The original group, with a few friends moving in and out of it, was one of many unsuccessful "skiffle" bands in Liverpool during the 1950s. They listened to everything from rhythm and blues to contemporary jazz and Presley. In a few years, imitating what they liked and improvising on what they heard, Lennon, McCartney and Harrison recapitulated much of the current history of pop music, a feat impossible in any but the acoustically equipped society in which we live.

In the spring of 1960 the Beatles, in their first significant club engagement, discovered the value of noise. The group, flat broke, owned four guitars but only two amplifiers and the booking was in a wild club on a noisy street in Hamburg. How were they going to be heard? McCartney recalled: "We didn't worry about arrangements or anything. If we had trouble with our overworked amplifiers—we had to plug two guitars into one—I'd just chuck everything in and start leaping around the stage or rush to the piano and start playing some chords . . . it was noise and beat all the way." The Germans loved it. When the police evicted the group from one club (they stamped their way through the floor at one point), the audience followed them to the next. Within a year the late Brian Epstein, then a twenty-six-year-old English businessman, offered to become their manager, and in the fall of sixty-one he became their official disciplinarian in charge of hair, clothes and manners. *Meet the Beatles,* their first album, appeared in 1964.

Twelve albums have been issued since then, the noise and beat progressively abating. Much as the medieval minstrel picked up artistic techniques from the more sophisticated *trouvère* of the period, the Beatles have appropriated the most artful devices available in their own time. Medieval modes and pentatonic scales appear in the songs of sixty-four and sixty-five, a baroque trumpet sings out "Penny Lane," and a classical string quartet performs the hauntingly beautiful "Eleanor

Rigby." George Harrison has studied with Ravi Shankar, the Indian sitar virtuoso, and first used the sitar in a song called "Norwegian Wood." All of his recent music and lyrics show the influence of Indian melody and Indian philosophy. Paul McCartney, studying music now in London, has become absorbed in the avant-garde works of Stockhausen and Luciano Berio. His attitude has changed: "I used to think that anyone doing anything weird was weird. I suddenly realized that anyone doing anything weird wasn't weird at all and that it was the people saying they were weird that were weird." Despite the careful handling of so many diverse musical tools, the legend of how Beatle music is made persists: Lennon whistles to McCartney and McCartney whistles back to Lennon.

In its essence the legend is accurate. But between the initial melodic impulse and the finished product more than cooperative whistling has taken place. When they record the men work a five-day week—from 7 P.M. to 2 A.M. They spent almost half a year recording their thirteenth album; it took twelve hours to make *Meet the Beatles*. From 1964 on, they have had the services of a gifted, well-trained musician, George Martin, who translates their unorthodox ideas into recognizable symbols for the regular symphony-orchestra musicians, who now complement their forces. Within the past year the Beatles have made music for French horn, oboe, clarinet, bassoon, piano, harmonium, tamboura and sitar. Not long ago Harrison said: "There's much more going on in our minds. There are things past drums and guitars which we must do. In the last two years we've been in a good vantage point inasmuch as people are used to buying our records. . . . We can do things that please us without conforming to the standard pop idea. We are not only involved in pop music but all music, and there are many things to be investigated."

The audience has responded. Today's population is literally turned on to listening; the record business grossed $892,000,000 in 1966 and the greater part of that was from rock. The Beatles' thirteenth album, *Sergeant Pepper's Lonely Hearts Club Band,* replete with dissonant sounds, unconventional phrasing and advanced electronic techniques had, within two weeks of its appearance, sold a million and a half copies in the United States alone. A salesman at Sam Goody's Manhattan record store compared the response to *Sergeant Pepper* to that which greeted the recording of Horowitz's initial return concert at Carnegie Hall.

Sergeant Pepper is an extraordinary work, not just comparable to a new sonata or opera, but far more important. It is a work of art that has sprung from unexpected, nonart roots. The salesman's comment was appropriate: "Sergeant Pepper" is to be listened to in the concert context and the Beatles set the tone right away. The beginning of the album simulates the sounds in a concert hall before a performance. Musicians tune instruments, people talk and move around, and an air of expectation prevails.

To the accompaniment of a distorted old-time English music hall sound, the Beatles begin Side I; their business is show business:

It was twenty years ago today,
Sergeant Pepper taught the band to play . . .

Side I is about illusion. The Beatles sing of particular methods people use to hide the truth from themselves. Ringo wears the stripes. He is Sergeant Pepper, the lonely outsider, the nonintellectual of the group who, as he concedes in the first song following the theme, gets by "with a little help from my friends." In a dialogue between the narrator and the sergeant, Ringo is asked:

Would you believe in love at first sight,
Yes I'm certain that it happens all the time . . .

Drugs are the subject of "I'm Fixing a Hole" and "Lucy in the Sky with Diamonds," an acrostic of LSD. Lavish verbal imagery and tonal distortions obtained by electronic manipulation suggest the visual hallucinations associated with "acid":

Picture yourself in a boat on a river
With tangerine trees and marmalade skies . . .

More familiar refusals to face the truth are treated in "Getting Better," a conventional rationalization, and in "She's Leaving Home." After their daughter has fled the house her parents sing:

We gave her most of our lives . . .
We gave her everything money can buy . . .

While the narrator chants, in contrapuntal fashion:

She's leaving home after living alone
For so many years.

Side I concludes with a return to the most obvious fiction of all: show business. The subject of the final song, "Mr. Kite," was inspired by an old-time theater poster.

Side II begins with a piece by George Harrison. It is the album's longest song, built on Indian ragas, and explicitly describes what Side I was all about:

> *the space between us all and the people who*
> *hide themselves behind a wall of illusion.*

The next three numbers treat life without drugs or hypocrisy. The Beatles sing of the sterile, ritualized roles people play. The first song wryly mocks the activities of an elderly couple; the second is a spoof on romantic love. A whore in Liverpool, who procures through her daytime trade as a meter-maid, was the inspiration for "Lovely Rita."

> *In a cap she looked much older*
> *And the bag across her shoulder*
> *Made her look a little like a military man . . .*

The third describes, in desolate terms, the disonance of an ordinary day:

> *Nothing to do to save his life call his wife in*
> *Nothing to say but what a day*
> *how's your boy been . . .*

There follows a reprise of the Sergeant Pepper theme—with a stunning difference. Sergeant Pepper is no longer the raucous fun man, promising smiles and good times. Avoiding the initial expression of these empty hopes the band starts shouting "Hup, two, three, four," pounding out the beat and the ultimate truth of Sergeant Pepper's inner life:

> *Sergeant Pepper's lonely* [repeated four times].

Thus Lennon and McCartney, the group's guiding spirits, commit themselves to the philosophy that Eugene O'Neill expressed in *The Iceman Cometh*—that man cannot live without illusion. The last song, "A Day in the Life," suggests that man cannot live with it either. It is a moving work, a desperate reflection of contemporary life, a song *Newsweek* described as the Beatles' "Waste Land."

The piece is, in a sense, a *roman à clef*. Shortly before its composition a close friend of the Beatles, the twenty-one-year-old son of a prominent British couple, smashed his car in the center of London while high on drugs. After telling of the accident, the narrator cites a film of the English army after it had won the war. In both instances the protagonist is removed from the core of the experience in much the manner of the central character in an Antonioni film. The only links with his friend's death are a news story and a photograph; the only connections with violent war, a film and a book. Lennon's voice, breaking with sadness, invites the listener: "I'd love to turn you on." The last word of this one-line refrain leads into an electronic passage in which a large orchestra, recorded on tracks laid upon tracks, builds up to a growling controlled crescendo, simulating a drug-induced "trip." An alarm awakens the narrator who continues his story to the accompaniment of a nervous jazz idiom. High-pitched voices intone a series of open, sensuous chords more suggestive of "pot" than "acid," after which John returns, reflects on the emptiness of everyone (the holes in Albert Hall are people), and invites the listener on still another trip. The nonpitched sounds return, increase in volume and duration until they dissolve, with suddenness, into one resonant, depressing, seemingly interminable terminal tonic chord.

At the bottom of the album cover is a burial plot covered with red flowers arranged to spell BEATLES. The original Beatles of the 1950s, joyous and innocent, are dead. Above and to the left are four standing figures in dark ties and dark suits. Madame Tussaud's wax reproductions of Brian Epstein's carefully groomed group of the early sixties. Sergeant Pepper's Lonely Hearts Club Band is pictured in the center of the cover. Its members are adorned with colorful, psychedelic costumes and are devastatingly unsmiling. They are the Beatles of today. Sergeant Pepper's Band, Madame Tussaud's figures, and a host of others, including Shirley Temple, Mae West, Fred Astaire, W. C. Fields, Marilyn Monroe, Timothy Leary, Edgar Allen Poe, Tom Mix, Bob Dylan, Karlheinz Stockhausen, Tony Curtis, and Lawrence of Arabia look down at the grave below. All mourn the loss of the youthful Beatles, the group Lennon recently referred to as "those four jolly lads."

Dealing with identity, illusion, loneliness, and death, the Beatles represent their generation and its overwhelming sense of anomie. Refusing to accept the status quo and take square places in a "straight" society, they reach everyone from the

Haight-Ashbury section of San Francisco to the Manhattan East Side discotheques. In this respect they differ most dramatically from the art musician of our time. Contemporary art composers are committed to a style of composition that is, in its essence, opposed to a dramatic expressionism that has prevailed in art music for the last few hundred years. Music as drama grew, in part, from tonality, a musical system in which one note, the "key," serves as the focus of an entire work. This single focus is placed into conflict with other keys throughout the course of the piece; the juxtaposition and resolution of the resulting tonal conflict weaves a dramatic, extramusical meaning into the musical fabric of the composition.

During the years in which Picasso and Kandinsky shattered the single focus of perspective in painting, Schoenberg and Varèse shattered the single focus of tonality in music. Schoenberg did it by organizing a new musical arrangement in which all twelve tones of the chromatic scale are equal and Varèse went even farther—by opening his music to all sound, not just pitched sound. Although a number of present-day musicians continue to rely on a traditional, tonal base for composition, the significant musical action of the 1950s and 1960s has centered on Milton Babbitt, John Cage, and the musicians working around both men. All make music that is intramusical; abstract, beatless and nonmelodic, it reaches only those trained in the highly complex manner of what is referred to as new musical expression.

Babbitt's highly structured form and Cage's negation of traditional form have a common base; both are expressions of a belief that tonality is no longer valid, that there is no *a priori* order, no God-given frame of reference. The particular tonal-expressive tradition that began with Monteverdi in the seventeenth century and culminated in the dramatic works of Richard Wagner has been overthrown. It is inevitable that serious art musicians write music the way that they do. The battle against dramatic expressionism in art music has been waged and won.

But the Beatles never had anything to do with a war. They replaced revolution with affable irreverence. Born in Liverpool, they grew up among the constantly shifting population and extremely high crime rate of a large seaport, where the standards and taste of bourgeois London mattered little and local guitar players enjoyed higher repute in the community than opera singers. Lennon, McCartney, Harrison and Starr emerged from this milieu as the antithesis of British tradition, classless kids who began their meteoric rise not musically but socially, by overstating the clothing and hairstyles of the educated Eton boy. Brashness and confidence have always distinguished their conduct. In Buckingham Palace McCartney criticized the condition of the carpets. And at a Royal Command Performance in London Lennon directed the audience: "People in the cheap seats can clap. The rest of you—rattle your jewelry!"

The Beatles' sense of freedom from the shackles of social tradition is matched by their freedom from the shackles of the hallowed styles of musical composition. Lennon, whose mother played the banjo (she died when he was thirteen), and McCartney, whose father had a jazz band thirty years ago, never had an awesome musical tradition to fight. At least ten years younger than the youngest of the recognized art composers of our day (the oldest Beatle is twenty-seven), and a generation younger than Babbitt and Cage, the Beatles grew up with transistor radios next to their ears. Bach's "Art of the Fugue" and Schoenberg's "Method of Composing with Twelve Tones" had as little relevance to them as English imperialism and the White Man's Burden. Despite the use of styles and techniques from various periods throughout the history of music, the Beatles and their youthful colleagues are essentially ahistorical. Born after the social and musical revolutions of the twentieth century, able simply to relax and use all the musical tools available, they have created something moving and altogether new.

Are we entering an era in which musical high art, as we have known it, is coming to an end? The medieval poet-musician, who passed on his art through an oral tradition, has a contemporary analogue in the rock-and-roll performer. He is a central, contributing member of a society that is moving steadily away from notation and inexorably toward the preservation of the musical object on record and tape. No notational system is capable of reproducing the complex texture of a Beatle record or the sophisticated manipulations the sound engineer immobilizes on it. What is preserved in the music is the performance itself; the record is the message. Marshall McLuhan's thesis that the visually oriented and literate society of Western man is being replaced by an acoustically oriented, electronic society receives its firmest confirmation in the most logical field. The compositional tradition associated with notation that has prevailed since the beginning of the Renaissance is being replaced by an overwhelmingly oral tradition—in both art and rock music. Art music, for the moment, has excluded all but the most cerebral, specialized listeners. Rock is all embracing, having absorbed elements of blues, folk, jazz, and the serious avant-garde.

Few other groups are as good as the Beatles, of course. The quality of rock is about as uneven as the quality of the songs of the jongleur; a small percentage of it is very good. But the best rock is moving with unprecedented speed into unexpected, more artistically interesting areas. Such a phenomenon has historical antecedents; vital popular forms have anticipated crucial stylistic changes in art music of the past. The street singers' *commedia del arte,* for instance, was in great part responsible for the flowering of the opera which, in turn, provided the source for the very dramatic expressionism that dominated art music until the second half of this century.

A few performers, composers, and scholars of traditional art music have begun to acknowledge that the boundaries between art and rock music are becoming less defined. Cathy Berberian, noted avant-garde singer for whom Igor Stravinsky, John Cage and Luciano Berio have written works, recently recorded an album of twelve Beatle songs, and commented that "Eleanor Rigby" was one of the most beautiful she had heard in years. And on CBS-TV Leonard Bernstein called the best of rock "irresistible." From the other end of the spectrum the Beatles, with their drooping Mexican mustaches, lugubrious faces, and increasingly bizarre clothing, are heard exploring progressively more intellectual and artistic frames of reference. Paul told a reporter that he vaguely minds anyone knowing anything he doesn't know and John said he would rather have the attention of two hundred people who knew what he was doing than two million who had no idea what was going on.

Despite the similarities, there is a crucial difference between the breeds. Art musicians have reacted to the absence of structure and system in contemporary society by imposing a highly complex structure and system upon their creative work or by annihilating form altogether. The Beatles, on the other hand, have reacted to the same sterility in an extramusical way—by immersing themselves in Eastern mystical theology and experimenting with psychedelic drugs. Because the intramusical aspect of their songs is unaffected by historical considerations, esthetic ideology, or the search for a meaning in life, their lyric buoyancy remains intact. It is in striking evidence in the rollicking single, "All You Need Is Love"—a wild and beautiful distillation of their sole and pervasive antidote to mid-century despair.

BEATLES NOT ALL THAT TURNED ON

●

ALAN ALDRIDGE

"There's a fog upon L.A. and my friends have lost their way," sings Beatle George Harrison in "Blue Jay Way," named for a road in the Hollywood hills. And there is a fog, one that has led to sundry articles, calls to talk radio stations, asides from disc jockeys and myriad conversations and arguments over the significance of Beatles' lyrics in such songs as "A Day in the Life," "Dr. Roberts" and "Strawberry Fields Forever."

All this crypto-analysis has produced more murk than light and, since Beatles records are the most-played, most-sold, most-memorized, most-discussed pop product of the decade, their meanings and intents—whether subliminal or superliminal—have heavy social impact. Realizing the magnitude of confusion, British writer-artist Alan Aldridge interviewed Beatle Paul McCartney to get a fountainhead perspective of their words. His article may answer some questions. Then again, it may not.

Alan Aldridge: It seems to me your songs appeal to two entirely separate audiences, the mass teeny-boppers who accept your work at a humming and dancing level, and the new semi-intellectual audience which analyzes and seeks hidden meanings behind the lyrics.

Paul McCartney: We write songs; we know what we mean by them. But in a week someone else says something about it, says that it means that as well, and you can't deny it. Things take on millions of meanings. I don't understand it.

A fantastic example is the inner track on the back of *Sergeant Pepper* that plays for hours if your automatic doesn't cut off. It's like a mantra in yoga and the meaning changes and it all becomes dissociated from what it is saying (the changing meaning of an endlessly repeated phrase is the subject of experiments by Dr. Chris Evans at the National Physical

Laboratory). You get a pure buzz after a while because it's so boring it ceases to mean anything.

Aldridge: To be honest it wasn't until I heard "Eleanor Rigby" ("she keeps her face in a jar by the door") that I became aware that your songs had a lot more to offer than "yea yea yea." Perhaps we could talk about this for a start?

McCartney: Well, that started off with sitting down at the piano and getting the first line of the melody, and playing around with words. I think it was "Miss Daisy Hawkins" originally; then it was her picking up the rice in a church after a wedding. That's how nearly all our songs start, with the first line just suggesting itself from books or newspapers.

At first I thought it was a young Miss Daisy Hawkins, a bit like "Annabel Lee," but not so sexy; but then I saw I'd said she was picking up the rice in church, so she had to be a cleaner; she had missed the wedding, and she was suddenly lonely. In fact she had missed it all—she was the spinster type.

Jane [Jane Asher] was in a play in Bristol then, and I was walking round the streets waiting for her to finish. I didn't really like Daisy Hawkins—I wanted a name that was more real. The thought just came: "Eleanor Rigby picks up the rice and lives in a dream"—so there she was. The next thing was Father MacKenzie. It was going to be Father McCartney, but then I thought that was a bit of a hang up for my dad, being in this lonely song. So we looked through the phone book. That's the beauty of working at random—it does come up perfectly, much better than if you try to think it with your intellect.

Anyway, there was Father MacKenzie and he was just as I had imagined him, lonely, darning his socks. We weren't sure if the song was going to go on. In the next verse we thought of a bin man, an old feller going through dustbins; but it got too involved—embarrassing. John and I wondered whether to have Eleanor Rigby and him have a thing going, but we couldn't really see how. When I played it to John, we decided to finish it.

That was the point anyway. She didn't make it, she never made it with anyone, she didn't even look as if she was going to.

Aldridge: Like "Dr. Roberts"—he seems to be a psychiatrist?

McCartney: Well, he's like a joke. There's some fellow in New York, and in the States we'd hear people say: "You can get everything off him; any pills you want." It was a big racket, but a joke too about this fellow who cured everyone of everything with all these pills and tranquilizers, injections for this and that; he just kept New York high. That's what Dr. Roberts is all about, just a pill doctor who sees you all right. It was a joke between ourselves, but they go in in-jokes and come out out-jokes because everyone listens and puts their own thing on it, which is great. I mean, when I was young I never knew what "Gilly Gilly Elsa Feffer Cats . . ." was all about, but I still enjoyed singing it. You put your own meaning at your own level to our songs and that's what's great about them.

Aldridge: Is that how you wrote *Sergeant Pepper?*

McCartney: I was just thinking of nice words like Sergeant Pepper, and Lonely Hearts Club, and they came together for no reason. But after you have written that down you start to think, "There's this Sergeant Pepper who has taught the band to play, and got them going so that at least they found one number." They're a bit of a brass band in a way, but also a rock band because they've got the San Francisco thing. We went into it just like that: just us doing a good show.

Aldridge: Why did you put all those people on the cover, like a school photograph gone wrong?

McCartney: These were all just cult heroes. George chose a few of his schoolmates he liked; and the rest of us said names we liked the sound of: Like Aldous Huxley, H. G. Wells, Johnny Weissmuller.

Those Indian people have amazing stories. There's one called Panmahansa Yogananda, who died in 1953 and left his body in an incredibly perfect state. Medical reports in Los Angeles three or four months after he died were saying, This is incredible; this man hasn't decomposed yet. He was sitting there glowing because he did this sort of transcendental bit, transcended his body by planes of consciousness. He was taught by another person on the cover and he was taught by another, and it all goes back to the one called Babujee, who's just a little drawing looking upwards.

You can't photograph him—he's an agent. He puts a curse on the film. He's the all-time governor, he's been at it a long time and he's still around doing the transcending bit.

Aldridge: These are all George's heroes?

McCartney: Yes. George says the great thing about people like Babujee and Christ and all the governors who have transcended is that they've got out of the reincarnation cycle; they've reached the bit where they are just there; they don't have to zoom back.

So they're there planning the spiritual thing for us. So, if they are planning it, what a groove that he's got himself on our cover, right in the middle of the Beatles' LP cover! Normal ideas of God wouldn't have him interested in Beatles music or any pop—it's a bit infra dig—but obviously, if we're all here doing it, and someone's interested in us, then it's all to do with it. There's not one bit worse than another bit. So that's great, that's beautiful that he's right on the cover with all his mates.

Whatever it is, it's what is doing all those trees and doing us and keeping you going; which someone must be doing.

The yogi goes through millions of things to realize the simplest of all truths, because while you are going through this part, there's always the opposite truth. You say, "Ah, well, that's all there is to it then. It's all great, and God's looking after you." Then someone says, "What about a hunchback then? Is that great?" And you say, "Okay then, it's all lousy." And this is just as true if you want to see it. But the truth is that it's neither good nor lousy; just down the middle; a state of being that doesn't have black or white, good or bad.

Aldridge: Is that what George's number is about?

McCartney: I think George's awareness has helped us because he got into this through Indian music—or as he calls it, "all-India radio." There's such a sense of vision in Indian music that it's just like meditation. You can play it forever; there's just no end to what you can play on a sitar and how good you can get.

Aldridge: It struck me that *Sergeant Pepper* is one of the first LPs and has looked at the idiom either like a symphony or a paperback: trying to present a complete show that lasts an hour.

McCartney: That's it. We realized for the first time that someday someone would actually be holding a thing that they'd call "The Beatles' new LP" and that normally it would just be a collection of songs or a nice picture on the cover, nothing more. So the idea was to do a complete thing that you could make what you liked of; just a little magic presentation. We were going to have a little envelope in the center with the nutty things you can buy at Woolworth's: a surprise packet.

Aldridge: "Late of Pablo Fanques Fair"—Where did you get that?

McCartney: John has this old poster that says right at the top, "Pablo Fanques Fair presents the Hendersons for the benefit of Mr. Kite," and it has all the bits of thing that sound strange: "Over men and horses, hoops and garters, lastly through a hogshead of real fire." "The Hendersons"—you couldn't make that up.

Aldridge: There's one part that must be one of John's puns: "Somersets" instead of "somersaults."

McCartney: No, that's from the poster as well.

Aldridge: The pop scene before you came along went to great lengths to create names. I suppose we ought to realize that you can't do better than real fact—your own actual experience of life.

McCartney: There's no need to make things up. We started on interviewers who would say, "What do you believe?" and we'd say, "We do not believe in gold-lamé suits: That's trying to glory it up and doesn't even do it well." That detaches you from the real thing. That's why Daisy Hawkins wasn't any good—it sounds like Daisy Made-up. Billy Shears is another that sounds like a schoolmate but isn't. Possibly one day we'll meet all these people.

Aldridge: One of the most obviously ambiguous of your songs, the one that everybody can see something in, is "Lucy in the Sky with Diamonds."

McCartney: This one is amazing. As I was saying before, when you write a song and you mean it one way, and then someone comes up and says something about it that you didn't think of—you can't deny it. Like "Lucy in the Sky with Diamonds," people came up and said, cunningly, "Right, I get it. L-S-D," and it was when papers were talking about LSD, but we never thought about it.

Aldridge: If you take LSD as a sort of pun, the whole song is a trip.

McCartney: What happened was that John's son, Julian, did a drawing at school and brought it home, and he has a schoolmate called Lucy, and John said, "What's that," and he said, "Lucy in the Sky with Diamonds"—so we had a nice title. We did the whole thing like an *Alice in Wonderland* idea, being in a boat on the river, slowly drifting downstream and those great cellophane flowers towering over your head. Every so often it broke off and you saw Lucy in the sky with diamonds all over the sky. This Lucy was God, the big figure, the White Rabbit. You can just write a song with imagination on words and that's what we did.

It's like modern poetry, but neither John nor I have read much. The last time I approached it I was thinking, "This is strange and far out," and I did not dig it all that much, except Dylan Thomas, who I suddenly started getting, and I was quite pleased with myself because I got it, but I hadn't realized he was going to be saying exactly the same things.

It's just that we've at last stopped trying to be clever, and we just write what we like to write. If it comes out clever, okay. You get to the bit where you think, if we're going to write great philosophy it isn't worth it. "Love Me Do" was our greatest philosophical song: "Love me do/You know I love you/I'll always be true/So love me do/Please" simple and true, means that it's incredibly simple.

Aldridge: People have told me that "Fixing a Hole" is all about junk, you know, this guy, sitting there fixing a hole in his arm.

McCartney: This song is just about the hole in the road where the rain gets in; a good old analogy—the hole in your make-up which lets the rain in and stops your mind from going where it will. It's you interfering with things as when someone walks up to you and says, "I am the Son of God." And you say, "No you're not; I'll crucify you," and you crucify him. Well that's life, but it is not fixing a hole.

It's about fans too: "See the people standing there/Who disagree and never win/And wonder why they don't get in/Silly people, run around/They worry me/And never ask why they don't get in my door." If they only knew that the best way to get in is not to do that, because obviously anyone who is going to be straight and like a real friend and a real person to us is going to get in; but they simply stand there and give off, "We are fans, don't let us in."

Sometimes I invite them in, but it starts to be not really the point in a way, because I invited one in, and the next day she was in the *Daily Mirror* with her mother saying we were going to get married. So we tell the fans, "Forget it."

If you're a junky sitting in a room fixing a hole then that's what it will mean to you, but when I wrote it I meant if there's a crack or the room is uncolorful, then I'll paint it.

Aldridge: "She's Leaving Home" is a great song, very simple, similar to "Eleanor Rigby."

McCartney: It's a much younger girl, but the same sort of loneliness. That was a *Daily Mirror* story again: This girl left home and her faither said, "We gave her everything, I don't know why she left home." But he didn't give her that much, not what she wanted when she left home.

Aldridge: Fine. What's "Lovely Rita" all about?

McCartney: I was bopping about on the piano in Liverpool when someone told me that in America they call parking-meter women meter maids. I thought that was great, and it got to Rita Meter Maid and then Lovely Rita Meter Maid and I was thinking vaguely that it should be a hate song: "You took my car away and I'm so blue today." And you wouldn't be liking her; but then I thought it would be better to love her and if she was very freaky too, like a military man, with a bag on her shoulder. A foot stomper, but nice.

The song was imagining if somebody was there taking down my number and I suddenly fell for her, and the kind of person I'd be, to fall for a meter maid, would be a shy office clerk and I'd say "May I inquire discreetly when you are free to take some tea with me." Tea, not pot. It's like saying "Come and cut the grass" and then realizing that could be pot, or the old teapot could be some thing about pot. But I don't mind pot and I leave the words in. They're not consciously introduced just to say pot and be clever.

Aldridge: After the line "a little like a military man" there's a fantastic "whoop whoop." How did you do that?

McCartney: It's done with a comb and paper. We had it in the bit after and it sounded too corny; it wasn't quite good enough to have twice, but in a way that's nice because you listen for it to come around again.

There's a lot of random in our songs—Strawberry Fields is the name of a Salvation Army School—by the time we've taken it through the writing stage, thinking of it, playing it to the others, writing it, and letting them think of bits, recording it once and deciding it's not quite right and do it again and then find "Oh, that's it, the solo comes here and that goes there," then bang, you have the jigsaw puzzle.

That happens with all our songs, except the ones we want to keep really simple, like, "When I'm Sixty-four" and "Fixing a Hole."

Aldridge: What kind of scene are you thinking of when you say "Took her home and nearly made it, sitting on the sofa with a sister or two"?

McCartney: That's it: There are a couple of sisters around so that is why I never made it.

Aldridge: I could see a whole scene of naked bodies writhing on the sofa . . .

McCartney: If it had been really made . . .

Aldridge: Then the tricky one that the BBC banned—"A Day in the Life." It's been said that this is a sort of requiem to Tara Brown [the heir to the Guinness Trust, killed in 1966 in a car crash in London].

McCartney: I've heard that. I don't think John had that in mind at all. The real words to that are "read the news today." There'd been a story about a man who'd made the grade, and there'd been a photograph of him sitting in his car. John said, "I had to laugh." He'd sort of blown his mind out in the car.

Aldridge: Literally, with a gun?

McCartney: No, he was just high on whatever he uses, say he was in this big Bentley, sitting at the traffic lights. He's driving today; the chauffeur isn't there, and maybe he got high because of that. The lights have changed and he hasn't noticed that there's a crowd of housewives and they're all looking at him saying "Who's that? I've seen him in the papers," and they're not sure if he's from the House of Lords. He looks a bit like that with his Homburg and white scarf and he's out of his screws.

That's a bit of black comedy. The next bit was another song altogether but it just happened to fit. It was just me remembering what it was like to run up the road to catch a bus to school, having a smoke and going into class. We decided, "The hell with this, we're going to write a turn-on song." It was a reflection of my school days—I would have a Woodbine then, and somebody would speak and I would go into a dream.

This was the only one in the album written as a deliberate provocation. A stick-that-in-your-pipe . . . But what we want is to turn you on to the truth rather than pot.

Aldridge: "Yellow Submarine" has connotations—I read that in Greenwich Village they call yellow phenobarbital capsules—Nembutals—"yellow submarines."

McCartney: I knew it would get connotations, but it really was a children's song. I just loved the idea of kids singing it. With "Yellow Submarine" the whole idea was, "If someday I came across some kids singing it, that will be it," so it's got to be very easy—there isn't a single big word. Kids will understand it easier than adults. "In the town where I was born/ There lived a man who sailed to sea/And he told of his life in the land of submarines." That's really the beginning of a kids' story. There's some stuff in Greece like icing sugar—you eat it. It's like a sweet and you drop it into water. It's called submarine; we had it on holiday.

Aldridge: But some of your songs are real places and real facts. Can you remember the little influences that made "Penny Lane," for example?

McCartney: Penny Lane is a bus roundabout in Liverpool; and there is a barber's shop showing photographs of every head he's had the pleasure to know—no that's not true, they're just photos of hairstyles, but all the people who come and go, stop and say hello. There's a bank on the corner, so we made up the bit about the banker in his motor car. It's part fact, part nostalgia for a place which is a great place, blue suburban skies as we remember it, and it's still there.

Aldridge: I've heard it said that George Martin writes most of your music.

McCartney: He always has something to do with it, but sometimes more than others. For instance, he wrote the end of "All You Need Is Love" and got into trouble because the "In The Mood" bit was copyrighted. We thought of all the great clichés because they're a great bit of random. It was a hurried session and we didn't mind giving him that to do—saying, "There's the end, we want it to go on and on." Actually what he wrote was much more disjointed, so when we put all the bits together we said, "Could we have 'Greensleeves' right on top of that little Bach thing?" And on top of that we had the "In The Mood" bit.

George is quite a sage. Sometimes he works with us, sometimes against us; he's always looked after us. I don't think he does as much as some people think. He sometimes does all the arrangements and we just change them.

Aldridge: Finally, many people in the trade tell me Ringo can't drum.

McCartney: That's extraordinary. He wasn't on our first record; with "Love Me Do" Ringo was on the LP and Andy White on the single, and you really notice the difference. What a long time ago that was.

THE BEATLES

●

MURRAY KEMPTON

To see the Beatles is to confront a gallery of eminent women of the nineteenth century. Women of character, of course, who got themselves criticized as masculine in their time as the Beatles are entirely masculine now.

But the hair is an all-enveloping mask; it is not just long, but Victorian long, great-lady long, bishop's-daughter long. The only comparisons are with women—all long dead; the image is so overriding that one's own mind turns womanly and the thought at the first sight of the Beatles in the flesh is what American ladies seem always to say when they first see the Queen: "My dear, that lovely British skin; it cannot be photographed."

So Ringo is George Sand, and Paul is Elizabeth Bennett in Jane Austen and John looks like the photograph of Florence Nightingale—"We are ducks," said her mother, "who have hatched a wild swan"—and George, the only one who occasionally lets the black devil of melancholy come through, is that Caroline Lamb who drove Lord Byron to such a frenzy of detestation that he begged only "to be spared from meeting her until we may be chained together in Dante's Inferno."

All the women the Beatles evoke were struggling with the problem of being women in the nineteenth century, when one was adored and never taken seriously and where the least little thing one said could make scandal, all of which is rather like being a Beatle.

The first question was to John about Viet Nam. He answered that he didn't like it.

"*We* don't like it," said George suddenly. His voice was grim; Caroline Lamb was declaring her independence. "We can elaborate on that if we want to in England."

The questions passed to John on Christianity.

"There's more people in America," Paul answered, "so

there's more bigots. We hear more from American bigots than we do from Rooshan bigots."

The Jane Austen heroine was offering the defense of wit against the stupid, accepted of course as the stronger.

There were countries, he said, where this sort of thing would not be taken up and misinterpreted as it was here.

"Here somebody will take it up and use it and not have too many scruples." He paused at the thought of the scandal that might be approaching him and his face automatically lied that he was just a child and that he did not mean it.

"It's just wonderful here," he finished. Everyone laughed.

And now that you've learned to play the sitar, someone asked George, will you be using it more and more?

"I haven't learned to play the sitar," George answered coldly. "Shankar hasn't learned to play it and he's been playing for twenty-five years."

The tone was bitter as of deprivation of adventure. You began to understand that, as women of the nineteenth century were, the Beatles are preserved and protected from the nonsense of the convention which surrounds them by the sweetness and safety of their home. They only try the sitar; Shankar lives by it. For only the men can go to the wars and bleed and die and hate; and one moment of Joe Turner singing that it's your dollar now but it's gonna be mine some sweet day is more than all they have ever said. What is raw and crude in life is not for them; they are only translators.

And yet, even though they know their loss, they translate all the meanness of the blues to us as charm and wit and gaiety; and they make us remember that the nineteenth-century woman, stay home though she had to, was something of a piece of goods.

THE MUSIC OF THE BEATLES

●

NED ROREM

I never go to classical concerts any more and I don't know anyone who does. It's hard still to care whether some virtuoso tonight will perform the *Moonlight Sonata* a bit better or a bit worse than another virtuoso performed it last night. But I do often attend what used to be called avant-garde recitals, though seldom with delight, and inevitably I look around and wonder: What am I doing here? Where are the poets and painters and even the composers themselves who used to flock to these things? Well, perhaps what I am doing here is a duty, keeping an ear on my profession so as to justify the joys of resentment, to steal an idea or two, or just to show charity toward some friend on the program. But I learn less and less. Meanwhile the absent artists are at home playing records; they are *reacting* again, finally, to something they no longer find at concerts.

Reacting to what? Why, to the Beatles, of course, whose arrival I believe is one of the most healthy events in music since 1950. What occurred around 1950 will be the starting concern of this brief essay, an essay with a primarily musical approach. Most of the literary copy devoted to the Beatles extols the timely daring of the group's lyrics while skirting the essential quality, the music. Poetry may be the egg from which the nightingale is hatched, though in the last analysis that nightingale must come first.

My "musical approach" will be that of what once was termed long-hair composer, somewhat disillusioned, nourished at the conservatory yet exposed all his life (as is any American, of necessity) to jazz. It will not pretend to a total appraisal, only to the fact that I and my colleagues have been happily torn from a long nap by the energy of rock, principally as embodied in the Beatles. Naturally I've grown curious about their energy. What are its origins? What need does it fill? Why should the Beatles—who seem to be the best of a good thing, who are, in my view, far superior to all the other groups who pretend to copy them, but who nevertheless are mostly American and perpetuating what once was an essentially American thing—why should the Beatles have erupted from *Liverpool?* Could it be true, as Nat Hentoff suggests, that they "turned millions of American adolescents on to what had been here hurting all the time . . . but the young here never did want it raw so they absorbed it through the British filter"? Do the Beatles hurt indeed? Are they really so new? Does their attraction, whether of pain or pleasure, stem from their words—or even from what's called their *sound*—or from their tunes? Those are the questions, more or less in order, that I'd like to examine.

Around 1940, after a rather dim puberty, American music grew up. Cut off from Europe, composers began producing an identifiably native product. By the war's end we had cultivated a group worthy of export. Symphonies of all shapes were being ground out; new operas were being performed in Mid-western towns; and vocal soloists were everywhere making themselves heard. On one side were Sinatra, Horne, and Holiday, stylists of a high order, wonderfully performing material of little musical interest (when not derived from Gershwin or Porter) and dim literary content. On the other side were specialized concert singers—Frijsh, Fairbank, and Tangeman—who, though vocally uneven, helped to create a new style by persuading certain youngish composers to make singable songs based on texts of quality.

By 1950 the export of American music was well under way. But we soon realized that no one abroad cared much. Jazz, of course, had always been an attraction in the Europe that dismissed American "serious" music as not very serious; Europe, after all, was also reawakening after the war. But that awakening was mainly concerned with the past, namely with the dodecaphonic system which in America had atrophied, and in Germany had been forgotten since the war. This device (no, not a device, but a way of thinking) was being revitalized not in Germany where it had all begun, but in France. By 1950 Pierre Boulez virtually single-handedly had cleared the path and set the tone that music would follow for the next decade. America took the cue, allowing her new-found individuality to dissolve into what ultimately became the bandwagon of International Academicism.

This turn of events suprised no one more than the composers themselves. Although Copland and Thomson, after Satie, had been reacting in the twenties against the complicated romantic Teuton soup in which music had wallowed for centuries, in the fifties complex systems were revived, literally with a vengeance, by certain middle-aged composers (Elliott Carter, Milton Babbitt, Arthur Berger, etc.) whom fame had by-passed during the forties, and by the young in general; while the randomness of Dada was reanimated by John Cage, Copland, on the other hand, became engaged in serial formality, this time with a straight face, as though intimidated by those deadly serious composers half his age.

These "serious" youngsters, in keeping with the times, were understandably more geared to the practical concerns of science than to "superfluous" considerations of self-expression. When they wrote for the human voice (which they did less and less often) it was treated not as an interpreter of poetry—nor even necessarily of words—but as a mechanism, often electronically revamped. Verse itself was no longer married to the music, or even framed *by* the music, but was illustrated *through* the music. There was little use left for live singers.

Live singers themselves, at least those of formal training, weren't interested anyway. Modern music was too difficult. Besides it had no audience any longer, nor did the classical song recital so beloved in the already distant years of Teyte and Lehmann. Young singers were lured away from *lieder,* from *la mélodie,* from the American "art song" until not one specialist remained. They had all been seduced by the big money and chance of celebrity of grand opera. Even today the few exceptional singers are mostly European: Schwarzkopf, Souzay, Fischer-Dieskau. Even the accurate Bethany Beardslee certainly makes no money, while her excellent West Coast counterpart, Marni Nixon, now does movie dubbing and musical comedy. But most modern song specialists have awful voices and give vanity concerts for invited guests.

Elsewhere the progressive, or cool jazz of Brubeck and Kenton and Mulligan was developing a rarefied expression that had nothing to do with song or dance. The Hit Parade was defunct, Negro stylists out of jobs, and the vulgar vocalists of college bands in low esteem. Song was out.

Meanwhile the wall separating so-called classical from so-called jazz was crumbling, as each division sought somehow to join with and rejuvenate the other. Yet the need for "communication," so widely lamented today, seemed to be satisfied less through music—any music—than through other outlets, particularly movies. Movies, in becoming accepted as a fine art, turned out to be the one medium which could depict most articulately the inarticulateness of today, even to intellectuals; whereas the intellectualization of music had ironically alienated the intellectual and has not much interested anyone else.

Myself and a handful of song-writing friends (Paul Bowles, Daniel Pinkham, William Flanagan, David Diamond) who began in the forties I consider as having come in at the end, as having attempted an irrelevant resuscitation of a creature with sleeping sickness. Most of us have written depressingly few songs lately, and those few emerged less from driving need than from ever-rarer commissions extended by die-hard specialists. Since there's little money, publication, recording, performance, or even concern for songs, our enthusiasm for that most gently urgent of mediums has been, alas, pretty much dampened.

But if the once-thriving Art of Song has lain dormant since the war, indications now show it restirring throughout the world—which is not the same world that put it to bed. When it fully awakens, its composition and interpretation will be of a quite different order and for a quite different public.

Since big-time vocalists like Leontyne Price are, for economic reasons, no longer principally occupied with miniature forms, and since "serious" composers like Stockhausen are, for scientific reasons, no longer principally occupied with human utterances (of which singing is the most primitive and hence the most expressive), and since a master like Stravinsky has never been famous for his solo vocal works, the artful tradition of great song has been transferred to the Beatles and their offshoots. Their music was already sprouting a decade ago through such innocent male sex symbols as Presley in America and Johnny Hallyday in France, both of whom were caricatured by the English in a movie called *Expresso Bongo,* a precursor of *Privilege,* about a none-too-bright rock singer. These young soloists (still functioning and making lots of money) were the parents of more sophisticated, more committed, soloists like Dylan and Donovan, who in turn spawned a horde of masculine offspring including twins (Simon and Garfunkel, the most cultured), quintuplets (Country Joe and the Fish, the most exotic), sextuplets (the Association, the most nostalgic), even septuplets (Mothers of Invention, the most madly satirical). With much less frequency were born female descendents such as Janis Ian or Bobbie Gentry (each of whom has produced one, and only one, good song) and the trio of Supremes. Unlike their "grandparents," all of these groups, plus some twenty other fairly good ones, write much of their own material, thus combining the traditions of twelfth-century troubadours, sixteenth-century madrigalists, and eighteenth-century musical artisans, who were always composer-performers—in short, combining all sung expression (except opera) as it was before the twentieth century.

For this expression one must now employ (as I have been doing here) the straightforward word song, as opposed to the misleading *lieder* which applies just to German repertory, or the pretentious *art song* which no longer applies to anything. (The only designation in English that ever really distinguished "serious art song" from what used to be named "pop tune" was "recital song.") Since pop tunes, as once performed by such singers as Billie Holiday and the Big Bands during an epoch not simply dormant but dead, are heard not only in night clubs and theaters but in recitals and concerts, and since those tunes are as good as—if not better than—most "serious" songs being composed today, the best cover-all term is simply song. The only sub-categories are good and bad. Curiously, it is not through the suave innovations of our sophisticated composers that music is regaining its health, but from the old-fashioned lung exercise of gangs of kids.

That the best of these gangs should have come from England is unimportant; they *could* have come from Arkansas. The Beatles' world is just another part of an International Academicism wherein the question is to be better rather than different. It seems to me that their attraction has little to do with "what had here been hurting" (as Hentoff implied), but on the contrary with enjoyment.

No sooner does Susan Sontag explain that "the new sensibility takes a rather dim view of pleasure," than we discover her "new" sensibility growing stale. Her allusion was to a breed of suspiciously articulate composers—suspicious because they spend more time in glib justification than in composition, and denigrate the *liking* of music, the *bodily* liking of it. Indeed, one doesn't "like" Boulez, does one? To like is not their consideration; to comprehend is. But surely fun is the very core of the Beatles' musically contagious expression: the Japanese, the

Poles (who ignore the poetic subject matter of suicide and bombs) love them as much as do their English-speaking fans. The Beatles are an antidote to the new (read "old") sensibility.

The Beatles are good even though everyone knows they're good, i.e., in spite of the claims of people under thirty about their filling a new sociological need like civil rights and LSD. Our need for them is neither sociological nor new, but artistic and old, specifically a renewal, a renewal of pleasure.

Why are the Beatles superior? It is easy to say that most of their competition (like most everything everywhere) is junk. More important, their superiority is consistent: each of the songs from their last three albums is memorable. The best of these memorable tunes—and the best is a large percentage ("Here, There and Everywhere," "Good Day Sunshine," "Michelle," "Norwegian Wood")—compare with those by composers from great eras of song: Monteverdi, Schumann, Poulenc.

Good melody—even perfect melody—can be both defined and taught, as indeed can the other three "dimensions" of music: rhythm, harmony, counterpoint (although rhythm is the only one that can exist alone). Melody may be described thus: a series of notes of varying pitch and length, which evolve into a recognizable musical shape. In the case of a melody (tune means the same thing) which is set to words, the musical line will flow in curves relating to the verse that propels it inevitably toward a "high" point, usually called climax, and thence to the moment of culmination. The inevitable element is what makes the melody good—or perfect. But perfection can be sterile, as witness the thousands of thirty-two-bar models turned out yesterday in Tin Pan Alley, or today, by, say the Jefferson Airplane. Can we really recall such tunes when they are divorced from their words?

Superior melody results from the same recipe, with the exception that certain of the ingredients are blessed with distortion. The Beatles' words often go against the music (the crushing poetry that opens "A Day in the Life" intoned to the blandest of tunes), even as Martha Graham's music often contradicts her dance (she gyrates hysterically to utter silence, or stands motionless while all hell breaks loose in the pit). Because the Beatles pervert with naturalness they usually build solid structures, whereas their rivals pervert with affectation, aping the gargoyles but not the cathedral.

The unexpected in itself, of course, is no virtue, though all great works seem to contain it. For instance, to cite as examples only the above four songs: "Here, There and Everywhere" would seem at mid-hearing to be no more than a charming college show ballad, but once concluded it has grown immediately memorable. Why? Because of the minute harmonic shift on the words "wave of her hand," as surprising, yet as satisfyingly *right* as that in a Monteverdi madrigal like "*A un giro sol.*" The notation of the hyper-exuberant rhythms in "Good Day Sunshine" was as elusive to me as some by Charles Ives, until I realized it was made by triplets over the bar; the "surprise" here was that the Beatles had made so simple a process *sound* so complex to a professional ear, and yet (by a third convolution) be instantly imitable by any amateur "with a beat." "Michelle" changes key on the very second measure (which is also the second word): in itself this is "allowed"—Poulenc often did it, and probably he was the most derivative and correct composer who ever lived; the point is that he *chose* to do it on just the second measure, and that the choice worked. Genius doesn't lie in not being derivative, but in making right choices instead of wrong ones. As for "Norwegian Wood," again it is the arch of the tune—a movement growing increasingly disjunct, an inverted pyramid formed by a zigzag—which proves the song unique and memorable, rather than merely original.

The Beatles' superiority, of course, is finally as elusive as Mozart's to Clementi: both spoke skillfully the same tonal language, but only Mozart spoke it with the added magic of genius. Who will define such magic? The public, in realizing this superiority, is right, though not for the wrong reason, as it was, say, ten years ago with *Lolita*. For while *Lolita* was accepted pretty much as just a naughty novel, the Beatles can legitimately be absorbed by all ages on all levels: one is allowed to dance or smoke or even have a funeral (playwright Joe Orton's in London) while listening to this music. I suspect that the same public when discussing the Beatles does not do so by relating them to others, but by relating them to aspects of themselves, as though they were the self-contained definition of an entire movement, or as though in their brief career they had, like Picasso or Stravinsky, already passed through and dispensed with several "periods" (which is true). For example, no sooner was the *Sgt. Pepper* album released than a quiver of argument was set off as to whether it was inferior to their previous album *Revolver,* or to *Rubber Soul.* A critic in the *Village Voice* disparaged "She's Leaving Home" as an imitation of "Eleanor Rigby." But if one must compare them—the songs are independent and incomparable—the point, as I wrote at the time, is that "Eleanor Rigby," though set to a poem of touchingly original and quasi-surrealist winsomeness, is a tune as predictable and banal as the average Kentucky carol. "She's Leaving Home," while set to less interesting verse, is a mazurka equal in melancholy and melodic distinction to those of Chopin.

And what's this one hears about their *sound,* those psychedelic effects produced from orchestration "breakthroughs" presumably inspired by Paul McCartney's leanings toward Stockhausen and electronics? Well, as first demonstrated in "Tomorrow Never Knows" and "Strawberry Fields," the sound proves less involved with content than with color, more with glamor than with construction. McCartney's composition has not been affected by these "innovations" which are instrumental tricks glossily surrounding the composition. Nor is any aspect of that composition itself more "progressive" than that of the old Big Bands, or the Cool groups of yesterday. The harmony at its boldest, as with the insistent dissonances of "I Want to Tell You," is basically Impressionist, not more advanced than Ravel's *Chansoms Madécasses.* The rhythm gets extremely fancy, as in "Good Day Sunshine," but nearly always falls within a 4/4 measure simpler than that in Bartók fifty years ago. The melodies, such as "Fixing A Hole" or "Michelle," are exquisitely etched, but evolve from standard modes—those with the lowered thirds and sevenths of the Blues. The counterpoint when strict, as in parts of "She's Leaving Home," is no more complex than "Three Blind Mice," and when free, as in "Got to Get You into My Life," has the freedom of Hindemith (which is really Bach without working out the problems presented by the rigors of eighteenth-century part-writing). The Supremes, not to mention instrumentalists like Ornette Coleman, go much further out than the Beatles in this domain. As for their form, most of the songs of *Sgt. Pepper* are less complicated than those of previous albums which, themselves, seldom go beyond a basic verse/chorus structure. It is not in innovation that Paul McCartney's originality lies, but in superiority. It remains to be seen how, if ever, he deals with more spacious forms. But of that miniature one, Song, he is a master. As such he is the Beatles' most significant member.

The lyrics, or rather the poems, of John Lennon have been analyzed beyond recognition. They are indeed clever, touching, appropriately timely, and (which is most important) well mated to the tunes. Yet without the tunes, are they really all that much better than the words of, say, Cole Porter or Marc Blitzstein? Certainly Blitzstein's music succeeds in spite of the dated commentary of his words, and Porter's songs remain beautiful with no words at all. We are often told (for instance by Korall in *Saturday Review*) that the Beatles "are shouting about important things," but are these things any more pertinent than "Strange Fruit" was yesterday, or than "Miss Otis Regrets"? And even if they are, could that be what makes the Beatles good? While the film *Privilege* portrays a rock singer so subversive he requires total control, the fact, as Gene Lees puts it, is that "thus far no rock group, not even the entire rock movement put together, has made a government nervous, as Gilbert and Sullivan did." Even if, in a pinch, poems can be successfully political, no music can be proved to "signify" anything, neither protests, nor love, nor even bubbling fountains, nothing. John Lennon's words do indeed expose not only current problems ("A Day in the Life") but suggest solutions ("Fixing A Hole"); and the music—which is presumably set to the verse, not vice versa—works. But that music is stronger; and, like the slow and meterless Gregorian chant which altered the "meaning" of the rapid and ribald street chanties it stemmed from, Lennon's words do or don't matter according to how they're sung.

With Billie Holiday it was not so much the song as her way with the song; like Piaf she could make mediocre material seem masterly. With the Beatles it's the song itself, not necessarily their way—like Schubert whom even a monster can't destroy. "Michelle," for example, remains as lovely but becomes more clearly projected when performed by a "real" singer like Cathy Berberian. Her diction (and the diction of nearly anyone) is better than theirs, at least to non-Cockney ears. Even if the words did not come second, the Beatles oblige you to judge the music first by virtue of their blurred diction.

As for George Harrison's excursions into India, they seem the least persuasive aspect of the more recent Beatle language. Like McCartney with electronics, Harrison seems to have adapted only the frosting; but in pretending to have adapted also the structure, his two big pieces, "Love You Too" and "Within You Without You," end up not hypnotic, merely sprawling. Harrison's orientalism is undoubtedly sincere but sounds as fake as the overdone pentatonicism of Country Joe and the Fish. Debussy, like all his colleagues, was profoundly influenced by the Balinese exhibits at the Paris World's Fair of 1900 which inspired his *Pagodes* and *Lindaraja.* These pieces were as persuasive in the same genre as were the concert works many decades later by Henry Cowell or Harry Partch or even Peggy Glanville-Hicks. But whereas these sophisticated musicians without concern for "authenticity" translated Eastern sound effects into Western jargons and then spoke those jargons with controlled formality, Harrison still flounders for faithful meaning where it just won't work: good will and "inspiration" will never provide him with the background—the birthright—which of necessity produced the music he would emulate.

Ringo Starr's projects, when not involved with his comrades, are unknown, though he does seem to be learning to sing with what is quite literally an unutterable charm. Nor have I seen John Lennon's war movie. Thus far, however, when the Beatles are creating their songs together (even more than as a performing unit), they are at their most interesting.

Just as today my own composition springs more from pristine necessity than from driving inspiration (I compose what I want to hear because no one else is doing it), so I listen—sifting and waiting—only to what I need. What I need now seems less embodied in newness than in nostalgia: How many thrilling experiences do we get per year anyway, after a certain age? Such nostalgia is most clearly engendered by the Beatles. There isn't much more to say, since structurally they're not interesting to analyze: they've added nothing new, simply brought back excitement. The excitement originates (apart, of course, from their talent) in their absolutely insolent—hence innocent—unification of music's disparate components—that is, in using the most conservative devices of harmony, counterpoint, rhythm, melody, orchestration, and making them blend with a contagious freshness. (Parenthetically, their recent "I Am The Walrus," seems a bit worrisome, more contrived, less "inspired" than anything hitherto. Though the texture may be Vaughan Williams with a bebop superimposition and all very pretty, the final effect becomes parody of self-parody, the artist's real danger. Though probably even the holy Beatles must be permitted an occasional stillborn child.)

The Beatles have, so to speak, brought *fiction* back to music, supplanting criticism. No, they aren't new, but as tuneful as the thirties with the same exuberance of futility that Bessie Smith employed. They have removed sterile martyrdom from art, revived the sensual. Their sweetness lies in that they doubtless couldn't care less about these pedantic explications.

LEARNING FROM THE BEATLES

RICHARD POIRIER

Has anyone been able completely to ignore *Sgt. Pepper's Lonely Hearts Club Band?* Probably not. But the very fact of its immense popularity with people of every age and persuasion is almost a guarantee of its not receiving the demanding critical attention that it calls for. It isn't enough to say that it is the latest and most remarkable of the thirteen albums composed and performed by the Beatles since 1964; some such claim could have been made for each album when it appeared. *Sgt. Pepper* isn't in the line of continuous development; rather, it is an eruption. It is an astounding accomplishment for which no one could have been wholly prepared, and it therefore substantialy enlarges and modifies all the work that preceded it. It sends us back to the earlier Beatles not for confirmation of the fact that they have always been the best group of their kind. Rather, we listen for those gestations of genius that have now come to fruition. And the evidence is there: in each album which, while being unmistakably theirs, is nonetheless full of exploratory peculiarities not heard on the others; in the way the release even of a single can set off a new surge of energy in their many imitators; in a self-delighting inventiveness that has gradually exceeded the sheer physical capacities even of four such brilliant musicians. The consequent necessity for expanded orchestral and electronic support reached the point where the *Sgt. Pepper* album had to be wholly conceived in studio with as many as forty-eight instruments. Meanwhile, still in their midtwenties, they have made two movies, *A Hard Day's Night* and *Help!,* which are in spots as good as the Marx brothers, and their most talented member, John Lennon, has written two books of Joycean verbal play that suggest why no one is ever in danger of reading too much into the lyrics of their songs. The Beatles are now beyond patronization, and this is especially satisfying to those like myself who have wondered how much longer the literary academic adjudicators could claim to be taking the arts seriously by promoting a couple of distinguished novels every year, a few films, some poems, maybe a museum show and, if they're really lucky, a play.

Of course to delay a revolution there are ways and ways of finally paying considered attention to the lower orders. One way is to sociologize in the manner, McLuhan or pre-McLuhan, that forces the good and the bad in the popular arts to lie down in the same categories. There'll surely be a piece announcing, say, that the Beatles "represent"—a favorite word in the shelving process—not just the young but an aristocracy of the young. And of course they are aristocratic: in their carelessness, their assumption that they can enact anyone else's life just for the fun of it, their tolerance for the things they do make fun of, their delight in wildness along with a disdain for middle-class rectitudes, their easy expertness, their indifference to the wealth they are happy to have, their pleasures in costume and in a casual eccentricity of ordinary dress, their in-group language not meant, any more than is Bob Dylan's—another such aristocrat—to make ordinary sense. That kind of accommodation is familiar by now, and so is another, which is to admit them into the company of their "betters." You know, the way jazz is like Bach? Well, sometimes they are like Monteverdi and sometimes their songs are even better than Schumann's. But that won't work either. Liverpool boys of their sort have been let into Eton before, and not on the assumption that it would be the style of Eton that would change.

It won't be easy to accommodate the Beatles, and that's nowadays almost the precondition for exciting the pastoral concern of Responsible Critics. Literary and academic grown-ups will discover that their favorite captive audience, the young in school, really have listened to the Beatles' kind of music and won't buy the yarn of significance that ensnares most adult talk about the other arts. Any effort to account for what the Beatles are doing will be difficult, as I've learned from this not very extensive and inexpert try, but only to the extent that talking about the experience of any work of art is more difficult than talking about the theory of it, or the issues in it or the history around it. The results of any such effort by a number of people would be of importance not just for popular music but for all the arts. People who listen to the Beatles love them—what about that? Why isn't there more talk about pleasure, about the excitement of witnessing a performance, about the excitement that goes into a performance of any kind?

Such talk could set in motion a radical and acutely necessary amendment to the literary and academic club rules. Since the exalted arts (to which the novel, about a century ago, was the last genre to be admitted) have all but surrendered the provision of fun and entertainment to the popular arts, criticism must turn to film and song if it is to remind itself that the arts really do not need to be boring, no matter how much copy can be made from the elaboration of current theories of boredom.

Critical confrontations initiated in this spirit could give a new status to an increasingly unfashionable kind of criticism: to close-up, detailed concern for performance, for enactment and execution in a work of art. Film and song, the two activities in which young people are now especially interested, and about which they are learning to talk fairly well, may yield something to other kinds of scrutiny, but they yield much more to this kind. So does literature, on the very infrequent occasions when it is so treated. The need is for intense localization of interest and a consequent modesty of description, in the manner of Stark Young's dramatic criticism, or Bernard Haggin's writing about classical music and jazz or Edwin Denby and, more recently, Robert Garis on ballet. Imagining an audience for such criticism, the critic thinks not of a public with Issues and Topics at the ready, but rather of a small group of like-minded, quite private people who find pleasure in certain intensive acts of looking and listening. Looking and listening to something with such a group, imaginary or real, means checking out responses, pointing to particular features, asking detailed questions, sharing momentary excitements. People tend to listen to the Beatles the way families in the last century listened to readings of Dickens, and it might be remembered by literary snobs that the novel then, like the Beatles and even film now, was considered a popular form of entertainment generally beneath serious criticism, and most certainly beneath academic attention.

The Beatles' music is said to belong to the young, but if it does that's only because the young have the right motive for caring about it—they enjoy themselves. They also know what produces the fun they have, by phrase and instrument, and they're very quick, as I've discovered, to shoot down inflated interpretations. They should indeed exercise proprietary rights. This is the first time that people of school age have been tuned in to sounds invented not by composers approved by adults but in to sounds invented by their own near contemporaries, sounds associated with lyrics, manners and dress that they also identify as their own. David Amram, the New York Philharmonic's first resident composer, is understandably optimistic that this kind of identification will develop an avidity of attention to music that could be the salvation of American musical composition and performance. Perhaps in some such way the popular arts can help restore all the arts to their status as entertainment.

To help this process along it isn't necessary that literary and academic grown-ups go to school to their children. Rather, they must begin to ask some childlike and therefore some extremely difficult questions about particular works: Is this any fun? How and where is it any fun? And if it isn't why bother? While listening together to recordings of popular music, people of any age tend naturally to ask these questions, and I've heard them asked by young people with an eager precision which they almost never exhibit, for want of academic encouragement, when they talk about a poem or a story. Their writing about this music isn't as good as their talk, at least in the magazines I've been able to get hold of, like *Vibrations, The Broadside* and, perhaps the best, *Crawdaddy*. In written criticism they display some of the adult vices, including at times a nearly Germanic fondness for categorization: the Mersey beat, the raving style, trip songs, the San Francisco school, the love sound, folk-rock and the rock-folk-pop tradition are typical of the terms that get bandied about with desperate and charming hope. Reviews of popular music in the major newspapers and magazines are much worse, however, and before the *Sgt. Pepper* album practically no space even for an intelligent note was given the Beatles in any of them. Now that they've begun to appear, any adult easily victimized by a reputed generational gap need only read reviews of *Sgt. Pepper* in the *New York Times* and the *Village Voice* by Richard Goldstein to discover that youth is no guarantee of understanding. In his early twenties, he is already an ancient. Some of his questions—does the album have any real unity?—were not necessary even when originally asked some two thousand years ago, while others are a bad dream of Brooks and Warren: the "lyrical technique" of "She's Leaving Home" is "uninspired narrative, with a dearth of poetic irony." The song is in fact one of *Sgt. Pepper's* satirically funniest cuts, though someone Goldstein's age mightn't as easily see this as someone older. Recognition of its special blend of period sentimentality and elegance of wit is conferred upon the listener not by his being chronologically young but by his having once lived with that especially English blend of tones from Beatrice Lillie or Noel Coward, and their wistful play about the genteel.

Nearly all the songs on the *Sgt. Pepper* album and the two singles released here since then—"All You Need Is Love" and "Baby You're a Rich Man"—are in fact quite broadly allusive: to the blues, to jazz hits of the thirties and forties, to classical music, early rock-and-roll, previous cuts by the Beatles themselves. Much of the comedy in these songs and much of their historical resonance, as in the stately Wagnerian episode in "A Day in the Life," is managed in this way. Mixing of styles and tones remind the listener that one kind of feeling about a subject isn't enough and that any single induced feeling must often exist within the context of seemingly contradictory alternatives. Most good groups offer something of this kind, like the Who, with the brilliant drummer Keith Moon. In songs like "Don't Look Away" and "So Sad About Us," Moon, working with the composer-guitarist Pete Townsend, calls forth a complicated response in a manner nicely described in *Crawdaddy* by Jon Landau, one of the best of the reviewers I've read: "Townsend scratches his chorus, muffles his strings, or lets the chord stand out full, depending on what Moon is doing—the result being a perfectly unified guitar-drum sound that can't help but make you feel happy even while the lyrics tell you to feel sad." The Beatles have often in the past worked for similar mixtures, but they now offer an additional nuance: especially in later songs, one of the interwoven strands is likely to be an echo of some familiar, probably clichéd musical, verbal or dramatic formula. These echoes, like the soap-opera background music of "She's Leaving Home" or the jaunty music-hall tones of "When I'm Sixty-four," have the enriching effect that allusiveness can have in poetry: of expanding a situation toward the simultaneous condition of pathos, because the situation is seen as recurrent and therefore possibly insoluble, and comic, because the recurrence has finally passed into cliché.

Any close listening to musical groups soon establishes the fact that as composers and performers the Beatles repay attention altogether more than does any other group, American or English. They offer something for nearly everyone and respond to almost any kind of interest. The Rolling Stones, the Left Banke and the Bee Gees are especially good, but in none of these is there an inventive productivity equal to that of Lennon, McCartney or their producer George Martin, whose contributions of electronic and orchestral notation really make him one of the group, particularly now that their performances are to be exclusively in studio. Only Dylan shows something equivalent to the Beatles in his combination of talents as composer, lyricist and performer. In performance the Beatles exhibit a nearly total theatrical power. It is a power so unencumbered and so freely diverse both for the group and for each of its members that it creates an element of suspense in whatever they do, an expectation that this time there really will be a failure of good taste—that attribute shared by only the greatest theatrical performers. They never wholly lose themselves in anyone else's styling, however, or in their own exuberance; they never succumb to the excitements they generate, much less those of their audience. It's unthinkable that they would lend themselves for the rock and wreck sequence of the Yardbirds in Antonioni's *Blow-up*. That particular performance, quite aside from what it contributed to a brilliant film, is a symptom of the infiltration even into popular music of the decadence by which entertainment is being displaced by a self-abasing enactment of what is implicit in the *form* of entertainment—in this instance, of group playing that gives way to animosities and a destructive retaliation against recalcitrant instrumental support. When the Beatles sound as if they are heading orchestrally into self-obliterating noise, it is very often only that they may assert their presence vocally in quite the opposite direction: by contrasting choirboy cooing, by filigrees of voice-play coming from each of them, as in the reprise of "Sgt. Pepper," for instance, or, as in "Lovely Rita," the little choral *oo*'s and gaspings—all of these suggesting, in their relation to solo, crosscurrents of feeling within an agreed area of play. Manners so instinctively free and yet so harmonious could not be guided from outside, either by an audience or even by directorial guidance, however much the latter did help in rescuing them from the tawdry enslavement to Elvis Presley, an otherwise profitable influence, in their first, fortunately hard-to-find recording of 1961 made in Hamburg, with Ringo's predecessor at the drums, Peter Best.

As is the taste of all great performers—in athletics, in politics, in any of the arts—the taste of the Beatles or of Dylan is an emanation of personality, of a self that is the generous master but never the creature of its audience. Taste in such instances is inseparable from a stubbornness of selfhood, and it doesn't matter that the self has been invented for the theater. Any self is invented as soon as any purpose is conceived. But the Beatles are a special case in not being *a* self at all. They are a group, and the unmistakeable group identity exists almost in spite of sharp individuation, each of them, except the invisible Martin, known to be unique is some shaggy way. There are few other groups in which even one or two of the members are as publicly recognizable as any of the Beatles, and this can't be explained as a difference simply in public relations. It is precisely this unusual individuation which explains, I think, why the Beatles are so much stronger than any other group and why they don't need, like the Who, to play at animosities on stage. The pretense doesn't communicate the presence of individual Who but rather an anxiety at their not instinctively feeling like individuals when they are together. The Beatles, on the other hand, enhance the individuality of one another by the sheer elaborateness by which they arrive at a cohesive sound and by a musical awareness of one another that isn't distinguishable from the multiple directions allowed in the attainment of harmony. Like members of a great athletic team, like such partners in dance as Nureyev and Fonteyn or like some jazz combos, the Beatles in performance seem to draw their aspirations and their energy not from the audience but from one another. Their close, loyal and affectionate personal ties are of course not irrelevant.

The incentive for what they accomplish seems to be sequestered among them, a tensed responsiveness that encourages from Harrison, as in "And Your Bird Can Sing," what sounds like the best guitar playing in the world and which provokes the immense productivity of Lennon and McCartney. The amount they have composed might be explained by commercial venture but not the daring and originality of each new single or album. Of course the promise of "new sounds" is itself a commercial necessity in their business, as the anxieties of the second album of the Jefferson Airplane indicate, but the Beatles will soon release their fourteenth, and it's not merely "new sounds" that they produce, an easy enough matter with orchestral support, electronics and Asiatic importations. They produce different styles, different musical conceptions and revisions of sentiment that give an unprecedented variety to an artistic career that had its proper beginning a mere four or five years ago. The freshness of each effort is often so radically different from the one before, as any comparison among *Rubber Soul, Revolver* and *Sgt. Pepper* will indicate, as to constitute risk rather than financial ambition—especially three such albums, along with a collection of earlier songs, *Yesterday and Today,* in a period just over eighteen months. They are the ones who get tired of the sounds they have made, and the testings and teasings that produce each new album are self-inflicted. If they are careerist it is in the manner not of Judy Garland, reminding us in each concert of "Somewhere Over the Rainbow" and the pains of show biz, but of John Coltrane who, when he died in July at forty, was also about to give up performance in public altogether, even though his reputation as one of the most influential musicians in jazz and its greatest saxophonist guaranteed him an increasingly profitable concert career. His interest in music was a continually exploratory one, an effort to broaden the possibilities, as the Beatles do now in studio, of his music and his instruments. Like Harrison with his guitar, he managed with the soprano sax to produce a nearly oriental sound, and this discovery led him to an interest in Indian music much as Harrison was led to the study of the sitar. And again like the Beatles, Coltrane's experimentation was the more intense because he and his sidemen, Elvin Jones and McCoy Tyner, achieved a remarkable degree of liberating, energizing empathy. Almost all such champions are extraordinary and private men who work with an audience, as the phrase goes, only when that audience is composed of the few who can perform with them. Otherwise, the audience is what it ought to be: not participants but witnesses or only listeners to a performance. The audience that in the theme song of *Sgt. Pepper* is so "lovely" that "we'd like to take you home with us" is a wholly imaginary one, especially on a record contrived as an escape from public performance.

Aloof from politics, their topicality is of music, the sentiments and the social predicaments traditional to folk songs, and ballads. Maybe the most important service of the Beatles and similar groups is the restoration to good standing of the simplicities that have frightened us into irony and the search for irony; they locate the beauty and pathos of commonplace feelings even while they work havoc with fashionable or tiresome expressions of those feelings. A particularly brilliant example is the record, released some weeks after the *Sgt. Pepper* album, with "Baby You're a Rich Man" on one side and

"All You Need Is Love" on the other. "Baby You're a Rich Man" opens with an inquiry addressed by McCartney and Harrison to Lennon, who can be said to represent here a starry-eyed fan's version of the Beatles themselves: "How does it feel to be/One of the beautiful people?" This and subsequent questions are asked of the "rich man" in a reverentially high but devastatingly lilting voice, to the accompaniment of bursts of sitar music and the clip-clopping of Indian song. The sitar, an instrument Harrison studied in India for six weeks with the renowned Ravi Shankar ("George," he reported, "was truly humble") here suggests not the India of "Within You, Without You" evoke on the *Sgt. Pepper* album, the India of the Bhagavad Gita. It is rather another India, of fabulous riches, the India of the British and their Maharajahs, a place for exotic travel, but also for josh sticks and the otherworldliness of a "trip." All these possibilities are at work in the interplay of music and lyrics. Contributing to the merely social and satiric implications of the song, the Indian sounds operate in the manner of classical allusion in Pope: they expand to the ridiculous the cant of jet-set, international gossip columns—"one of the beautiful people" or "baby, you're a rich man now," or "how often have you been there?" But, as in Pope, the instrument of ridicule here, the sitar, is allowed in the very process to remain unsullied and eloquent. The social implications of the song carry more than a hint of self-parody since the comic mixtures of verbal and musical phrasing refer us to similar mixtures that are a result of the Beatles' fantastic fortune: Liverpool boys, still in their twenties, once relatively poor and now enormously rich, once socially nowhere and now internationally "there," once close to home both in fact and in their music but now implicated not only in the Mersey beat but in the Ganges sound, in travel to India and "trips" of a kind for which India set the precedent for centuries.

Most remarkably, the song doesn't sort out its social satire from its implicitly positive treatment of drugs. Bob Dylan often puns with roughly the same intention, as in "Rainy Day Woman # 12 & 35," a simple but effective example: "Well, they'll stone you when you're trying to be so good, / They'll stone you just like they said they would." In the Beatles' song, the very same phrases that belong to the platitudes of the "beautiful people" belong also, with favorable connotations, to the drug scene. The question, "And have you traveled very far?" is answered by Lennon, the "beautiful" person, with what socially would be a comfortable cliché: "Far as the eye can see." But the phrase is really too outmoded for the jet age and thus sends us back to the original question and to the possibility that the "travel" can refer to a "trip" on LSD, the destination of which would indeed be "as far as the eye can see." Most of the lyrics operate in this double way, both as social satire and drug talk: "How often have you been there? / Often enough to know," or "What did you see when you were there?/Nothing that doesn't show" or "Some do it naturally" (presumably an acid-head by nature) to which the answer is "Happy to be that way." The song could pass simply as social satire, though to see that and that only is also to be the object of satire, of not knowing what implications are carried even by the language you make fun of for its imprecisions. The point, and it's one that I'll come back to, is that the argot of LSD isn't much different from the banalities of question and answer between a "beautiful" person and his bedazzled interviewer. The punning genius of Lennon is evident here perhaps more effectively than in his two books, *In His Own Write* and *A Spaniard in the Works,* with their affinities to Edward Lear as well as to the Joyce of *Finnegans Wake.*

The Beatles won't be stuck even within their most intricate contrivances, however, and they escape often by reminding us and themselves that they are singers and not pushers, performers and not propagandists. The moment occurs in "Baby You're a Rich Man," at it does in other songs, near the end, in the question "Now that you've found another key/What are you going to play?" Necessarily the question refers us to their music while at the same time alluding to the promised results of drugs—a new "key" to personality, to a role as well as to the notes that one might "play." Similar uses of words that can allude both to the subject of the moment and to their constant subject, musical creation, occur in "All You Need Is Love" ("Nothing you can sing that can't be sung"), with implications we'll get to in a moment, and in the second song on the *Sgt. Pepper* album, "A Little Help from My Friends." Sung by Ringo the "help" refers most simply to affection when there is no one around to love and it also means pot supplied by a friend. However, at the beginning of the song it explicitly means the assistance the others will give Ringo with his singing, while the phrases "out of tune" and "out of key" suggest, in the broadest sense, that the number, like the whole occasion, is in the mode not of the Beatles but of Sgt. Pepper's

Lonely Hearts Club Band: "What would you think if I sang out of tune, / Would you stand up and walk out on me? / Lend me your ears and I'll sing you a song, / And I'll try not to sing out of key. / Oh, I get by with a little help from my friends, / Mmmm, I get high with a little help from my friends, / Mmmm, going to try with a little help from my friends."

One of the Beatles' most appealing qualities is their tendency more to self-parody than to parody of others. The two are of course very close for performers who empathize with all the characters in their songs and whose most conspicuous moments of self-parody occur when they're emulating someone whose style they'd like to master. At such moments their boyishness really does shine forth as a musical virtue: giving themselves almost wholly to an imitation of some performer they admire, their necessary exaggeration of his style makes fun of no one so much as themselves. It's a matter of trying on a style and then—as if embarrassed by their own riches, by a self-confident knowledge that no style, not even one of their own invention, is more than a temporary exercise of strength—of laughing themselves out of imitation. Listen to the extravagant rendering on *Beatles '65* of Chuck Berry in "Rock and Roll Music" or their many early emulations of Presley, whose importance to their development is everywhere apparent, or the mimicry of western music in "Act Naturally" on one of their very best albums, *Yesterday and Today*, or the McCartney imitation of Little Richard singing "Long Tall Sally" on the *Beatles Second Album*. It's all cowboys and Indians by people who have a lot of other games they want to play and who know very well where home is and when to go there. Parody and self-parody is frequent among the other groups in the form of persistent stylization, but its object is almost always some clichéd sentiment or situation. Parody from the Beatles tends usually, and increasingly, to be directed toward musical tradition and their own musical efforts. This is at least one reason why "All You Need Is Love," recorded on the reverse side of "Baby You're a Rich Man," is one of the most important they have ever done, an indication, along with the *Sgt. Pepper* album, of so sophisticated an awareness of their historical achievements in music as to make it seem unlikely that they can continue much longer without still further changes of direction even more radical than their decision not to perform henceforth for live audiences. "All You Need Is Love" is decisive evidence that when the Beatles think about anything they think musically and that musical thinking dictates their response to other things: to "love," in this instance, to drugs and social manners in "Baby You're a Rich Man" and throughout the *Sgt. Pepper* album.

I doubt that any of these subjects would in itself prove a sufficient sustenance for their musical invention until first called forth and then kindled by some musical idea. At this point in their career it is impossible, given their and George Martin's musical knowledge and sophistication, that the title "All You Need Is Love" should mean what it would mean coming from any other group, namely hippie or flower love. Expectations of complications are satisfied from the outset: the repetition, three times and in a languorous tone, of the phrase "love, love, love" might remind us of the song of the aging Chaplin in *Limelight,* a song in which he keeps repeating the word throughout with a pitiable and insistent rapidity. Musical subterfuge of lyric simplicity occurs again when the title line, "all you need is love," picks up a musical trailer out of the thirties ballroom. The historical frequency of the "need" for love is thus proposed by the music, and it is as if this proposition emboldens the lyrics: "Nothing you can do that can't be done," "nothing you can sing that can't be sung," "nothing you can know that can't be known," "nothing you can see that can't be shown—it's easy"—this is a sample of equally ambiguous assertions that constitute the verbal substance of the song, even while the word "love" is being stretched out in choral background. And like the ambiguous language of "Baby You're a Rich Man," the phrasing here sounds comfortably familiar—if you had love you could do anything. Except that isn't really what the lyrics imply. Rather, the suggestion is that doing, singing, knowing, seeing have in some sense already been done or at least that we needn't be in any particular sweat about them; they're accepted as already within the accustomed range of human possibility. What has not been demonstrated to anyone's satisfaction, what hasn't been tried, is "love." "Love" remains the great unfulfilled need, and the historical evidence for this is in endless musical compositions about it. Far from suggesting that "love" will solve everything, which would be the hippie reading of "all you need is love," the song allows most things to be solved without it. Such a nice bit of discrimination issues from the music and thence into the lyrics. Interestingly enough, the lyrics were meant to be simple in deference to the largely non-English-speaking audience for whom the song was especially written and performed on the BBC worldwide TV production of *Our World.* "Normally," the Beatles' song publisher Richard James later observed, "the Beatles like to write sophisticated material, but they were glad to have the opportunity to write something with a very basic appeal." But so was Shakespeare at the Globe, and we know how unsophisticated *he* could be. The simplicity is entirely in the initial repetitions of title line and the word "love," a verbal simplicity first modified by the music and then turned into complications that have escaped even most English-speaking listeners.

Lennon and McCartney's recognition through music that the "need" for love is historical and recurrent is communicated to the listener by instrumental and vocal allusions to earlier material. The historical allusiveness is at the outset smart-alecky—the song opens with the French National Anthem—passes through the Chaplin echo, if that's what it is, to various echoes of the blues, and boogie-woogie, all of them in the mere shadings of background, until at the end the song itself seems to be swept up and dispersed within the musical history of which it is a part and of the electronics by which that history has been made available. The process begins by a recurrence of the "love, love, love" phrase, here repeated and doubled as on a stalled record. It then proceeds into a medley of sounds, fractured, mingled musical phrases drifting into a blur which my friend Paul Bertram pointed out to me is like the sounds of a radio at night fading and drifting among the signals of different stations. We can make out fragments of old love songs condemned to wander through the airways for all time: "Green Sleeves," a burst of trumpet sound I can't identify, a hit of the thirties called "In the Mood," a ghostly "love you, yeah, yeah, yeah" of "She Loves You" from the *Beatles Second Album* of 1964 and, in the context of "All You Need Is Love," a pathetic "all together now . . . everybody!" of the old community sing. Far from being in any way satiric, the song gathers into itself the musical expression of the "need" for love as it has accumulated through decades of popular music.

This historical feeling for music, including their own musical creations, explains I think the Beatles' fascination with the invented aspects of everything around them, the participatory tenderness and joy with which they respond to styles and artifact, the maturity with which they have come to see the coloring of the human and social landscape of contemporary England. It's as if they naturally see the world in the form of *son et lumière*: as they say in a beautiful neighborhood song about Liverpool, "Penny Lane is in my ears and in my eyes." Not everyone their age is capable of seeing the odd wonder of a meter maid—after all, a meter maid's a meter maid; fewer still would be moved to a song of praise like "Lovely Rita" ("When it gets dark I tow your heart away"); and only a Beatle could be expected, when seeing her with a bag across her shoulder, to have the historically enlivened vision that "made her look a little like a military man." Now of course English boys out of Liverpool can be expected, it says here, to be more intimate than American boys from San Francisco with the residual social and cultural evidences from World War II and even from the First World War. In response to these and other traces of the past, however, the Beatles display an absolutely unique kind of involvement. It isn't simply that they have an instinctive nostalgia for period styles, as in "She's Leaving Home" or "When I'm Sixty-four," or that they absorb the past through the media of the popular arts, through music, cinema, theatrical conventions, bands like Sgt. Pepper's or music-hall performers. Everyone to some extent apprehends the world in the shapes given it by the popular arts and its media; we all see even the things that are new to us through that gridiron of style that Harold Rosenberg imagines as a debilitating shield in front of the British Redcoats even as they first entered the American terrain. No, the Beatles have the distinction in their work both of *knowing* that this is how they see and feel things and of enjoying the knowledge. It could be said that they know what Beckett and Borges know but without any loss of simple enthusiasm or innocent expectation, and without any patronization of those who do not know. In the loving phrases of "Penny Lane," "A pretty nurse is selling poppies from a tray, / And tho' she feels as if she's in a play, / She is anyway."

It isn't surprising that drugs have become important to their music, that they are leading an effort in England for the legalization of marijuana, partly as a result of the conviction and sentencing on drug charges of two of the Rolling Stones, and that in response to questions, Lennon, McCartney and Harrison have let it be known that they've taken LSD. At least four of the songs on the *Sgt. Pepper* album are concerned with taking a "trip" or "turning on": "A Little Help from My Friends," "Lucy in the Sky with Diamonds," "Fixing a Hole" and "A Day in the Life," with a good chance of a fifth in "Getting Better." Throughout the album, the consciousness of the *dramatis personae* in the songs is directed more or less by inventions of media or of the popular arts, and drugs are proposed as one kind of personal escape into the freedom of some further invention all on one's own. Inventing the world out of the mind with drugs is more physically risky than doing it by writing songs, films or wearing costumes, but danger isn't what the songs offer for consideration, and it's in any case up to the Beatles alone to decide what they want for their minds and bodies. Instead, the songs propose, quite delightfully and reasonably, that the vision of the world while on a "trip" or under the influence of a drug isn't necessarily wilder than a vision of the world through which we travel under the influence of the arts or the news media. Thus, the third song on the album, "Lucy in the Sky with Diamonds," proposes that the listener can "picture" a "trip" scene without taking such a "trip" himself. Here, as in "Baby You're a Rich Man," the experience of a "trip" is wittily superimposed on the experience of ordinary travel: "Picture yourself on a train in a station, / With plasticine porters with looking-glass ties, / Suddenly someone is there at the turnstile, / The girl with kaleidoscope eyes." Of course the images could come as easily from Edward Lear as from the experience of drugs, and Lennon has claimed that the title of the song is not an anagram for LSD but was taken from a drawing his son did at school. Lennon, the author of two books of Joycean punning, knows to the point of hilarity that one meaning denies the presence of another, which it has hidden inside, only to all strangers and the police. Still his reticence is obviously a form of the truth. The Beatles won't be reduced to drugs when they mean, intend and enact so much more. "Acid," Harrison told the Los Angeles *Free Press* in August, "is not the answer, definitely not the answer. It's enabled people to see a little bit more, but when you really get hip, you don't need it." Later, to Hunter Davies of the London *Sunday Times,* McCartney announced that they'd given up drugs. "It was an experience we went through and now it's over we don't need it any more. We think we're finding other ways of getting there." In this effort they're apparently being helped by Maharishi Mahesh Yogi, the Indian founder of the International Meditation Society, though even on the way to their initiation in Bangor, North Wales, Lennon wondered if the experience wasn't simply going to be another version of what they already knew: "You know, like some are EMI and some Decca, but it's really still records."

The notion that we "picture" ourselves much of the time anyway without even willing it, that we see ourselves and the world in exotic images usually invented by someone else, is suggested throughout the *Sgt. Pepper* album, even on the cover, with its clustered photographs of world-shaping "stars" of all kinds. In "A Day in the Life," the last song and a work of great power and historical grasp, the hapless man whose role is sung by McCartney wants to "turn on" himself and his lover—maybe us too—as a relief from the multiple controls exerted over life and the imagination by various and competing media. The sad little "oh boy" interjected by McCartney's sweet, vulnerable voice into orchestral movements of intimidating, sometimes portentous momentum, expresses wonderfully how the victim is further confounded by the fact that these controls often impose themselves under the guise of entertainment: "I read the news today, oh boy, / About a lucky man who made the grade, / And though the news was rather sad, / Well I just had to laugh, / I saw the photograph. / He blew his mind out in a car, / He didn't notice that the lights had changed, / A crowd of people stood and stared, / They'd seen his face before, / Nobody was really sure if he was from the House of Lords. / I saw a film today, oh boy, / The English Army had just won the war, / A crowd of people turned away, / But I just had to look having read the book. I'd love to turn you on." The news in the paper is "rather sad" but the photograph is funny, so how does one respond to the suicide; suicide is a violent repudiation of the self but it mightn't have happened if the man had followed the orders of the traffic lights; the victim isn't so much a man anyway as a face people have seen someplace in the news, in photographs or possibly even on film; and while a film of the English Army winning the war is too dated for most people to look at, and maybe they don't believe in the victory anyway, the man in the song has to look at it (oh boy—a film) because he has read a book about it and therefore it does have some reality for him. "Turning on" is at least a way of escaping submission to the media designed to turn on the mind from the outside—quite appropriately the song was banned on the BBC—and loving to turn "you" on, either a lover or you, the listener, is an effort to escape the horror of loneliness projected by the final images of the song: "I read the news today, oh boy, / Four thousand holes in Blackburn Lancashire, / And though the holes were rather small, / They had to count them all, / Now they know how many holes it takes to fill the Albert Hall. / I'd love to turn you on." The audience in Albert Hall—the same as the "lovely audience" in the first song that the Beatles would like to "take home" with them?—are only many holes: unfilled and therefore unfertile holes, of the earth and therefore holes of decomposition, gathered together but separate and therefore countable, utterly and inarticulately alone. Is this merely a bit of visionary ghoulishness, something seen on a "trip"? No, good citizens can find it, like everything else in the song, in the daily news—of how Scotland Yard searched for buried bodies on a moor by making holes in the earth with poles and then waiting for the stench of decomposing flesh.

Lennon and McCartney in their songs seem as vulnerable as the man in "A Day in the Life" to the sights and sounds by which different media shape and then reshape reality, but their response isn't in any way as intimidated, and "turning on" isn't their only recourse. They can also tune in and play the game, sometimes to show, as in "A Day in the Life," how one shaped view of reality can be mocked out of existence by crossing it with another. They mix their media the way they mix musical sounds of cross lyrics of one tone with music of quite another—with a vengeance. It's unwise ever to assume that they're doing only one thing or expressing themselves in only one style. "She's Leaving Home" does have a persistent cello background to evoke genteel melodrama of an earlier decade, and "When I'm Sixty-four" is intentionally clichéd throughout, both in its ragtime rhythm and in its lyrics. The result is a satiric heightening of the love-nest sentimentality of old popular songs in the mode of "He'll build a little home / Just meant for two / From which I'll never roam / Who would, would you?" The home in "When I'm Sixty-four" is slightly larger to accommodate children, but that's the only important difference: "Every summer we can rent a cottage / In the Isle of Wight, if it's not too dear / We shall scrimp and save. / Grandchildren on your knee / Vera Chuck & Dave." But the Beatles aren't satisfied merely with having written a brilliant spoof, with scoring, on their own authority, off death-dealing clichés. Instead, they quite suddenly at the end transform one cliché (of sentimental domesticity) into another (of a lonely-hearts newspaper advertisement), thereby proposing a vulgar contemporary medium suitable to the cheap and public sentiments that once passed for nice, private and decent: "Send me a postcard, drop me a line, / Stating point of view. / Indicate precisely what you mean to say, / Yours sincerely, wasting away. / Give me your answer, fill in a form, / Mine for evermore. / Will you still need me, will you still feed me, / When I'm sixty-four."

The *Sgt. Pepper* album and the singles released here just before and after it—"Penny Lane," "Strawberry Fields Forever," "All You Need Is Love" and "Baby You're a Rich Man"—constitute the Beatles' most audacious musical effort so far, works of such achieved ambitiousness as to give an entirely new retrospective shape to their whole career. Nothing less is being claimed by these songs than that the Beatles now exist not merely as a phenomenon of entertainment but as a force of historical consequence. They have placed themselves within a musical, social and historical environment more monumental in its surroundings and more significantly populated than was the environment of any of their early songs. Listening to the *Sgt. Pepper* album one thinks not simply of the history of popular music but of the history of this century. It doesn't matter that some of the songs were composed before it occurred to the Beatles to use the motif of *Sgt. Pepper,* with its historical overtones; the songs emanated from some inwardly felt coherence that awaited a merely explicit design, and they would ask to be heard together even without the design.

Under the aegis of an old-time concert given by the type of music-hall band with which Lennon's father, Alfred, claims to have been associated, the songs, directly or by chance images, offer something like a review of contemporary English life, saved from folksong generality by having each song resemble a dramatic monologue. The review begins with the "Sgt. Pepper" theme song, followed immediately by "A Little Help from My Friends": Ringo, helped by the other Beatles, will, as I've already mentioned, try not to sing out of "key," try, that is, to fit into a style still heard in England but very much out of date. Between this and the reprise of "Sgt. Pepper," which would be the natural end of the album, are ten songs, and while some are period pieces, about hangovers from the past, as is the band itself, no effort is made at any sort of historical chronology. Their arrangement is apparently haphazard, suggesting how the hippie and the historically pretentious, the genteel and the mod, the impoverished and the exotic, the Indian influence and the influence of technology are inextricably entangled into what is England. As I probably shouldn't say again, the Beatles never for long wholly submerge themselves in any form or style, so that at the end of the Indian, meditative sonorities of "Within You Without You" the burst of laughter can be taken to mean—look, we have come through, an assurance from the Beatles (if it *is* their laughter and not the response of technicians left in as an example of how "straights" might react) that they are still Beatles, Liverpool boys still there on the far side of a demanding foreign experience. This characteristic release of themselves from history and back to their own proper time and place occurs with respect to the design of the whole album in a most poignant way. Right after the reprise of the "Sgt. Pepper" song, with no interval and picking up the beat of the "Sgt. Pepper" theme, an "extra" song, perhaps the most brilliant ever written by Lennon and McCartney, breaks out of the theatrical frame and enters "a day in the life," into the way we live now. It projects a degree of loneliness not to be managed within the conventions of Sgt. Pepper's Lonely Hearts Club Band. Released from the controls of Sgt. Pepper, the song exposes the horrors of more contemporary and less benign controls, and it is from these that the song proposes the necessity of still further release. It does so in musical sounds meant to convey a "trip" out, sounds of ascending-airplane velocity and crescendo that occur right after the first "I'd love to turn you on," at midpoint in the song, and after the final, plaintive repetition of the line at the end, when the airplane sounds give way to a sustained orchestral chord that drifts softly and slowly toward infinity and silence. It is, as I've suggested, a song of wasteland, and the concluding "I'd love to turn you on" has as much propriety to the fragmented life that precedes it in the song and in the whole work as does the "Shantih, Shantih, Shantih" to the fragments of Eliot's poem. Eliot can be remembered here for still other reasons: not only because he pays conspicuous respect to the music hall but because his poems, like the Beatles' songs, work for a kaleidoscopic effect, for fragmented patterns of sound that can bring historic masses into juxtaposition only to let them be fractured by other emerging and equally evocative fragments.

Eliot is not among the sixty-two faces and figures, all unnamed and in some cases probably quite obscure, gathered round the Beatles on the cover, a pictorial extension of the collage effect which is so significant to the music. In making the selection, the Beatles were understandably drawn to figures who promote the idea of other possible worlds or who offer literary and cinematic trips to exotic places: Poe, Oscar Wilde, H. G. Wells, along with Marx, Jung, Lawrence of Arabia and Johnny Weismuller. They are also partial to the kind of theatrical person whose full being is the theatrical self, like W. C. Fields, Tom Mix, Brando and Mae West, who has delightfully adapted such Beatle songs as "Day Tripper" to her own style. Above all, the cover is a celebration of the Beatles themselves who can now be placed (and Bob Dylan, too) within a group who have, aside from everything else, infused the imagination of the living with the possibilities of other ways of living, of extraordinary existences, of something beyond "a day in the life." So it is indeed like a funeral for the Beatles, except that they'd be no more "dead" than anyone else in attendance. There they are in the center, mustachioed and in the brassed and tassled silk of the old-time bands, and, with brilliant, quite funny implications, they are also represented in the collage as wax figures by Madame Tussaud, clothed in business suits. Live Beatles in costumes from the past and effigies of the Beatles in the garb of the present, with the name of the Beatles in flowers planted before the whole group—this bit of slyness is of a piece with not sorting out past and present and promised future in the order of the songs, or the mixed allusiveness to period styles, including earlier Beatles' styles or the mixing and confoundings of media in songs like "When I'm Sixty-four" or "A Day in the Life." The cover suggests that the Beatles to some extent live the past in the present, live in the shadows of their own as well as of other people's past accomplishments, and that among the imaginative creations that fascinate them most, the figures closest at hand on the cover, are their own past selves. "And the time will come," it is promised in one of their songs, "when you will see we're all one, and life flows on within you and without you." As an apprehension of artistic, and perhaps of any other kind of placement within living endeavor, this idea is allowable only to the very great.

NEW MUSIC IN A NEW WORLD

●

WILFRID MELLERS

The ultimate, rediscovered primitivism of a Cage or a Feldman has parallels, we have seen, in the surrealistic trend in modern jazz. Most interestingly, it is also paralleled by mid-century developments in pop music. Thirty, or even twenty years ago, pop music was still commercial jazz, tied to the Sousa-Foster tradition of hedonism or escape. Today pop music seems, no less than "straight" music, to be affecting another kind of return *ab ovo*, to rhythm and to the most rudimentary line as incantation. The music of Cage or Feldman on the one hand, the Beatles and Bob Dylan on the other, may seem poles apart; nonetheless they have in common a distrust of the personal, of "individual" expression, and both attempt to return to magic, possibly as a substitute for belief. To neither does the Christian ethic, which implies guilt and conscience and the duality of harmony, seem relevant. In the music of Cage there is virtually no corporeal rhythm left; the Mersey beat has nothing much except corporeal rhythm. Yet both, by their complementary if opposite paths, effect a dissolution of Time and of consciousness.* In a very literal sense the rows of nubile young females who faint away at a Beatle performance have found the Nirvana that Tristan was seeking, and the ecstasy of being "sent" becomes a communal and collective activity which is also a sundering of identity. The fact that young people dance *alone*, not with partners, to beat music is interesting in itself. They evade the togetherness of relation-

* "It is perhaps the essential character of consciousness that it is not just a picture of what is happening at one instant of time or an infinitely thin cross-section of process. Consciousness introduces the time-dimension as a reality, linking the no-longer-existing past with the actual present in what is called perception or recognition, and forecasting a merely possible future on lines influenced by wish and purpose. Process and purpose are thus inseparable in our minds from the beginning. . . . It is significant in this connection that the repressed unconscious mind is said to be 'timeless,' suggesting that the loss of 'span' is one of the factors in repression." (Ian Suttie: *The Origins of Love and Hate.*)

ship with another person (a love relationship, however joyful, will also inevitably hurt) in order to enter into a collective unconsciousness. There's no coming together of individuals; their lonesomeness merges into a corporate act, and belonging to the group asserts one's livingness, such as it is. In this way the ritual value of the sound is inseparable from its musical nature. Its melodic and harmonic material is rudimentary, its rhythmic appeal obvious in its excess (contrary to popular opinion beat music never swings, only beats, for jazz-swing implies a subtle tension between metrical accent and melodic phrasing). The essential characteristics of beat music are that its phrases are very brief and are hypnotically repeated; that its rhythm is obvious and unremitting; and that its sonority is very loud. Through its rudimentariness, its unremittingness, and its loudness it provides a substitute for security, or a pretense that we, the young, in an insecure world, can stand—or dance—on our own feet.

One may doubt whether it is pervasively erotic, for the eroticism of jazz depends precisely on the swinging equilibrium between line and rhythm which beat music lacks. In this connection it is interesting that the musical origins of beat music were not in traditional jazz or even in the commercialized forms of jazz which were the pop music of the thirties and forties; rather, they were in the most primitive and rudimentary form of the country blues, which had begun not as a music of social (let alone sexual) intercourse, but as the solitary "holler" in the empty fields. Created by a deprived, dispossessed, alienated, persecuted minority, the country blues became the impetus to the mass-music of young people in a mass-civilization. We can trace the process whereby this happened by listening to some specific examples. Howlin' Wolf, yelling a field holler, attempts to "send" himself beyond personal distress by the monodic, incantatory repetition of a three-note wail, basically pentatonic, using techniques of pitch distortion and rhythmic elipsis that have the remotest and most primitive ancestry. This folk tradition still survives in the urban blues, as we can hear in "Fare Well Blues" as performed by a white singer, Barbara Dane. The effect of this most moving performance depends largely on the fact that the "primitive" elements in vocal inflection and rhythmic displacement are at odds with the hymnbook-derived harmony of the blues guitar; the age-old monodic melancholy of the voice seems the more searing against the harmonic prison of "civilization."

As folk art merges into pop, the prison, at least at a superficial level, has to be accepted. Two stages in this process can be observed in different versions of "Alabama Bound." Leadbelly and Woody Guthrie still employ primitive folk techniques of vocal production and rhythmic distortion, while at the same time subduing these wilder qualities to a regular beat and a simple *harmonic* pattern suggested by white vaudeville music, blackfaced minstrel music and hillbilly harmonica playing. The strange, disturbing hiatus between vocal and instrumental elements, typical of Barbara Dane's blues, has gone. This is still more the case in a typical rock-'n'-roll performance, wherein the primitive blues has been metamorphosed into pop. Ray Charles's version of "Alabama Bound" is an excellent example. He preserves the blues inflection in pitch and rhythm, which gives the music its characteristic "lift," an intensity of feeling beneath the exuberance and bounce; we feel he knows what he's singing about when he tells us that he's banished the heebie-jeebies. Nonetheless, the drive of the music, scored for big band, is that of the powerhouse. The country blues, streamlined, seems to have entered the world of commerce.

Up to this point this tradition in pop music, stemming from a deliberate revival of the most primitive form of blues, has followed a predictable path, gradually increasing in sophistication and in technical expertise. With the appearance of the Beatles, however, something odd happens, which may not be unconnected with the fact that they are British, outside the main tradition of American pop culture. Rock-'n'-roll music incorporated folk elements into conventions deriving from Tin Pan Alley, whereas the melodic, rhythmic and harmonic texture of the Beatles' songs is itself primitive; at least it has more in common with conventions of late medieval and early Renaissance music than it has with the harmonic conventions of the eighteenth century and after. Consider one of the Beatles' most celebrated songs, "She Loves You." The key signature is the three flats beloved of pop convention; however, the opening phrase is pentatonic, or perhaps in an Aeolian C which veers towards E flat, and much of the effect depends on the contrast between the ascending sharp sevenths and the blue flat sevenths of folk tradition. Nor is the final chord of the song simply an added sixth cliché; or if that's what the guitar chord is, the melody suggests that C, not E flat, is the root. Again, "A Hard Day's Night," the theme song from the Beatles' first film, has no conventional tonic-dominant modulations. Instead, it has a distinctively plagal, "flat" feeling, beginning with the dominant seventh of the subdominant. The tune itself is pentatonic until the chromatic extension in the final phrase (which doesn't alter the harmony), and the verse section depends entirely on alternations between the tonic and the chord of the flat seventh (between C and B-flat triads). After the double bar we have mediant substitutions for dominants, while the coda phrase alternates sharp thirds with blue flat thirds in a manner characteristic equally of the true blues, and of the fase relations of sixteenth- and seventeenth-century English music. None of these features would be found in post-eighteenth-century textbook harmony: the flat seventh-chord flourish in the guitar postlude is strikingly similar to passages in the keyboard music of Farnaby or Gibbons!

Of course this doesn't necessarily mean that the Beatles have ever heard, or even heard of, medieval or Renaissance music, any more than the peasant folk singer knew he was singing in the Dorian mode. It's rather that their melody and harmony, welling up in their collective subconscious, discovers authentic affinities with music of a relatively early, less "harmonic" stage of evolution, and thereby reinforces the primitivism of their rhythm. Even the noise of the electric guitar, though in part commercially dictated because of the sheer volume necessary to get across to vast audiences, emulates the "primitive" sound of the multi-stringed Blue Grass banjo, a white folk music. In their most recent discs (1965), the Beatles have, indeed, employed far more primitive instrumental techniques, imitating the guitar-picking styles of the most rudimentary country blues and using an electronic organ to suggest harmonica, bagpipes, jew's-harp and still more basic rural instruments. At first George's use of the Indian sitar in place of banjo or guitar was no more than a pleasing new sonority applied to the Western-style tune "Norwegian Wood." On their latest disc, however, the characteristic Merseyside electronic noises merge into sonorities and techniques that are specifically Eastern; and the Beatles couldn't do this so effectively if they were merely picking up fashions from the sophisticated world. There is a genuine connection between what is happening in pop music and what is happening in "art" music and in jazz. The remarkable song "Tomorrow Never Knows" begins with jungle noises very similar to Coleman's or Coltrane's "free" jazz, and employs both vocal and instrumental techniques which we may find both in Ornette

Coleman and in Stockhausen! Interestingly enough, the words of the song tell us to "Turn off your mind; relax and float downstream: it is not dying. Lay down all thought; surrender to the voice: it is shining. That you may see the meaning of within: it is being." One couldn't wish for a more unequivocal abnegation of Western "consciousness"; and the disturbing quality of the music certainly suggests that we're not meant merely to take it ironically.

Naturally enough, the Mersey sound has been, at least in its earlier and cruder manifestations, commercially manipulated. Yet the impressive nature of their recent development suggests that it always was the spontaneity and authenticity of the Beatles' return to "beginnings" that has given their music, no less than their characters, its obsessive appeal, and has distinguished it from that of groups who have made a more conscious attempt to imitate primitive models. Moreover, it's interesting that when sophisticated composers such as Burt Bacharach produce pop numbers, they exploit knowingly the techniques which, in Beatle music, were instinctive. Bacharach's "Anyone Who Had a Heart," made famous by Dionne Warwick, uses the same mediant transitions and shifting sevenths as characterize the Beatles' songs. There are more of them, in somewhat more surprising relationships, but the principle is the same, and equally remote from post-eighteenth-century convention. Again, the tune itself has a pentatonic tendency, while the irregular groups of repeated notes suggest an affinity with folk monody, derived from the inflections of speech. Perhaps there's even a link with folk tradition in the words' and tune's simple, suffering, numbing resignation. It's the opposite pole to the Beatles' bounce, but it isn't, like the Stephen Foster-derived Tin Pan Alley ballad, self-pitying.

The intrusion of folk elements into the songs of a sophisticated pop composer like Bacharach hints that there may be a growing together of pop culture with real folk-song revival movement: a hint which is reinforced by the recent phenomenal success of Bob Dylan. This American lad, after an abortive career at a provincial college, wandered the country with his guitar, a new-style hobo, writing and singing his own songs. Ray Charles, back in the days of rock-'n'-roll, lustily sang, the Beatles boisterously shout, Bob Dylan rustily croaks; this apparent decline in musical significance, however, is accompanied by a progressive increase in verbal significance. Dylan writes his own words, which are always *about something*, usually of urgently topical and local import. Quite often these words are of poetic intensity, resembling real ballad poetry, the nursery rune, or even on occasions the songs of Blake; they have to be listened to, if the experience is to mean anything. Whereas a typical Beatle performance may be totally inaudible beneath the screams of appreciation, a similar mass audience of young things will listen to Bob Dylan in a silence in which the proverbial pin could be heard dropping. Attention presupposes a rebirth of consciousness. Bob Dylan's primitivism, in succession to the Beatles', may mean a new start.

Basically, Dylan's music is far more primitive than that of the Beatles, or even the Rolling Stones. "The Ballad of Hollis Brown," for instance, tells a (true) story of the poor white who "lived on the outside of town, with his wife and five children and his cabin fallin' down." His baby's eyes look crazy, the rats get his flour, bad blood gets his mare, his wife's screams are "stabbin' like the dirty drivin' rain." He kills his family and himself with a shotgun, and the song ends, "There's seven people dead on a South Dakota farm. Somewhere in the distance there's seven new people born." The tune of this ballad could hardly be more primitive, for it is entirely pentatonic and most of the time is restricted to four notes, while the guitar part oscillates between the tonic and dominant. The restricted vocal range, the obsessive ostinato, have a dramatic function, suggesting the numbing misery of poverty; the deliberately antilyrical, dead-pan vocal production has a comparable effect, which is by no means merely negative and deflationary. The primal simplicity of the tune and accompaniment carries its own affirmation, even resilience. The end isn't Nirvana; life goes on, however insignificant one's personal destiny.

In "Masters of War" Dylan uses a similarly nagging pentatonic tune and reiterated ostinato to build up a cumulative fury. But not all his songs are musically as primitive as this. His social-satirical protest songs more commonly derive from white hillbilly style, rather than from the Negro blues. "With God on Our Side" has a swinging arpeggiated tune in slow waltz rhythm; Dylan's hiccups and hiatuses, and the occasional melismatic twiddle, point the irony of the words, which tell the bitter story of American martial history: "Oh the history books tell it, they tell it so well, / The cavalries charged, the Indians fell, / The cavalries charged, the Indians died, / Oh the country was young, with God on its side." The song goes down through the Spanish-American War and the two World Wars, with an especially biting melisma for the Second World War, after which "we forgave the Germans and we were friends, / Though they murdered six million, / In the ovens they fried, the Germans now too / Have God on their side." After stanzas about the Russians, chemical warfare and the atom bomb, the song reaches its climax: "In many a dark hour I've been thinkin' all this, / That Jesus Christ was betrayed by a kiss. / But I can't think for you, / You got to decide, / Whether Judas Iscariot / Had God on his side."

The guileless tune, and the harmonica ritornelli which seem to come from another Eden, make the savagery of the words the more trenchant; it's not surprising that even in an "affluent" society, young people listen to Dylan croaking these words in an electrically tense silence.

In many of his songs Dylan adapts both the words and tunes of traditional folk ballads to contemporary ends. Thus, "A Hard Rain's Gonna Fall" is a version of Lord Randal: "Oh, what did you see, my blue-eyed son? / I saw a new-born baby with wolves all around it, I saw a highway of diamonds with nobody on it, I saw a black branch with blood that kept drippin', I saw a roomful of men with their hammers a bleedin', I saw a white ladder all covered with water," etc. "Who Killed Davy Moore?" transforms Cock Robin into an anecdote and parable about a calamity in the boxing ring, with social and political overtones. The mainly pentatonic tune is very fine, the words at once witty and scary, naturalistic yet with a flash of poetry when the boxer falls "in a cloud of mists." This isn't so far away from the authentic folk-revival tradition as represented by Joan Baez, who has her protest song "What Have They Done to the Rain?," with its obsessive rhythmic ostinato, its plagal flatness which is possibly a mixolydian G. The fusion of pop and modern folk seems to be consummated when a Baez disc enters the Top Ten.

Many Bob Dylan tunes have been sung recently by folk singers such as Joan Baez, Odetta and Pete Seeger. The latter's version of "Davy Moore" is especially impressive and interesting because he sings it not in Dylan's deadpan, uninvolved manner, but with considerable passion. That he makes it a *dramatic* song-story is significant, since despite the Beatles' and Dylan's primitivism we know that the situation today isn't really the same as it was in primitive societies. Once having experienced knowledge and power, man cannot be entirely ignorant of moral choice; he's bound to ask, even if he's a pop artist dealing in myths rather than in personal expression, whether some myths aren't "better than" others. So the pop artist is inevitably an artist, once more making choices, using conscious techniques better or worse, *for* better or worse, as we can see from the Beatles, however spontaneous their creative origins may have been. What matters is how effectively he can learn to be reborn through the absorption of "preconscious" folk techniques, notwithstanding the commercial pressures he's submitted to.

Bob Dylan is said to be worried that he, the hobo troubador, now nets an income of $500,000 a year. No doubt he is bearing up pretty well; if his art does so too, even as well as that of the Beatles, it may not be extravagant to say that youth's new world is winning through. In this context we should beware of the glib assumption that a capitulation to commercial techniques is necessarily a capitulation to commercial values. It's easy to say that Dylan's recent discs, employing electrically amplified guitar instead of the natural folk guitar and sometimes calling for the souped-up, big-band sound, corrupt his folk-like authenticity. Sometimes this is true, sometimes it isn't; and it is surely more, not less, "natural" for a folk singer living in an electronic age to exploit, rather than to spurn, electronic techniques. The folk purists are also the escapists; Dylan has proved that it is possible to be a myth-hero and an artist at the same time, and to carry the integrity of the rural folk artist into a world of mechanization.

There is thus a true parallel between a Dylan's desire for a rebirth, using, not refusing, the techniques of an industrial society, and the concern with a new birth of a Cage or a Feldman. It is interesting that the most insidiously haunting of all Dylan's songs should be a recent number, "Mr. Tambourine Man," which, far from being a socially committed protest, looks superficially like an escape from life to dream. In a sense it is, for the tambourine man is a marijuana peddler; yet Dylan specifically says that he is "not sleepy," even though there ain't no place he's going to. Drug addiction is not, of course, itself a positive solution; but the song suggests that the impulses that have driven young people to it *could* have a positive outcome. We can sense this because the song is so beautiful. Like the tranced music of Cage or Feldman, it appeals for a different kind of commitment; it's a Pied Piper myth encouraging us to follow the unconscious where spontaneously it leads us, and this is most movingly suggested both by the wavery ballad-like refrain and also by the irregularity of the verbal and musical clauses which pile or float up, one after the other, like smoke rings. The metaphor of smoke rings actually appears in the verses which transport Dylan, a "ragged clown," beyond the "twisted reach" of sorrow. Release from the mind's tension, for Dylan no less than for Cage and Feldman, is a necessary step toward rediscovery; losing the self, in the ancient biblical phrase, in order to find it, we are encouraged to forget "consciousness" today so that we may recharge our spiritual batteries for tomorrow. Such a pop song haunts us so disturbingly because its mythology plumbs unexpectedly deep; indeed, one might almost say that it not only links up with the extremism of Cage and Feldman, but also reminds us how the avant-garde has not been without effect even on the central, humanistic and Christian traditions of European music. Though this is unlikely to have been a matter of direct influence, it's an indication that, in Dylan's phrase, "the times they are a-changin'."

NOTE: THERE IS NO EVIDENCE TO Suggest that the "Tambourine Man" is a Junk Pedlar. He is variously taken to be the pied piper, J.F. Kennedy, and Dylan himself. However, the Most likely answer is none of these. Much of Dylans work is concerned with Religious Quest, only natural for an ashamed Jew. I would argue that the "Tambourine Man" is an unattainable target, representative of the God for which Dylan looked, but was not to find until 1978. Thus the Song is a confused, sometimes hysterical account of Dylans Search for God + Meaning; a quest which most often led him to look deep into himself.

See also "ISIS" on "Desire", 1976. CBS

FUGS

UPI

THE NEWPORT

PERFORMER

PHOTOGRAPHS BY ELLIOTT LANDY

THE CAST IN ORDER OF APPEARANCE

Pablo Light Show, The Fugs
Joan Baez
Janis Joplin
Jim Morrison
Metropolitan Airport, Detroit, Sam Andrew
Jimi Hendrix
Dressing room, Country Joe MacDonald
Albert King
Backstage, Newport Folk Festival, Sam Andrew
Press conference, Lennon and McCartney
(l-r) Levon Helm, Rick Danko, Bob Dylan, Robbie Robertson
Janis Joplin
Rob Tyner
James Gurley
The Incredible String Band
Frank Zappa

A FAMILY ALBUM

ALFRED G. ARONOWITZ

NEW YORK, 1967—Scrooge McDuck is in mourning. Crew-cut Benson has just come home from two years of V-C hunting with his duffle bag half full of grass. A lady in Paducah, Kentucky, says that Mars is taking integrated couples. Smog is blowing in the face of New York. California department stores are selling electrical bananas. A group in London is planning to knock off Big Ben and Andy Warhol is coining uptown silver.

What's happening in the music business? Someone has designed a miniskirt for men.

Eighteen-year-old Suzanne Tumbler, who used to paper the walls of her room with pictures of Paul McCartney, Brian Jones and her high-school principal, has split from her mother's $50,000 California ranch in Basking Ridge, New Jersey, to go to work as a salesgirl in a New York psychedelicatessen, one of those charming little boutiques that specializes in anything you need to take drugs and be happy. She's been disinherited by her millionaire father because she'd rather live with her unemployed long-haired boy friend than finish her high school education in a convent her father has picked out for her.

"There isn't the same excitement in the music scene that there used to be," she recently said while being interviewed for a job as a topless waitress by Gregory Smith, a notorious Macdougal Street hawk, "I mean there's no more of this kid stuff. I mean even Murray the K has grown up."

Murray the K survived his short-lived career as the Fifth Beatle to become a respectable disk jockey on WOR-FM, a New York station that broadcasts rock-and-roll for adults. "The entire music industry has matriculated to a point where everybody is articulating in a different way," says Murray, who began to talk like that after he started writing books.

Suzanne Tumbler's father has become a regular listener to WOR-FM after having divorced Suzanne's mother. He tuned in by accident one day and, mistaking it for WQXR's dinner music, he now listens endlessly while riding in his chauffeur-driven limousine with his girl friends, each of them at least old enough to be Suzanne's twin sister.

NEW YORK, 1963—"If the establishment knew what today's popular music really is saying," explained one musician, "not what the words are saying, but what the music itself is saying, then they wouldn't just turn thumbs down on it. They'd ban it, they'd smash all the records and they'd arrest anyone who tried to play it."

NEW YORK, 1964—Brian Sommerville is a balding thirty-two-year-old Londoner whose eyes lie dully behind his glasses and whose jaw juts out like the southeast corner of England when he thinks he is about to say something important. At New York's Kennedy International Airport last February 7, Sommerville's jaw extended beyond his ability to express himself.

A thousand screaming teen-agers were trying to wriggle through the spaces between one another to the thin white line of nylon rope that had been stretched across the terminal lobby. Another three thousand were screaming discordantly from behind bulging metal railings atop the observation roof.

At Sommerville's arm a phalanx of British correspondents were complaining that the police wouldn't let them into the press box without New York credentials. Disk jockeys equipped with miniature tape recorders were pointing cylindrical microphones at the mob in a crossfire. Strobe lights and flash bulbs lit up faces that were open-mouthed in ecstasy. From the back of the lobby came word that two girls had fainted.

"I haven't seen press coverage like this since Kennedy was assassinated—or, for that matter, since Elizabeth Taylor and Richard Burton were chasing around Rome," remarked one reporter.

Hemmed in and harassed, Sommerville's jaw signaled a pronouncement. "This," he said in the intonations of a nation that has been accustomed to ruling the world, "has gotten entirely out of control." Brian Sommerville is the press officer of a British rock-and-roll group known as the Beatles. Their plane had just landed.

LIVERPOOL, 1964—Liverpool is a gray city, the stone houses below mirroring the almost constant overcast above, but its grayness merely camouflages the true colors of its passion. Its people throb in bodies that are made small, tough and wiry by the spare diets and frequent malnutrition that comes with the factory wages in Northern England—when wages come. Liverpool has one of the highest unemployment rates in England, something else which sets it apart from the rest of the country.

A seaport on the slimy mouth of the Mersey River, with streets that look dirty in the grayness even though they are scrubbed clean every day, Liverpool is an immigrant city, with one-third of its population awash from the Irish Sea.

There was a time when Liverpool issued its own money, and there are still iron rings on the docks where the slaves were chained before trans-shipment to the colonies in open defiance of the Crown. The big colonnaded stone mansions on Upper Parliament Street and Gambia Terrace were built by profits from slave trade, but, as John Lennon points out, "It's the coloreds who won out in the end, isn't it? Now it's them that live on Upper Parliament Street."

The mansions have been broken down into the tiny flats of Liverpool's Harlem, and Lennon himself used to live in one of them on Gambia Terrace when he was a student at the Liverpool Art Institute, across the street. His friends still talk about the winter he chopped up the furniture to heat the flat and about the time a London newspaper sent a photographer to take pictures of it for an article on England's Beat Generation. Lennon threw the photographer out. Lennon's roommate, Stuart Sutcliffe, co-founder of the Beatles but now dead and buried in Hamburg, Germany, was reading the poetry of Allen Ginsberg in those days.

Liverpool, the slum of England, has the championship football team of the United Kingdom. Of its 750,000 population, it also has Harold Wilson; Miss Brenda Blackler, Miss England of 1964; the Royal Liverpool Philharmonic, acclaimed as the best symphony orchestra in the country; and, of course, the Beatles.

"Except," says thirty-four-year-old Allan Williams, the short, poetic, but ready-fisted owner of Liverpool's all-night club, the Blue Angel, "the Beatles don't belong to Liverpool any more, they belong to the world. You know, I used to be manager of the Beatles. It was all done on a handshake. One bloody nasty paper said I now cry myself to sleep. That's ridiculous. I couldn't have done what Brian Epstein did for them. Nor what he did for Gerry and the Pacemakers. That's another one of my sad stories. I used to manage Gerry, too.

You wouldn't believe it could all happen to one fellow, would you?"

LONDON, 1964—Derek Taylor threw a cablegram across the neatly piled clutter of his desk top. "Here," he said with a smile that seemed to wish it could be broader, but couldn't because his face was too thin. "Here," he said, "have a look at this."

The address on the cablegram was simply, JOHN LENNON, THE BEATLES, LONDON, but it had been delivered safely to the offices of Nems Enterprises Ltd., where Derek Taylor, thirty-two-years-old and dressed to the teeth of his grin, was sitting in a seat formerly occupied by one Brian Sommerville, recently resigned as press officer of the Beatles.

UNDERSTAND THROUGH WEST COAST SOURCE, the cablegram said, THAT YOU PLAN TO LEAVE BEATLES. CAN UNDERSTAND TRAVELING MOST TIRING AND YOUR DESIRE TO SETTLE DOWN. WHILE WE HAVE NO IMMEDIATE OPENINGS ON KLIF DEEJAY STAFF, WE OFFER YOU THE MUSIC CRITIC'S POSITION ON NUMBER ONE STATION IN DALLAS. SUGGEST YOU REMAIN WITH GROUP UNTIL BEATLES APPEAR HERE IN SEPTEMBER. IT WILL SAVE YOU TRAVEL MOVING EXPENSES. PLEASE ADVISE. CHARLES F. PAYNE, MANAGER, KLIF DALLAS, TEXAS.

"It's incredible, absolutely incredible!" said Derek Taylor. "Here are these four boys from Liverpool. They're rude, they're profane, they're vulgar, and they've taken over the world. It's as if they've founded a new religion.

"In Australia, for example, each time we'd arrive at an airport, it was as if De Gaulle had landed, or better yet, the Messiah. The routes were lined solid with people; cripples threw away their sticks; sick people rushed up to the car as if a touch from one of the boys would make them well again; old women stood watching with their grandchildren, and as we'd pass by, I could see the look on their faces. It was as if some Saviour had arrived and people were happy and relieved as if things somehow were going to be better now."

The telephone rang. It was a newspaper reporter asking for tickets to the forthcoming Beatles' Royal Premiere. "Utterly out of the question!" said Taylor, trying to sound apologetic. "I'm sorry," and he hung up.

"If I were a Beatle," he said, "this would be the ultimate. The Royal Premiere would be the ultimate—except for the Sermon on the Mount. The only thing left for them is to go on a healing tour."

AUSTIN, 1965—*Reporter:* What do you consider yourself? How would you classify yourself?

Bob Dylan: Well, I like to think of myself in terms of a trapeze artist.

Reporter: Speaking of trapeze artists, I've noticed in some of your recent albums a carnival-type sound. Could you tell me a little bit about that?

Bob Dylan: That isn't a carnival sound, that's religious. That's very real, you can see that anywhere.

Reporter: What about this "Ballad of the Thin Man"? This sounds as though it might have been dedicated to a newspaper reporter or something.

Bob Dylan: No, it's just about a fella that came into a truck-stop once.

Reporter: Have the Beatles had any influence on your work?

Bob Dylan: Well, they haven't influenced the songs or sound. I don't know what other kind of influence they might have. They haven't influenced the songs or the sound.

Reporter: In an article in *The New Yorker,* written by Nat Hentoff, I believe, you said you sang what you felt and you sang to make yourself feel good, more or less. And it was implied that in your first two albums you sang "finger-pointing songs," I believe.

Bob Dylan: Well, what he was saying was, I mean, I wasn't playing then and it was still sort of a small nucleus at that time and by the definition of why do you sing, I sing for the people. He was saying, "Why do you sing?" and I couldn't think of an answer except that I felt like singing, that's about all.

Reporter: Why is it different?

Bob Dylan: Come on, come on.

Reporter: What is your attitude toward your "finger-pointing" songs? He implied that you thought they were just superficial.

Bob Dylan: No, it's not superficial, it's just motivated. Motivated. Uncontrollable motivation. Which anyone can do, once they get uncontrollably motivated.

Reporter: You said before that you sang because you had to. Why do you sing now?

Bob Dylan: Because I have to.

Reporter: Your voice in here is soft and gentle. Yet in some of your records, there's a harsh twang.

Bob Dylan: I just got up.

Reporter: Could you give me some sort of evaluation as far as your own taste is concerned, comparing some of the things you did, like old music, say, "Girl from the North Country," which I consider a very beautiful-type ballad? Perhaps some of the things that have come out in the last couple of albums—do you get the same satisfaction out of doing this?

Bob Dylan: Yeah, I do. I wish I could write like "Girl from the North Country." You know, I can't write like that any more.

Reporter: Why is that?

Bob Dylan: I don't know.

Reporter: Are you trying to accomplish anything?

Bob Dylan: Am I trying to accomplish anything?

Reporter: Are you trying to change the world or anything?

Bob Dylan: Am I trying to change the world? Is that your question?

Reporter: Well, do you have any idealism or anything?

Bob Dylan: Am I trying to change the idealism of the world? Is that it?

Reporter: Well, are you trying to push over idealism to the people?

Bob Dylan: Well, what do you think my ideas are?

Reporter: Well, I don't exactly know. But are you singing just to be singing?

Bob Dylan: No, I'm not just singing to be singing. There's a much deeper reason for it than that.

Reporter: In a lot of the songs you sing you seem to express a pessimistic attitude toward life. It seems that "Hollis Brown" gives me that feeling. Is this your true feeling or are you just trying to shock people?

Bob Dylan: That's not pessimistic form, that's just statement. You know. It's not pessimistic.

Reporter: Who are your favorite performers? I don't mean folk, I mean general.

Bob Dylan: Rasputin . . . Hmmm . . . Charles de Gaulle . . . the Staple Singers. I sort of have a general attitude about that. I like just about everybody everybody else likes.

Reporter: You said just a minute ago you were preparing to go to classical music. Could you tell me a little about that?

Bob Dylan: Well, I was going to be in the classical music field and I imagine it's going right along. I'll get there one of these records.

Reporter: Are you using the word classical perhaps a little differently than we?

Bob Dylan: A little bit, maybe. Just a hair.

Reporter: Could you explain that?

Bob Dylan: Well, I'm using it in the general sense of the word, thumbing a hair out.

Reporter: Any attention to form?

Bob Dylan: Form and matter. Mathematics.

Reporter: What is your belief in a God? Are you a Christian?

Bob Dylan: Well, first of all, God is a woman, we all know that. Well, you take it from there.

NEW YORK, 1966—American colleges and universities began adding Contemporary Popular Music to their curricula, teaching it as if it were Business Administration. In Greenwich Village two entrepreneurs of hip bought out stock of a theatrical-costume company sight unseen, and in a matter of days sold five thousand costumes to people who wore them into the street.

Senator Everett McKinley Dirksen, the fabled honey of his voice dripping off the wax black edges of a 45 rpm single, recorded an orchestrated oration called "Gallant Men" and, with an "I didn't know you can get paid for doing this too," announced plans for another record of himself reading from the Bible.

Otherwise the nation's Top 40 radio stations steadfastly maintained their traditions. In Federal Court a company called Coed Records, alleging it had paid $19,000 to disk jockeys, claimed that payola was so commonplace it ought to be allowed to deduct the money from its income tax as a business expense. When the Rolling Stones released a record called "Let's Spend the Night Together," the radio stations played the other side, "Ruby Tuesday." The Stones nearly walked off the Ed Sullivan Show when Sullivan insisted they mumble the line, "Let's spend the night together," during a performance of the song. While American radio kept busy trying to keep its turntable clean of records that dealt with sex and drugs, American songwriters kept busy outwitting the censors with lyrics that had double, triple and sometimes multiple meanings. America's new generation was creating its own culture and as part of that culture it was creating its own music and its own language.

LOS ANGELES, 1967—As clean and machine-finished as fresh Saran Wrap, the Monkees in six months seemed on the way to becoming the most popular group in the world. Their success stunned even their manufacturers, who had designed the Monkees primarily for a weekly half-hour comedy television show. When the show went on the air last September [1966], it was almost booed right off by the ratings.

Then the Monkees' records were released and the sales figures started rising beyond anybody's belief. The first single sold 1,200,000 copies, the first album sold 3,300,000, the second single sold, 3,100,000 and by the time the second album was put on the market, in three weeks advance sales totaled 2,500,000. "I think the Monkees are outselling Elvis Presley and the Beatles at the same point in their careers," one RCA Victor official cautiously volunteered.

On the other hand, the Monkees, packaged and marketed in the same way that their sponsors produce a box of sugar-coated crisp, had begun to feel that their own personalities had as much to do with the success of the package as the vacuum-sealed silver foil they came wrapped in.

"It's like somebody predicted it," said one musician, viewing the whole pop scene with the amusement of someone who had bought his fame with ten years of one-nighters, playing country-blues guitar in every town that ever canceled a postage stamp. "That three years after the Beatles, someone would get the idea of putting a group together like the Monkees and putting them on television, and they'd become very big, almost as big as the Beatles, and that after they got very big they'd start hassling their producers and want to do their own stuff. But they seem pretty groovy; they seem like they'd be able to do their own thing and not have to worry about it. Did you know that Mike Nesmith wrote 'Mary, Mary'? That's a groovy song. Even Paul Butterfield recorded 'Mary, Mary.' "

"The amusing thing about this," taunted the magazine *Crawdaddy!*, "is its supreme unimportance—after it's all over, and they've outsold everyone else in history, the Monkees will still leave absolutely no mark on American music."

At last report, according to one witness, "they were having this big meeting in this hotel room, and Mike Nesmith got mad and said he was sick and tired of putting out cruddy records. He wanted to put out a product worthy of the Monkees' image. The Monkees are getting worried about what their hippie friends in Greenwich Village and Haight-Ashbury are going to think about them."

NEW YORK, 1967—"Dylan has been doing nothing, absolutely nothing," said Jaime Robertson, Dylan's guitarist, to an inquiring reporter. "He's been looking at the gate around his house and training his dogs how to bite." But that was just a contribution to the Dylan mystery. Actually, Dylan was writing ten new songs a week, rehearsing them in his living room with Robertson's group, the Hawks, and trying to complete a one-hour film TV special for ABC-TV, which said it couldn't use the program because it was delivered seven months late.

LOS ANGELES, 1967—In his office on the Sunset Strip, Derek Taylor lit another filtertip cigarette. Once he had been the press officer for the Beatles; now he was the publicity agent for a dozen Top 40 recording artists. On his desk was a newspaper clipping about a Catholic priest who for two years had been touring the country giving lectures based on a *Saturday Evening Post* article which had quoted Taylor as saying that the Beatles were anti-Christ.

Taylor was talking music: "The myth is that the industry has grown up. All the marvelous elements have come together, all the groovy people are now in command. Okay. But when the awards come out at the end of 1966, you open *Record World* and what do you find? The top vocalist of the year is Staff Sergeant Barry Sadler. I'm sure Barry Sadler is a very good soldier, but what has that got to do with music? All right. The most promising male vocal group is Tommy James and the Shondells. Here's a group that made one record that hung around for two years because nobody would touch it. Then, by some freak, it sells more than a million copies—'Hanky Panky,' the all-time definitive piece of crap, a very poor recreation of 'Be Bop a Lula,' a famous Gene Vincent song—and on the basis of *that,* they're voted the most promising male vocal group in the single market.

"In *Cash Box,* somewhere on their list is Bob Dylan, who has just beaten out John Gary, but above Dylan is *Al Martino.* All of which goes to prove that it's quite untrue that the record industry has grown up. And the reason is that there's no growing up of the public taste. The same crap is being bought that was bought ten years ago. Let's look at *Record World* again.

The most promising male vocal group in albums in 1966 was the Monkees. Now, the Monkees are a workmanlike group put together like a play is put together, through casting. But if the most promising group of 1966 was the Monkees, the industry is in a mess."

Through the sunglow of his office windows, the grass of the Hollywood Hills could be seen spreading up to the castled doorsteps of the aging Lords of Entertainment. But things had changed. Marilyn Monroe used to watch the flashing thunderbolt of the RKO studio from her girlhood bedroom. Now the children of Los Angeles looked out their picture windows to see America's Mount Olympus dancing to acid-rock rhythms in their heads.

From behind the electric gates of his mountaintop stronghold on Mulholland Drive, Frank Sinatra had founded a dynasty. From another craggy peak in Bel Air, Dr. Jules Stein, who rose to power as a booking agent for bandleaders like Guy Lombardo, still reigned as the Bernard Baruch of show business. But on another hill was Brian Wilson of the Beach Boys, holding water ballets in his heated swimming pool under the eye of a television camera and millions who would watch the program.

The Byrds were up there, too, all nestled in the same neighborhood, close enough to one another for Byrd Jim McGuinn to take videotape films with his home TV camera when Byrd Chris Hillman's house burned down. McGuinn sold his tapes to a Los Angeles TV station for its late-night news broadcast. And on another hillside were John and Michelle Phillips, who, as half of the Mamas and the Papas, lived in a mansion where Gene Raymond and Jeanette MacDonald had once inspired the old-fashioned lovers of the world.

Down on the flatlands below, the groupies were trying to crash the sound stage where the Monkees were filming their TV show. It wasn't hard. A select few were allowed in each day to brighten the set.

At night, the Los Angeles Sheriff's office was using armored buses to enforce the 10 P.M. curfew for kids under eighteen, and the authorities were acting to close down the Sunset Strip rock-and-roll clubs by rescinding their teen-age dance permits. Dressed in paisley and suede and any costume they could dig up from the days of Charlie Chaplin, the mini-masses were fighting back with protest marches. Walt Disney was dead, but amid the young mobs that walked the Strip at night, the police were arresting life-long Mickey Mouse fans on charges of possession of narcotics.

WOODSTOCK, NEW YORK, 1967—Bob Dylan's eyes drew you into them like whirlpools, so you had to look away to keep from being drowned in his charisma. He was sitting at an electric piano while a Japanese windchime played random melodies on the porch outside. Dylan had owned the house for quite a while before he finally moved into it, a rambling American chateau of mahogany-stained shingles that clung to a mountaintop above the point where the mountaintop kept its head in the clouds. It seemed as if God and nature had joined in the conspiracy to help draw the veil of mystery and seclusion which had surrounded Dylan and his activities since he broke his neck in a motorcycle accident last year.

He wore a beard now and rimless Benjamin Franklin eyeglasses, and from behind his incognito he sang a new song he had written.

"*You can change your name but you can't run away from yourself . . . You can change your name but you can't run away from yourself . . .*"

"Do you like that song?" he asked a friend.

"I think it's great," the friend said.

"I don't like that song," Dylan said.

The friend was crestfallen. Later, Dylan sang another new song.

"I like that one better than the other one," the friend said.

Dylan turned to Jaime Robertson.

"See," Dylan said, "we shouldn't keep any music critics around here. We just lost another song."

BAEZ AND DYLAN: A GENERATION SINGING OUT

●

RICHARD FARIÑA

When Bob Dylan drove across the Berkeley campus with his songs in a hip pocket and a station wagon full of friends, it was as if the undergraduates had been whispering of his imminent arrival for months. They seemed, occasionally, to believe he might not actually come, that some malevolent force or organization would get in the way. From north into Oregon and as far south as Fort Ord, near Monterey, college-age listeners had found time to make the trip, secure tickets, and locate seats in the mammoth Berkeley Community Theatre. They had come with a sense of collective expectancy, some attracted by already implausible legend, some critical of an idiom that seemed too maverick to be substantial, but most with an eye to taking part in a passing event that promised more than usual significance for their generation.

Each of Dylan's concerts this past year had had a way of arousing the same feeling. There was no sensation of his having performed somewhere the previous night or of a schedule that would take him away once the inevitable post-concert party was over. There was, instead, the familiar comparison with James Dean, at times explicit, at times unspoken, an impulsive awareness of his physical perishability. Catch him now, was the idea. Next week he might be mangled on a motorcycle.

The Berkeley performance did little to set anyone at ease. It often looked as if it were calculated to do the opposite, as a result both of its haphazard form and the provocative nature of its content. There were songs about the shooting of Medgar Evers, the Mississippi drowning of Emmet Till, the corporate tactics of munitions executives, even a fiercely cynical review of American war history called "With God on Our Side." Dylan appeared as usual in well-worn clothes, said whatever occurred to him at the time, and sang his songs in no particular order. When he surprised everyone by introducing Joan Baez from the wings, the students were electrified. Their applause was potent, overwhelming, unmitigated. Had a literary audience been confronted by Dylan Thomas and Edna St. Vincent Millay the mood of aesthetic anxiety might have been the same.

To professional observers—and I talked to a good many—this mood threatened to overreach the abilities of the unassisted performers. They spoke of the fragility of the two people on stage, the lack of props and dramatic lighting, the absence of accompanying musicians, the banality of costume. A writer from one of the new folk magazines told me, "They can't be *that* confident, man; sooner or later they're going to play a wrong chord." But he was talking in terms of show-business proficiency, while the performers themselves were concerned with more durable values. They never doubted their capacity to equal the ovation, and, if anything, they felt applause was a dubious reward for their efforts.

They claimed to be there not as virtuosos in the field of concertized folk music, but as purveyors of an enjoined social consciousness and responsibility. They believed they were offering contemporaries the new musical expression of a tenuous American legacy, a legacy that threatened to become the most destructive and morally inconsistent in the nation's history. They felt the intolerability of bigoted opposition to civil rights, the absurdity of life under a polluted atmosphere, and they were confident that a majority of their listeners felt the same way. "I don't know how they do it," said a San Francisco columnist, "but they certainly do it." When they left the stage to a whirlwind of enthusiastic cheers, it seemed that the previously unspoken word of protest, like the torch of President Kennedy's inaugural address, had most certainly been passed.

Significantly, when Joan and Dylan are together and away from the crush of admirers and hangers-on, the protest is seldom discussed. They are far more likely to putter with the harmonies of a rock-'n'-roll tune or run through the vital scenes of a recent movie than consider the tactics of civil disobedience or the abhorrence of biological warfare. Like many another person in his early twenties, they derive a sense of political indignation from the totality of everyday conversations and media that surround them—a process more akin to osmosis than ratiocination. And because of this subjective approach to the problems at hand, metaphor is better suited than directness to their respective dispositions.

"I don't like the word 'bomb' in a song," Joan said one evening, watching a fire in her sister's small Carmel cabin. The flames were the kind that hissed and crackled, causing small coals to pop and sometimes explode with surprising violence. They seemed to reinforce her feeling that simple, explicit reference to heat and radiation was too easy to slough off, that this never evoked anything more than superficial interest and sympathy in an insufferable situation. Speaking or singing with regard to megatons, fall-out, Strontium 90, nuclear deterrents, overkill ratios, genetic mutation, all in so many facile phrases, might have been necessary for raising the initial indignation of the populace, but it was certainly not sufficient. "People don't listen to words like those," she said. "They hear them, sure, but they don't listen."

Certainly popular American reaction to these concepts had already proved, on the whole, nothing short of apathetic. A more meaningful vocabulary was needed to loosen fundamental feelings. Students across the country were helplessly aware of this fact whenever their civil or political protests were met by blatantly bureaucratic response from public officials, elders, and even fellow students. Posters scrawled with "Ban the Bomb" or "No More Jim Crow" were invariably treated with a disdain that belied any awareness of the gravity of the causal situation. The students, seeking a more profound language and finding such language in folk music, looked to folk musicians as their spokesmen; and the musicians said and sang what they could. Last year, however, the vivid and topical imagery of a self-styled Midwestern folk-poet finally lent their arguments more vigorous meaning. And even from the point of view of the bureaucrats, this meaning was difficult to evade.

"It ain't nothin' just to walk around and sing," Dylan said, "you have to step out a little, right?" We were strolling in the pre-dawn London fog a year and a half ago, six months before he made the now historic appearance at the Newport Folk Festival. "Take Joanie, man, she's still singin' about Mary Hamilton. I mean, where's that at? She's walked around on picket lines, she's got all kinds of feeling, so why ain't she steppin' out?"

Joan quite possibly had asked herself the same question. As much as any of the young people who looked to her for guidance, she was, at the time, bewildered and confused by the lack of official response to the protesting college voices. She had very little material to help her. At one point she was enough concerned about the content of her repertoire to consider abandoning public appearances until she had something more substantial to offer. Traditional ballads, ethnic music from one culture or another were not satisfactory for someone whose conception of folk singing extended so far beyond an adequate rendering. Her most emphatic song was "What Have They Done to the Rain?" and she was, one felt, more personally moved by the image of a small boy standing alone in a tainted shower than by the implication of the remaining lyrical content.

By May, 1963, however, she had a firsthand opportunity to hear Dylan perform at the Monterey Folk Festival in California. His strong-willed, untempered, but nonetheless poetic approach to the problem filled the gap and left her awed and impressed. Moreover, by the time she had finished going over the songs he left behind, it seemed his lyrics would finally provide the substance for her continuing role as a soulful representative of the generation, a young woman whose very function seemed defined by an ability to mirror alternatives to the malaise of the times.

Meaningfully enough, the highest personification of these social concerns was not indifferent to Joan's role. Just weeks before the Dallas assassination ended an era of Washington style that was based in part on an implicit acceptance of contemporary arts, Joan received a telegram from Lyndon B. Johnson asking her to perform for the President. Since that time, the invitation was renewed, and on May 26 she sang for President Johnson at a Democratic fund-raising show. Yet it speaks for her place in the company of essentially interpretive artists that she has never strayed very far from the sensibilities of those closest to her age.

By living the life many university students would like to live, were it not for the daily concerns of textbooks and money from home, and by spending most of her public time in and around the nation's campuses, she has had no trouble keeping a half-conscious finger on an eager college pulse. Young people are very much aware that she drives an XKE and that it has been in the repair pits an inordinate number of times. So much so that a recent *Channing* television show used the car as an insipid symbol of the paradox of high speed and homely folk tradition. Some who live nearby are also used to seeing her chug down the Big Sur coast at midnight with four dogs in a red jeep, to watch the moon above the Pacific. To most students it comes as no surprise that she is refusing to pay 60 per cent of her income tax, a figure that corresponds to the government's allotment for defense.

Occasionally one gets the feeling that people try too hard to relegate her to a premature immortality, and the subsequent rumors are in kind: She has come down with a mysterious paralysis and will never sing again; she has been arrested at the Mexican border with a Jaguar full of narcotics; she is living with Marlon Brando on a Choctaw Indian reservation. In what many would call the alarming calm of her California surroundings, the exoticism of these stories seems absurd.

It was to her home in Carmel that Dylan came last spring just after the Berkeley concert. He was on his way to Los Angeles in the station wagon, traveling with Paul Clayton, once the most recorded professional in the folk revival; Bobby Neuwirth, one of the half-dozen surviving hipster nomads who shuttle back and forth between Berkeley and Harvard Square; and a lazy-lidded, black-booted friend called Victor, who seemed to be his road manager. They arrived bearing gifts of French-fried almonds, glazed walnuts, bleached cashews, dried figs, oranges and prunes. Here again the legions of image-makers might well have been disappointed by the progress of the evening. How could so volatile a company get itself together without some sort of apocalyptic scene dominating the action? Instead, Joan's mother, visting from Paris, cooked a beef stew. We talked about old friends, listened to the Everly Brothers, and finally got Clayton to do a number of songs that few others can sing with such understated composure. The only overt references to Dylan's music came when Joan said she might want to record an entire album of his songs and he told her, "Sure thing."

The college student's reaction to Dylan has been somewhat more complex than their acceptance of Joan, however. It was clear from his initial entry on the folk scene that he was neither as musically gifted and delicate, nor as consistent in performance as she. Yet Robert Shelton, now the editor of *Hootenanny* magazine, predicted that these very qualities would contribute to his popularity. "He's a moving target," Shelton said in New York, "and he'll fascinate the people who try to shoot him down." In the beginning, when he was better known for his Huck Finn corduroy cap than his abilities as a composer, he jumped back and forth between Boston and New York, developing a style and manner that brought the manifestation of the pregnant pause to uncanny perfection. Some still found a discomforting similarity to Jack Elliott, or too much affectation in his droll delivery; but everyone agreed his smirk implied a certain something left unsaid and that whatever it was, if he got around to letting you in on the secret, it would be worthwhile.

It developed that this something was his writing. In no time, Dylan nearly abandoned established material for songs of his own composition. The transition from one to the other was nearly imperceptible since he had the good sense to keep his overall cadence within the framework of familiar traditional music. He begged and borrowed from the established ballad styles of the past (in some cases quite freely), from the prolific works of Woody Guthrie, from the contemporary production of friends like Clayton. But the stories he told in his songs had nothing to do with unrequited Appalachian love affairs, or idealized whorehouses in New Orleans. They told about the cane murder of Negro servant Hattie Carroll, the death of boxer Davy Moore, the unbroken chains of injustice waiting for the hammers of a crusading era. They went right to the heart of his decade's most recurring preoccupation: that in a time of totally irreversible technological progress, moral amelioration has pathetically faltered; that no matter how much international attention is focused on macrocosmic affairs, the plight of the individual must be considered, or we are forever lost.

Such a theme has often been associated with the output of folk poets; in fact, since the time John Henry laid down his hammer and died from the competition of the industrial revolution, they have celebrated little else. But even including the dynamic figures of Guthrie and Leadbelly in this century, no creator of the idiom has ever received such a wide cross section of public attention. It is quite possible that already, within the astonishing space of a single year, Dylan has outdistanced the notoriety of still another spiritual forebear, Robert Burns. And like Burns he has the romantic's eye for trading bouts of hard writing with hard living. He often runs the two together, courting all the available kinds and degrees of disaster, sleeping little, partying late, and taking full-time advantage of the musician's scene in New York's Greenwich Village, where he keeps a small apartment. Using a blowtorch on the middle of the candle is less aesthetic than burning it at both ends, but more people see the flame. He can dip in and out of traditional forms at will, shift temperament from cynical humor to objective tragedy, and never lose sight of what people his age want to hear.

This wanting is in no way a passive or camouflaged matter. It is part and parcel of a generation's active desire to confront the very sources of hypocrisy, which in early years deceived them into thinking that God was perforce on their side, that good guys were always United States Marines, that if they didn't watch the skies day and night the Russians, Vietnamese, North Koreans, tribal Africans, and Lord knows who else would swoop down in the darkness and force them all into salt mines. Dylan feels a very critical trust was betrayed in these exaggerations. He feels further, in what amounts to a militant attitude, that it is up to him to speak out for the millions around him who lack the fortitude to talk themselves.

Because he speaks for them, undergraduates in many ways seek to identify with his public image, just as they have with Joan's. They search for the same breed of rough Wellingtons and scuff them up with charcoal before wearing. They spend weekends hitchhiking, not so much to get somewhere as to log hours on the road. I've even come across an otherwise excellent guitarist and harmonica player from Fort Ord who tried a crash diet with Army food in order to achieve the necessary gaunt look. The image, of course, has shifted with Dylan's increasing maturity. Some fans are reluctant to accept his early attempts at playing with his past. Last winter, an article in *Newsweek* went to great pains recalling his middle-class upbringing in Hibbing, Minnesota, and alluding to a prior, less attractive surname, which had been removed by the courts. After the Berkeley concert a nineteen-year-old girl in a shawl told me, "He has a knack for saying what younger people want to hear. It's only too bad he had to change his name and not be able to accept himself." I reminded her that she liked his music, but she went on: "People want an image. They carry it around to make their scene look more important. There're so many guys wanting to be something they're not that Bobby makes a nice alternative. At least he has integrity."

The seeming paradox between name-changing and integrity is significant. His admirers enjoy possessing a certain amount of private information and using it against him as insidiously as they try to hasten Joan's premature immortality. But he has done something they will never do: stepped so cleanly away from his antecedents and into the exhilarating world of creative action as to make the precise nature of an early history look insignificant. Behind the college students of America today, no matter what their protest against segregation, injustice, and thermonuclear war, are the realities of their parents, the monthly check, and their hometown. *The Freewheelin' Bob Dylan,* as the title of his second album sets him up, lives in a world that is the realm of their alter ego.

But in the meantime the word still has to be passed, and both Joan and Dylan go to the campuses to make sure that it gets there. After the evening of the French-fried almonds and beef stew, both of them journeyed into Southern California—Dylan with his friends in the station wagon, Joan in the XKE. There was some anticipatory talk of getting together at one or more of the concerts, but circumstances were not propitious and they went their separate ways. Dylan stayed at the Thunderbird Motel in Hollywood, drifting out to parties and local folk nightclubs between engagements; Joan stayed with friends of the family in Redlands, lying in the sun, going to bed early. She sang at her old high school one afternoon and was moved to tears by the standing ovation. When she did an encore, her mention of Dylan's name brought cheers. That same night, he returned the compliment to a devoted audience in Riverside.

It could be said that during these respective performances, as with each of their concerts before predominantly young crowds, their specific relationship to their generation is most unhindered and best understood. They utter a statement of unmistakably mortal grievance against what they stand to inherit as a result of the blunders of their immediate forebears. In the one case this statement is from the source, in the other through interpretation, but in neither is there any distance between expression and experience. To the young men and women who listen, the message is as meaningful as if it were uttered in the intimacy of their own secluded thought.

BOBBY DYLAN—FOLK-ROCK HERO

LAWRENCE GOLDMAN

The phrase "the Dylan problem" sounds rather peculiar. After all, no one is talking about the Baez problem or the Van Ronk problem. But Dylan is different; Dylan is more than a folk singer, more than an entertainer; he is a culture hero. Scores of people, from Playboy bunnies to Harvard undergraduates, regard him as a mentor, a bard, a force.

Culture heroes tend to be as numerous as Chevrolets in this frenetic, escapist pseudo-culture of ours, but what is significant about Dylan is that, unlike James Dean and Charlie Parker, two of his spiritual predecessors, he came out of a radical bohemian environment, the Village scene, which is profoundly hostile to the dominant American political and cultural values. Some people, including many of his former admirers, claim that Dylan has only attained his present position of eminence by betraying the values of this environment.

Dylan's critics claim that his new addiction to electric guitar and the amplified sound associated with folk-rock is merely a callow attempt to gain entree into the lucrative field of pop music. In addition they argue that his present work is inferior to the music of such old time rhythm-and-blues singers as Lightnin' Hopkins and John Lee Hooker. But the most serious charge brought against Dylan, the one that in a sense lies behind all the others, is that he has deserted the Cause, given up his concern with injustice and the threat of war, and retreated into an annoying and often meaningless obscurity.

Dylan has his defenders, of course, but the controversy itself is a waste of time. The real significance of this argument is what it reveals about the culture that nurtured Dylan and which he reflected for a time in all its defensive, moving and terribly earnest inauthenticity.

Bob Dylan has been called the voice of the sixties on innumerable occasions, the voice both of the "movement" and of those who distrust all movements. This is undoubtedly true. Still, certain important questions remain: What is Dylan saying? Who, or rather, what is he?

The most important thing that can be said about Bob Dylan, and the key to a good deal of his success, is that like Jay Gatsby, he arose out of some sort of Platonic Conception of himself. He created himself, which is not unusual, but he was more extreme than most of us; he created himself, name and all, from scratch, and rejected all the elements in his past except those which fit in with his carefully constructed personal mythology.

Dylan came from a middle-class family in Minnesota and was always restless. He ran away from home several times and left his state university after a few months of fruitless study. During his adolescence he developed a deep affection for his two earliest folk-music influences, Big Joe Williams and the now legendary Woody Guthrie. It is interesting to compare these two singers with Dylan. Big Joe and Guthrie, for all their inevitable differences, both sing about a series of experiences that were imposed upon them, very often against their will. Dylan chose his situation and decided at one point to become a vagabond, an outsider and a follower of circus shows and blind street singers. I am not making any value judgments, but simply observing that Dylan had options which were not open to Williams and Guthrie.

However, Dylan's original choice of roles was refined and defined during his stay in the Village or rather in that particular sub-world of the Village which is bounded on one side by the Folklore Center and on the other by Folk City. This little sub-world is necessary because it fulfills the very genuine needs of the hundreds of thousands of adolescents who journey to it every weekend on the IND. At the same time this world is unreal and inauthentic in a very important way, and was never less real than when Dylan came to it in 1961, a time when the political attitudes of the nineteen fifties were much more influential than they are today.

At that time the folk music world was composed to a large extent of the rebellious children of ex-radical middle-class families. These families had once been active, often in support of causes associated with the Communist Party. They were still sympathetic to radicalism and regarded themselves, whether they were active or not, as "progressives." It should be remembered that in the nineteen fifties the Left consisted of a small band of harried and desperate people, divided by ancient quarrels, persecuted by the McCarthyites, abused by the cold war liberals and betrayed by the Khrushchev Report and the Hungarian Revolution. They were tired, impotent and unsure of where they were going or why they were going there.

To protect and preserve itself the Left created a series of myths which, though originally based on a careful analysis of the political situation, had become, after a time, a means of avoiding reality. The Left came to talk of the Negro rather than Negroes, of the Worker rather than workers, of the Thirties rather than the fifties, and of the People rather than people. The folk music world was one of the few places left in American cultural life, aside from the novels of Howard Fast and the criticism of Mike Gold, where those myths still retained their emotional force.

The most vociferous defenders of these myths had by the nineteen fifties become solid middle-class citizens, and more often than not restricted their political activities to baiting Richard Nixon when he appeared on TV. Their children, who noted this passionate passivity, felt betrayed by their parents who they accused of selling out. At the same time they were alienated from the stagnant, mindless and conservative country in which they lived and were searching for new directions. The painful paradox was that they rebelled against the apostasy of their elders in the name of the very myths their elders had bequeathed to them. These embittered and thwarted adolescents wrapped themselves in the myth of the thirties to keep out the cold. They tried to turn themselves inside out and become "working class" even though they did not have the faintest notion of what this working class was or how it functioned. And it was these adolescents who spread the myths and sang the songs which gave the Village folk community its peculiar political complexion.

Dylan was a natural for this world.

Dylan recognizes the times have changed, but obviously wishes they hadn't; I can't help but wonder if Woody Guthrie felt the same way. In any event Dylan had found his proper milieu. The corduroy cap, the dungarees, the deliberately ungrammatical language, the "folk" spelling of words like "the," the mannerisms, the consciously simplistic stance and the way in which Dylan protested against injustice were all symptoms. They reflected a deep-seated drive of Dylan's the will to make himself into a type: the vagabond folk-poet of the thirties, the hungry, restless, freedom-loving friend and comrade of the oppressed. Many of the younger Village folk enthusiasts who formed his earliest admiration society were responding to this image, this persona of Dylan's rather than to his singing or to his harmonica playing. It was not until Dylan's second record, *The Freewheelin' Bob Dylan,* which, unlike his first record, presented him not simply as a singer but as a folk bard, that Dylan began to acquire a large following. This may be a natural process in the world of music, but the fact remains that Dylan became very popular only when people began treating him as a seer as well as a singer.

The image that Dylan projected had less to do with his experience than it did with what he wanted his experience to be. Dylan was, like many of the young people who admired him, a disturbed, unconventional, rebellious and confused young internal exile from an affluence he could have had, but did not want. Dylan had no intention of deceiving anyone—quite the contrary. He did not write songs about his actual situation because of the kind of persona he felt he had to acquire in order to be a folk singer.

Indeed, for all of Dylan's jagged and angular singing power, most of his protest songs do not quite come off. Compare "Blowin' in the Wind," one of his best protest songs, with Guthrie's "Pastures of Plenty," Hooker's "Down Child," any of the songs of the freedom movement or Big Bill Broonzy's "Get Back." These songs are all personal statements. They move, as genuine feeling most often does, from the specific to the general. By involving the listener in their particular predicament, the singers automatically involve him in the more universal predicament this problem reflects. In comparison "Blowin' in the Wind" seems abstract and impersonal, retreating very often into easy clichés and vague generalities. Songs like "Masters of War" and "Pawn in Their Game" are trite, simplistic and often misleading. "A Hard Rain's A-Gonna Fall," one of his best songs, is not a protest song at all in the accepted sense of the word. In fact, only once, in "The Lonesome Death of Hattie Carroll," does Dylan actually create anything as concrete and moving as the songs mentioned above.

Yet there were two traits which saved Dylan from becoming simply a creature of his own insubstantial mythological world. These two traits, again typical of his generation, were an exact and unsentimental feeling for the nuances of his personal relationships, especially with women, and a morbid and surprising sense of humor which always seemed to confront total chaos in a deadpan, understated and unnerving manner.

Dylan's love songs are often bitter, which is certainly true, but in songs like "It's All Over Now, Baby Blue," "Don't Think Twice, It's All Right," "It Ain't Me, Babe," and "Love Minus Zero/No Limit," Dylan has managed to make fresh and touching statements about essentially hackneyed situations. Dylan's lovers are all anti-heroes, restless, almost never dependable, concerned but cynical, guarded and resigned to inevitable failure. The fact that some of these songs are sung with a rock-and-roll background and others are not is completely irrelevant. "Like A Rolling Stone" says something and was successful in the popular music field where most songs say nothing.

In songs like "Talking World War III Blues," "A Hard Rain's A-Gonna Fall," and especially "Ballad of a Thin Man," Dylan shows himself to be a skillful and disturbing black humorist. His eerie, improbable landscape, peopled by clowns and dwarfs, is constantly threatened by chaos and destruction. Dylan's attitude toward Mr. Jones in "Ballad of a Thin Man" is revealing. Mr. Jones is a hip intellectual, successful and secure in his rationalism, thrust suddenly and brutally into an insane and malicious world where he does not know what to do. What lies at the center of these songs is not anger, though these are genuinely angry songs, but terror, a peculiar terror, half humorous and half despairing. Here, if anywhere, Dylan is the voice of his generation.

It is not at all surprising that Dylan rebelled against this image of himself as a protest singer and songwriter. His rebellion took the form, as he saw it, of a rejection of politics and political action. And yet this is not quite accurate. He was not rejecting politics, because in this era it is impossible. No one can step outside the war in Vietnam, for instance, and by saying nothing about it Dylan is supporting American policy. What Dylan actually rejected was a false image of politics, the abstractions he had confused with political thought and the clichés he had confused with political reality. He said, in rejecting political action, that he felt he was being stereotyped. He was wrong only insofar as his view was limited. He was becoming one more stereotyped progressive in a gallery full of radical wraiths, but he himself had contributed at least one picture to the gallery wall, a self-portrait in fact. He had come to the Village seeking a myth, had walked and talked and sang and wrote that myth and had no one to blame for what happened as a result of his behavior.

But now that Dylan is free of politics he is beginning to create another myth, starting to don another mask. His new persona is rather hard to describe while still in its formative stage. At this point it seems to involve motorcycles, the deliberate destruction of all meaning, with Dylan coming on mysteriously as a kind of hip Hell's Angel, a pop art folk-bard, a wild combination of Steve McQueen, John Lennon, Marisol and Bo Diddley. Again Dylan has hit upon something that satisfies a profound need, for him as well as his audience, though in this case his admirers are the adventurous and far-from-simple adolescents who move restlessly about on the outer fringes of the middle class.

It seems that Dylan, having once lost himself inside a self-made myth, can only function as a performer by creating a new myth. Possibly this mythic persona has become an integral part of Dylan's artistic personality. And yet, paradoxically, the other part of him which touches reality, which confronts terror and love, is still very much there. Despite himself Dylan continues to communicate.

JOHN WESLEY HARDING

●

JON LANDAU

White rock is moving in a single direction at this time. The trend is unmistakably toward the redefinition of the musical structures that have been identified with it during its existence as a recognizable musical idiom. Bob Dylan alone stands outside this development. He alone moves in circles, not lines. Or at least Dylan is the only major artist in the field whose circularity has become evident. For the space between *Bob Dylan* and *John Wesley Harding* is that between birth and rebirth, not that between beginning and end. Unlike the Beatles, whose basic identity has been totally altered in the space between *Meet the Beatles* and *Magical Mystery Tour,* Dylan achieves a continuity through growth seldom found in the development of a popular artist. (Although the Beatles may bring it all back home yet.)

This continuity was more evident in the progression of Dylan's first seven albums than it is on his latest, *JWH.* The source of that continuity was derived from every facet of his recordings: the continuity of his use of the blues, his humor and, especially, his reliance on the melodramatic and the mythical. Musically, continuity has been sustained by the self-imposed limits he has placed on the structure of his melodies, his guitar style and his almost static use of the harmonica. (John Lennon gave that up after *Hard Days' Night.*) With the advent of *JWH* Dylan has totally redefined himself by breaking with much that was consistently in evidence on the albums immediately preceding this one. And the breaks with the past that he has made here are of greater import than any of his earlier breaks with his own past—such as the shift away from pure self-accompaniment. Yet the major break I wish to discuss—Dylan's abandonment of myths and melodrama that dominated all of his earlier albums—evidences Dylan's growth as an artist and when fully understood heightens the sense of continuity one can derive from his entire career. It is a break which allows Dylan to get more in touch with himself and with his audience.

The myth to which I refer has certainly not been a static one. Dylan has redefined it with each successive album, including *JWH*. However, the underlying myth of *JWH*, namely, Bob Dylan, a moderate man, is a qualitatively different kind of myth than all the previous ones Dylan has created about himself. And to really understand its importance one has to look at his development from the beginning to see how Dylan has used myth, how he has defined his myth at each successive stage in his career and how, on *JWH*, he completely shatters the vestiges of the myths that had dominated all of his previous recordings.

The Dylan process began with a folk-singer stance. On his first album, *Bob Dylan*, he defined himself as a son of Woody Guthrie. Obviously the image was only skin deep. The comparison between Guthrie and Dylan was an incongruity from the very beginning—yet Dylan did his best to come on like the comparison was real. In a most un-Guthrie-like gesture, Dylan's first subject emerges on the album as "death." The album ended with "See that My Grave Is Kept Clean," which is an inherently melodramatic selection for ending an album and an inherently absurd one for anybody but Blind Lemon Jefferson to have recorded. While Dylan seems to have wanted to live up to his image very much he had already been overinfluenced by the urban folk-types' concern with bigness and overstatement. The self-consciousness which separates this type of artist from a Woody Guthrie unfortunately fell very heavily on Dylan even on his earliest work. Even on the lovely "Song to Woody" the attempt at understatement at the end of the song simply magnifies the feeling of overstatement that Dylan's vocal mannerisms impart to the song. In fact, the obvious affectations illustrate that for all his folk antiquarian and eclectic impulses the earliest Dylan was uncomfortable with his material. It doesn't seem to say enough to satisfy him. Most of his interpretations are really whole new songs like his "Freight Train Blues," which has nothing to do with Roy Acuff's version. The overall feel of the album is a tension between Dylan and his material, Dylan's need to impose his own drama on the drama of the originals. The resulting attempts at saying something important, something big, will contain the seeds of the Dylan myth of the creative genius, the artist as a totally free man and the totally self-reliant and unique individual.

The fact that Dylan did choose to create his style out of the sources of the past, however, cannot be overlooked, for his antiquarianism, his love of the simple, has a tendency to reassert itself at times you least expect it throughout his career. And his consistent use of the blues—the folk style he has been most at home with and most competent at—shows that his feel for music never gets too far ahead of his sense of the past.

The transition from folk singer to folk writer and in turn to folk prophet is the substance of *Freewheelin'* and *The Times They Are A-Changin'*, and it is in these two works that Dylan's myth and melodrama define themselves. In this regard a song like "Masters of War" is most revealing. It is, of course, a song of deep hatred and it illustrates Dylan's polarizing and dualistic tendencies. The Masters are on one side and he is on the other. Neither his own righteousness (as the first person of the song) nor their wickedness is ever questioned. Not only does he end up by wishing the death of his enemies but he wants to bury them himself and then stand over their graves until he is sure that they're dead. What is jarring here is not Dylan's political judgments—they are unobjectionable by themselves—but the unreality of Dylan's response to this situation. He is creating an abstraction, a stereotype, upon which he can justify his hatred, not the other way around. His response is not to someone he knows, but to someone he imagines, and the only possible result is a mythical picture of his subject and his feelings. The overstatement and the overkill of the imagery and narrative of the song strain the credibility of even those fully in agreement with the political implications of the song. The entire conception suffers from its one-dimensionality. Yet it was a dimension that Dylan could put his finger on very well indeed. His vocal style, his droning guitar, the charisma of his performance, elevated the song to a very high level of kitsch. There is a "touchability" and a monomania that give the work great power, not unlike the power of a demagogue. Yet it never goes beyond the boundaries of myth and it proves to be a short step indeed between Dylan creating a myth and becoming its prophet.

I am not unaware of the fact that there was more than "Masters of War" on *Freewheelin'*. It is obvious that songs of this type constitute only a fraction of Dylan's work, even on this particular album. However, I do think it the most revealing strain to look at for purposes of comparison with *JWH* for reasons that will become evident shortly. There is, in fact, a continuing tension between Dylan's continually evolving mythical view of himself and society and his own desire to get outside of it. Hence, "Corrina, Corrina" falls completely outside the frame of reference I am using to discuss Dylan's early work. But "Don't Think Twice," which on the surface seems very little like "Masters of War," is lyrically really not so different. Dylan casts himself in the same light, with reference to his subjects, i.e., above them. Also, his lack of sympathy for the girl, the totalness of the putdown, the necessity to come right out and say it, the lack of subtlety, are all characteristics of Dylan's one-dimensional myth-making. It's just that in "Don't Think Twice" the beauty of Dylan's vocal-guitar-harmonica performance doesn't really say what the words do, and; in fact, really transforms the verbal meaning of the song into something much deeper and much less coarse.

Nor is all of this myth talk to criticize the early Dylan —an irrelevant function at best. Dylan created a myth that already existed. In a very real sense we could call it the myth of the adolescent, the myth of self-righteousness, the myth of our own purity. Dylan was the only one on the scene who had the self-awareness, charisma, talent, imagination and lack of repression to give structure to this world view. This would tend to explain why he attracted the following he did, in contrast to his numerous and minor contemporaries. Beyond that, we can say that Dylan was not only able to put his finger on the world view, but he was, unlike some of his adulators, never satisfied with what he created for very long. He has always had an unrelenting capacity to grow, a capacity which is too great to sustain any particular myth for too long, or for him to lose control of it. Part of his genius—a word not to be used lightly—is certainly his capacity to always remain one step ahead of the game.

When we come to *The Times They Are A-Changin'* the myth is unquestionably the dominating force, and this album, along with *Highway 61*, is the one which is most dominated by Dylan's melodramatic and stereotyping tendencies. The imagery on *Times* goes back to the grand myth, Christianity. The song "Times" parrots the New Testament "the first will be last," and thereby gives expression to Dylan's new verbal love, the apocalypse. Dylan's apocalyptic vision manifests itself throughout the album. First, there is his religious optimism: the times are changing. An inevitable, unquestionable change. An inexorable change. That is the feeling that the almost droning guitar and Dylan's voice impart to the lyrics. The change is also to be all-encompassing. And then the specific, biblical imagery: "rattle your walls," "beyond your command," "first one now will later be last" and "the curse it is cast." This Dylan could have been preaching in the church where Otis Redding learned how to sing. Again, there is the lack of subtlety, the all-encompassing nature of the vision, the lack of self-doubt.

Even more so than the title song of the album, "When the Ships Come In" showed off the apocalyptic myth of this Dylan. The entire imagery is biblical: "Pharaoh's tomb," "the foes will rise," the use of the ship itself as an image and the concluding wish that the foes will drown. Shades of "Masters of War." This song is truly frightening in its righteous zeal. It is vengeful in the Old Testament sense of the word. It is the work of a profoundly religious mentality, but Bob Dylan didn't have to go any farther than the good old USA to get into this kind of religion. And if this wasn't enough, Dylan ends this album with "Restless Farewell." (When he was doing this material at concerts he would finsh the concert with "Ships" and encore with "Restless Farewell.") It is hard to conceive of what could follow Dylan's vision of destruction, but "Restless Farewell" does the trick. After having sold his audience on the impending revolution Dylan tried to tell them that he is not really a prophet, that he cherishes his freedom, that he wishes to stand alone, that he will bid them all farewell and not give a damn. That desire, combined with the self-pitying last verse of the song, offers very strong parallels with a self-destructiveness not uncommon to messianism of any kind. Yet one can't help but feel listening to the album in retrospect that Dylan himself realizes that his apocalypse in a quasipolitical setting has played itself out. It has degenerated into a Hollywood production—into pure kitsch—and Dylan, seeing that, tries to break with it on his next album—unsuccessfully.

In the poems on the back of *Another Side of Bob Dylan,* Dylan shows his sensitivity to the fact that he has backed himself into an artistic corner and that he now wants out. The problem with the myth of the apocalypse is that there is no place you can go with it. Jesus promised he would come again—a promise that never actually materialized. What could Dylan promise after telling us of the time when the good will win and the bad shall lose. It *clearly* was time to de-escalate and on the surface that is what it appears Dylan did. With this de-escalation Dylan's political-minded enthusiasts began to feel sold out. What they of course failed to realize was that Bob Dylan never was political. He was simply acting out a religious allegory on the political landscape of contemporary America. His primary concerns were on the face of it moral, and moral in a religious, Jewish, Christian sense. If he had lived fifteen hundred years ago he would probably have been a Talmudic moralist, and two thousand years ago an apostle or savior. What happens on *Another Side* is that Dylan begins to discard the political landscape, but retains the mannerisms, style and content of an essentially one-dimensional moralist.

Only now he is a poet instead of a prophet. There are attempts at understatement, subtlety and depth, like on "Spanish Harlem Incident," just as on *Times* there had been the jarringly out of place "One Too Many Mornings" and the pre-apocalyptic "Spanish Boots." Yet Dylan has at best only begun to pick up the pieces of reality. "I Don't Believe You" was his first real rock-and-roll song and was a pure delight, giving off the kind of charm and cuteness Dylan is so capable of and uses so rarely another brilliant example is "If You Got to Go Now, Go Now" the best recording of which was done by Mannfred Mann). He should record it with a band someday, if he wants to. "My Back Pages," with its denouncement of the old myth, shows Dylan's vast capacity at self-analysis and criticism and his ability to be honest with both himself and his audience. Yet the advances remain on the surface. Dylan still sounds like he is singing about the apocalypse—and Dylan's voice always tells us so much more than his words. Even when he renounces the fantasies of the past in "My Back Pages," he creates new ones in "It Ain't Me, Babe." And the "Chimes of Freedom" shows that his love of the majestic, big, epic type of material is an all but permanent side of Bob Dylan. How many artists would come right out and say they are singing for "every hung-up person in the whole wide universe"? Yet, for all its obviousness, the album had undeniable power, especially when it first came out. The fact that we were buying the records shows where we all were at. There seems to be all the signs of the search for the constant, static truth. And just as on *Times,* after Dylan completely wins his audience over he ends on a note of rejection—"It Ain't Me, Babe."

When Bob Dylan switched to an electrified sound the furor that ensued was indicative of the emotional investment so many of his fans had put in him. I was at Forest Hills for his first real electric concert, and the response he evoked from those who six months earlier had thought him a semi-deity showed the frightening possibilities Dylan possessed as "spokesman for his generation." The absurd thing of course is the fact that ten months after the hostility and the boos, these same people found themselves standing in line to buy *Blonde on Blonde.* As usual it was just that he was a little too far ahead of the game.

The reason why Dylan switched to electrified instrumentation is fairly obvious. He had simply exhausted all the possibilities of his guitar-harmonica accompaniment. In that his brilliant melodic sense is essentially limited in its range, Dylan undoubtedly found that by adding a band he could extend his range without having to transcend the limitations of his compositional abilities. In addition, perhaps he had gotten a little tired of the lone-man-against-the-world image. Maybe he just liked the company.

Bringing It All Back Home had the electrified sound. But. interestingly, with the exception of one cut, they were all blues. I think it reasonable to say that a very strong side of Dylan had already recognized the ultimate vacuity of the previous stances. The blues side of this album was another attempt to de-escalate. However, de-escalate or not, Dylan has never been able to get too far away from high seriousness. Consequently we got side two, which contains some of Dylan's best serious songs prior to *JWH.* The two particularly arresting numbers were "Mr. Tambourine Man" and "It's Alright, Ma," both notable because they clearly take Dylan beyond the one dimension of his earlier seriousness. The multilevelness and diversity of imagery in "Mr. Tambourine Man" is comparatively innovative. The simplicity of Dylan's requests, the lack of up-tightness and the artistic perspective with which this song was both written and performed, the fact that the Byrds could do it justice by performing it in their cyclical, unmelodramatic style, all this points up the fact that this song is a break with Dylan's chain of dialectical myth, his polarizing tendencies.

"It's Alright, Ma" does exactly the opposite. It is the ultimate statement of the earlier myth, only this time the depth of Dylan's vision created a reality that transcends the purely mythical quality of something like "Chimes of Freedom." The polarity is there but voiced so honestly and with such brilliance and sense of awareness of where both Dylan and this country are at, that the song is totally credible. Hence, on *Bringing It All Back Home*, we get the ultimate dialectic within a dialectic: Dylan himself has become polarized between an aesthetically brilliant statement of what all his past work has led to, and an aesthetically brilliant attempt to transcend the limitations of the self-created myth. And as on the previous two albums, he ends on a note of rejection with "Baby Blue." The resolution of the conflict in Dylan's work, to the extent that there has been one, is quite delayed, and on *Highway 61* the old myth reasserts itself, although in a somewhat disguised manner. In a sense this disguise is embodied in the brilliant accompaniment that dominates the album as well as in Dylan's superb vocal work. Dylan is one of the finest singers of rock-and-roll who ever lived—the truest slogan that Columbia's PR people have ever come up with is the "Nobody sings Dylan like Dylan" thing—and it is on this album that his abilities as a vocalist begin to come into full bloom. He is truly at home with the band (the instrumental work on the previous album was really not very good at all), and when he sings a beautiful song like "It Takes A Lot to Laugh, It Takes A Train to Cry," he can be really relaxed and drive the thing home. (The song itself impresses me as being a superior statement of the "Don't Think Twice," "It Ain't Me, Babe" theme.)

Despite the musical virtues contained on this album compared to previous ones, there are some real problems. Dylan's basic antipathy and hostility to all kinds of people has multiplied itself many times over and the most powerful works on this album are flat-out putdowns. On the back of this album he talks about the wipe-out factory, but on the album it is he who seems intent on wiping out things, not unlike what he was trying to do in "Masters of War." "Like A Rolling Stone" is of course a putdown, most likely the best Dylan ever wrote. What is annoying about it to me is its self-righteousness, its willingness to judge others without judging oneself, the proselytizing in disguise for Dylan's own way of life. Let me hasten to add, apropos Dylan's particular genius, that the structure of the song, his vocal performance and the instrumental arrangement are perfectly suited to communicating his hostility. The first two lines of each verse have an ascending chord progression of c-d-minor-E-minor-F-G. Each line moves straight up in a perfect creation of a melodramatic feeling. And the cry of "aah" before the fourth verse is simply brilliant vocal work. It is Dylan's genius again that no matter where he is at he has the power to make you feel it and to pull you along, perhaps because none of us is so far removed from where he is at that we can't grasp what it is he is trying to communicate.

The bitterness of "Like A Rolling Stone" is magnified still further in "Ballad of A Thin Man." Dylan's mood in this instance can be characterized as one of overkill. When he sang "Only A Pawn In Their Game," he seemed to have realized that sometimes even the most guility are not the most guilty, that they are a product of situations created by people other than themselves. In this song he wants to blame Mr. Jones for things that aren't his fault and the result is, to me, an embarrassingly hateful putdown of unreal and wholly fictitious entity. It is a meaningless attack on forces which Dylan doesn't really understand at this point, or forces that he simply can't control. At the other end, however, "Desolation Row" must be counted a logical extension of the "It's Alright, Ma" mode and is a fantastic achievement. Those two songs taken together, in fact, give us a fantastically real picture of the good old U.S.A. 1968. This Dylan is infinitely more political than the earlier one, and in a much more real way. Yet what Dylan himself says about where he was at this time should not be overlooked. He wrote on the back of the record involvement was lifelessness. Most of the songs on the album show that he really meant it.

And then came *Blonde on Blonde* and involvement was no longer the enemy and all of a sudden Dylan was writing about love again. The only other album where this theme had been central was *Another Side* and there it was still tied to Dylan's religious, epic style and was as unreal as everything else during that phase. On *Blonde on Blonde* Dylan shows phenomenal abilities in the area of love songs. His selection of Charlie McCoy's Nashville band to accompany was an act of genius. Those musicians showed themselves capable of the kind of fluid yet structured sound that Dylan utilized so brilliantly when just performing alone. While at times this fluidity seems to be excessive to the point of liquidness, resulting in the observation that the sound is not unlike Muzak in its overall effect, what is overlooked in this insight is Dylan's contribution to the total sound. For the purpose of this instrumental fluidity is simply to give Dylan a point of reference against which he can create a genuine artistic tension. (Nobody has ever said Dylan's voice reminds them of Muzak.) The smoothness of the band is a perfect counterweight to Dylan's toughness. The height of this type of interaction is reached on the chorus of "Memphis Blues Again," in which Dylan gives us "Oh, mama, could this really be the end," over the perfectly symmetrical organ-drum sound. It should be recalled how nicely Kenneth Buttrey shatters the fluidity at the end of the line. A most un-Muzak-like gesture.

On the whole this is instrumentally Dylan's finest pre-*JWH* album, and his own performance is beautifully relaxed, controlled and yet soulful. The hostility is vastly reduced. He is smiling again and not the cynical smile of *Highway 61*, either. "Rainy Day Women, #12 & #35" really did set the tone for this work. I was particularly taken with the richness and complexity of "Visions of Johanna," perhaps the high point of the album (especially Dylan's vocal and the drumming), and the power of "Sooner or Later." About this last number there is great reliance on the clichés of "Like A Rolling Stone" but the impact is vastly different. Because on *Highway 61* he could put down involvement and on this cut he could sing "I really did try to get close to you." Or elsewhere, "You break just like a little girl."

Concurrently with this verbal opening up by Dylan, there is a striking revitalization of his blues style on "Obviously Five Believers," possibly his best blues performance. The vocal here is truly the entire message and on this cut we are listening to a genuine blues artist.

One of the most pleasing things about *Blonde on Blonde* is that by shifting the focus from the impossible epics of earlier works to subjects which were closer to himself personally Dylan was able to create a more powerful and lasting artistic tension than he ever was out of things like "With God On Our Side." The tension of a painfully real work like "Visions of Johanna" is infinitely more pervasive and lasting than that of the earlier work because, whereas "With God On Our Side" becomes less real with successive listenings, "Vision" becomes more so. And anyway, if you don't like what he is saying, you can just move your mind over to those musicians and to just Dylan's vocal. For the Dylan of *Blonde on Blonde* is in many ways a performer, a musician before he is a lyricist, and his actual performance as a singer on this album is one of the most brilliant rock performances ever recorded.

With *Blonde on Blonde* Dylan was well on the way to closing the first cycle in his artistic development, the jorney from folk singer to rock star, which took him five years to accomplish. In that time he explored and eventually exhausted the artistic potential of his recurring stances as prophet and polarizer, teller of truths, moralist and creator of epics. The originator of the eight-minute rock song, the arch foe of all authority, the extreme resistance to involvement (he did end three albums in succession with songs indicating as much), the stance of the self-reliant artist, in fact, the entire metamorphosis, from "Song To Woody" to "Ballad of A Thin Man," had come to an end. His first recording after the interim of a sixteen-month absence is a thoroughly startling redirection for him, and justifies being called a new birth of his artistic potential, for it is clearly the beginning of a new Dylan myth—the myth of the moderate man. The new myth is the product of an adult Dylan. The essentially adolescent quest for certain truths, static imagery, finality and the underlying hostile world view which allowed him to create his compelling but ultimately unsatisfying visions have been superseded. We will get no more "When the Ships Come In," "It's Alright, Ma," "Chimes of Freedom" or "Like A Rolling Stone" from Bob Dylan. For whatever the virtues of these works, they have been abandoned along with their faults in favor of "a whole other level."

John Wesley Harding is a profoundly egotistical album. For an album of this kind to be released amidst *Sgt. Pepper, Their Satanic Majesties' Request, Strange Days* and *After Bathing At Baxter's*, somebody must have had a lot of confidence in what he was doing. Hence the first noteworthy fact about this album is its essential lack of insecurity. Dylan seems to feel no need to respond to the predominant trends in pop music at all. And he is the only major pop artist about whom this can be said. The Dylan of *John Wesley Harding* is a truly independent artist who doesn't feel responsible to anyone else, whether they be fans or his contemporaries. It is implicit, in fact, in his rejection of the formal basis of a rock band on this album that Dylan does not accept what is happening in pop music at the moment.

Of course Dylan's independence from much of what passes for the scene these days is not the product of deliberate intent but simply the result of a fundamentally different level of awareness of what is going on all around us. He appears to be one of the few intellectuals making popular music at this time and he doesn't appear to be interested in the same bill of goods that everyone else is. I doubt whether Bob Dylan would have ever pushed a Maharishi Mahesh Yogi on us. Rather, what I hear on this album is two things. The first is a fundamentally American artistic statement. That is to say that Dylan's influences and sources are primarily peculiar to American culture. The second thing is that out of his identity being tied to what is happening in this country, Dylan manifests a profound awareness of the war and how it is affecting all of us. This doesn't mean that I think any of the particular songs are about the war or that any of the songs are protests over it. All I mean to say is that Dylan has felt the war, that there is an awareness of it contained within the mood of the albums as a whole. (The only other recent pop album that strikes me in the same way is *The Notorious Byrd Brothers.*) Dylan's songs acknowledge the war in the same way that songs like "Magical Mystery Tour" and "Fool On the Hill" ignore it. They acknowledge it by attemping to be real, by attempting to not speak falsely and by playing fewer games than ever before. Bob Dylan, 1968, could not write a song analogous to "Magical Mystery Tour" just because he knows too much.

The Dylan of *JWH* is profoundly moral. Of course Dylan has always been a moralist; on this album the nature of his moralizing is drastically altered. In the past his judgments were the inevitable results of unreal, stereotyped depictions of good against bad. They were the kitsch moralisms of young America—pop moralizing at its best. The type of moral judgments Dylan is making on this album are really more of a prudential kind of wisdom which is the outgrowth of very real narratives that avoid the one-dimensional stereotyping of the past. "Don't go mistaking paradise for the home across the road" is a form of moral advice, a moral suggestion, not a final answer or an exaggerated dividing up of what is good and what is bad as on *The Times They Are A-Changin'*. The same is true of the earnest plea that "If you don't underestimate me, I won't underestimate you."

This difference in the quality of Dylan's moral outlook is shown in the difference in vocal style he now uses to communicate his lyrics. In the past Dylan's vocal style has been a perfect vehicle for the melodramatic myths of his youth. On this transitional album he redefines his vocal style more than he ever has before. There is genuine understatement, there is an attempt at expressing different moods through different styles and there is an attempt to be honest without affecting honesty. He doesn't always succeed—some of his singing is painfully awkward, as on "I Pity the Poor Immigrant"—yet he is really trying to do things differently and it is good to hear it. His two best vocal performances on this album, "All Along the Watch Tower" and "I'll Be Your Baby Tonight," reflect a vocal sophistication and honesty you won't hear anywhere else these days. Dylan's charisma, timing and coloration, when functioning at their best, transcend just about anything.

To round out his own performance vocally he again chose Charlie McCoy and Kenneth Buttrey to accompany him. Buttrey is a great drummer, especially for Dylan, and McCoy's bass playing is without flaw. It must astound people that these two crackers (that's what McCoy calls his new band) have just been floating around Nashville spending their talents on studio sessions. And then somebody tells us that this is the way that all those Nashville cats play.

What I see on *JWH*, then, is a Dylan prepared to confront reality without many of the crutches of the past, with a new flexibility to vocal style and musicians who can sustain that flexibility, and a Dylan with a lyrical sense that is unafraid to judge but that judges differently and more responsibly than before. He achieves a genuine detachment from his work that allows him to do several things at once without seeming to contradict himself. On this album he is above all a musician, a singer first, and in looking at how these overall characteristics manifest themselves on the particular songs of the album, it will help us to look especially at how Dylan is using his voice.

The four songs on the record I want to talk about are "All Along the Watch Tower," "Dear Landlord," "Along the Cove" and "I'll Be Your Baby Tonight." The first lends itself to a certain amount of interpretation, but ultimately one is prevented from coming up with anything too concrete due to the lyrics' incongruities, if one confines oneself to just the lyrics. Rather than see the song as something to be interpreted, I tend to see it as an evocation of a mood, a mood created primarily by the way Dylan sings his words. Suppose he sang "There must be some way out of here" softly, in ¾ time. Supposing he was laughing while he sang it. That would change the meaning, such as there may be, drastically. But now suppose he scatted in place of using words, and that he did the scatting precisely as he sings the words. You'd probably respond quite similarly, except your response would be less specific due to the lack of words to focus on. That is, I think that the line "There must be some way out of here" is a great line to sing in the tone of voice Dylan uses, not the other way round.

Of course the words give you a good alternative way at getting to what it is he is singing about. They can be the same kind of tip-off that the card in *Don't Look Back* reading "Dig Yourself" was. It's just that I think it more natural to respond first to the music and then to the words when one is listening to a song, and I think that is in fact what most people probably do.

Or, finally, to put it another way, in *Don't Look Back* Dylan tells the *Time* man that he is as good a singer as Caruso. And, in fact, Dylan is comparable to an opera singer because at his best he is using his voice to say things for him and is not just relying on verbal levels of meaning. On some songs he could probably sing the whole thing in French and it wouldn't be that much harder to understand him. Just like you can understand the Beatles when they sing "I Wanna Hold Your Hand" in German.

All of which is not say that the lyrics are of no importance. Particular lines in "All Along the Watch Tower" give tremendous focus to the emotive qualities of the vocal. Lines like "life is but a joke," "you and I have been through that," "let us not speak falsely" and, of course, the opening line. The overall impression that I get is of a kind of updated "My Back Pages" in which Dylan is trying to communicate his realization that life is not a joke, that the hour is getting late, that unlike the earlier stages of his career, perhaps recently he hasn't been serious enough. The overwhelming feeling is that of immediacy, but a controlled immediacy—it is not, for example, desperation. Perhaps the one word to use is forceful.

"Dear Landlord" is similarly given a recognizable layer of meaning which is in turn obscured somewhat by incongruent images. And again, more striking than the words in and of themselves is Dylan's interpretative powers as a vocalist. While the landlord has been thought to represent all manner of authority—everyone from his manager to the government—that type of speculation is unimportant. What is important is

Dylan's attitude toward the subject. He is not out for blood, yet at the same time he isn't willing to give in. He is empathetic but realistic. "If you don't underestimate me I won't underestimate you." I will recognize you but you are going to have to deal with me. This is a truly incredible transformation in attitude when seen in contrast with "Ballad of A Thin Man." The role of the vocal is totally complimentary to the verbal level of meaning. What I particularly dig is the firmness in Dylan's voice. No reliance on exaggerated mannerisms but a simple and direct statement. Also, the melodic structure of the song is one of the most sophisticated Dylan has ever devised and his piano playing is quite incisive and competent.

Dylan's greater reliance on vocal style is most in evidence in the last two songs on the album, both of which are singer's songs. In "Down Along the Cove" and "I'll Be Your Baby Tonight" he has given us very little to interpret verbally, possibly because he wants to make himself perfectly explicit, and possibly because he wants his singing to do his talking for him.

"Down Along the Cove" is a blues without the artifacts we have come to expect from white blues: no Mike Bloomfield. The words border on cuteness but basically there is no real barrier between Dylan's voice and our response to it. The need for words at this point is more habit than anything else. "Lord have mercy, sure is good to see you coming today," "Down along the cove I spied my little bundle of joy," and "Everyone knows we're in love, yes they understand," clichés all of them, but given new life in the act of Dylan's singing them. It just feels so right that after all the bigness Dylan should wind up writing and feeling something so simple and so basic. The marvelous demonstrativeness with which he renders the vocal lines is just perfect.

And then "I'll Be Your Baby Tonight" and we go from the blues to c&w without even thinking about it: the bridge is perfectly crossed. And again we are given clichés which aren't clichés and that fantastically expressive voice. This song shows Dylan's absolute mastery of the sources of his music. The break in which he sings "You won't regret it" is so like rock-and-roll and so much more than we have come to expect, so much more personal. There is an easiness and a relaxed quality to it all that is coupled with a realization that he really means it that is virtually cathartic. Such a simple performance, yet so subtle and so complex. And, please note, this album ends on a note of acceptance in marked contrast to the three albums that ended with "Restless Farewell," "It Ain't Me, Babe" and "Baby Blue."

What we are forced to see on *JWH* is Bob Dylan growing up. In every possible respect. On this album Dylan's songs are no longer just him, they are separate identities which exist apart from their author. And we see Dylan moving toward an identity of himself as a classical artist, not as just a pop artist. He sees the distinction himself and is willing to accept it. I think we are also beginning to see a Dylan who is prepared more than ever before to accept uncertainty, to give up the search for the finite, a Dylan who no longer feels that each of his songs must tell us everything he knows. He is prepared to look at the pieces of reality, and let the miller tell his tale.

As a musician we can see him as he sees himself—seriously. It isn't all just something he does so that we will hear his words. He seems to realize that on a record his musical performance has always been, and will always be, pre-eminent, and he is prepared to utilize his fantastic talents as a vocalist to their fullest, even though he hasn't begun to approach his potential in this area.

At both levels he seems determined to search for authenticity, which is perhaps what was most often lacking in his earlier work. And to the extent that he is able to approach that state of being able to create without the aid of the earlier myths, to the extent that he can sustain an identity of being a "moderate man"—which he certainly does on *JWH*—to that extent he will come much closer to approaching the tradition of the genuine folk-artists whom Dylan modeled his career after in the beginning. With the reduction in the need for a self-conscious stance, he has made the first step toward becoming a very real kind of modern folk singer, for when I hear Dylan now, and this is of course simply my own response to what is happening on *JWH,* I am reminded of Woody Guthrie and of Robert Johnson. And the Bob Dylan of *JWH* may well bear more in common with either of those men than he does with anyone else who is performing in April of 1968.

ROCK LYRICS ARE POETRY (MAYBE)

●

ROBERT CHRISTGAU

Until it narrowed its programming, there was one hip radio station in New York, the station of the college kids and the bright suburban adolescents and the young professionals and the hippies—your station, if you're within range: WOR-FM. Not that there was much choice—AM radio in New York is antediluvian. But for a while, WOR-Stereo did seem to try. Its playlist was flexible and enormous and its deejays enjoyed much freedom. WOR was the home of the born-again Murray the K, with his "attitude music" and his tell-it-like-it-is (baby) cool, and coming up strong behind was the latetime (ten-to-two) jock, a spade named Rosko. Rosko emcees at the Village Theater, which is a story in itself, but not this one. This one is about Rosko and Kahlil Gibran, now-deceased author of a dozen or so quasi-poetic, pseudo-religious texts, the most famous of which is *The Prophet.**

Rosko quit WOR when the station decided to chase after the post-adolescent AM audience with a tight oldies playlist, but he had more in common with all the screaming-meemies than he probably suspected. Just like Cousin Brucie or B. M. R., he did not so much announce a show as preside over a ritual. Cultism is not confined to teenyboppers. All four jazz fans out there should remember Symphony Sid, who played virtually the same cuts night after night for literally years, announcing the same Stan Getz / Oscar Brown, Jr. / Nina Simone / Willie

* Already I can hear the screaming. You *like* Kahlil Gibran, right? So let's have it out. A critical essay—consider yourself forewarned—illumines nothing so much as the prejudices of its author. My tastes in music derive largely from Alan Freed and Thelonious Monk, but my tastes in poetry and philosophy were pounded into me by a phalanx of Ivy League professors. I think Kahlil Gibran is the worst kind of trash, much worse than Harold Robbins, say, because good people take him seriously.

Bobo / Miles Davis in the same throat-cancer growl. Rosko did Sid one better. He played the same stuff every night, Beatles / Stones / Dylan, plus hip hits and various cult heroes—Richie Havens, Vanilla Fudge, Jimi Hendrix, Big Brother, Judy Collins. Then, to ice the cake, he would climax his show with a reverent reading from Kahlil Gibran. "And he who has deserved to drink from the ocean of life deserves to drink from your little stream"; "The soul unfolds itself, like a lotus of countless petals"; "Vague and nebulous is the beginning of all things, but not their end, and I would fain have you remember me as a beginning," et cetera. In the background was poor Ravi Shankar, who hadn't been so ill-used since that nameless film poetaster discovered the quadruple-exposure raga. Rosko's fans loved it. They flooded the station with requests for printed versions, which Rosko answered with the sweet suggestion that they buy the book. A Gibran boomlet—you may even have been part of it.

I hope not. Admirers of books like *The Prophet* crave the enthrallment of poetry without the labor. For poetry—the Greek *poiein* means to construct or make—involves labor, in the creation and the understanding. Perhaps even too much so. Ever since the Industrial Revolution moved art out of the mainstream and produced the artistic rebel, whose avant-garde art comprises virtually all the good work in this century and much in the last, the arts have moved slowly and sadly beyond ordinary people. Artists have turned inward and concerned themselves with form. Not without superb results, either—whatever disservices they are done in the classroom, Proust, Yeats, Pollock, Stravinsky, and all the others have produced work which is not only marvelous technically, but very real emotionally, to those who know the language. The problem is, not many do—art is still not very respectable, and it's a lot more trouble than it used to be. What's worse, many who take the trouble succeed imperfectly, and turn to mass art or kitsch.

I want to say right now that none of the categories I'm going to be using are worth much. All but a few artists resist categories; the good ones usually confound them altogether. So a term like "rock" is impossibly vague; it denotes, if anything, something historical rather than aesthetic. "Mass art" and "kitsch" are pretty vague as well. Let's say that mass art is intended only to divert, entertain, pacify—Mantovani, Jacqueline Susann, *Muscle Beach Party,* etc. Kitsch is a more snobbish concept, and a more sophisticated product. It usually has the look of slightly out-of-date avant-garde in order to give its audience the illusion of aesthetic pleasure, whatever that is. An important distinction, I think, is that many of the craftsmen who make kitsch believe thoroughly in what they are doing. That may be true of the creators of mass art, too, but their attitude is more businesslike—they don't worry about "art," only commercial appeal.

I think it is just because they didn't worry about art that many of the people who ground out the rock-and-roll of the fifties—not only the performers, but all the background people—were engaged (unconsciously, of course) in, making still another kind of art, folk art. If longevity is any criterion, then I say the Five Satins will be remembered longer than the Weavers, because consciousness tends to kill what is vital in folk art. Like any rule, this one is far from perfect. Paul Anka's songs were horrible even though he didn't worry about art; Pete Seeger did, and his stuff was good. Or take a better example. In 1944, James Agee wrote an essay called "Pseudo-Folk" that deplored contemporary jazz; Duke Ellington was marvelous in his way, Agee argued, but he was also effete, and gimme that Jelly Roll. Like everything Agee wrote, "Pseudo-Folk" was sensible and heartfelt. But as it was written a young alto-sax played named Charlie Parker was creating jazz that had all the vitality of folk art plus all the complexity and technical inventiveness of the "higher" arts. You never can tell.

The same kind of transformation may be occurring right now in what used to be called rock-and-roll. It is certainly fashionable to think so. But despite all the happy praise, no one really seems to understand what is going on. Here is Robert Shelton of the New York *Times:* "More than a few conservatives in and out of the academy will be quick to dismiss serious writing by pop stars as commercial gimmickry, box-office ploys and faddist ephemera. Time, I submit, will strain out the worthless and leave us with some valuable creative works, in music and in literature, by a wholesome group of new writers." Shelton's facts are okay, but there is something dreadfully wrong about his tone—wholesome indeed. Does time really "strain out the worthless," or is it merely that we judge what is present and what is past by two entirely different and entirely proper standards? Does Shelton want to imply that "commercial gimmickry, box-office ploys and faddist ephemera" are necessarily inconsistent with "valuable creative works"? The Beatles have long since pulverized that cliché. Another example comes from Leonard Bernstein, who told a nationwide TV audience, "Many of the lyrics, in their oblique allusions and wayout metaphors, are beginning to sound like real poems." In a way Bernstein was right. Many rock lyrics sound like poems, especially to those who don't read poetry, which is almost everyone. But then, so does Kahlil Gibran.

The songwriter who seems to sound most like a poet is Bob Dylan. Dylan is such an idiosyncratic genius that it is perilous to imitate him—his faults, at worst annoying and at best invigorating, ruin lesser talents. But imitation is irresistible. Who can withstand Paul Nelson of *Little Sandy Review*, who calls Dylan "the man who in every sense revolutionized modern poetry, American folk music, popular music, and the whole of modern-day thought"? Or Jack Newfield of the *Village Voice*, wandering on about "symbolic alienation . . . new plateaus for poetic, content-conscious songwriters . . . put poetry back into song . . . reworks T. S. Eliot's classic line . . . bastard child of Chaplin, Celine and Hart Crane," while serving up tidbits from Dylan's corpus, some of which don't look so tasty on a paper plate? However inoffensive "The ghost of electricity howls in the bones of her face" sounds on vinyl, it is silly without the music. Poems are read or said. Songs are sung.

Dylan gets away with it simply because there is so much there. The refrain of "My Back Pages," his renunciation of political protest—"I was so much older then, I'm younger than that now"—may be the finest line he has ever written. Its opening—"Crimson flames tied through my ears"—may be the worst. The song bulges with metaphors and epithets, some apt, some stuck in to fill out the meter. The tired trick of using a noun for a verb to spice things up reaches an all-time low with the word (?) "foundationed." Dylan's obsession with rhyme (which he has lately begun to parody: "Hear the one with the mustache say, jeeze/I can't find my knees") compels him to match "now" with "somehow" three times in six stanzas. Twice this is totally gratuitous. But the third time—"Good and bad, I define these terms, quite clear no doubt somehow"—"somehow" becomes the final qualification in a series of qualifications, and works perfectly: a typical hit among misses.

"My Back Pages" is a bad poem. But it is a good song,

supported by a memorable refrain. The music softens our demands, the importance of what is being said somehow overbalances the flaws, and Dylan's delivery—he sound as if he's singing a hymn at a funeral—adds a portentous edge not present just in the words. Because it is a good song, "My Back Pages" can be done in other ways. The Byrds' version depends on intricate, up-tempo music that pushes the words into the background. However much they mean to David Crosby, the lyrics—except for that refrain—could be gibberish and the song would still succeed. Repeat: Dylan is a songwriter, not a poet. A few of his most perfect efforts—"Don't Think Twice," or "Just Like a Woman"—are tight enough to survive on the page. But they are exceptions.

Such a rash judgment assumes that modern poets know what they're doing. It respects the tradition that runs from Ezra Pound and William Carlos Williams down to Charles Olson, Robert Creeley, and perhaps a dozen others, the tradition that regards Allen Ginsberg as a good poet, perhaps, but a wildman. Dylan's work, with its iambics, its clackety-clack rhymes, and its scattergun images, makes Ginsberg's look like a model of decorous diction. An art advances through technical innovation. Modern American poetry assumes (and sometimes eliminates) metaphoric ability, concentrating on the use of line and rhythm to approximate (or refine) speech, the reduction of language to essentials, and "tone of voice." Dylan's only innovation is that he sings, a good way to control "tone of voice," but not enough to "revolutionize modern poetry." He may have started something just as good, but modern poetry is getting along fine, thank you.

It is fortunate that Dylan's most prominent disciple, Donovan, is not an imitator. His best stuff crosses Dylan's surrealist bent with the jazzy cleverness of thirties' songwriters like Cole Porter. Donovan makes demands on his listeners (tossing off an elliptical image like "To a leopard's you've been changin'" or devoting whole songs to his medieval fetish) and he delights in obscurity (everyone loves "Mellow Yellow" and "Sunshine Superman," but no one understands them—and don't tell me about bananas, but once again he is a songwriter, and in a much less equivocal way than Dylan. With a few tricks so well tried that they are legitimate *lingua franca,* at least for his special audience (that is us), he is working to deliver songwriting from superannuated sentimentalists like Johnny Mercer and shrewd camp followers like Tommy Boyce and Bobby Hart. In another way, Mick Jagger and Keith Richard are doing the same thing. They began by writing pungent pseudo-blues from their peculiar, ironic vantage—"Heart of Stone," "The Last Time," etc. Now, while sticking to old forms, they have allowed their sense of themselves to dominate their sense of blues tradition, producing a body of work that is as consistent and various as anything this side of Lennon-McCartney, but still song, not poetry. In the atmosphere that they and Donovan and especially Dylan have created, dozens of intelligent craftsmen—from folk-rockers like Marty Balin and John Sebastian to commercial talents like Neil Diamond and Mike Nesmith—are working down below to return popular songwriting to the honest stature it had in the thirties and beyond. The new songwriters are sentimental, not about the way the world is, but about their feelings toward it. That is a great step forward.

Dylan's influence has not always been so salutary. Lennon-McCartney and Jagger-Richard would have matured without him. But had there been no Dylan to successfully combine the vulgar and the felicitous, would we now be oppressed with the kind of vague, extravagant imagery and inane philosophizing that ruins so much good music and so impresses the Kahlil Gibran fans? I doubt it. Gary Brooker and Keith Read of Procol Harum, for an instance, obviously have a lot of talent. The opening of "Homburg" ("Your multilingual"—piano chord—"business friend") is my choice for line of the month, and the transformation of Bach in "A Whiter Shade of Pale" was brilliant and well executed. But is "A Whiter Shade of Pale" poetry? From the ads London placed in the trades, you might assume it was Shakespeare, newly unearthed. In fact there is a rumor that it was adapted from an Elizabethan poem. No matter. Full of obscure clichés ("skipped the light fandango"; "sixteen vestal virgins") with a clever (admittedly) title phrase and refrain, the overall archaic feel reinforced by literary reference ("the miller told his tale"), it sold because it did such a successful job of sounding like poetry, which, as we all know, is obscure, literary, and sort of archaic. Pure kitsch. Not much better is the self-indulgence of the Doors' Jim Morrison. "Twentieth Century-Fox," "Break on Through," "People Are Strange" and "Soul Kitchen," listed in ascending order of difficulty, all pretty much succeed. But Morrison does not stop there. He ruins "Light My Fire" with stuff like "our love becomes a funeral pyre"—Ugh! what does that mean? Nothing, but the good old romantic association of love and death is there, and that's all Morrison wanted—and noodles around in secondhand Freud in "The End." Morrison obviously regards "The End" as a masterwork, and his admirers agree. I wonder why. The music builds very nicely in an Oriental kind of way, but the dramatic situation is tedious stuff. I suppose it is redeemed by Morrison's histrionics and by the nebulousness that passes for depth among so many lovers of rock poetry.

The Doors and Procol Harum are good groups. Each has given me much pleasure. But I don't think "The End" and "A Whiter Shade of Pale" are just bad tries. I think they grow out of a bad idea, the idea that poetry—a concept not too well understood—can be incorporated into rock. This idea is old fashioned and literary in the worse sense. But young rock groups write "symbolic" lyrics that they like only because they wrote them, and they set them to music, and the cycle starts again. In a sense Morrison and Brooker-Reed are responsible for these kids in the same way Dylan is for them.

This phenomenon obviously has limitless depths (though in fairness it should be said that most groups—most of the ones you hear, anyway—avoid them), but I think its heights have been reached by a songwriter who has in abundance the one quality that Dylan, Morrison, and all their lessers lack. The songwriter is Paul Simon, and the quality is taste. Simon is so tasteful the media can't help but love him. Even Richard Goldstein has guessed that "chances are he's brought you closer to the feel and texture of modern poety than anything since the big blackout." Goldstein does pin down the reason for Simon and Garfunkel's popularity, though: "They don't make waves."

Paul Simon's lyrics are the purest, highest, and most finely wrought kitsch of our time. The lyrics I've been putting down are not necessarily easy to write—bad poetry is often carefully worked, the difference being that it's easier to perceive flaccidly—but the labor that must go into one of Simon's songs is of another order of magnitude. Melodies, harmonies, arrangements are scrupulously fitted. Each song is perfect. And says nothing.

What saddens me is that Simon obviously seems to have a lot to say to the people who buy his records. But it's a shock. Like Kahlil Gibran all he's really doing is scratching them where they itch, providing some temporary relief but coming nowhere near the root of the problem. Simon's content isn't modern, it is merely fashionable, and his form never jars the sensibilities. He is the only songwriter I can imagine admitting he writes about that all-American subject, the Alienation of Modern Man, in just those words. His songs have the texture of modern poetry only if modern poetry can be said to end with early Auden—Edwin Arlington Robinson is more like it. Poets don't write like Robinson any more because his technical effects have outlived their usefulness, which was to make people see things in a new way. And even in such old-fashioned terms, what Simon does is conventional and uninspired. An example is "For Emily, Wherever I May Find Her," in which "poetic" words—organdy, crinoline, juniper (words that suggest why Simon is so partial to turn-of-the-century verse) and "beautiful" images (softer-than-the-rain, wandered-lonely-streets) are used to describe a dream girl. Simon is no dope; he knows this is all a little corny, but that's okay because Emily is an impossible girl. Only in order for the trick to come off there has to be an ironic edge. There isn't, and "For Emily" is nothing more than a sophisticated popular song of the traditional-fantasy type.

This kind of mindless craft reaches a peak in Simon's supposed masterpiece, "The Dangling Conversation," which uses all the devices you learn about in English class—alliteration, alternating concretion and abstraction, even the use of images from poetry itself, a favorite ploy of poets who don't know much of anything else—to mourn wistfully abut the classic plight of self-conscious man, his Inability to Communicate. Tom Phillips of the *New York Times* has called this song "one of Paul Simon's subtlest lyrics . . . a pitiless vision of self-consciousness and isolation." I don't hear the same song, I guess, because I think Simon's voice drips self-pity from every syllable (not only in this song, either). The Mantovani strings that reinforce the lyric capture its toughness perfectly. If Simon were just a little hipper, his couple would be discussing the failure of communication as they failed to communicate, rather than psychoanalysis or the state of the theatre. But he's not a little hipper.

Still, maybe he's getting there. A new album should be out shortly (there is one more track to record at this writing) and could be a surprise. Simon is going through changes. He has released almost nothing new since *Parsley, Sage, Rosemary and Thyme,* which contains "For Emily" and "Dangling Conversation." Last winter's "At the Zoo" is more concrete and less lugubrious than his other work, just a whimsical song about Central Park Zoo, and despite an occasional kernel of corn ("It's a light and tumble journey"), the metaphors work because they are fun: "Zebras are reactionaries/Antelopes are missionaries." "Fakin' It" is more serious, but the colloquial diction that dominates the song—in the first, third, and fifth sections, there is no word that isn't among the most common in the language: "The girl does what she wants to do/She knows what she wants to do and I know I'm/Fakin' it/I'm not really makin' it"—adds a casual feel; even when the verbiage becomes more Simonesque, it is seasoned with a dash of the colloquial: "A walk in the garden wears me down/Tangled in the fallen vines/Pickin' up the punch lines." In addition, the song contains an extraordinarily subtle switch. "I own a tailor's face and hands/I am the tailor's face and hands." No image-mongering there, just one little changeover, from a clever metaphor to a painful identification.

In an oblique and probably unconscious way, I think "Fakin' It" is true rock poetry, an extension of a very specific tradition. The pop that preceded rock, and still exists today, was full of what semanticist S. I. Hayakawa has listed as "wishful thinking, dreamy and ineffectual nostalgia, unrealistic fantasy, self-pity, and sentimental clichés masquerading as emotion." The blues, by contrast, were "unsentimental and realistic." Rock-and-roll combined the gutless lyrics of pop with the sexual innuendo of blues music and delivery. What this meant in practice was that it had no lyrics at all. Most rock fans just ignored what inane content there was in favor of the sound and the big beat. So rock diction became imbecilically colloquial, nonsense syllables proliferated, and singers slurred because nobody cared. Be-bop-a-lula, you can really start to groove it, caught Aunt Mary something and she ducked back in the alley. In "Fakin' It," the basic-English diction, the eleven repetitions of the title, and that almost inaudible changeover not only avoid Simon's usual pretensions; combined with the big-beat arrangement, they create a mood that asks "Why should this mean anything?" Only it does.

It is by creating a mood that asks "Why should this mean anything?" that the so-called rock poets can really write poetry—poetry that not only says something, but says it as only rock music can. For once Marshall McLuhan's terminology tells us something: rock lyrics are a cool medium. Go ahead and mumble. Drown the voices in guitars. If somebody really wants to know what you're saying, he'll take the trouble, and in that trouble lies your art. On a crude level this permits the kind of one-to-one symbolism of pot songs like "Along Comes Mary" and "That Acapulco Gold." "Fakin' It" does other things with the same idea. But the only songwriters who seem really to have mastered it are John Phillips and Lennon-McCartney.

Phillips possesses a frightening talent. "San Francisco—Flowers in Your Hair," catering to every prurient longing implicit in teenage America's flirtation with the hippies without ever even mentioning the secret word, is a stunning piece of schlock. A song like "Once Was A Time I Thought" (as if to say to all those Swingle Singer fans, "You thought that was hard? We can do the whole number in fifty-eight seconds") is another example of the range of his ability. You have the feeling Phillips could write a successful musical, a Frank Sinatra hit, anything that sells, if he wanted to.

Perhaps you are one of those people who plays every new LP with the treble way up and the bass way down so you can ferret out all the secret symbolic meanings right away. Personally I think that spoils the fun, and I suspect any record that permits you to do that isn't fulfilling its first function, which pertains to music, or, more generally, noise. The Mamas and Papas' records are full of diversions—the contrapuntal arrangements, the idiot "yeahs," the orchestral improvisations, the rhyme schemes ("If you're entertaining any thought that you're gaining by causin' me all of this pain and makin' me blue, the joke's on you") and Phillips' trick of drawing out a few words with repetitions and pauses. Perhaps this isn't conscious. In songs like "California Dreamin'," "12:30" and many others, Phillips is obviously just a good lyricist (with a lot of tender respect for the fantasy world of pure pop that critics like Hayakawa derogate so easily). But his lyrics are rarely easy to understand. Maybe it's just me, but I wonder how many of you are aware that a minor track on the second album, "Strange Young Girls," is about LSD. No secret about it—there it is, right out in the open of the first stanza: "Strange young girls, colored with sadness/Eyes of innocence hiding their madness/Walking the Strip, sweet, soft, and placid/Off'ring their youth on the altar of acid." But you don't notice because there's so much else to listen to.

My favorite Phillips song is "Straight Shooter." By now, everyone knows "Straight Shooter" is about drugs. They printed it right in the *Times* and everything. But its genius is that it doesn't have to be—it works equally well as one of those undefined, meaningless love songs that have always been the staple of rock. Oh, there are a few little aberrations—baby is suspected of holding anything, not anyone, and the "half of it belongs to me" doesn't make sense. But this is rock-and-roll. It doesn't have to make sense. Even the "just get me high" has all sorts of respectable precedents, like the "I get highs" in "I Want to Hold Your Hand," which may be about spiritual high but is no drug song. In addition there is the irony of this bright, bouncy melody being all about some needle freak. It's a characteristic trick—Phillips likes to conceal the tone of a lyric in a paradoxical melody (the perfect example being the gentle-sounding "Got a Feelin'"). Every level of uncertainty makes the song more like the reality we actually perceive. Yet the whole effect occurs within a strict rock framework.

Phillips achieves rock feel with his arrangements. The lyrics themselves are closer to traditional pop—Rodgers and Hart's "My Heart Stood Still," on the second album, sounds less out of place than Bobby Freeman's "Do You Wanna Dance?" on the first. Lennon-McCartney do it with diction. Their early work is all pure rock—the songs are merely excuses for melody, beat and sound. Occasionally it shows a flash of the subtlety to come, as in the sexual insinuation of "Please Please Me" or the premise of "There's A Place" ("There, there's a place/Where I can go/When I feel low, when I feel blue/And it's my mind"). More often it is pure, meaningless sentiment, couched in the simplest possible terms. By the time of *A Hard Day's Night* the songs are more sophisticated musically, and a year later, in *Help!*, the boys are becoming pop songwriters. *Help!* itself is a perfect example. Words like "self-assured" and "insecure" are not out of rock diction, nor is the line: "My independence seems to vanish in the haze." This facet of their talent has culminated (for the moment) in songs like "Paperback Writer," "A Little Help from My Friends," and "When I'm Sixty-four," which show all the verbal facility of the best traditional pop and none of the sentimentality, and in deliberate exercises like "Michelle" and "Here, There and Everywhere," which show both.

Other songs like "Norwegian Wood," "Dr. Roberts," "Good

Morning, Good Morning" are ambiguous despite an unerring justness of concrete detail; little conundrums, different from Dylanesque surrealism because they don't fit so neatly into a literary category (Edward Lear is their closest antecedent). Most of the songs since *Rubber Soul* are characterized by a similar obliqueness. Often the Beatles' "I" is much harder to pin down than the "I" in Donovan or Jagger-Richard, a difficulty that is reinforced by their filters, their ethereal harmonies, and their collective public identity. This concern with angle of attack is similar to that of poets like Creeley.

Lennon and McCartney are the only rock songwriters who combine high literacy (as high as Dylan's or Simon's) with an eye for concision and a truly contemporary sense of what fits. They seem less and less inclined to limit themselves to what I have defined as rock diction, and yet they continue to succeed—the simultaneous lushness and tightness of "Lucy in the Sky with Diamonds," for instance, is nothing short of extraordinary. They still get startling mileage out of the banal colloquial—think of the "oh boy" in "A Day in the Life," or the repeating qualifications in "Strawberry Fields Forever." But they have also written two songs which are purely colloquial—"She Said She Said," and "All You Need Is Love."

"She Said She Said" is at once one of the most difficult and banal of Beatle songs. It is a concrete version of what in "The Dangling Conversation" (despite all those details) remains abstract, a conversation between a hung-up, self-important girl who says she knows "what it's like to be dead" and her boy friend, who doesn't want to know. (If Simon had written it, the boy would have argued that he was the one who knew.) The song uses the same kind of words that can be found in "She Loves You" (the quintessential early Beatles song), yet says so much more. Its conceit, embodied in the title, is meaningless; its actuality is a kind of ironic density that no other songwriter (except Dylan at his best) approaches. One of its ironies is the suggestion that callow philosophizing is every bit as banal as the most primitive rock-and-roll.

"All You Need Is Love," deliberately written in basic English so it could be translated, makes the connection clearer by quoting from "She Loves You" while conveying the ironic message of the title. Is love all you need? What kind of love? Universal love? Love of country? Courtly love? "She Loves You" love? It's hard to tell. The song employs rock-and-roll—dominant music, big beat, repeated refrain, simple diction—

and transforms it into something which, if not poetry, at least has a multifaceted poetic wholeness. I think it is rock poetry in the truest sense.

Maybe I am being too strict. Modern poetry is doing very well, thank you, on its own terms, but in terms of what it is doing for us, and even for the speech from which it derives, it looks a bit pallid. Never take the categories too seriously. It may be that the new songwriters (not poets, please) lapse artistically, indulge their little infatuations with language and ideas, and come up with a product that could be much better if handled with a little less energy and a little more caution. But energy is where it's at. And songs—even though they are only songs—may soon be more important than poems, no matter that they are easier too.

Once there were bards and the bards did something wondrous—they provided literature for the illiterate. The bards evolved into poets and the poetry which had been their means became their end. It didn't seem to matter much after a while, since everyone was literate anyway. But semiliteracy, which is where people go when they're not illiterate any more, is in some ways a worse blight.

The new songwriters think there should be bards again and they're right, but the bardic traditions are pretty faint. Too many of them are seduced by semiliteracy—mouthing other people's ideas in other people's words. But they are bards, and that is very good. Maybe soon it will be a lot better.

This essay was written (too fast, like most journalism) in the early fall of 1967 for *Cheetah,* now sadly departed. Though I haven't been able to resist a few stylistic fixes, I have left it mostly as is. If the piece seems dated to me now, in the fall of 1968, then any revisions would no doubt seem dated by the time they appeared. Journalism ought to survive with its limitations of time and place intact.

Nevertheless I feel compelled to put things in some small perspective and right a few wrongs. I'm probably guilty of overkill on Paul Simon, who has since gone on to his just reward as the writer of a Number One filmscore, but when I wrote this he was still taken seriously by people who deserved better. And though I love "Mrs. Robinson" and consider *Bookends* S&G's finest album, I don't think Simon has lived up to the promise I discerned in "Fakin' It." As for John Phillips, I am now convinced the Mamas and the Papas are destined to become high camp, but that doesn't change what they were and sometimes still are for us, and I stand by my praise.

What I describe as the poetry of rock has to do with surprise, and it is still relevant: the effect of a lyric by John Kay of Steppenwolf, say, or even Gerry Goffin and Carole King, is frequently enhanced by indirection. But since last fall there have been only two completely successful examples of this tradition, the ultimate test being how broadly they sold: Lennon-McCartney's "Hello Good-bye" and Peter Townshend's "I Can See for Miles." I am beginning to think such specimens will become increasingly rare. The technique is based on one overriding assumption: that no one takes rock seriously. It can only survive as long as that assumption is viable, if not as a present truth then as a living memory. But even the memory seems to be dying. It may be that the most lasting verbal effect of what I can only call the rock ambience may be a new eloquence in popular songwriting, typified by a figure like Randy Newman, whose work has little to do with rock per se.

The key figure in all this is Bob Dylan, who as a vocalist and a writer has pointed out all sorts of new directions for song. I think I misunderstood what Dylan did for those of us who always knew he was a rotten "poet." It was his very badness that attracted us. His overwriting was the equivalent in folk music of the happy energy of the Beatles. He loved language enough to misuse it. Of course, if he hadn't had the genius to use it brilliantly as well, that would hardly have been a virtue. But he did, and so revitalized areas of language that had seemed exhausted. The songwriter who has learned most from this is Leonard Cohen, with his wry exultation in silly rhymes and inconsistent or overly consistent images. It may be, by the way, that poets have learned something from Dylan's freedom as well. In any case I know now that the work of poets like Robert Creeley was no longer really central when I wrote this. Anyone who would like to sample what has replaced it should refer to *Bean Spasms,* by Ted Berrigan and Ron Padgett.

THE AESTHETICS OF ROCK

●

RICHARD MELTZER

Bob Dylan's greatest dive into the rock-'n'-roll domain, "Like a Rolling Stone," represents an attempt to free man by rescuing him *from* meaning, rather than free man *through* meaning. John Lennon's two collections of writings, *In His Own Write* and *A Spaniard in the Works,* have shown his desire to denigrate all meaning and thus throw intentional ambiguity into all domains of meaning. And very definitely *all* meaning is similar, beginning with the most "authentic" and continuing down the line. When told by Paul McCartney about a girl he encountered with the idea that God had advised her to marry Paul, "I was trying to persuade her that she didn't in actual fact have a vision from God, that it was—" George Harrison interrupted with, "It was probably somebody *disguised* as God." Meaning by any other name, smells about the same. John and Ringo destroy P. F. Strawson's argument for separation into logical and empirical primacy:

John: We're money-makers first, then we're entertainers.
Ringo: No, we're not.
John: What are we then?
Ringo: Dunno. Entertainers first.
John: O.K.
Ringo: 'Cause we were entertainers before we were money-makers.

Whereas James Joyce attempted to salvage meaning from semantic chaos, John would rather attain a cool semantic oblivion, and thus has written two books intentionally inferior to James Joyce's works.

One of Lennon and McCartney's maneuvers is to present meaning in such a role that it becomes trite. Thus is the use of "in spite of" in a positive sense reduced to triviality in "Yes It Is":

Please don't wear red tonight . . .
For red is the color that will make me blue
In spite of you . . .

This very spirit of the song, with its assertively positive title, presents a frightening ambiguity between arrogance and possession of a unique vulnerability. "When I Get Home" plays upon the mere appearance of a single word, "trivialities":

> *Come on, if you please,*
> *I got no time for trivialities,*
> *I got a girl who is waiting home for me, tonight.*

In the midst of apparent "tragedy" in realizing a sudden revulsion at his semiadulterous involvement with another girl, he can hesitate to give it the meaning of "triviality." But the five-syllable word is so strange in such a monosyllabic context that it is rendered incredibly inappropriate, and the need for meaning collapses.

Barry McGuire's "Eve of Destruction" presents a plethora of such words: "coagulatin'" "legislation," etc. The very appearance of such "serious" subjects as war and segregation in a rock context is a denigration of their original significance. His absolute overstatement of theme renders disaster cool; his "Don't you know we're on the eve of destruction" is so affirmative that one can feel comfortable with such knowledge. England's banning of this song is a really fine misunderstanding of how McGuire has rendered *Weltschmerz* trite.

In a world of such things as random values, metaphysical inconsistency, and the constant unavoidable interruption of pure aesthetic perception by random events from within and without, eclecticism is the only valid position; and other stances may be measured by virtue of their distance from the eclectic. Andy Warhol has devised one of the simplest of all schemes, the selection of a popular motif, from Troy Donahue, to floral prints, to Campbell's soup, followed by mechanical multiple reproduction of this motif, with the consistency and inconsistency being a function of the mechanism of creation. Rock-'n'-roll, however, cannot rely upon the selling power of random circumlocution of the originally acceptable motif, but turns toward the utter compression of popularly acceptable, yet eclectically arranged images. "A Little Bit Better" by Herman's Hermits begins with the instrumental introduction from the Four Season's Coca-Cola commercial, proceeds with the sinister spirit of the Rolling Stones' "Play with Fire" (of course rendered innocent by Herman's contradiction), sung with the vocal style of the Zombies, to the tune of Chuck Berry's "Memphis," and in possession of a title clearly reminiscent of the recent hit by Wayne Fontana and the Mindbenders, "A Little Bit Too Late." Wayne Fontana himself sounded like a clear version of the Kingsmen in his first hit, like the Searchers in his next. The Beatles have taken from visceral jazz saxophonist John Coltrane in "Love Me Do," the gay Four Seasons in "Tell Me Why," Larry Williams in "I'm Down," and Bob Dylan and Scottish marching bands in "You've Got to Hide Your Love Away." They have used elderly African drum in "Mr. Moonlight," violins in "Yesterday," timpani in "What You're Doing" and "Every Little Thing," packing case in "Words of Love," and unusual amplification maneuvers in "I Feel Fine" and "Yes It Is." They have used double tracking on several records, sometimes so obviously that it can be easily noticed (in *Hard Day's Night,* John Lennon's harmonica line can be heard while he is singing lead vocal in "I Should Have Known Better." It does not matter if part of the Beatles' formula is visible; after all, even Lennon's bathing suit is clearly visible in a bathtub scene).

Teilhard de Chardin's philosophy of education as expounded in *The Phenomenon of Man* is readily visible in the eclecticism of rock. Just as branches of life strive for continuation, sometimes to succeed and sometimes to reach a dead end, with nature always using a multiplicity of interrelated strivings in its drive toward the "Omega Point," rock-'n'-roll is clearly viewable in terms of crude persistence. As long as a fixture "works" in the Allan Kaprow usage of the term, it remains in the forefront and shouts its presence; when it ceases to work it is relegated to relative obscurity until a new context presents itself and allows for favorable reacceptance. No branch can ever really become extinct if it continues to function in the memory, even dormantly, and old but undiscovered branches from both the "within" and "without" of things past, as Chardin uses these terms, can always appear in active functions in contemporary rock. The almost forgotten 1957 minor hit by Kathy Linden, "Billy," features an expectation of obscenity in it's final passage:

And when I sleep . . .
I always dream of Bill.

This anxiety of waiting for the impossible use of "sleep" in the last line is not too overtly common in rock of any period, but suddenly in the summer of 1965 it arose in Tom Jones' "What's New Pussycat?" "Pussycat lips," "pussycat eyes" and other "pussycat" features are mentioned until, with the final verse, the singer is hesitatingly approaching something more openly sexual and finishes, "You and your pussycat . . . nose." Here is the appearance of a branch of rock with now at least two evolutionary members, a branch which I can call the "pussycat school." Rock has had its "rain school" ("Raindrops," "Teardrops," "Rhythm of the Rain," "Walking in the Rain," etc.), a fine eclectic grouping which is ambiguously between the inner and outer world of artistic evolution. Cousin Bruce Morrow of WABC has used even flimsier branches, as the branch of all songs with "tell" in their titles ("I'm Telling You Now," "Tell Me," etc.), and that composed of "animal" titles. Rock has implicitly operated on this infinitude of random, eclectic evolutionary pathways, something merely suggested by Thomas Pynchon in his *V.* My categories "ponytail rock" (the group the Poni-Tails; "What Is Love?" which describes this emotion as "five feet of heaven with a ponytail"; "Chantilly Lace," with its reference to the hairpiece as a criterion of socio-sexual adequacy), "fear-of-loss-of-being rock ("Going Out of My Head"; "Remember"; Dion and the Belmonts' absolutely obscure "I Can't Go On, Rosalie"), and "march rock" (Little Peggy March; the beat of "I'll Never Dance Again"; the timpani of "Every Little Thing"; "Calendar Girl," which declares, "March, I'm gonna march you down the aisle") are as valid as such categories as "folk rock," "Motown rock," or even "rock-which-legitimately-renders-human-experience" or "that-which-consistently-conforms-to-the-standards-of-classical-music-rock."

At the same time rock has transcended any difficulties encountered in the sociology of knowledge. Because it is so wantonly eclectic, any moment's linear connections can bear contradictory relationships to those of the next without difficulty. "I Can't Stop Loving You" has succeeded "I've Had It," "Tequila" has led to "Too Much Tequila," and "Eve of Destruction" and "Dawn of Correction" have appeared almost concurrently. William James has seen the impossibility of viewing philosophical constructs separate from the temperament which has led to them; rock has never for a second viewed the construct and temperament as anything but the same phenomenon, or noumenon for that matter. Quine has noted, "The unit of empirical significance is the whole of science." The unit of rock significance is the whole of rock-'n'-roll, and this is not merely the result of the failure of reduction, as Hegel's unit of historical significance as all of history seems to be. Just as permissible, anyway, is the Jamies' position in "Summertime, Summertime," which resembles Hegel's end of history, "No more studyin' history."

The possibility of artistic evolution presupposes questions of evolving legitimacy and illegitimacy. Once a new approach has been legitimatized through acceptance it may be repeated; in the case of rock-'n'-roll the very process of legitimatization itself can pertain to rock-'n'-roll's total picture, and this repetition of course is driven into the ground, just as I have obliterated the concept of repetition by overuse so far in this very essay. But when the mere juxtaposition of a still extraneous element can lead to either friction within an art or between it and the audience (which to rock is equally internal), more than simple vulgarity and tastefulness are in question. Moreover, rock has dealt with legitimacy and illegitimacy in a manner which frequently annihilates the distinction. Often something is capable of being observed as both at home in a rock context and utterly alien. When Elvis Presley followed his early hardcore rock hits with a ballad, "Love Me Tender," the music of which had been taken from Stephen Foster, several questions arose. Could Elvis now be considered a popular musician in the "adult," Muzak-oriented sense? Was rock-'n'-roll, not even three years old as an identifiable movement, on the verge of fusion with this popular mainstream? Pat Boone built his entire early career on music ambiguously legitimate to both pop and rock, with titles like "Love Letters in the Sand," "Anastasia," "There's a Gold Mine in the Sky," "April Love," "When the Swallows Come Back to Capistrano," and the Quaker "Friendly Persuasion." Perhaps he was interested mainly in attaining pop legitimacy for his own songs, imbued already with a pseudo-rock energy, without concentrating upon how that energy might enhance what he conservatively judged to be legitimate. The Platters, perhaps the biggest group during the early days of rock-'n'-roll, strained to sound so "legitimate" that they have completely vanished. As rock developed, a significant change took place: ballads became illegitimate. That is, they were no longer ambiguous "good" music but were now eligible for use by rock-'n'-rollers. Beauty could now reenter rock-'n'-roll with full "badness" to it; there was no longer a need to equate beauty with the submundanely pretty, as Muzak necessitates: beauty was now free and ontologically energized. "Soul" encountered a similar problem, resolved completely by Ray Charles. His early blues and gospel contained an intense, lyrical poignancy that seemed unbreachably removed from rock's trivial sentimentality. Charles' "What'd I Say" and "Swanee River Rock" alienated his work from its earlier more conservative legitimacy and introduced to rock a variety of soul far more "righteous" than that of rhythm and blues. One of the first great ballads of this new era of rock was Conway Twitty's "It's Only Make Believe," perhaps an indicator of the self-cognition necessary for such a transition beyond limitation by dubious distinction: "People see us everywhere/ They think you really care/ But myself I can't deceive/ I know it's only make believe." The problem of delegitimatization has sometimes been reduced to a problem of trivialization. The Righteous Brothers' "Unchained Melody" is a song recorded scores of times in a "legitimate" context, but only they (actually only one Brother sings on the record, a dubious trivialization itself) could make it completely renderable through a rock context. The trick was to slur the phrase "your love," in the final "God speed your love to me," so that it is not clearly audible, even inaudible on a faulty transistor radio. Bob Dylan has brought his harsh folk songs of protest into rock-'n'-roll by following the latter's pleasure principle, recording for single releases (separate from his record albums) those songs which are the most aurally pleasing, as "Like A Rolling Stone" and "Positively Fourth Street."

The usual labels for segments of artistic evolution, baroque and rococo, are really superficial manifestations of this deeper activity. A cursory examination of the terms used to designate success, the accepted song, is revelatory of an orientation different from that of the traditional forms to which those labels were originally applied. A song can be a "hit," a "blast," a "smash," or even a "gasser"; kinetic destruction is inherent in kinetic success.

Above all the Beatles have established the necessity of at least watching the "action." When the Dave Clark Five produced its revival of the Contours' "Do You Love Me," they strongly emphasized the phrase, "Watch me now!" What to the Contours meant the observation of the lamenter's dancing, "now that I can dance," is to the D. C. Five a metaphor of universal nascent consciousness.

The Beatles have in their own work mirrored the entire development of rock-'n'-roll. They began with primitive emotional music ("Love Me Do"), went on to hardcore affirmative kineticism ("She Loves You") and triviality (Ringo's wail, "Okay, George," during "Boys"), progressed to highly sophisticated arrogance ("I Should Have Known Better") and straightforward profundity ("I'll Be Back"), pessimism ("Things We Said Today") and modern "tragedy" ("No Reply"), while at all stages relating themselves to the roots with revivals ("Dizzy, Miss Lizzie") and retrogressions to early noncognitiveness, written themselves ("I'm Down"). They have noted the evolution of multitracked recording, with "Help!," a single-tracked recording, at its pinnacle. In this work juxtaposed Greek-like lead and chorus seem separate in echoing each other, suggesting that the Beatles' self-restraint in limiting the song to a single track divided between George and Paul and John is a self-conscious comprehension of the effect of one being fully capable of echoing himself and yet refusing, a queer addendum to a movement continuously felt throughout rock-'n'-roll history. Representing the evolution of rock made conscious of itself (just as Chardin asserts man to be the crown of the natural evolution of the universe, made conscious of itself), the Beatles have made ontologically important the concept of anachronism. Just as the Parmenidean One "at all times . . . both is and is becoming older and younger than itself," Beatlistic unity implies anachronism in its novelty, not just infinite extension of nostalgia.

Stylistically Conway Twitty resembles closely Elvis Presley, who is echoed by Terry Stafford, who sounds just like Del Shannon. Marianne Faithful can be thought of as an anemic Joan Baez; Adam Faith is essentially the same as Jimmy Soul both stylistically and nominally. By a convenient raunch epistemology, Dee Dee Sharp has resembled the Orlons, who in turn resemble the Marvelettes. The "late great" Buddy Holly was posthumously heard in the singing of Tommy Roe and Bobby Vee, who has even used Buddy Holly's Crickets. The instrumental sounds of the Tornadoes and of Johnny and the Hurricanes display no distinct difference. Mel Carter is not readily distinguishable from the "late great" Sam Cooke. Some vocals and harmonica solos by Dylan and Lennon have sounded so related that one rock-'n'-roll magazine said that they might be the same person in different disguises. Jay and the Americans sound like the Fortunes, who sound like the We Five, who sound like the Ivy League, who sound like the Beatles, who sound like the Zombies, who sound like the Searchers, who sound like the Everly Brothers, who sound like a multitude of white country-blues singers, who sometimes sound like Negro country-blues singers, who can sometimes sound like urban Negro blues singers, who sound like the Rolling Stones, who sound like the Nashville Teens, who do not even look like Jay and the Americans.

An epilogue adds to a body of writing what occurs temporally after the main action or what occurs to the writer after he has written about the main body of action. Often it is the summation of all the excess energies still residual after this main body has been explicated, but necessary to fully explain it. Actually, an idea should be quite visible when first mentioned, and continuous attention to it should beat it to death. Thomas Mann's novels contain this type of idea expansion and elaboration. Thomas Pynchon's novel, *V*, whose main character, Benny Profane, envisions himself as a yo-yo, proceeds like a yo-yo to expand and elaborate the idea that it is silly yet essential to expand and elaborate to infinity. Pynchon's epilogue, quite naturally, is a flashback to an event forty-six years before the time of main action.

Often an epilogue can contain what would have been too boring to develop in the preceding body. John Lennon's epilogue to *In His Own Write,* entitled, "About the Awful," states the following gibberish:

> "I was bored on the 9th of Octover when, I believe, the Nasties were still booming us led by Madalf Heatlump (who had only one). Anyway they didn't get me. I attended to varicous schools in Liddypool. And still didn't pass—much to my Aunties supplies. As a member of the most publified Beatles my and (P, G, and R's) records might seem funnier to some than this book, but as far as I'm conceived this correction of short writty is the most wonderfoul larf I've ever ready. God help and breed you all."

George Harrison, in *Hard Day's Night,* remarks upon boredom as the preclusion of continuity of expression in his description of a television personality: "She's a drag, a well-known drag. You turn down the sound and say rude things."

An epilogue should be an afterthought on afterthought. "About the Awful" appears on the back cover of the book, a perfect mechanical epilogue. "Mr. Moonlight" and "Everybody's Trying to Be My Baby," the two most trivial of the songs contained in *Beatles '65,* appear last respectively on side one and side two, a perfect mechanical incorporation of essential triviality. The Beatles' trivialization scheme has been this reflexive afterthought.

The Rolling Stones' trivialization scheme has been more elusive. Although the Rolling Stones appear timid in the face of a creative universe of triviality, one which the Beatles visit frequently, they have allowed a truly trivial American, Joey Page, to accompany them on tours. His distinctively abominable television performance on *Hollywood a Go-Go* exonerates the Stones: they are unafraid of triviality, at least by proxy. And this significant key to a great mystery of the Stones remains invisible to the American follower of rock-'n'-roll unless he is either degenerate or sophisticated enough to appreciate the unique experience of this television program. Here we have an empirical approach not dependent upon dispositions of human perception but upon dispositions of human sentiment. The Rolling Stones have not relied upon reflexive afterthought.

So what?

At the close of Plato's *Symposium*, Socrates has clinched complete control of the situation and has, by keeping his listeners on the verge of boredom and sleep, forced them into acceptance of anything he chooses. "Socrates was arguing with others—not that Aristodemus could remember very much of what he said, for, besides having missed the beginning, he was still more than half asleep. But the gist of it was that Socrates was forcing them to admit that the same man might be capable of writing both comedy and tragedy—that the tragic poet might be a comedian as well." Socrates here has spoken of tragedy and comedy alone as a matter of drunken brevity. John Lennon, in a similar position, would group together many more things, likely tragedy, comedy, pornography, melodrama, structured philosophy, mathematics and psychology, history, limerick, babble. Dulled beyond speech he might still indicate his conception of the One as dullness beyond speech. Mick Jagger actually offers a variation of this position at the conclusion of the Stones' "Walking the Dog," babbling, "Duh-duh-duh-duh-duh . . . just a-walkin'." Struck by profound revelation, he is ambiguously wounded and removed of his power to speak coherently or so awestruck that coherent speech is no longer necessary. Anyway, he just babbles.

John Lennon focuses upon the dead toward which all solutions, although utterly successful, may move, in a two-page cartoon in *A Spaniard In The Works.* Shown on the left-hand leaf is a very thin blind man, standing upright upon a cane with a trumpet at his lips and a pot of coins at his feet. Even his seeing-eye dog is cadaverously thin and it is furnished with a pair of sunglasses as is his master. He has only two toes on each foot, and his tragic despair is evident in his upright resignation. His "I am blind" sign is his only objective label. Opposite him on the right-hand page is someone who has seen beyond the inadequacies of tragic authenticity and bears "I can see quite clearly" on his chest. He is fat, has three toes on each foot, owns a well-fed, smiling dog who is roaming freely at the end of a leash, and from his jovial expression and carefree, slovenly stance, he appears quite successful for one endowed with the limitation of sight. The creative genius of the second trumpeter has carried the tin-cup experience about as far as it can possibly be extended both artistically and financially while still toying with an ambiguous level of authenticity. Although he has a great solution, perhaps the only viable one, standing on a street corner will reduce to sheer boredom for him in about three hours. He has seen and rejected the tragic possibilities of blindness, with all its metaphysical and poetic implication, would generate a new potency for man, as a Nietzschean trumpeter might. But now he is about to become simply bored, so he may pack up his earnings and pay the debts he owes his brother-in-law. Even the genius Sisyphus might eventually produce a scheme whereby he can scratch pornographic drawings with his thumb; after fourteen or fifteen successful attempts Sisyphus would then finally get bored by this newly found experience. But Sisyphus is entrapped by his situation: he cannot completely say, "So what?" to his fate worse than death. But the seeing trumpeter and John Lennon share a fate worse than life. They can become fully bored; this capability limits their ability to sustain aesthetic expression while it simultaneously allows an escape.

Cognitive "solutions" can be more awesome in their manifestations than Nietzsche imagined, additionally awesome because they are doomed to burn out as brilliant sparks awaiting a noncognitive rekindling. Writer for children, Dr. Seuss has given insight into a related aspect of solution: " 'If I ran the zoo,'/ Said young Gerald McGrew,/ 'I'd make a few changes,/ That's what I'd do.' "

FRANK ZAPPA INTERVIEW

●

FRANK KOFSKY

Kofsky: When I read into what you're trying to do in your music is not just play music, but also agitate and educate—

Zappa: And synthesize . . .

Kofsky: It strikes me as a kind of musical version of Berthold Brecht. Might that be a correct inference?

Zappa: Well, I'm not a Brecht fan because I don't know that much about what he does, but people keep saying that, so maybe it's true. I've read hardly any of his stuff. I've heard the "Three-Penny Opera"—like half of it one time—couldn't sit through the rest.

Kofsky: I don't necessarily mean that you were copying him. It just seems to me that his idea was that you could use art to galvanize people into some kind of action.

Zappa: Oh, I think we can definitely galvanize people into some kind of action. We galvanized somebody into singing "Louie, Louie" tonight, who was asleep. [In the Mothers' first show at the Garrick Theatre that evening, a young man who was apparently tripping out at the time had volunteered to come up from the audience and sing "Louie, Louie" accompanied by the Mothers.] From zero to "Louie, Louie" in ten seconds is not bad. We can generate that sort of wave, and I hope that once we get on a footing where we can reach more people at once, more mass-media exposure, then we'll be able to get more of that happening. Some of the stuff we get for fan mail, although it's not huge in quantity, what those letters are saying, no other group in the world is getting. We get fantastic letters from anarchists, nineteen years old: "Help me in my town," and all that stuff.

Kofsky: Are those the people you want to appeal to, or is that what you want people to do then—destroy the system?

Zappa: No, not exactly destroy it. I want it modified to the point where it works properly. A lot of people think that a new political movement, the ideal new political movement, is to bust it all up and start all over again with tribes and feathers in your hair and everybody loves everybody else. That's a lie. Those kids don't love each other; they're in that because it's like another club—it's like the modern-day equivalent of a street gang. It's clean *pachucos,* a little hairier perhaps. But it's not right.

First of all, the idea of busting it all down and starting all over again is stupid. The best way to do it, and what I would like to see happen, what I'm working towards, is using the system against itself to purge itself, so that it can really work. I think politics is a valid concept, but what we have today is not really politics. It's the equivalent of the high school election. It's a popularity contest. It's got nothing to do with politics—what it is is mass merchandising.

Kofsky: Then your kind of politics is something that raises real alternatives: say, a thorough revamping of American foreign policy—doing away with the American Empire; really discussing the issues that exist and not simply running two television candidates.

Zappa: Right.

Kofsky: How do you envision the connection between what you're doing now and generating that kind of a movement?

Zappa: First of all, I would like to manufacture a thing called the Interested Party—I'm taking steps in that direction now—which would be a third party that lives up to its name.

Kofsky: Then it would be a *second party,* really.

Zappa: Actually, yes. The people that would be active in such a venture would have to be the ones . . . in every small town there's a little guy that lives there that knows what's happening and everybody thinks he's a creep, and he's the only one who's right, you know? We have a way of reaching these people, because they come to us, they find us, because they say, "Maybe there's a chance." So suppose we don't sell ten million albums. We've reached most of those kids in those towns. A lot of them have written to us, and the other ones have heard and at least been made aware that somebody is thinking in the direction that they're thinking. I think what we do is really constructive, although a lot of people are repelled superficially by the sound of it, the way we look, and some of the grotesque action on stage. But those are all therapeutic shockwaves.

Kofsky: Sometimes when you insult the audience, as in "You're Probably Wondering Why I'm Here," and in the notes to the first album—this is all part of the thing of stinging them into action, isn't it? You're trying to arouse them and make them angry instead of apathetic.

Zappa: Yes, yes, I think that it's easier to make somebody mad than to make somebody love. And seeing as how hate is the absolute negative of love, if you can evoke hate and it's really there, you can polarize it, and then you really could have love.

Kofsky: Don't you think that this emphasis on love that we see among hippies really reflects not so much their ability to love at the moment, but their desire to create the kind of society where it will be possible to love?

Zappa: No, I think that what they do is a definite indication of their inability to love, because the whole hippie scene is wishful thinking. They wish they could love but they're full of shit, and they're kidding themselves into saying, "I love! I love! I love!" And the more times they say it, the more times they think they love. But like it doesn't work, and most of them don't have the guts to admit to themselves that it's a lie.

Kofsky: Do you think that this is because it's an early phase of the thing?

Zappa: Oh yeah, I see it growing into something that really works. I'm glad the kids are pretending they're dropping out, because when they find out that that doesn't work they'll be ready for some sort of action.

Kofsky: Revolutionary action?

Zappa: Sure. I think a revolution—not the sloppy kind, but the kind that really works—you know, it's about time for that.

Kofsky: Do you want to distinguish between sloppy kind and—?

Zappa: The sloppy kind is blood-in-the-street and all that bullshit. Today, a revolution can be accomplished by means of mass media, with technical advances that Madison Avenue is using to sell you washing machines and a loaf of bread and everything else. This can be used to change the whole country around—painlessly.

Kofsky: How so?

Zappa: Because all those facilities are available, and facilities that the people are using now on Madison Avenue—there are techniques above and beyond that which they aren't aware of and which I think I've come into—things that they're not ready to believe exist yet. Because they have a tendency to get into a formula, like they get into their bag with their motivational researchers with their degrees, who have only scratched the surface of what the youth movement is about. They don't know youth from shit. And that's the market. You know, they're still selling products to the youth on a glandular level. There are ways to move the youth to action through their brains and not through their glands. You have to start off part of the thing on the glandular level just to get their interest.

Kofsky: As you do now.

Zappa: But we're not nearly as glandular as most of the rock and roll bands, because we're not selling sex that much.

Kofsky: Well, you insult people too much to be really glandular. You challenge them.

Zappa: But we've got enough so they don't lose interest in us completely. If we tried to just be straight up there and sing our songs and go away, we wouldn't make it, because we're old men compared to rock-and-roll standards, and there's no sex appeal to an old man singing a straight song. So if we do something that makes us bizarre, we got that happening for us.

Kofsky: The thing that occurs to me at this point is, we know the powers that be in this country are pretty much opposed to people revolutionizing their society—witness the way Johnson deals with Vietnam when the Vietnamese try to do that. Do you think that those same powers would be any more lenient with you if it looked like you were trying to take everything they had away from them?

Zappa: First of all, it will never look to them like I'm going to take everything away from them, because I'm not taking it all away from them—I have no intention of taking it *all* away from them.

Kofsky: Well, taking their power. I didn't necessarily mean taking their personal possessions. But their power right now is the ability to command what the man on the street thinks through their control of the mass media and so on and so forth.

Zappa: That's where I have one basic human drive on my side that they can't defeat—greed. You see, they're so greedy, and the powers that be are not necessarily the government, but you're talking about big industry and the military and all, and that's greed-motivated activity. Industry wants to make money; and I'm getting into a phase now where I'm being used by industry to move products. A lot of the industries now are aware of the fact that they're in a vicious cycle: in order to sell their goods to the youth market, which accounts for the major market of most of American products, that same market that buys most of the records, you have a weird situation where in effect record companies especially are helping to disseminate the information which will cause the kids to wake up and move and eventually destroy what they stand for, and they can't help it.

Kofsky: Ralph Gleason tells me that this is happening by kids in the Haight-Ashbury in particular, by simply turning their back on big-corporation society and going out and creating a parallel society of their own.

Zappa: That doesn't work.

They can't survive. That's like saying, "We're going to secede from the union; we'll have our town secede from the union." That's stupid.

Kofsky: In a sense, I agree with you, but it also seems to me that there's a certain element of wishful thinking in what you propose, too. In my rigid Marxist bag, it does seem to me that the power Elite (or ruling class), when you get to that point where it looks as though you are somehow going to emancipate the population from taking orders from them, they simply aren't going to let you have it that easily. They are going to try to do the same thing they tried to do to Fidel Castro or to Ho Chi Minh . . .

Zappa: That's all a question of how you perceive what I'm trying to do. I'm not trying to take power.

Kofsky: No, I'm not saying you're trying to take power, but you are trying to—

Zappa: You originally brought up the question of power. Now, power is a thing that bears on this case, but what we're really talking about is modifying the system just so it works. The present principles of democracy that were originally set up when they invented it aren't being applied today, and I think that with an educated population, democracy works. So what we need are things that would change the shape of education.

Kofsky: I didn't mean that you personally wanted to take power, but I do think that you meant that you wanted to undermine the power of those people who have it now—the power to control people's minds.

Zappa: It's like this. A person likes to feel useful in the society; people have certain things that they can do. I happen to have a knack for doing that sort of thing, and if I can apply it to good use, it gives me satisfaction just to know that I'm functioning. Where normally, you know, I wouldn't have a chance to use my trade, because what I can do is spread out over a broad range of activities. I like to do them all because it feels good to do that. If I can help at the same time, that's groovy. If it works, fine. If it doesn't work, at least I kept myself occupied for a while.

Kofsky: So in other words, this isn't some rigid prescription that you're trying to force on people?

Zappa: No! If I thought it was like that, I'd be wearing armbands or be out there with a costume on—the robe—and doing it with some showmanship. But we've taken our time about presenting our case and the scene itself has been developing at a rate—it seems like its developing slower than I wanted it to. But, I am not in a position of where I can govern the growth rate.

Kofsky: No, isn't it a question of feedback from your audience to you, I would imagine?

Zappa: Yes and no. We keep track of what's going on out there, but what they do and what they say doesn't have a hell of a lot of bearing on what we're going to do for them. Except that I try to forecast certain social-political events. We have some material that's going into the next album about the concentration camps in California—you're seeing this before the world even knows what the tune is because I turned these out the other day. These are going on the album, *The Mothers and Lenny Bruce,* which is due for September release.

Kofsky: Well, how does that go? Is it going to be real Lenny Bruce on there?

Zappa: Yeah. I'm editing the tapes of Lenny's and interspersing these special tunes, so we come up with an oratorio thing, and the name of the album is *Our Man in Nirvana.*

Kofsky: I suspected that you and I had a lot in common, and one of the things we had in common was being turned on by Lenny Bruce.

Zappa: Yeah.

Kofsky: Besides growing up in Los Angeles, putting twin pipes on our car and reprimering the right front fender and going to drive-ins. I wonder if anybody understands all of that kind of thing?

Zappa: They don't.

Kofsky: That whole album *[Freak Out!]* is Southern California. Nobody else knows what a swimming pool *is.*

Zappa: No, this is a new type of lyric that I'm getting into. These are also social-political things. This is straight bizarre lyric, based on—I made research tapes of behavior of some seventeen-year-old kids in Ontario, California, and this is based on those tapes.

Kofsky: How long do you carry some of this stuff around in your head?

Zappa: Well, "Call Any Vegetable", for example, was written two weeks after we finished *Freak Out!*, when we were in Hawaii, and it took a year to learn how to play it. "Son of Suzy Creamcheese" took a year to learn how to play. Can you tell why? The time, the time—it's fantastic. It's four bars of 4/4, one bar 8/8, one bar of 9/8—OK? And then it goes 8/8, 9/8, 8/8, 9/8, 8/8, 9/8, then it goes 8/8, 4/8, 5/8, 6/8, and back into 4/4 again. To get it together now, we just toss it off and it becomes a flop.

Kofsky: Are there a lot of splices on "Absolutely Free"? I thought I detected places where there were very abrupt changes, and it hadn't been like you paused and changed tempo. but that you'd spliced one part into another. Am I right about that?

Zappa: Oh, yeah. There was a lot of editing. Since that time, we've adjusted our playing so we can sound like we've been edited. I like that effect.

Kofsky: When I've heard jazz groups change tempos, they usually pause and make it quite apparent that the tempo is being changed.

Zappa: That's silly though.

Kofsky: Yes, it is silly.

Zappa: Because you lose the impact.

Kofsky: Yes. Why aren't the lyrics to "Absolutely Free"—

Zappa: More intelligible?

Kofsky: No. Let me back up. I've heard rumors—I know rumors are unreliable—that there was some censorship problem in making this album.

Zappa: Yes, there were.

Kofsky: And I wondered if you deliberately made the lyrics unintelligible.

Zappa: No. The censorship problem was not in the lyrics being unintelligible on the record. I wanted to print the libretto as the liner notes.

Kofsky: That was my next question. Why wouldn't they let you?

Zappa: There's a legal difference between what's on the record and what's on paper.

Kofsky: In other words, you can say it and not get—

Zappa: You can sing it, and that's part of a work of art; but the liner notes to an album are not—you can't defend that in court as a work of art.

Kofsky: Who's the genius who decided that?

Zappa: M-G-M legal department. And this is the one that'll *really* kill you. You see that copy [of the libretto to "Absolutely Free"] you've got in your hand?

Look what they censored out of it—the word "thirteen"! "She's only thirteen and she knows how nasty" [from "Brown Shoes Don't Make It]. You know what they took out? The word "thirteen," not nasty. Yes, they wanted us to say that she was . . .

Look: "Magnificent Instrumental, Ejaculation Number 1." They had to cross it out and change to "Climax." [Laughter]

You dig? They wanted to change, "I'd like to make her do a nasty on the White House lawn," [from "Brown Shoes" . . .] they wanted to change it to—

Kofsky: White House bathroom?

Zappa: No, "I'd like to make her do the crossword puzzle on the back of *TV Guide*."

Kofsky: Are you kidding?

Zappa: Read it. You want to know something else? M-G-M says, "Now, we know—you and I both know—that you want to make her do nasty on the White House lawn can mean only one thing: you want to make her shit on the White House lawn."

Kofsky: Oh! Wow!

Zappa: That's what he said. "Now, look, there are some things that are in bad taste. . . ."

Kofsky: Napalm, of course, is perfectly in good taste. . . .

Zappa: Like dig the way these guys think, man. Also, "she's only 13 and I hear she gets loaded," ["Brown Shoes" . . . again] M-G-M says, "We might run into trouble, because in some states—"

Kofsky: You're not supposed to *drink* until you're eighteen. You know, in some states the legal drinking age is eighteen.

I reviewed the record and I reviewed it without the libretto; and I admit I was very uptight by not having the libretto at hand; and I kind of thought that this might be some kind of publicity or money-making gimmick on your part.

Zappa: The whole logic behind that is, the only way you can teach an American is by example, because they've gone past the point where they'll believe what you tell them.

That's the way it is. They have to get it from a different source. They have to be shown by example. So—in other words, the American advertising system, which is one of the main evils of contemporary society—the whole idea of making people buy things that they don't need is morally wrong. And the only way you're going to mak'em know is to do it, really overdo it—buy, sell, cram. Until they finally say, "What the f—— is this?" Now, the way the libretto is going to be handled is it's going to be printed in *Evergreen Review*, I believe, either *Evergreen* or *Ramparts*. The idea is to carry the whole liner notes; and it will also be available in booklet form, if they want to send for it.

Kofsky: It seems to me very coincidental that the Beatles' new record *Sgt. Pepper's . . .* came out the same time "Absolutely Free" did. I find a great similarity. The Beatles seem to be rejecting the idea that you have to be enslaved to commodities; and that when you're sixty-four years old, all you have is two weeks summer in the Isle of Wight.

Zappa: I think it's probably more subjective than that. It sounds to me like, "what's going to happen when we're sixty-four? Are you still going to buy our shit?" It's a humorous treatment of what happens when a rock and roller gets old.

Kofsky: I didn't get that impression. I juxtaposed that track with the George Harrison thing in front of it ["Within You Without You"], which was talking about, "We could change the world with our love." It seems that what they're saying, "On the one hand you can go off and be free if you want. On the other hand, you can enslave yourself to buy, buy, buy, buy, buy."

Zappa: I believe in what George Harrison says that you can change the world with love—if you really got it. If you really care, you can do it.

Kofsky: Can you love in a society that only teaches hate?

Zappa: Why not? Just to be contrary, you can do it. If you really want to be a rebel, honestly try and love something. And if you really want to be gross about it, try and love the society that's shitty—try and love it enough to do something about it. If you can get enough zealots out there that believe in that sort of activity, you can't stop them, no matter what they look like and where they live, because those are the kind of people that move mountains and you can't do anything about it. They won't take no for an answer.

Kofsky: Let's put in a note here when this thing is edited for the magazine not to take the word "f——" out and the word "shit" out, and so forth, because that would be contrary to the spirit of the interview.

Zappa: Well, like if they're going to substitute any words substitute "do-do" for "shit," got that? And for "f——" we'll have "hunchy-punchy."

[*Society has become very permissive in its acceptance of the use of four-letter words, especially in serious publications. We admit to being rather conservative but do permit the use of some four-letter words as this interview indicates. We recognize that in the future it will be difficult for a responsible periodical to omit the use of all four-letter words.* Ed.]

Kofsky: California is clearly the center of the new popular music. I wonder how you relate the Mothers to some of the Northern California groups like the Jefferson Airplane, and the Grateful Dead, and though it's a Southern California group, Love. I'm curious as to how you see the relationship between you and your audience compared to the relationship between them and their audience.

Zappa: The whole San Francisco scene is promoting a love relationship between the audience and the group. The group is supposed to love the audience to death.

Kofsky: Do you think this exists in practice?

Zappa: No, I don't think so.

Kofsky: Have you seen this firsthand?

Zappa: Sure. Because I find it equally as nonexistent as—well, you go to the Avalon Ballroom and they pass out feathers and bells. That's it, man. That's phony. That's like if we were to pass out Molotov cocktails in the lobby, it'd be just as phony. It's childish, because it's like a club. The key club—you bring a feather and a bell.

Kofsky: What do you think is the relationship between, say, the Airplane and its following, then, if it isn't really love? Do you think it's just, as you suggested earlier, a street gang without fights?

Zappa: I can't really evaluate other band's followings, because I don't know that much about the inner workings of their promotion. All I can say is that people who like the Jefferson Airplane like'em, and people who like the Grateful Dead, they like'em. People have different tastes.

Kofsky: How about the relationship between the Mothers and their audience?

Zappa: It's a little bit different, because our initial appeal is to the outcasts, the weirdos.

Kofsky: Especially the L.A. weirdos. Your whole thing is steeped in the L.A. mystique.

Zappa: Well, we're definitely a product of our environment. That whole band grew up in L.A.

I don't see how people can lump us in with the San Francisco bullshit scene, because it doesn't sound like San Francisco music to me, no matter how objective. . . . Anyway, the people that we hear about that like us—I could show you some of the fan letters. They're just unique, man. These are really the cream of the weirdos of each town, and they're coming from all over. We're getting letters from very strange places.

Kofsky: Do they think in political terms, or what?

Zappa: Some of them do. Some of them think just in terms of like, "I feel funny because people think I'm strange." And, "Say that you like me, please, Mothers of Invention, so that I'll keep on being strange and I'll stay alive in my small town."

Kofsky: What do you do with those letters?

Zappa: We haven't answered any of them yet. We're just now setting up our correspondence. We've got a total of about three hundred fan letters for the past year.

Kofsky: You take this pretty seriously, then?

Zappa: Sure. Why not? Those are live people out there. If you can think of it as somebody who paid four dollars for an album, that's one way to do it, and then you send him an autographed picture. But I'll show you the material we've been preparing for fan consumption.

Kofsky: [Quoting Mothers' first answer to fan mail:] "We could have sent you a cheesy form letter, all purple and mimeographed, something that would probably say, 'The Mothers of Invention want to thank you blah blah for writing such a nifty letter blah and they love their fans who are so loyal and thoughtful blah and blah. But they are so busybusybusybusy that it would be virtually impossible for them to even begin to attempt to consider the possibility of any sort of warm personal reply, blah, blah, blaaahhh.' We could have sent you *that* sort of cheesy letter, instead we have sent you *this* cheesy letter, the text of which reads:

" 'Dearest Wonderful and Perceptive Person: The Mothers of Invention want to thank you blah blah for writing us such a nifty letter, some of which you have written to us on toilet paper—how wonderfully original. Golly gee, we are so awful busy being thrown out of restaurants and hotels in Montreal, ignored by taxis in New York—have you had that trouble too—it's getting so you don't even have to be black not to be picked up—mugged by policemen in Los Angeles and scrutinized by the censors of all major U.S. media. Willikins! It takes so much time to do all that crap we hardly have any time to answer each of you in a warm, personal way. So: If you are a worried girl and you wrote to us because we turn you on and you want our bodies and/or you think we are cute, here is your own personal section of the letter. The answer to any and all questions is, yes, we love you even if you are fat, with pimples. If you are or are considering the possibility of becoming a boy and you think you are very hep and swinging and you wrote to us on a piece of toilet paper, this section is for you: Keep up the good work. We would like to encourage you to become even more nihilistic and destructive. Attaboy. Don't take any gas from your metal shop teacher or that creep with the flat top in physical education who wants to bust your head because you are different. Give them all the finger, just like we would give you the finger for writing to us on a piece of toilet paper.' "

Zappa: Solid! End letter. That's not all; I have to type up a few more sections. OK, that's the initial reply to a fan letter, which has to be modified, because I understand that there are legal complications to saying anything sexual in a form letter.

Kofsky: There are legal complications to everything. Then follows: "Would you be interested in joining what's called a fan club for the Mothers? The official name of the organization is the United Mutations. We call it that because we are certain that only a few special people might be interested in active participation. It will cost you three dollars and you must fill in the accompanying questionnaire. Name, age, sex, height, weight, address, state, zip, father's name, profession, mother's name, profession. Answer these questions briefly: Who is God? ESP? Yes? No? Describe. Best way to describe my social environment is: If I had my way I would change it to: How will you change your social environment? When? What are you afraid of? What sort of help can the Mothers give you?

"On another sheet of paper describe your favorite dream, or nightmare, in clinical detail. Send both sheets with three dollars to the address above and in return we will send you useful information about the Mothers, a small package with some other things you might be interested in. Thank you. Your signature in ink, please."

This is the follow-up letter that accompanies the package:

"Hello. Thank you for responding to our initial proposal. It is necessary to know a few more things about you. We hope you won't mind answering another form letter, but our files require it for continued membership. If you are interested in this worthwhile program of let's call it self-help, please be advised that our work can be continued only if your membership is kept paid yearly and we have periodic reports of your activities within the context of our program. You will be notified by mail for your next membership report. For now, please fill in this form and return it to us and read the enclosed material carefully. We are happy you took an interest in us. Answer these questions briefly. Please enclose a small photo of yourself.

"Are you a mutation? What can you do to help us? People's minds: how many do you control? Why not more? How do you control your subjects? Do they know? Do other people know? How do you avoid problems? Do you group think? Is there another operator near you? Who? Does he/she belong to our association? If no, why not? Describe your relationship with your parents. How can the Mothers assist you? Your signature in ink, please. Date."

Kofsky: I take it you're mostly interested in young people, in particular high school students?

Zappa: Well, they seem to be the only ones left alive.

Kofsky: Perhaps this is a mis-estimate on my part, but so much of your thing seems to be directed towards the high school scene, for example, "I'm losing status at the high school" [from "Status Back Baby"]. For people who know what the public education system is, they're obviously going to be in sympathy with you. They won't be *convinced* because you've already reached your conclusions on their own. They don't need any more propagandizing. And the ones who aren't convinced, they're not going to be convinced by that, because they're not even going to listen to that record, or if they do, they won't listen to it a second time. So then, who is going to be—

Zappa: Influenced by "I'm losing status at the high school?"

Kofsky: Yeah, and that whole genre: "You're Probably Wondering Why I'm Here," and "Mr. America, walk on by" [from *Hungry Freaks, Daddy*].

Zappa: Unfortunately, that's the genre that brought these fan letters to us.

Kofsky: So there are, in small towns and so forth, all these people who really think that there's something wrong with them because they're losing status at the high school?

Zappa: That's right. Think about this for a minute: If you were to graphically analyze the different types of directions of all the songs in the *Freak Out!* album, there's a little something in there for everybody. At least one piece of material is slanted for every type of social orientation within our consumer group, which happens to be six to eighty. Because we got people that like what we do, from kids six years old screaming on us to play "Wowie Zowie." Like I meet executives doing this and that, and they say, "My kid's got the record, and 'Wowie Zowie's' their favorite song."

Kofsky: How did the kid get the record in the first place?

Zappa: They may have an older sister or brother who got hold of the thing and who played it at the house, but the young kids that hear it like "Wowie Zowie," and then there are other high school kids—they're all trying to find something on there that they can identify with. I've gotten a lot of replies that kids like the "Watts Riot song" (*Trouble Comin' Every Day*).

Kofsky: That's a beautiful song; I'm surprised you don't do that more.

Zappa: But the heaviest stuff on there is "It Can't Happen Here" and "Who Are the Brain Police?" Nobody's penetrated "Brain Police"—yet.

Kofsky: Who *are* the Brain Police?

Zappa: I can't tell you that—it's a religious song. But the ones who say they like "Brain Police" like it because it's got some screaming and they love it. The ones that like "Help I'm a Rock", you know that mumbling part at the end, haven't come to realize what the musical structure of that is. They'll perceive it because it's got some gag lines in it.

Kofsky: Who played the piano solo on it?

Zappa: I did.

Kofsky: That's what I thought. Hence, "If you want to become a piano player, go out and buy a Cecil Taylor record." [As Zappa stated in *Hit Parader*].

Zappa: That whole *Freak Out!* album is to be as accessible as possible to the people who wanted to take the time to make it accessible. That list of names in there, if anybody were to research it, it would probably help them a great deal.

Kofsky: The list of names preceded by, "We have been influenced by ——, do not hold it against them?"

Zappa: Yeah.

Kofsky: There again you seem to be very conscious of packaging, promoting, that sort of thing.

Zappa: Of course. The Mothers were packaged two years before we actually put the band together, because I had been doing motivational research in the field, watching successes and failures of other people in the industry.

IN PERSON: THE MOTHERS OF INVENTION

●

DOON ARBUS

The Mothers of Invention remember it well. They remember white bucks and pompadours and pimples and going steady. They remember rock-and-roll in the days of its innocence: songs of self-affirmation ("Rock-and-roll is here to stay/It will never die"); songs of adolescent agony ("I'm so young and you're so old/This my darling I've been told"); the shameless glorification of romantic woe ("Goin' to the river/Gonna jump overboard and drown"); and the eloquence of nonsense lyrics ("pa pa oom mow mow," "dombee doobee dom," or "*sha* da da da, *sha* da da da *da* da"). Alan Freed, the lindy, or even the real Elvis Presley already seem like part of history, but the Mothers were there in their late teens and *they remember.*

Frank Zappa, composer, conductor, lead guitarist and unquestionably the leader, ambles on stage. He is wearing a purple high-school cardigan, knit pants, and butterscotch-colored shoes with pointy, turned-up toes. His face is made of planes and angles, like a house of cards, and is framed by a mantle of squiggly, black curls. The mustache and abrupt goatee form an upside-down anchor. He is like a wild, woodsy hermit, either very benign or very ferocious.

The other six Mothers follow at their leisure. They make an incongruous group. Each seems a distinct, Technicolor character, as identifiable as Hollywood. Billy Mundi, the rotund, unjovial drummer, is a baker from the French Revolution. Roy Estrada, caressing his electric bass, looks perplexed and determined, like a Polish anarchist. Don Preston sits within the circle of piano, organ and clavichord, well intentioned and vague, a Don Quixote before the windmill encounter. Bunk Gardner, absorbed in his collection of wind instruments, appears oblivious to everything except the anticipation of playing music. With his silver hair and trim beard he exudes the unruffled elegance of a riverboat gambler. Jim Black, the wry-eyed, bowlegged beater-of-the-gong, looks like a Mexican *bandido*. Ray Collins, credited with lungs and ingenuity in the program, is a high-browed Viking.

Zappa has not even glanced at the audience yet. He has been adjusting dials and tuning his guitar. He has chatted inaudibly with Don, tied the shoelaces of his butterscotch shoes, and sipped pale coffee from a glass mug. His nonchalance is, of itself, a kind of frenzy. Finally he approaches the center microphone and peers past the lights, scanning rows like a surveyor.

"Hello, pigs." A few people giggle briefly.

Zappa speaks thickly, deliberately, like a 45 rpm record played at 33⅓. It makes him seem supremely dispassionate.

"We're gonna lay some 'thick black sounds' on ya," he says, quoting a phrase from a *New York Times* review of a Mothers' performance.

It begins with a medley of "My Boy friend's Back" ("a rock-and-roll song which some of you may have gotten pregnant to"), followed by "I'm Gonna Bust His Head," and "Ninety-six Tears." Ray is singing and making literal, illustrative gestures. He hunches his shoulders and strides forward, the football-hero boy friend coming back. He places one hand on his hip and swats the air as he sings, "I'm gonna give him such a *smack*." All the Mothers are ravenous mimics; the source of inspiration is not always detectable.

Between numbers a few Mothers wander around stage. Others carry on pantomime conversations with each other or exchange quips. Zappa often talks to the audience. "The *New York Times* said we show contempt for our audience. See," he says, holding up his mug of coffee, "con-temptuously I drink this." He spews a mouthful out towards the audience. Most of it lands at the end of the stage. Ray, almost smiling, sweeps up the mess with a broom. They have made an art of silliness.

In the middle of the show Zappa introduces "this strange little person in her mod clothes," who is called Uncle Meat. She is a very young, expressionless girl with silky hair, who sings, sometimes in duet with Ray. They stand with their arms around each other rubbing chests and looking tender and mournful. They even dance with each other, separated by a century of style. Uncle Meat also gazes through a kaleidoscope or rattles a hypnotic rhythm on the tambourine or parries Ray's carrot swordplay using a lettuce leaf for a shield.

They are much more fun to watch than listen to, so that towards the end, when they begin to tire and the singing becomes sporadic and the kidding around loses its fervor, the music becomes relentless. It goes on and on, the volume and insistence making listening to it like a day at the ocean: Afterwards, nothing can be seen but waves. And when it is all over, ending very abruptly (Zappa says, "Good night," and all seven leave the stage), the music seems to go on without them, an engulfing, independent rhythm, like a complementary image of the show.

ZAPPA AND THE MOTHERS: UGLY CAN BE BEAUTIFUL

●

SALLY KEMPTON

It is 1 A. M. on a Friday night and the Mothers of Invention are recording part of the soundtrack for their forthcoming movie. Ian is playing the harpsichord and Bunk is playing the flute. They huddle together in a cluster of microphones, Bunk leaning over Ian's shoulder to read the music propped up on the harpsichord stand. Bunk wears a goatee and a matching moustache, and his long thick hair is gray (in the studio light it looks like a powered wig). Resembling a figure in an old etching, he bends closer to Ian, his flute poised, and Ian straightens his back and places his fingers on the harpsicord keys. Poised like musicians at a nineteenth-century musicale, they wait for a signal to begin. One feels they are waiting to play a Mozart sonata.

Inside the control booth Frank Zappa, wearing a T-shirt bearing the legend "Herzl Camp, Garner, Wisconsin," is fiddling with knobs on the control board. "You're going to have to do the parody notes more staccato, Ian," he says through the intercom.

"You want a little bebop vibrato on that too?" calls Ian.

"Yeah, a little bebop a go go," says Frank. Dick Cunk, the engineer, flips the "record" switch.

"OK, for fame and stardom," says Frank. "You ready?"

Ian and Bunk begin to play a series of dissonant, rhythmic, oddly beautiful chords. The people in the control booth listen intently.

"This is going to be a nice soundtrack," someone says.

Frank Zappa is bent over a music sheet, writing out the next piece. "Yeah," he says. "This is one the folks can enjoy listening to at home."

Frank Zappa is an ironist. He is also a serious composer, a social satirist, a promoter, a recording genius, but his most striking characteristic is his irony. Irony permeates his music, which is riddled with parodies of Charles Ives and Guy Lombardo, of Bartòk and the Penguins and Bo Diddly and Ravel and Archie Shepp and Stravinsky and a whole army of obscure fifties rhythm and blues singers. It permeates his lyrics, which are filled with outlandish sexual metaphors and evocations of the culture of the American high school and the American hippie.

Irony is the basis of his public image. In pursuit of absurdity he has had himself photographed sitting naked on the toilet. His latest album is titled *We're Only in It for the Money.* And he has appeared on television speaking in well-rounded periods about music and society and The Scene, all the while emanating a kind of inspired freakishness. Zappa's is the sort or irony which arises from an immense self-consciousness, a distrust of one's own seriousness. It is the most modernist of defense mechanisms, and Zappa is an almost prototypically modernist figure; there are moments when he seems to be living out a parody of the contemporary sensibility.

And now he and his group are teenage idols, or anti-idols, and Zappa's irony, which, because it is so often expressed through contemporary clichés, is the most accessible part of his musical idiom, turns on audiences and makes the Mothers, in addition to everything else, a splendid comedy act. Until recently Zappa's voice, the paradigm California voice, could be heard on the radio doing "greasy teen-age commercials" for Hagstrom Guitars. During the Mothers' live appearances he sits on a stool, his expression deadpan above his bandillero moustache, and occasionally he will lean over and spit on the floor under the bandstand, saying to the audience: "Pigs!"

"Actually, we don't turn on audiences," he said the other day. "Not in the sense that other groups do, anyway. I think of that sort of thing as the strobes going and everybody dancing and love-rock-at-the-Fillmore bullshit—if anybody felt like that about us it'd be for the wrong reasons. Last week we were playing in Philadelphia and we got seven requests, so we played them all at once. It was fantastic. Sherwood was playing the sax part to one song: the whole thing, even the rests. It was really great. But nobody knew what we were playing. They couldn't even tell the songs apart. Half the time, when we're really doing something, the audience doesn't know what it is. Sometimes the guys in the band don't know."

But the Mothers' first album sold a quarter of a million copies and the second has done almost as well. And when they played a long stretch at the Garrick last summer they were beset by loyal groupies. Perhaps the groupies sensed the presence of a governing intelligence, perhaps they simply dug perversity. In any case, the Mothers have an audience.

Frank Zappa is twenty-seven years old. He was born in Baltimore and began playing drums in a rock-and-roll band in Sacramento when he was fifteen.

"It's almost impossible to convey what the r and b scene was like in Sacramento," he says. "There were gangs there, and every gang was loyal to a particular band. They weren't called groups, they were called bands. They were mostly Negro and Mexican, and they tried to get the baddest sound they could. It was very important not to sound like jazz. And there was a real oral tradition of music. Everybody played the same songs, with the same arrangements, and they tried to play as close as possible to the original record. But the thing was that half the time the guys in the band had never heard the record—somebody's older brother would own the record, and the kid would memorize it and teach it to everybody else. At one point all the bands in Sacramento were playing the same arrangement of 'Okey Dokey Stomp' by Clarence Gatemouth Brown. The amazing thing was that it sounded almost note for note like the record."

Zappa was lying in bed, eating breakfast and playing with his three-month-old baby. He lives with his wife, Gail, and the baby, in a long basement apartment in the West Village. The apartment has a garden and its walls are papered with posters and music sheets and clippings from magazines; there is a full-length poster of Frank in the hall and a rocking chair in the living room with a crocheted cover that says "Why, what pigs?"

Frank was in bed because he had been up all night before, recording. "The reason I can stand New York is because I spend all my time here or at the studio," he said.

"Mostly at the studio," said his wife, smiling.

"Let's see, my life," he said. "Well, when I was sixteen my father moved us to a little town out in the country. That was terrible, I hated it. I was used to Sacramento, you see. I was the strangest thing that ever hit that high school. They were so anxious to get rid of me they even gave me a couple of awards when I graduated. After that my father wanted me to go to college. I said no, I was interested in music, I didn't want to go to college. So I hung out at home for a while, but there was nobody to talk to, everybody else being at college, so I finally decided I should go too. That was very ugly. I stayed for a year. In the meantime I had shacked up with this girl and married her. We stayed married for five years during which time I held a number of jobs" (he listed the jobs). "Then in 1963 we were living in Cucamonga and there was a recording studio there which I bought for $1000, also assuming the former owner's debts. He had hundreds of tapes, among them such big hits as" (he named three or four obscure songs) "and I took the tapes and the equipment and began fooling around. About that time I got divorced and moved into the studio. I spent all my time experimenting; a lot of stuff the Mothers do was worked out there."

A year later the studio was torn down to make room for a widened road, but by that time he had gotten the Mothers together. "We were playing at local beer joints for like six dollars a night. I finally decided this would not do, so I began calling up all the clubs in the area. This was in 1965, and to get work you had to sound like the Beatles or the Rolling Stones. You also had to have long hair and due to an unfortunate circumstance all my hair had been cut off. I used to tell club managers that we sounded exactly like the Rolling Stones. Anyway we finally got a booking in a club in Pomona, and were something of a hit. It was more because of our act than because of our music. People used to go away and tell their friends that here was this group that insulted the audience.

"Then M-G-M sent someone around to sign us to a contract. Their guy came into the club during a set of 'Brain Police' and he said, 'Aha, a protest rhythm and blues group,' so they paid us accordingly. The fee we got for signing was incredibly small, particularly considering the number of guys in the group."

Nowadays, of course, Zappa runs something of an empire. He has an advertising agency ("mostly to push our own products, at least so far"), and a movie coming out which someone else shot but for which they are going to do the soundtrack. The movie is a surrealistic documentary called "Uncle Meat"; it is shot in a style Zappa refers to as "hand-held Pennebaker bullshit," and it will be edited to fit the music.

"Then we're going to do a monster movie in Japan—Japan is where they do the best monster work. And we're starting our own record company. We'll record our own stuff and also some obsure new groups."

It was time for him to go to the studio. The Mothers have rented Apostolic Studios on Tenth Street for the entire month of January. "One hundred and eighty hours—not as much time as the Beatles use, of course, we can't afford that"—and that is where Zappa spends most of his time. He puts on a brown leather greatcoat, pulls a red knitted cap over his ears, and sets out, talking about his music as he walks.

"Stockhausen isn't really an influence," he says. "That is, I have some of his records but I don't play them much. Cage is a big influence. We've done a thing with voices, with talking, that is very like one of his pieces, except that of course in our piece the guys are talking about working in an airplane factory, or their cars.

"It was very tough getting the group together in the beginning. A lot of guys didn't want to submit to our packaging. They didn't like making themselves ugly, but they especially didn't like playing ugly. It's hard getting a musician to play ugly, it contradicts all his training. It's hard to make them understand that all that ugliness taken together can come out sounding quite beautiful."

The studio, when he arrived, was nearly deserted, except for Mother Don Preston, who sat at the organ wearing earphones and playing a piece audible only to himself. "Can you run a playback on the violins?" he asked when Frank came in.

"Sure," said Frank. "We recorded this thing last night. I found some violins in a closet and I gave them to three of the guys. None of them had ever played a violin before. They were making all these weird sounds on them, and then in the middle I got them to add some farts. It's a concerto for farts and violins."

But instead of playing back the violin thing, Dick put on a tape of "Lumpy Gravy," one of the Mothers' new records, an instrumental piece, framed at the beginning and end with cocktail music, and interspersed with quiet, hollow, surreal voices talking behind a continuous hum of resonating piano strings. The music has overtones of Bartòk and Ives, but by some stylistic alchemy it ends by sounding like nothing but Zappa. It is an impressive record. Three or four people had drifted into the control room while it was playing, and after it was over someone said, "I love that piece."

"Yeah, but will the kids go for it," said Frank.

"It's good to have it out," said Don, "so people will know what you can do."

"No, no," Frank said. "It's good to have it out so I can take it home and listen to it."

ROCK-AND-ROLL WOMAN

•

MICHAEL THOMAS

John Cooke had a party a couple of months ago in an iron-lung factory in Cambridge, Massachusetts. It belongs to J. H. Emerson and Co., that's his uncle. Picture all these people, say a hundred odd, following little red arrows through three floors of sinister, nay baroque, hospital supplies, any number of artificial limbs and pleural suction pumps and special rocking beds (they're for people with polio, he will explain), now and then picking up a straggler who lost his way, counting out ten paces as the sign stuck to the micro-manipulator says, and turning left up tiny wooden staircases, it's like sneaking in and out of all the doors you even saw that say *Do Not Enter,* you keep looking over your shoulder and you talk in whispers if at all, parties at J. H. Emerson and Co. are like hanging out in the attic at Dr. No's house. Finally you come to a door with Spider Man on it, and that's where John Cooke lives when he's in Boston. Inside, there are deviled eggs and chili beans and booze and all, and everybody Jim Kweskin knows in town.

John Cooke, Harvard '62–'63, sometimes photographer, weekend movie maker (he was on the Pennebaker crew at Monterey), refugee guitarist from the Charles River Valley Boys (he's the one who used to sing "Yes, It Is"), has a new gig. He's the gentleman road manager for Big Brother and the Holding Company. Which means he wakes up the boys in the band and gets them on a plane to Detroit in time, he makes sure everybody has television in their rooms, and he explains to Albert B. Grossman, manager, just how surprised you feel when you wake up in the morning on a sunny Boston day and find five thousand dollars' worth of equipment was heisted the night before from the Psychedelic Supermarket and there's two sets to play that night and a concert tomorrow afternoon and you can't even get into the club because there's a symposium on the Boston sound going on and all the hippies of Massachusetts Avenue are there wearing buttons that say "I Love the Ultimate Spinach," under the delusion, their's and M-G-M's, that

Boston's where it's at this year. (Oh, Grossman, *he* just grins like a bear, he grins and says, "Make the club pay.") And it also means getting in some Southern Comfort for the party, and then Janis Joplin grins that San Francisco grin. She grins all the way home when she's feeling good.

At John Cooke's party I was trying to get the last butterscotch out of a Callard and Bowser's package, but my finger kept slipping on the silver foil and I finally had to tear it open, and Janis Joplin came in, in a not-so-brand-new pillbox fur hat, with a fur handbag on her arm and bells jingling against the tight blue silk on her thighs, a quart of Southern Comfort under her arm and beads around her ankle.

"It's one-hundred-percent proof," she said to someone at the door. Her voice rasps like she's got sand in her throat. She'd just come from a concert in Providence and she was weary, but was grinning. "It was groovy. All the kids were, like, hippies."

Her face is pale, almost chalky, but she looks as though she spends a lot of time outdoors, her forehead is furrowed and her cheeks are plump, her hair is raggedy, it's the kind of face to catch the eye of whoever it is draws *Li'l Orphan Annie,* except that her eyes roam too far and stare too hard. She looks like a beautiful barmaid with beads. She cackles when she laughs.

"We were playing in a club in L.A. (and you know we don't know anybody in L.A.), and we walked into the dressing room, and there's thousands of empty beer cans and Southern Comfort bottles and whiskey bottles all over the place, and drunks sitting all over the floor, and Leary sitting cross-legged in the middle with his beatific smile. And Peter comes lurching over to him and drunkenly talked to him for about thirty minutes, incomprehensible, and Leary sat there, just like a bird, sweet and clear. He was real nice. Did I ever say he wasn't nice? He didn't drink, though. But then, we didn't take acid, did we?"

That's Peter S. Albin, Gemini, bass player for Big Brother, who wrote a song that goes, "*I'm a pterodactyl,*" repeated three times, followed by "*Flying for your love,*" also repeated three times. He's always the most gregarious. It was he who somehow got himself locked into an iron lung at the party. A big wooden box, it was, like an electric chair with a lid and a Plexiglass helmet on top. A bunch of people came to look, one or two blew smoke down his airhole, he looked pretty bashful after a while.

I first saw Big Brother about a year ago, it was the first time I'd ever been to San Francisco and the first time I'd been to the Fillmore. And, if you remember, it was before the hippies became a middle-class phenomenon and a national embarrassment, and Haight Street was not yet the Atlantic City boardwalk of the underground, not quite. It was when, if you'll forgive the rank nostalgia, a hippy was a hippy and not a *Time* Magazine stringer with a borrowed flower in his hair, when a freak was a freak and not necessarily Frank Zappa. It was when the Fillmore still had a little fresh air.

I went to see Howlin' Wolf in his overalls. But before he came bebopping out with his soulful broom, while I was still trying to find a good place to sit on the floor and take in the light show, Big Brother came on, and somebody I knew from New York who was shooting a film in there, a mild man with a love of Mozart, give me the warning. I wouldn't believe Janis something, he promised, *he* couldn't believe her and *I* wouldn't believe her, she was fan*tas*tic.

Now the band was ragged, the music was manic, overblown, most of the time incoherent, they played fast and loud but nothing much went anywhere, it was an anarchic psychedelic jerk-off. But Janis something was, truly, something else. She was *so* tough. She sang like a rock-and-roll banshee and leaped about the stage like a dervish. It was the raunchiest, grittiest, most attacking rhythm-and-blues singing I'd ever heard, it made the fifteen-year-old kid next to me feel so good he spilled a bottle of orange Day Glo all over my shoes.

"Who's that?" I asked him.

"Oh, it's Janis Joplin," he said. "Look at your shoes."

She sang like a down-home psycopath. She threw the microphone from hand to hand, she straddled it and threatened to eat it whole, she tossed her head and stamped her foot and punched her thigh and shook her fist at the audience and she shivered all over; she wasn't pretty, she was just plain shake-that-thing erotic. ("A sex goddess," said John Cooke. "You're fired, John," said she.)

Gonna knock ya, rock ya, sock it to ya now! she sang. It wasn't a promise, it was more of a threat.

"I think the way that you're *good* at anything, I mean I can't say for anything else, but I know for me, when I'm singing, I can't be thinking about my moti*va*tion, you know, I can't be thinking about any kind of bullshit like that. I've gotta just close my eyes and get inside my head and sing. And when I'm singing, it's really like a *rush,* do you know what I mean, it's such a *heavy* moment. When it's gone, it's like, you can rem*em*-ber it, but you can't ever be aware of it again until it happens again. And then it's all there again, and then it goes. It's, like, just a great moment, you know? It's like an orgasm, you can't rem*em*ber it, but you remember it."

All I'd ever known about Big Brother and the Holding Company was that they were another Haight-Ashbury neighborhood band, and something someone once told me about a singer they had, modest fellow, name of Buddha.

"Oh, the Buddha, he's like Vito, he was just a character on the San Francisco scene for a while. He'd just get up and lay his trip on everyone. The guys would play, like, a long jam, and he'd say, 'Everybody groove,' and 'Everybody touch everybody,' it was just a thing, a group exhortation. He performed with the band about three or four times, that's all."

The band in fact came together in 1965 in the way bands did in San Francisco that year. Peter spoke to Sam and Sam called Jim and everybody knew Chet Helms (because a Family Dog is a band's best friend), and David gave up painting for a while, and they all got together at somebody's house, and what else would they choose to be called but Big Brother and the Holding Company, the year being 1965 and the place, San Francisco by the sea. Says long tall Sam, "First time I ever met Peter, he had this weird idea for starting a rock group which would speak to all the children of the nation in their own language. I thought, What's this nut trying to do, what trip is he on?"

They'd all been playing a little rock-and-roll, a little bluegrass, a little folk music, Sam had even been playing classical guitar, and Janis was singing a little blues in the bars round about.

"I went to California at a very young and fucked-up stage, about eighteen. I used to sing in a little bar outside of Austin, Texas, called Thredgill's. Fantastic bar. All kinds of real-live hillbillies come in every Saturday night, and everybody brings their guitars and sits around a big wooden table and drinks free beer and plays. I sang Rosie Maddox songs. But I didn't really sing hard until I got with this band."

They began playing in the ballrooms and the parks, rabid

blues-country-freak-rock, if not for all the children of the nation, at least for all their friends and neighbors in the California sun. They even cut a record for Mainstream about that time, but it didn't get released until after the Monterey Pop Festival, Mainstream not being the most considerate of record companies, Mainstream being, in fact, the kind of merchant company that makes lots of records and sits on them with their fingers crossed until something like the Monterey Festival happens along and they wake up on Monday morning and find Big Brother and the Holding Company is all of a sudden worth at least an ad in *Billboard*. It's a funky kind of record, it sounds like it was recorded on a six-transistor portable, not too loud so as not to wake the neighbors. Nobody takes any risks, but still, its ballsy, it's like a Kodak Brownie snapshot, not too well exposed, but you can tell what was going on and there are suggestions of what it might have been.

"The reason that the record is so bad is because we were young and naïve and we were misproduced and we had no manager and we were, if not ill advised, not advised at all, and we didn't know what we were doing and they took advantage of us. They gave us three days to do that whole album, and like, if we tried to do anything creative in the studio, they would have thrown us out. If we couldn't get a song down in ten takes, they'd say, 'Play an easier one,' you know what I mean, they didn't want us to do anything good, they just wanted to get us out as quickly as they could. Then they just held it until, you know, our name got to be big after the Monterey Festival, and then they released the album. Until then they had no plans of releasing it or promoting it or pushing it or anything. Because of *our* efforts our name is worth something, and they put out an album recorded a year and half previously to capitalize on our name."

(Janis manages to run it all down in one breath; in her rusty voice it always sounds like she's got catarrh.)

"It's not really *that* bad," says David Getz, the drummer, B.F.A., M.F.A., Fulbright Fellow, sometime second cook and "freak with no context," who came to San Francisco fresh from a year playing with jazz groups in Poland. I forgot to ever ask him about that.

Big Brother is a better band now, they play better and she sings better than they were at Monterey, and they were better at Monterey than they were when they made their first record. And with luck, they're a better band than they were the Friday night in March when Bill Graham decided to bring some of that San Francisco charisma to New York, and christened the Village Theater the Fillmore East, and Big Brother got up and set out to fit the battle of Jericho right there and then and lost. They fell victim to their own reputation. What I'm trying to say is, they're getting better all the time, but, unhappily, they're getting louder too, and there's not much a good old girl can do but scream to be heard, so that Big Brother, at best, walks a thin red line between music and noise, and that night, when the sound was on (and lousy sound it was), they were appalling. She hollered like a fishwife.

I wanna show you, baby, that a woman can be tough, she sang. I felt like the guy in a Jules Feiffer cartoon of the mind, who went up the mountain with a flower, and a bell, and a joss-stick, and a pair of crystal spectacles, and a Ravi Shankar tape catridge, all prepared to glimpse eternity in a snowflake, only to find he'd been burned, and the pill he held in his hot little hand was, say, 750 micrograms of Compoz. It was a rude awakening. Any good band plays a down set now and then, but Big Brother does it with what seems like vengeful glee. It's entropical, it's flabby.

"At the beginning of the year we each bought two pounds of speed, see . . ." says Sam, but they all cry nay.

"Like, at a point, it seems to me, at some tenuous point, I wouldn't be able to say when it was, our attitude towards, like, how we were going to do the songs changed. Where *my* head is at is that I don't like to improvise a whole lot. Improvising vocally is very hard, we do put some of that into our songs, I have parts where I improvise, but I'm not going to go on stage for a forty-five minute set and just improvise, man, I'm just not. So I want what we play to have, like, well, possibly, you narrow down your range from how good you can be, down to where you're more better every time, and you don't have such a variance. I think the music ought to get to where, like, at your worst, you're good, and when you're inspired you're much better, you know what I mean? And, in order to get to where you're at least good, you've gotta learn the tune. You can't rely on inspiration every night."

Sometimes she looks as tough as Bonnie Parker in the old photographs, sometimes she looks like a motherless child. I wasn't at Monterey, but I've read the book and seen the movie, and Janis Joplin singing *Love Is Like a Ball and Chain,* wrenching it out of some deep dark nether region of her Texas soul, is one of the very very heavy moments in rock-and-roll. She stands with her legs apart, pawing the ground with one foot, clutching the microphone as though it might disintegrate if she let go, her eyes closed, her nipples hard under her knit silver shirt, fracturing the lyric, wringing it out, and at that moment she stopped being the girl who sings with Big Brother and became a rumor. The voodoo lady of rock.

"It was such a fine time, really fine."

The day I saw the film was the day I saw the poster (it was pinned to the door of the ladies' room at the studio), that big black-and-white photograph of Janis in sulky disarray, more to the point, Janis with her shirt open to the waist. Her hair hangs down, but part of the rumor (like the Jim Morrison rumor) has to do with photographs like that.

("A new *kind* of sex goddess," said John Cooke.

"I don't know about that. I don't think I can relate that way. I still sing the same. Maybe better.")

Snapshot: at the Psychedelic Supermarket in Boston she sat on an amp, her leg swinging to and fro, her arms folded, sipping a can of beer like a raggamuffin Mae West, grinning that San Francisco grin. She enjoys herself. Janis is the last rock-and-roll singer I can ever imagine sashaying off after the Maharishi. You can't sock "Hare Krishna" to anyone.

"No, man, we're on a whole opposite trip, the other end. I'm not saying anything about his validity, it's just where we're not at. He's on, like, a non-everything trip, purifying your soul, you know, and we, well I can't speak for everybody but I know where we're at, you know, getting stoned and taking care of your head that way. You know what I mean, there's like stonedness and freedom and letting go and getting inside your head and wailing and *not* rising above it all. Acid scares me, it's a little too heavy, and I won't take STP. I have to set aside several days if I want to take acid, you know what I mean. I take it, I have taken it, and I'll take it again, but I don't like to take it a whole lot."

Right now I'm a little tired of California sympathy. I'm tired of being patted on the head and being told how unhappy I must be because I don't live on the Coast, I'm tired of being pitied by the bland and beautiful people of Laurel Canyon and the funky ones from the San Francisco Bay because I haven't crossed over to the sunny side of the street, poor fellow, stranded in the sunless uptight wastes of New York City, where everything is dark and dirty, threatened on every side by speed freaks and Poor Immigrants, the whole rote-California-Blue Jay-Way riff is becoming as mannered and as wanly familiar as a Derek Taylor press release or an Andy Wickham poem (Englishmen both, nobody *comes* from California). But there's no denying that the Fillmore East is a lot less agreeable than the Fillmore West. And West Coast bands, and especially San Francisco bands, *do* seem to have a lot more fun than East Coast bands, even with all those New York speed freaks messing up the vibrations with their colds in the nose.

"In San Francisco, we play for free in the park. You can't find a better audience that that, they're beautiful," says Janis.

"It's so very warm, and it's about two blocks from all the liquor stores. You buy a bit of juice and come down and in a little while everybody turns on and watches music," says Sam.

"It's like a park," says Peter.

Big Brother and the Holding Company are Haight Street natives, they don't give away free food on the streets, but they are conspicuous in the community and some of their best friends are Diggers. It's an ethnic group.

"Chocolate George, one of the Angels, got killed, and they threw a free thing in the park. We got lots of beer, and they got the Dead and us. It was just a beautiful thing, all the hippies and Angels were just stoned out of their heads, passing DMT, you couldn't imagine a better funeral. It was the greatest party in the world," says Janis.

"We sent him off just like he would have wanted, man," says Sam.

"Everybody was fucking in the bushes," says Jim, the lead guitarist (he also plays Kelp horn), who doesn't talk much, but has an eye for important details. (At John Cooke's party he was all but assaulted on the livingroom rug by a buxom wench from Providence, but he kept his cool like the true Capricorn he is.)

Stand in a queue for a concert any time nowadays and you'll find out things about your friends they never knew themselves. There may never been an underground, but if there was, it couldn't keep from surfacing, and by the time Janis Joplin got to New York, the rumor had spread river deep and mountain high. Why, while I stood in fear of my life in the crowd outside the Fillmore East last March, there were kids to my left who could've told me her bra size if I'd asked, and kids to my right whose cousin's best friend's roommate at Berkeley had told them for a fact she never wears one. New York was already and waiting for her, they knew what the band could do better than they did themselves.

"It's been much nicer than we expected, the whole East Coast trip, about twice as good as we expected."

But then, Big Brother is in steady hands now, none other than the ever-so-nimble fingers of Albert B. Grossman, the Big Daddy of managers. They'll get all the time they need for their next Columbia record, and all the advice they could possibly want.

"He's just mashed potaters," says Janis.

They get their photo taken by Richard Avedon these days.

The band is Big Brother and the Holding Company, but she's not Big Brother. ("The name is just a head trip. It doesn't mean anything. Before I joined the band it was called Big Brother and the Holding Company, and we said as a joke I was Big Brother because I was the girl and the least likely one to be Big Brother. Now people think that it's really true.") She's not Big Brother, she's just the Great White Beautiful Bitch of rock-and-roll, right out of the heart of Texas, "a great broad," says Bill Graham, and maybe the best rock-and-roll presence in the country.

And John Cooke may be host of the year.

JAMES BROWN IS OUT OF SIGHT

●

DOON ARBUS

I had been waiting for hours outside the part castle-part hacienda home of James Brown, while somewhere inside the great man lay sleeping. He's been working very hard these days, and he's made it big: "Pappa's Got a Brand New Bag" and "I Got You" both sold over a million copies, and he tours the country with his own show three hundred and thirty-five days a year. He performs for an average of five thousand people a day.

I had only seen him once before, on the TAMI show: James Brown and the Famous Flames. It was filmed in Electronovision, which may account for his looking so peculiar. Everyone else did as well: Lesley Gore and the Beach Boys and the Supremes. But he looked strangest of all. The giant head and broad shoulders. And the rest of him progressively smaller. Short legs. Tiny feet.

Someone finally does let me in the house after he wakes up and says it's okay. Nobody does anything without orders from the boss. But when he wakes up and gives the word, someone lets me in, through the back door, to a den which looks like a gymnasium—all upholstered in black leatherette with a great post in the middle of the room. It's very bare. Photographs of him crowded onto the wall above the imposing curved bar. Photographs of him, beaming proudly as he accepts an award, or demonstrating enthusiasm as he signs an autograph for a child, or sweating luxuriously on his knees over the microphone. They hang in a cluster amidst the rows of bottles, and there are shelves with rows of placques and trophies engraved with praise—*To The Hardest Working Performer.* Three large white B's are emblazoned on the black upholstered wall at the staircase.

Every few moments someone wanders into the den and pauses in the middle of the room distractedly, standing there muttering about the cold, or the time, or a lost shoe, or what car to take to the airport. Then wanders out again. James

Brown has to catch a four o'clock plane to Virginia Beach for a show that evening. A few people who are still here will fly down with him: Bobby Byrd and Bobby Bennett and Lloyd Stallworth, the three Famous Flames. All the other members of the show have already left. The musicians in the band and the band leader, Nat Jones; and James Brown's own girl group, The Three Jewels; and all the members of the unaccountably popular burlesque-comedy acts. They have gone ahead in the private bus. The equipment and the instruments have left in the two-ton truck. And all the costumes have been packed away in the black plastic garment bags, each with a white "B" on the front, and driven down by car. That's the way it always is when the James Brown Show is on tour.

Nobody seems to know exactly how many people travel with the show. Or if they do know, they're not sure if it mightn't be some kind of betrayal to reveal the exact number. So some say forty and some say fifty and some just say "a whole lot." Cautious and guarded. Afraid to say anything that might be used against him. ("What are you trying to find out? You looking for the good things? Or you just wanna know bad things?")

Bobby Bennett, one of the Famous Flames, has come into the den from upstairs. He wears a shiny brick-red suit and black Nylon socks and the big jeweled ring that cost him $10,000 which he has to remember to give to someone to hold for him before he goes on stage.

Bobby goes into a small room off the den. It has all sorts of black appliances in it: a black refrigerator, a black sink, a black washing machine. And it also has an ironing board. That's what Bobby needs. He has come to iron his clothes. "Yes sir. You gotta learn to do everything yourself. No one's gonna do it for you, so you learn. 'Cause there's a twenty-dollar fine for having wrinkles in your clothes. Or making a bad goof on stage. Or gettin' in trouble. It's like the army," he explains cheerfully. "You gotta have discipline. Otherwise, where are you at? Without discipline, nothin' gets done right." The fines go into the treasury to pay for parties and other fun things.

Mr. Brown is upstairs in curlers under the dryer. Bobby has just finished putting Mr. Brown's hair up in curlers and Mr. Brown under the dryer. He does it every day. To get the kinks out, to make Mr. Brown's hair big and round. Bobby says I can't go up yet. Nat Stillwell, the chauffeur, in his elegant blue-gray uniform, comes to collect the suitcases.

There are three cars in the garage. The purple Cadillac limousine, the red Stingray with "Mr. Dynamite" painted on the side, and the white Cadillac, the '66. That's the one Mr. Brown has decided to take to the airport. It's very roomy. Bobby goes upstairs to check on Mr. Brown's hair. Nat Stillwell goes outside with the suitcases to check on the white Cadillac.

Bobby calls from upstrais, "You wanna come up now? It's okay." Up the winding staircase into the main hall with the bright glass chandelier and the spongy green carpet protected with long strips of plastic. Yes. He is there, bethroned on a straight-backed kitchen chair against the wallpaper of orange and yellow flowers. His head of curlers resting lazily against the wall. He looks like the blackest man on earth. Actually, though, he is lavender, a wierd, superhuman, deathlike lavender. Or mauve; the great mauve face with the deep grooves about his mouth and across his forehead. Almost like scars. And the grave hollows under his cheekbones. He seems to blot out the light where he sits.

"Just call me James." He smiles grandly. Magnanimously. His teeth set in a neat, gleaming row.

Bobby is taking out the curlers. Ceremoniously, one by one. He teases each lock into place. Leaning over from behind to get at the front, careful not to obstruct James's view of things. He has learned not to interfere with conversations when he's doing James's hair. Creating the great round head.

The short kimona robe hangs open at his chest. A silver thing strung from a chain around his neck rests against his chest. Rests there noticeably. Ah, but he won't tell what it is. And like a spell, his not telling makes it impossible to guess.

The radio is on. They are playing his song. They are playing "I Got You" by James Brown. It is number three on WABC. "*I feel good. I knew that I would now. I fee-eel good. I knew that I wou-ould. So good. So good. 'Cause I got you.*" It makes him feel real good. He raises his hand and everyone freezes. Silent and motionless. Listening. But no one listens as well as he. He gazes deep into nowhere. He is part of it. It is part of him. Very good. He starts to sing with it. "I like that. '*Sugar and spi-ice.*'" The two voices of James Brown. The two incredible, hoarse voices of James Brown. Straining together, a Brown fugue.

We check in at the Admiralty Motel in Virginia Beach. The five of us: James and Bobby Byrd and Bobby Bennett and Lloyd and I. James has armed me with one of his suitcases and a pad and pencil. Insisting that I carry the pad and pencil all the time. To prove that I'm a traveling reporter. To guard against the assumptions of some dirty Southern minds. The pinched-featured white desk clerk with the plastered tan hair straightens up as we enter. He is marvelously meek. "Yes, Mr. Brown. Your room is all ready, Mr. Brown. Suite A-20, sir. It's all made up. And we have the three gentlemen in A-18, A-16 and A-14. But as for the young lady," he says, his eyes shifting uneasily from James to me and back again, "well, I'm terribly sorry, but the closest room we have is C-115. I do hope that's all right."

James winks. He isn't surprised that they "forget the B's. Just left 'em out *all* together. Playin' it real safe." He knew it would be that way. He hadn't wanted me to come at all at first. Back in the house in St. Alban's when I'd asked him if I could. He tried to dissuade me. Not just because his Negro fans in the South wouldn't understand if they got the idea he was going around with a white girl. It wasn't just that. He was worried for my *safety*. Because it's *dangerous* down there. "You remember what happened to President Kennedy."

But he seemed to have changed his mind at some point. Sometime while he was dressing. Because when he came downstairs again in his shiny purple shirt and purple pants, two inches taller than before thanks to the heels of the pale suede boots, he winked confidentially. "Don't you worry about *nothing*. You'll go wherever I go. I'll look after you. And if you write this the way it really happens, it's gonna be like *I Passed for White*. Only the other way 'round."

Suite A-20 wasn't very grand for a suite. Just a huge living room with a couch and two chairs, a dressing alcove, a bedroom and two bathrooms. Both television sets are on, one in the bedroom and one in the living room. James is sprawled opulently in one of the chairs, talking on the telephone. Bobby is doing his hair again, wielding the expert, inobtrusive comb. Gert pours champagne for all. James knows a groovy way to drink it. Pour salt in it: it makes more bubbles and stings. It also helps you burp. There is some fried chicken. "You dig *hot sauce?*" Eat. Drink. Have a ball. "So long, baby. I'll call ya." He hands Bobby the telephone to hang up. "She's in *love* with me," he laughs negligently. "Well, like I'm *all man,* you know." Lots of them are in love with him. It can sure make life *complicated*. He reaches for some more chicken. A real *hot piece.* It's *out o' sight.* He fixes on me. Fixes on me with those invincible black eyes. As if there's no one but him and me. He's giving me the James Brown Story.

You wouldn't *believe* how poor he was when he was a kid living in Augusta, Georgia. *Real* poor. He had to pick cotton and shine shoes and dance in the streets for people who would throw nickels and dimes and sometimes even quarters at his feet. That's what it was like. "I had a *real* big family. I didn't have no brothers and sisters. But a lot of *close* relatives. Know what I mean? And I had to help support 'em." He started out as a prizefighter. Former boxing champ, Beau Jack, spotted his incredibly fast footwork and offered to coach him as a fighter. "Boxing. That's *all work* and none of the *fun.*" Later, he started playing baseball. "I was an extraordinary pitcher," he confesses, with a chance to play professional baseball but he injured his leg. That put an end to his career as a ball player. He organized The Famous Flames and started out in show business, singing Gospel-derived songs for predominantly adult audiences in the South. But the whole thing really began in 1955. In Macon, Georgia. He and The Famous Flames made an unaccompanied recording of "Please, Please, Please." A local disc jockey played it on his radio show as a personal favor to James Brown. Well, since then he hasn't needed many favors. His record sales total well over 5,000,000. A huge following of adult and teenage fans all around the country. But he's gotta find the true challenge. Expand to the limits of himself. Or further. So he can't stop. Not with singing. He's got to be moving on. "Maybe into the acting field. I think I'm gonna be an actor next."

"It can be pretty scary up where I am. I mean like everybody's watching. Know what I mean? The whole world. Black and white. I'm carrying the whole thing. Right now, in what I'm doin', I'm doin' more for the Negro cause than *any* of them *other* cats. I'm talkin' about *Soul.* Forgettin' that other stuff. That's silly. I'm talkin' about bein' *alive,* man. About *feelin'.*

"I am one of the most alonest guys. You hip to that? Like I'm a very serious person. Know what I mean? I've got *alot* of problems. I'm real *confused,* you know. But I gotta keep it all to myself. All inside me. 'Cause there ain't no one I can really talk to. Not *really talk.* You dig?"

That's why he's got to do everything himself. Can't trust anyone to do it for him. He's got to know what's going on all the time. He's got to know firsthand. That doesn't just mean with the songwriting, the arranging, the choreography and the designs for all the costumes in the show. Sure he does all that. But also, he's got a publishing company, Try Me Music, Inc. and he and his agent, Ben Bart, each own 50% of a record production company, Fair Deal Records, Inc. On top of that, James Brown makes a special point of overseeing the whole business end of things: the publicity, the bookings, the contracts. Everything. So he's gotta be able to deal with all kinds of people in all kinds of fields. He's gotta keep his personality changing all the time. "A person who knows me from the way I am when I'm doin' the show would never recognize me as a business man."

"I gotta be hip to what's goin' on all the time. Know what I mean? When you write songs it's the same with doin' anything creative. You gotta be able to *reach* people. So it ain't enough just to know all there is about any one special thing. Like music. You gotta be diggin' *everything that's happening*. You gotta be *at least* eighty-five per cent up on everything. And you gotta try for one hundred per cent."

The Best of James Brown is in his performance. It begins in that tremulous moment before he comes on stage. That moment when the whole audience knows he is about to appear. Those rows and rows of clean-cut white college kids packing the arena on a school night. All there to see James Brown. The girls in fuzzy pastel sweaters with their hair in pert flips. The languid-limbed boys in impeccably casual, open-necked shirts. All of them waiting. Much more than just polite. Revelling in the suspense. Breathless with a tension they cannot explain. All eighteen musicians are standing in a row, rocking back and forth as they play something soft and full of promise. The five dancing girls shimmer themselves in the velvety blue and red lights. And small sad-eyed Danny, the quiet stage manager, the master of ceremonies, sits at a desk high up on some box, delivering his introduction. It doesn't much matter what he says. No one really cares. They're all too intent on waiting to be able to listen.

". . . And here he is, ladies and gentlemen. The star of many other exciting television shows *and* movies. The *one* and *only* James Brown and the Famous Flames."

The audience screams. First come the Flames. In a row. Trotting in time to the music over to the microphone where they dance the ritualistic dance. All three of them doing the same step. Leaning out toward the audience, leaning back, thrusting out their arms. The three of them look so hopelessly different. Three different sizes, three different shapes. Even the identical gold jackets can't hide it. But they move as one. And the crowd never stops screaming.

When he appears at the opposite side of the stage in the glamour of a brown-checked, waist-length jacket, matching vest and sleek brown pants, it all gets wilder. Not just the screaming. But the music, too. And the gyrations of the dancing girls. And the enthusiasm of The Flames. Because he is coming out to give the audience what he's got. Moving with a jaunty stride and a lot of purpose. Like he has come to do something he must do, something he knows how and loves to do. He smiles at them, too, a huge, generous smile full of glinting white teeth. He grabs at the microphone impatiently and starts to sing.

"*Odansze* edjerk.
*Pbapasinder*szing.
Aindyuooo hip
*Tdwotdat noobreed*szayn.
Ainno draaaag.
*Pbap*pas *got*da *brannoooo*bag . . ."

Snapping his elbows to his sides to hike up his pants. Flinging out his arms for a fresh start at the beginning of each new phrase. Pantomiming the lyrics. A phenomenal conglomeration of things: burlesque, Gospel, sports, silent films. It is Super-Fine. James cups his ear. "Come on, John. Play your horn. Play your horn." Cups his ear. "Your baritone." John rocks up to the microphone, feigning a limp. Stepping with one foot and sliding the other to meet it. Blowing his horn. John takes over at the microphone so James can do his stuff. He smiles at John. Come on John. And then his feet are shuffling quadruple time, never leaving the floor, carrying him miraculously all over the stage. So easily. His arms are outspread. He is erect. His knees are bending. He is sinking toward the floor. He is rising again. And all the while his feet are working with that phenomenal ease. He claps a hand behind his head, raises one leg, and watches as one foot moves him along with that slippery motion. And then he stops. He bends over his leg, smoothing an expert finger along the crease of his pants. The crowd howls its approval. He slides back to the microphone to relieve John.

"*Hehy*hey
*Come*ohn
*He*hey
*Yuhszetmeup*dtight.
*Yuhrouttas*zight."

There is no pause between the end of one song and the beginning of another. No pause at all. Not even the deafening applause which often drowns out huge portions of his sing.

"*Mebbede*lass *tdime.*
*Mebbedelasstdimeweshake*hans.
Mebbedelasstdimewemake roma-ance.
Oh-o whah, *Oh-o whah,* Ahcumon."

The Flames are cooing, "Hup hup doo-wee-ooo. Hup hup doo-wee-ooo." The dancing girls are holding up their index fingers and saying silently, "Oh why, Oh why, I don't know." The band takes over so James can dance with the Flames. They face the audience all in a line, each with his left hand on his left hip. Watching each other. They hop right and bump. They hop left and bump. They each execute a smooth turn and face each other in two rows: James and Bobby Bennett facing Bobby Byrd and Lloyd. Each with his left foot forward, opposite toes almost touching. Bouncing their weight on and off the forward leg. They are smiling. They are really looking at each other and smiling. They love it. All at once their heads bow and four arms shoot forward. And then four more. "Oh why. Oh why, I don't know."

"*Yiaaaaiih. Ahmalla*lohn.
"*Yiaaaaiih. Ahmalla*lohn.
*Ahaintgohtnoh*body *tocahlma*hohn.
*Causeahdoh*nohftmaybedelass*tdime.*
Lookahrounyanovahanhovahagai-ain.
*Shakehanswid*yoh*bes*fren.
*Yahmighdt*nevahevah*seedemagai*-ain.
*Shakehanswid*yoh*bes*fren.
*Shake*hans*widyoh*bes fren."

He is back at the microphone. Telling them where it's *really at.* He is holding out his right hand toward The Flames. And one by one they move toward it. First Bobby Bennett, then Bobby Byrd, then Lloyd. They each shake his hand. And then, inspired, fortified, eager, they stroll cheerfully to the edge of the stage, stretching out their hands to the crowd. They want to shake hands. They want to shake *everybody's* hand. They move along the edge of the stage with their hands reaching out, inviting.

But it isn't only The Flames who want to shake hands. It can't be because two men in tuxedos are moving out from the wings, forbiddingly. Each grips one of James' arms as he goes to the edge of the stage where they are waiting for him, they don't get their turn. Reaching up for James' hands which are scarred by the greedy fingernails or past crowds. He moves all along the edge of the stage, gleaming and glowing, submitting himself happily to the contest as they try to drag him down to them and the men in the tuxedos tug his arms away. Lots of the time it almost looks as if the men in the tuxedos may lose him. But they never have. One girl faints. Just collapses in a heap under all those frenzied feet and the cops have to come and fight off her hysterical friends and pick her up and carry her out of the theater.

"*Ahdlahktuhtellyah*somemoh.
So-horry. *Ahgotta*go-hoh."

And then suddenly it all stops. Everything. For a bare moment the musicians are quiet. The dancing girls are frozen with their heads bowed. The Flames have turned their backs. The light is deep purple and James cries into the stillness, "Pleeeeeze. Pleeeeze, please. Pleee-eeeze." His shoulders heave and he flops to his knees, dragging the microphone with him. Pleading over it.

The crowd is hysterical. Shattering the stillness. The band music is sighing, the Flames are moaning. The five girls high up on their platforms are jerking in mourning. Isolated screams from the audience, erupting out of its momentary silences. Sometimes a particularly long pleeze does it. Or a shake of his head. Or a shiver of his back. Because the pace is so insistently slow and the mood so sad. When it's like that, the balance is very delicate.

"*Pleeeze. Pleeeze. Pleeeze.*
*Ohdahlin*pleee-eeeze*dohngoh-who-aho*-owho*aa*ho-o!
*Ah*luhv*yah*sooo-o."

He is in an ecstasy of agony. Clinging to the neck of the microphone. Dripping sweat. Or tears. Or both. Screaming out his misery in that coarse voice which rakes relentlessly over the vowels. Bobby can't let him do it. Can't let him do this to himself. Nor can Danny. They approach him, Danny with a great purple cape to drape over James' kneeling body. They raise him to his feet, swathing him in the robe. Bobby pats his back comfortingly, in time to the music. They guide him toward the wings, still singing. But he stops halfway there. He stops and they can't move him any further. He just won't go. He has to say more. He stamps his feet like a child having a tantrum. No no no no no. In quickening succession. He flings off the cape defiantly. Stalks back to the microphone. Grabs it and sinks to his knees with it again.

> "*Bay*bay! *Yahdone me*wrohng.
> *Weee-e-eh. Yahdone me*wrohng.
> *Yah*nohw*yah*duhn *duhnme*wrohng.
> *Yahtuhk*mahluhv *nowyah*goh-hone."

Danny comes out with a gold cape this time. He and Bobby pull James up from the floor. Drag him to his feet. Limp and still crying out his song. Telling them about Soul. And they understand. Danny and Bobby each put an arm around his shoulders. Trying to tell him it's all right. It's all gonna be all right. As if he could ever get over it, drowning, as he is, in his anguish. He stamps his feet again. Again, he flings off the cape. He is back on his knees with the microphone. Back where he belongs.

> "*Ahjuswannaheahyahsay Aaiii.*
> *Aaaiii. Aaaiii. Aaaiii. Aaaiii.*
> *Aaaiii. Aaaiii. Aaaiii. Aaaiii.*
> *Dahlin*pleee-eeeze*dohn*goh-whoah-*oho-ohyeah*-oho-o.
> *Ahluhvyah*soh-hoh."

The audience is still howling, "Aaaiii" as they come for him once more. Danny and Bobby. They wrap him in a flowing black cape. They raise him very gently, very firmly. He is the victorious fighter, exhausted by the contest, shoulders heaving spasmodically, weak with the strain of exorcising his misery. He stops again. It isn't possible for him to come back for more. It's just not humanly possible. He raises his arms proudly and the black cape slides off his back into Danny's waiting hands. Expertly, he unfastens his cuff links and before anyone has a chance to guess what he is about to do, he flings them out to the audience in one last glorious gesture and all alone, without any help, he strides away into the wings.

The audience is overwhelmed. Overwhelmed and delighted by the relentless intricacy of it all. The music is still playing. The dancing girls are still swaying. The Flames are still warbling. And the audience is still wondering why they go on. What more could there possibly be. Wondering until James appears again, triumphant in a clean tan suit, swinging a small suitcase at his side. "Out O' Sight" it says. He stalks across the stage with it. His parting benediction.

It is over. This elaborate personal dream out of the head and body and sweat of James Brown. James Brown who really believes in the head and body and sweat of James Brown. Believes so fervently that the whole crowd is ready to follow him, even if he can only lead them to some private narcissistic vision of himself. They know it is not for them to ask what it all means. All that really matters is the sheer energy of his belief.

Backstage James sits at a long white dressing table cluttered with hair sprays and make-up kits and soda cans and packages of exotic cigarettes. He is transformed. The magnificence of his presence on stage has vanished. Almost as if it had all been a dream. Grease-paint is congealed in the creases of his face. Washed there by streams of sweat. It makes his face look cracked and stiff. And undefinably cruel. The metamorphosis is shocking.

Some open cuff link boxes are arrayed on the dressing table, displaying their goods. He uses 1000 pair a month to toss into the audiences. The boxes have been placed there by Gert or Danny for James to chose from. Bold, jewelled links, shining in the mirror lights. A gold encrusted pair set with a small black stone in the center seems truly elegant. "Ya like 'em? Ah'll give 'em to ya," cries James expansively.

He strokes on fresh grease-paint, surveying the room in the lighted mirror like some feudal lord. Bobby works patiently, repairing James' hair. Gert is hanging up the costumes, rearranging them on the rack. The 120 glistening shirts, the slacks, meticulously creased, the jackets, the ample capes. She attends each article with pride. Good old reliable Kenny is straightening the 80 pair of shoes and boots. Setting them out in neat rows against the far wall. He is harassed. He's always harassed. Which is what makes him reliable. James knows that. "When a fellow stops worrying about his job, that's when I gotta start worrying. Right?" he says. Danny is hiding something behind his back. It's a surprise for James.

Danny unfurls the huge sheet and lays it before James on the dressing table. There are eight costume designs. One looks like Prince Charming. Another like Napoleon. Another like a riding habit. And one like Sherlock Holmes. "Yeah," purrs James. He stabs a finger at Sherlock Holmes. He really *digs* that one. Everybody agrees that it's out o' sight. He flips through the swatches of material Danny has given him. He wants it made up in brown. Brown like this. With straight stove-pipe pants. 'Cause as long as it's tight from *here* to *here*. That's where the action is. That's where it's happening.

It's the private word of the show. The James Brown World. Warm, intimate and impenetrable.

And there's always something to rehearse after a performance. Some little thing to go over. Maybe Bobby Byrd has to be straightened out about one of the dance routines. He will come to the dressing room and do it for James, going over it a few times until it's just right. Or may be the leader of the dancing girls has to be warned to make sure the girls are covered up as much as possible. Can't have it looking like a burlesque show. Not when there's a fickle audience who could easily go either way. An audience that has to be wooed into the confidence that what they're seeing is something it's okay for them to like. Or maybe there's a phrase of music that's imperfect. Nothing gets left dangling. Anything short of perfection has got to be repaired. Nat Jones, the band leader, is summoned to the dressing room for instructions on the introduction to "I Got You." Because the way it is now, it's common. The way *any* old band would play it. It's not right for The James Brown Show. Where everything is *super-fine*.

A WHITER SHADE OF BLACK

JON LANDAU

Traditionally there have been three types of Negro musicians in pop music. The first consists of artists who for either aesthetic or financial reasons have chosen to sever their ties with specifically Negro music and instead work in the general field of pop. Richie Havens, as an exponent of the contemporary urban ballad in the Ochs-Dylan-Paxton tradition, and Jimi Hendrix, as an exponent of freaking out, are good examples. The second class consists of performers who are still working in one of the basic Negro musical forms but who seek to alter their approach enough to make it appealing to a large part of the white audience. Motown is the ideal example, but someone like Lou Rawls also falls into this category. Finally there is the hard core: performers who won't or can't assimilate, and therefore just continue to do their thing. If the white audience digs what a performer in this group is doing, it's just gravy; the performer never expected it. This category contains all of the independent r&b labels, most importantly the Stax-Volt group in Memphis, Tennessee.

Obviously the first group identified above is irrelevant in a discussion of Negro music because performers in this group are working in musical idioms which are not distinctively Negro. Motown, as the basic representative of the second group, seeks a white audience but maintains a basically Negro identity, and is a logical starting point for any survey of Negro pop.

Motown is two things above all. It is a place and a form. By the first I mean that it is a community, obviously tightly knit, made up of a group of people all aiming at the same thing. By the second I mean that the music that this community makes is stylized to express precisely what Motown wants it to by use of recurring techniques, patterns, and other devices. In the evolution of Motown the community clearly came first, and a brief look at how Motown began will help us clarify what the Motown form is, and why it takes the form that it does.

When Motown began is not altogether clear. Legend has it that Berry Gordy, Jr., the man who runs the place, quit a job on a Detroit assembly line nine or ten years ago, borrowed some money, and began his rise to success instantly. The history of Motown shows us that it was not all that simple. It is a fact that almost a decade ago Berry Gordy was already in the music business writing for one of the greatest of all Motown performers, although he has never recorded on a Motown label, Jackie Wilson. (Wilson, who was clearly a major influence on Smokey Robinson, has always recorded for Brunswick.) The first records that Gordy produced for his own labels were written by himself, starting around 1960, perhaps earlier. Two of the earliest Motown tunes were Barrett Strong's "Money" and the Contours' "Do You Love Me?" Both of these songs seem remarkably unsophisticated compared to what the typical Motown song-writing team of today throws out, even for flip-side material. Both of these records were in fact indistinguishable from the general r&b of the day. "Do You Love Me?"—the later of the two—even has the old-fashioned twist drumming, a rarity on the oldest of Motown records.

It appears that the first major move Gordy made in his attempt to build Motown was to bring William "Smokey" Robinson into the picture. At first Gordy collaborated with Smokey in writing tunes for Smokey's legendary Miracles. After four or five duds, their joint labors resulted in the spectacular "Shop Around." This was one of the early big ones for the Motown organization and it was not only a financial success but an aesthetic one, with Robinson's faultless lead earmarking the Miracles as something far above the rank and file of r&b vocalists.

Smokey gradually moved up in the organization. But while he was struggling to make a name for the Miracles, other talent was being brought into the picture. Mary Wells, Marvin Gaye, the Marvelettes, Little Stevie Wonder, and the Supremes were all gradually added to the roster. When back-up vocalists were needed for records by big stars, a former Motown secretary named Martha Reeves organized a trio—Martha and the Vandellas. Motown soul records with big booming commercial arrangements were making it into the pop charts. Marvin Gaye put two straight blues, "Wonderful One" and "Can I Get a Witness," right up there, and a little twelve-year-old kid named Stevie Wonder sold a million copies of one of the freakiest Motown records ever, "Fingertips, Pt. II." The community was clearly developing at breakneck speed in the early sixties, but there was still no form. Individual successes were common but they were not based on any specific Motown style. Motown was still just an electric grouping of artists not readily distinguishable from the rest of souldom except by virtue of the fact that they generally did what they did better than anyone else around.

The Motown form came in 1963–64, with the advent of the Supremes. During the pre-Supremes era a Motown vocalist named Eddie Holland had been occasionally releasing singles, mostly poor imitations of Jackie Wilson. Over a period of time he, Bryant Holland, and Lamont Dozier formed a song-writing-and-producing team. They had their first significant opportunities to develop their style with Martha and the Vandellas, and they wrote and produced many of the girls' early hits: "Come and Get These Memories," "Quicksand," "Livewire," and "Heatwave."

Apparently the Vandellas could only go so far. Martha has a straight, tough, soul voice and probably was not the right type for the more commercial records being planned. So attention was soon turned to the Supremes. The one advantage Diana Ross had over Martha, on a record, was her cooling sexy voice. This was coupled with the consumated Holland-Dozier-Holland writing-producing concept, and the result, after a few failures, was fantastic financial success. There can be no doubt that "Where Did Our Love Go" and the follow-up, "Baby Love," set the direction for the future of Motown. With these two records, H-D-H and the Supremes had created the Motown definition of success. Each of these records was the product of a carefully thought out, highly distinctive musical form that had been a long time in coming. When the formula paid off, Motown lost no time in refining the form, stylizing it, and imposing it on all of their artists, one way or another.

What then is this Motown style? It is a distinctive approach to all facets of record making, especially rhythm, melody instrumental sound, and vocal arranging. With regard to rhythm the most important thing is Motown drumming. Up until the time of H-D-H the most common pattern of drumming was for the drummer to hit the snare on the second and fourth beats of every measure. That was changed to the drummer hitting the snare on every beat. While this aspect of the style was not present on the earliest H-D-H productions, with the Vandellas and the Supremes, it soon became a Motown staple to the point where it would be safe to say that seventy-five percent of the records recorded in a Motown studio since "Baby Love" have this style of drumming. In addition, over a period of time production techniques were developed to give added emphasis to the drums, and to give them a distinctive sound. Tambourines were added on some records and in general anything that would deepen or solidify the effect of the beat was thrown in. The Motown beat was to become the key to public identification of the Motown sound.

Motown changed things around melodically as well. Prior to the Supremes there were two basic pop music forms: the blues form and the ballad form. Motown changed all that. Repetition was the new order. "Baby Love" is a circle of repetion. Its form is very close to a-a-a-a. Motown writers were among the first to realize that they were writing for the car radio and they learned early in the game to keep it simple. By and large the songwriting chores were turned over to a select number of teams such as H-D-H or the team of Stevenson-Gaye ("Dancing in the Streets"), all of whom stuck to the basic credo of keeping the melodic structure relatively simple and easy to follow. However, it must be added that within easy-to-follow melodic structures Motown has often produced melodies and chord progressions of surprising sophistication for a pop song.

Perhaps the part of a Motown record that is easiest to recognize is the overall instrumental background. In addition to the distinctive beat, already discussed, Motown has always presented the public with highly regimented, stiff, impersonal back-up bands. Even the solos so common on Motown singles are totally lacking in spontaneity. It's easy to see where the charge of black Muzak comes from. Of course this approach succeeds commercially because it keeps things simple, predictable and danceable, and besides, lots of the basic arrangements are pretty. (Like on "Stop in the Name of Love.")

Equally as important as the instrumental back-up style is the vocal back-up. Here Martha and the Vandellas can take full credit for stylizing the pattern of beginning sentences with high-pitched "Ooh's" and ending them with "di-doo-doo wah's" You can hear them do it perfectly on Marvin Gaye's "Stubborn Kind of Fellow" or throughout their own *Dance Party* album.

Such is the fourfold path to the Motown sound. However one other thing not strictly a part of the musical form must be mentioned. It is the Motown approach to the lead vocal. I haven't included this as one of the basic characteristics of the Motown sound because I feel there is too great a variation among the Motown lead vocalists and because I don't believe vocals can be stylized in the same way that other aspects of pop music can.

In discussing Motown vocals the first thing to realize is that Berry Gordy, Jr., knows that you can give a singer everything, but if the guy can't sing he won't sell any records. Therefore Motown makes damn sure that everybody who they sign has the basic raw material. Motown takes these vocalists and of course tries to give them a style. But most of the successful Motown artists have retained a strong degree of individual identity.

Within the context of many individual vocal styles, two basic approaches can be identified. One is symbolized by Diana Ross (of the Supremes), one of the most successful vocalists of all time. Diana's approach is to stick closely to the form. She rarely steps out on her own, seldom improvises, and never gets in the way. She restrains herself so as to fit perfectly into the prerecorded instrumental tracks that she dubs her voice into. Consequently she is the least jarring of Motown vocalists, the least disturbing, and the most able to reach a car-radio audience. I wouldn't deny for a second that she has a fantastic voice for what she is doing, that she oozes sex, and that she is a fine vocalist. But she seldom goes beyond what was planned for her by the production team.

The other type of Motown vocalist is seen in Levi Stubbs (lead singer of the Four Tops). His thing is breaking through the barrier that the regimented background sticks him with. All his shouting, his frenzy, his individuality, is something that Motown can't quite control or make predictable. He is an artist who can be told what to say only within certain limitations—once within them he is on his own and there is no telling what he will do. The dichotomy between Levi's style and Diana's is simply this: Diana strives for unity whereas Levi creates conflict. Diana's approach is to roll with the given version of the Motown sound she is to record. She will try to fit snuggly into the overall framework. A very commercial, good record will then be produced, but one without much artistic merit because it contains no tension. It becomes too smooth. The best example of this is Diana's performance on "You Can't Hurry Love." The alternative to this approach is Levi's method of attacking the song, and in the process creating his own dynamic. Levi's style is based on creating tension between the lead vocal and everything else that happens on the record. It is the same dynamic that Stevie Wonder creates when he sings "Uptight," and that David Ruffin creates when he sings "I'm Losing You." When the artist chooses this path the record as a whole improves because the background and the beat no longer have to stand on their own but can act as counter-weights to the vocal. And when a record is created in which all the different parts are interacting in this fashion then the listener is suddenly able to appreciate individual excellence on the part of the musicians as well as the vocalists, and you may find yourself digging the fantastic thing the bass is doing on "Bernadette," or the fact that the drummer is socking it to you on "Uptight." This is Motown at its finest.

Having gone this far in identifying a Motown style, it should be noted that things do not remain pat or static within the context of the basic sound. Refinements are constantly taking place and there are always some limited forms of experimentation going on. For example, Smokey's "Tracks of My Tears," one of the classic Motown lyrics, also was notable for the un-Motown-like use it made of the guitars. The Four Tops have been doing songs which have clearly been influenced by the Dylanesque technique of incessant repetition, as Richard Goldstein correctly noted some time ago. However, one thing Motown will never do is go against the grain of its highest value—success. It may dabble here and there in electric variations on its style, but if these variations don't sell records, forget it. Smokey Robinson's activities as songwriter and producer have recently been curtailed, presumably for that reason.

Of course, since the Supremes era began, success has never really been in question at Motown. They have the style and they have the talent, and by God, they sell the records. But success means many things to many people, and here is the rub. The head of the Motown corporation picked up some pretty perverse notions as to what constitutes success, somewhere along the line. It hasn't been enough to just break out of the soul charts and radio stations. It hasn't been enough to outsell the top pop stars in every field. Berry Gordy's idea of success is to be able to put each one of his groups into the big nightclub scene. As I write this the Temptations are at the Copa wowing them with "Swanee," according to the latest issue of *Variety*. As a result of this philosophy Motown has weighed down its artists with absurd album material (Would you believe the Four Tops singing "Strangers in the Night" on their *On Broadway* album?) and absurd live nightclub acts. There is no sense in laboring the point, because things are going to get worse before they get better. But it should be pointed out that such a policy may put big Motown stars into high-paying clubs but lose them some of their hard-core, record-buying audience in the process.

It has been suggested that Berry Gordy's experience as an auto worker in Detroit before his entrance into the music business has given him too rigid an idea of how to run a record company, and it is certainly true that he likes to run things in assembly-line-like fashion. The Temptations are going to do the Copa bit because that is what Motown stars are expected to do when they reach a certain level of success. And the fact that David Ruffin doesn't sound good singing "The Best Things in Life Are Free" isn't going to keep him from doing it.

This rigidity in management is particularly evident in the Motown album approach. Motown policy here is not hip to the concept being developed by the big pop stars that an album is a whole thing, not just your latest hits and some junk. As a result the best Motown albums are in the "Greatest Hits" series, because such albums at least retain the uniform high quality of Motown singles. They also sell quite well. The best of these is *The Temptations' Greatest Hits*. Only a few Motown albums outside this series are listenable. *Dance Party* is certainly one of these, but I don't know how many others could be named. This is a quick-money policy based on the concept that a few hits will sell an album. But as the Doors and the Airplane have recently proven, an album which builds up a reputation of being good unto itself doesn't need big hits on it to sell. Both *Surrealistic Pillow* and *The Doors* sold extremely well before any of the album cuts made it as singles. And *Sgt. Pepper* doesn't have any singles on it at all.

In general, Motown must base its reputation on singles. "Reach Out I'll Be There" is certainly the best record the Four Tops ever made and probably the best record ever produced at Motown. There are simply no flaws. No dumb instrumentals. A beautiful lyric and a very sophisticated chorus. Perfect tension between artist and orchestra. Fantastic use of verbal repetitions in the vocal back-up. It's a record that cuts through, that transcends all the limitations of the recorded rock form. In my opinion if there is any one thing that makes the difference on this record it is the power and absolute conviction of all four vocalists. When Levi sings you know he is not kidding. His voice literally drives that band through the floor of the record . . . And the rest of the Tops push even Levi that one step further with their perfectly timed responses to him, and their "Aahs" at the beginning of each verse.

As manufacturers of single records Motown is unparalleled in both artistic and financial success. From the Supremes on there has always been an abundance of first-rate Motown records. "Shotgun," "Ooh, Baby, Baby," "Heatwave," "Ain't That Peculiar," "Tracks of My Tears," "Baby I Need Your Loving," "Uptight," "Dancing in the Streets": it's positively remarkable what this company has achieved within the limited form they have chosen to produce their music in. And in the last year important steps have been made to broaden that form. increased virtuosity, particularly of the rhythm instrumentalists, is being featured. The level of songwriting for singles is fantastically high. (Just off the charts: "I Was Made to Love Her," "Ain't No Mountain High Enough," and "More Love.") New production people are being added who are doing good things, like Harvey Faqua.

The night before I started this article I saw Stevie Wonder on Joey Bishop's late-night show. He performed "Alfie," which I think is a decent song, on the harmonica. As they were introducing him I got upset thinking to myself that this was going to be dreadful. Stevie played it beautifully; he really did. And that—right there—showed me the power, the freedom the artist has to transcend the ephemeral, like the particular song he is playing, or the particular band he is working with. And after writing all this if I had to say what makes Motown work, when it does work, I would say it is the combination of the limitations that are imposed on Motown's artists, and their capacity, which manifests itself only occasionally, to shatter them with some little nuance that no one could have predicted. Motown is the transcendence of Levi saying "Just look over your shoulder." And the beautiful thing is that the way Levi says that—that could never be formalized or stylized. The beauty of Motown is that it gives great artists something to work with and against. It gives them salable good songs and a beat and a producer and musicians and supervisors. But it doesn't give its vocalists their voices, their talent, or their soul. When Smokey sings "This is no fiction, this is no act, it's real, it's fact," or when Stevie sings "No one is better than I/ And I know I'm just an average guy," we are no longer listening to a thing called Motown. We are participating in the transcendence of a particular artist, we are drawn into an individual vision of reality. From every aesthetical point of view possible it can truly be said that when these moments occur there is no longer Motown, but only music.

THE WAY WE ARE TODAY

•

PAUL WILLIAMS

Very small pieces of paper, not allowing a great many words, but perhaps the right ones. "Yesterday's a song without a name/ Now both our tomorrows are the same." Sometimes just the smell of things remains. Memory of a year is recollection of the way the air felt one day on Beacon Hill; and the distance between 1962 and 1965 has nothing to do with the distance between 1965 and the present. *Babes in Toyland.* Unless we can hear the background music, we don't really have a good perspective on what's going on. Earth Opera. Background music for the present. Joni Mitchell. Remembrance of the way we are today.

Babes in Toyland? Well, because it's been running through my head and it might really be nice to do a newsreel roundup of the week's events, with *Babes in Toyland* as theme music. See how they run, as the Beatles are hung up on. And Earth Opera send familiar Stephen Vincent Benét chills down my spine as they look in on the temporally local world scene with crisp and calm awareness and the incredible and true unspoken implication that this awareness is not shared, not on an emotional level. What should the texture of this 1968 year be?

Certainly the music is confusing us. We like, perhaps, Cream (none for me, thanks), Traffic, Blood Sweat & Tears, Randy Newman, Love, the Byrds, certainly *John Wesley Harding,* maybe even Simon & Garfunkel or the U.S.A. How can we integrate this stuff? Textures, back in the days when "Mr. Tambourine Man," "Can't Help Myself" and "Satisfaction" were the number one song, were complicated; today, when you find yourself liking "Cry Like a Baby," things really seem confused. I mean it's tough to keep your "rock" records all on the same shelf, and impossible to find reasonable categories to separate them off into.

And the political or emotional content of the world is worse. What's really important? McCarthy, riots in Germany, spy ships in Korea, the demise of the *L.A. Oracle,* an auto accident in Kansas, the looting and fires in Chicago, new evidence on who the assassin of Kennedy or King might really have been, a report on the price of milk in Britain? It's impossible to guess what really matters, and you can't avoid the dull suspicion that it's really none of the above. And when you get into such items as who's in love with whom, or what's a good book to read, or what should I do in the summer, it's hard to remember what anything feels like at all. In times of transition, whole dictionaries lose their meaning and there's a different face in every mirror. Where do we look for the truth?

Joni Mitchell (Reprise 6293) and *Earth Opera* (Elektra 74016) are recently released record albums, and it may be important that they are extremely textured, soft and rich albeit specific and even abrasive at places (last cuts on the first sides), comfortable, they fill the air, you can relax and bury your face in what they have to sing. They don't bring up other problems; they are self-contained and indeed obscure other matters, smoothing them over in your mind, consciously directing you toward concerns of their own.

Joni Mitchell is a young lady from Saskatchewan, simply an adventurer, off to seek her fortune in the States and meeting all these people and living in these places and having things happen to her. She is very much a peer of the young, of you or me who did or didn't go to college but anyway were looking for something and also finding things out at the same time, "I came to the city and lived like old Crusoe" and bumping up against people, which is the part that seemed to make a difference. I describe her as a peer and will do the same for Pete Rowan of Earth Opera, not because I think I know who you are but because it is unusual these days that "rock" people actually sing about themselves, and particularly unusual that they do it in a manner so mixing the general and the specific that it is comfortable and natural to "identify" with them in their songs. It is easy to see what and why Pete Rowan sees in the world he encounters in his album; it seems natural to feel how and what Joni feels of the things that happen in her songs. The very best music can be related to as an immediate reflection of the listener's life (just as the *I Ching* is the most personal of books), and even better music is that which reflects you and yet tells you of me.

Joni Mitchell's particular triumph is that girl singers or girl artists of any kind who have really gotten at what it is to be a woman can be counted on the fingers of one hand (if you're generous, use some fingers twice); and this record is a profound expression of I, a woman—I have yet to meet a girl who doesn't feel that Joni speaks for her. Most girls think and speak on a fairly simple level, but feel on a deeply complex one; a song like "Cactus Tree" many say what anyone would be clever enough to say of themselves ("but she's so busy being free"), but in its entirety—the mounting impact of the verses and the change in that line as it is repeated, the way the vocal struts and fumbles the defensiveness and pride, the sound of all those notes and thoughts (have you ever noticed how much more important is the sound of a woman's voice than what she says with it?)—"Cactus Tree" holds all the fullness and complexity of "this is where I am now," this is what I feel I know, a feeling one achieves in an afternoon alone and might not be able to begin to express in a month of conversations.

Peter Rowan is a person as complex, more elusive, more direct, frequently as successful and beautiful in his music as Joni; his focus, rather than people and places, is feelings—not that there aren't just as many feelings in Joni's songs in the long run, and even people in Peter's, but each approaches a song with a different concept of what a song is for. At their closest, Peter uses a situation to express a certain mood, and Joni reflects a particular feeling directly out of a situation she's describing. What a songwriter think he's doing is only the starting point for the nature and direction of the world his finished recording holds in the listener's mind. That both these persons sound like they feel what we're feeling is ultimately what brings them, and us, close together.

And, close together, what do we hear in their minds? Peter Rowan, lead singer and songwriter of Earth Opera, seems sensitive, uncertain, willing to explore but not eager to rush too blindly, quite deliberate, very very conscious and perhaps a little bitter as a result; but both bitterness and joy are luxuries he seems slightly ashamed of enjoying. The word "seems" is important here—I do not think Pete Rowan *is* uncertain, his music is more controlled and more together than that of almost anyone composing in rock, but it is an important part of the music's impact that it seems hesitant, exploratory, filled with awe and humility—there is a sense of footsteps taken cautiously and yet deliberately in the new-fallen snow. There! I have made that statement, yes, I shall leave another print right here; the footprints, if they are sacrilege, are final and most incriminating—one is willing to take responsibility for them, but does not want it to seem that he has clambered thoughtlessly through the unbroken landscape. The appearance of caution is the radical humanist's uncompromising way of showing respect.

More on Pete Rowan: his world is sparse and rich. He has a true economy of style, perceives only that which is relevant or perhaps is able to make all that he perceives relevant to his view. And it seems only natural that one with such control of such familiar words would also, if he had a head full of melodies, know precisely the one to apply to his song and, were he a singer, would be completely comfortable at rationing, through his voice, the music's flow of time. Everything is both precise and natural, this album breathes an air unburdened by asbestos and soot. Evil is absolute. Nothing is condemned, though the desire to condemn is always present; Rowan's efforts are to make us inescapably aware of what we attempt to be blind to. By using few words and tunes and the right ones, he makes his perception accessible. And with the richness of those words and that music, he draws us as the flame the moth. Joni Mitchell says of herself, "She has brought them to her senses." Peter Rowan, like some character in a Hawthorne short story, presents us with a world-view we cannot misconstrue nor turn away from nor ever forget. Like all good artists, he has linked us with the Overmind.

And Joni, well, she's a thousand different people, and knows it: she understands everything just up to here and knows nothing at all beyond this point, which is just as it should be. She disclaims nothing, demands no credit, spends her present walking unswervingly into the future, in harmony with her world because she has accepted nothing without first understanding it and has never rejected that of herself that she did understand; what I'm getting at is she hasn't tried to choose who she is or who she will be. So she writes songs that are simple and straightforward and enormously perceptive, she makes no presumptions, she really likes people and is quite cautious—careful not to like them for the wrong reasons. In "Michael from Mountains" she really conveys how and sort of why a woman could love a man and desire a man, and that's no everyday achievement. A great many ladies have their heads so full of all they've read and heard and seen about why a man loves a woman they can think of little save how lovable they are. But Joni even knows that a woman can have a will ("know that I will know you") without being unfeminine or unyielding herself. She is also most sensitive to other women ("Marcie" is not a song about herself; but you can see her seeing herself in her friend—empathy. Wonderful.) and she even knows that there's no one to blame. No one to name as a traitor here. Harmony. Peace and beauty. Five stars for good vibrations.

Earth Opera/Joni Mitchell are an aspect of experience, as well as the product of same; what we are today and soon is shaped by what we hear of them. And we are you and me. Our understanding of the world is daily added to, crossed out, erased, struck over, pasted together by various cyclones and breezes that blow through. If we do not listen to music, if we fail to read books or talk with each other, if we seldom look on human beauty or deep-felt expression or accidental creation, we diminish ourselves. Which somehow means there is a life-energy passed through art, through communication that is also expression (which indicates a kind of moreness or fullness) . . . don't we feel the need to fill our world with us, and ourselves with the world, not in the sense of three billion different people all producing until they suffocate in the stuff, but in the sense of three billion who are one sharing their perception, reducing the experiential distance between themselves?

Joni and Peter are aided and abetted by everyone from their studio engineer to the guy who sold you the record; let's mention the producers. Both are new to the task and brilliant; David Crosby, once (and hence always) a Byrd, has succeeded in giving the listener to Joni Mitchell's album one of the best front-row center seats ever available on record. Peter Siegel has somehow put Earth Opera's music on stage, in the sense of theater; distance is, on this album, very subtle, very palpable, the music moves among the instruments as in a ballet—this is a function of the music, and the way the group plays, but also very much a result of the producer's concept of what it is he's trying to capture on plastic. Crosby's achievements are the restraint and perfection of Joni's album, the expressiveness of her voice and (particularly) her guitar-playing, which requires great attention and much producerly love, and the resonance of the album's sound (achieved at least partly by standing Joni beside a grand piano and miking the strings as she sang—an invention of David's that gave him great joy last January). Siegel's triumphs are as subtle—and in a way harder to measure, since we know what Joni sounds like as she sings and plays guitar, but no one can know what Earth Opera would have sounded like in a recording studio with a less competent and imaginative guru. Suffice it to say that both Peter and David have carried the good news from Aix to Ghent, and should be considered among our leading producers.

Joni Mitchell's album (which has a name, *Song To A Seagull*) is divided in two parts—I Came to the City & Out of the City and Down to the Seaside—and ten parts—her songs. Each song has a consciousness, each has its clockwork, its secrets, its soul. "I Had a King" tells of a particular old man, a particular event in the history of a life and also a general state in the relationship between men and women: "You know my keys won't fit the door/ You know my thoughts won't fit the man"—and aren't those words clever, and charming, and right? "He lives in another time." She really perceives things; her words are a delight to be hit over the head with. And the games are played so unobtrusively . . . "the queen's in the [Cocoanut] grove till the end of the year" . . . everything you want is there, and more, and seldom too much, and for all the words you're still most impressed by the music.

The songs are singable. The melodies are so specific you know she knew just what she wanted and found it every time and was delighted. Everything is a whole, a painting in which paints and colors and subject matter and movement and forms and paintress all are one in the act of creation, united through clarity of vision and will. Phrases return, are altered, sing across each other, simple patterns move their quiet movements and leave the touch of fingers on guitar to make announcements. Embellishment is the work of the performer; the composer has done the jobs of framework and appeal. Joni-as-performer appreciates and makes full use of the achievements of her composing self; as a team, these Jonies are as efficient and effective as any playwright-actor team could be.

She plays guitar like someone smiling at you; she knows the communicating impact of every movement each speaking finger makes. Her singing is not quite so clarion; it is harder to listen to your own voice, it takes more years to know; she is learning; she explores and oh so often she succeeds. And she is trying, and knows how to try; where to make the effort, which means half the battle won. The listener can hear that, cannot help but be pleased, cannot help feeling more-than-content.

And she is pretty, which means her words and voice and face and music, and she's alive, which means the album; it is something you should welcome in your world.

Earth Opera is not exactly pretty, although its beauty takes the breath away; it is an album of omen, of perception and fear, or not quite fear, and understanding. There is a great deal of exploration, presentation of a feeling and then unrestrained musical exploration of that feeling—the lyrical guitar and keyboard solos in the middle of "As It Is Before" or "Dreamless." And yet at the same time that it is exploration, excited and free, the music is absolutely planned and conscious, part of a grand structure so flawless and specific that a single wrong moment would stand out like an explosion.

You get the feeling that the album is a score, performed by an orchestra long experienced at playing this piece of music and throwing themselves into it because that's their thing, the unleashing of the exact is their expression of passion. Everything feels predetermined, but absolutely liberated; the medieval concept of freedom. It's a joyous form for contemporary music—the Doors use it in a different way—because it allows the studio and the tedious exactness of electronics and repeat-until-correct to become as much a part of the moment as the Grateful Dead jamming in the park. The ending of "Home of the Brave" is like Pete Townshend's stage act with the Who, where you *know* he's going to destroy that guitar, and it's kind of a drag that you *know*, in fact it even makes the whole thing kind of anticlimatic, and then Peter uses that expectation of anticlimax in you, drawn out unbearably, as straight man for the real climax, wow! He can't possibly be getting into it but somehow he is, great passion is unleashed on stage in the unexpected attempt to transcend anticipated anticlimax, and since little was expected, it works overwhelmingly . . .

Earth Opera reminds one of Brecht, reminds one of the Doors and Procol Harum, reminds one really of no one else at all and therefore of everyone—their music is as thoroughly fresh as anything that's happened to us in years. It's one of those albums where the songs play continually in my mind, they can't be turned off and it's a different one every few days, the music has become fully a part of my experience and is as expressive to me as thinking. At that point I can scarcely write about the music; I wander about inside it, certain that there is enough here to explore for months, if only I can stand back far enough to describe to someone else what I'm exploring.

Music is a staple in my section of the world. It's something I breathe, something I live with, something I cannot live without producing (though for me it takes the form of words on paper; music could really be described as any dance of form-experiences—sounds, shape-textures—in time), something that is very much a part of the guise the life-energy wears on this planet. If I talk of the structure of Pete Rowan's songs—they mesh, they have great freedom because they flow back on themselves so well—I do it because I care about my world, and want to bring it to our consciousness. If I carry on about the way Joni Mitchell's words *touch* the feelings of the people who hear them, I do it to hear myself say it and see if it's true, and let you turn it into truth in your mind, and let you know I also feel that way. Music is just a form of something, writing about music is just another form of that same thing, listening and reading are as inseparable a part of singing and writing as one side of a piece of paper is of the other side. Art is animate when it is attached to people. Sensations, concepts, forms and feelings; these are things to exchange with each other. We provide ourselves with knowledge of the way we are today.

NASHVILLE: THE SOUNDS AND THE SYMBOLS

●

GENE LEES

Nashville is a pallid, tasteless town (population, 170,874) on the Cumberland River, somewhat to the north and west of central Tennessee. Since 1843 it has been the state capital.

Though it has a few attractive residential areas, it is, like most cities of the Middle South, architecturally undistinguished, its buildings a potpourri of preposterous borrowings and anachronisms. There is even a full-scale replica of the Parthenon, built in concrete by some well-meaning but artless philanthropists. It stands there, in a public park, to startle the unsuspecting passerby, and then make him smile.

Decent hotel accommodations exist, but they are scarce, and Nashville has a reputation for being the worst restaurant city in the United States. Nashville people explain with a sigh that religion is the reason. Smack in the Bible Belt, crowded with churches, Nashville is saddled with blue laws: its hotels and restaurants are not allowed to sell liquor. This makes it difficult to run either one at a profit, so the food in most restaurants is all but inedible, the big hotel chains won't build there, and those hotels that do have adequate accommodations maintain smaller staffs than they really need—which means that service is miserable. New Yorkers going to Nashville are often advised: "Take canned food."

This improbable place is one of the major music capitals of the world. It is second in this country only to New York as a recording center, turning out more releases even than Los Angeles. There are ninety music publishing firms listed in the Nashville telephone directory, headed (both alphabetically and economically) by the powerful Acuff-Rose. Both RCA Victor and Columbia Records maintain magnificent studios here, and every label of consequence has offices in Nashville. Another large studio is operated by Fred Foster, owner of Monument Records, and cubbyhole "demo" studios are scattered all over town. All of them stay busy. Indeed, the Columbia Studios, expanded at a cost of half a million dollars in 1965, have already been outgrown. They frequently record on a round-the-clock schedule, doing not only their own work but custom recording for other labels, including Decca, M-G-M, ABC-Paramount, United Artists, Mercury, and Capitol. Don Law, Columbia's executive producer in Nashville, happily complains that he has to book time weeks in advance to get into his own studio. RCA Victor's nearby studios are just about as busy.

Some of this recording is devoted to gospel music, some to rock-and-roll—Elvis Presley made his first records in Nashville. But the vast majority of the time, energy, and effort of Nashville's booming music business goes into country and western music, which in the last ten years has burst its regional boundaries to build a following among people all over America and in all walks of life.

The country and western explosion put Nashville on the map. At one time, certain of the city fathers wanted WSM's Grand Ol' Opry—the radio show around which the city's music business was built—to get out of Nashville. They thought it projected a foolish image for the city. But now that country and western is a major Nashville industry (some say it's the city's second largest), they're delighted about the whole thing. "Now that we're bringing in money, we're respectable," observes Victor's Chet Atkins wryly. With self-conscious arrogance but not without a certain accuracy, Nashville has taken to calling itself Music City, U.S.A.

For all its obvious significance to the record industry, it is impossible to get a statistical estimate of the scope of country and western sales, either in terms of unit sales or dollar volume. This is due to the smudging in recent years of the division lines between Country and Western and other forms of popular music. Says Andy Tomko, who is in charge of statistical services at *Billboard*, the music-business trade magazine, "It's a matter of semantics. Do you consider Eddy Arnold country or pop?"

Arnold, long a mainstay of the country and western field, has, like other performers of country music, taken to recording with string sections, brass, and reeds, which is a far remove from the guitars and banjos usually associated with this kind of music. His songs still have a Nashville flavor, as witness his recent hit "Somebody Like Me," but another song in the same album, "At Sunset," is almost a beguine. A capable singer with a relaxed style—he sounds somewhat like a countrified Perry Como—Arnold has built himself a non-country and western audience. Yet by style and experience both, he *is* a country and western singer. In which column, then, do you put his record sales?

The same thing applies to eccentrically brilliant Roger Miller, whose amusing, earthy songs have become major national hits, "King of the Road" probably being the biggest to date. So wide has Miller's appeal become that network television was willing to spot him in his own show. The show didn't find a following large enough to sustain it, but TV demands preposterously large audiences for a show to be considered successful—and besides, in an attempt to slick Miller up and package him, the producers took all the edge off his work, so that even many of his admirers gave up watching it after a time or two. The significant thing is the network estimate in the first place that his appeal was broad enough to carry a show. To which side of the ledger, then, do you assign Miller's record sales?

And the music business is more than recording. It is also publishing. Many country and western songs, such as the late Hank Williams' "Cold Cold Heart," have crossed the line into straight pop territory to become hits or even standards. The late Nat Cole and Ray Charles, among others, have recorded many songs imported from country and western land.

Clive Davis, Executive Administrative Vice President of CBS Records (which includes Columbia and Epic), agrees with Tomko that it is impossible to get clear and meaningful figures. "But it is possible to get an idea of what's happened," he says. "For example, we used to consider that we had a big country and western hit when we sold fifty thousand singles, limited to a special geographical area—roughly the South. Now the figures will go up to a few hundred thousand. The principal strength of the music remains in the South, of course, but its appeal has spread all over the country. In the West, Midwest, and East there are many radio stations that now operate on country and western programming. There's a country music station in Newark, aimed at the New York metropolitan area."

The reason for this increment in the appeal of the music seems to lie in its growing diversification and, paradoxically, its growing homogenization. On the one hand there is the borrowing from other forms of popular music that includes more complex (though still comparatively simple) harmonies and the use of string sections and other non-country instruments. This brings part of country music closer to the mainstream of the American popular song. On the other hand, such performers as Johnny Cash and Roger Miller have taken highly individualistic courses, leaving behind the quaintly naïve ah-luhv-yeeou lyrics and the hearts-and-flowers sentiment that so long characterized country music. Cash's work—both his singing and his material—has a singular quality of stern realism. Miller's sly, obtuse comments on contemporary society have lifted drollery to the level of a subtle musical art.

Country and western also embraces the work of Merle Travis, the unusual and gifted songwriter who composed "Sixteen Tons" and other intelligently bitter portraits of life in the coal-mine country of eastern Kentucky. It includes the work of sophisticated parodists Homer and Jethro. And, of course, it includes bluegrass music, which is its purest extant form. Thus, a music that at first hearing seems to sound all alike (as does opera, jazz, or any other kind of music, for that matter) turns out to be richly varied, its quality ranging from the trashy and trite to some of the most shrewdly perceptive songs of our time.

All of it descends from southern Appalachian folk music, which in turn descends from Elizabethan balladry. Out of this heritage eventually grew country bands, made up for the most part of men who made their livings in other trades and go together for weekend dances and parties. With the improvement in transportation came the rise of the professional—and itinerant—musician, who had to be recorded wherever and whenever the record companies could catch up with him.

One of the elder satesmen of country music is Don Low, who has been with Columbia Records and its predecessor companies for forty years. English-born, Law still has a vestigial precision in his speech, which sounds out of place in drawling Nashville.

"In the early days I did most of my recording in Dallas, El Paso, and Houston, usually in hotel rooms," he said. "At that time we recorded on waxes which had to be preheated. You couldn't play them back without ruining them, so you had to be right. It was a little hectic. Sometimes it was so crowded in those hotel rooms that we'd have to put the bass player in the bathroom—which was all right, in a sense, since the sound there was very live!"

The years have made Law an appreciator of country music, though he admits that his own private listening usually is to Scarlatti and Bach. "But I've learned to understand this music," he says, "and I like it. I like the spontaneity, the naturalness."

Another veteran of the field is Steve Sholes, RCA Victor's Vice President in Charge of Popular Artists and Repertoire. In his long career Sholes has recorded every kind of music in the catalogue, but he seems to have a particular affection for country music and jazz. Sholes first started recording in Nashville in 1949 and, like Law, has watched the gradual gravitation of the country and western industry to that city. The pull was Grand Ol' Opry, the one medium through which the country-and-western performer could hope to become a star. That has changed somewhat, but the program still is a powerful force.

One of the artists Sholes signed to his label was a young guitarist from a small town in the impoverished eastern part of Tennessee, named Chet Atkins, who says, "I was lucky to get out of there. A lot of people didn't."

Atkins played on many Sholes dates. "In his own low-pressure way," Sholes said, "he'd make suggestions. Right then and there he became a co-producer." Sholes paused and smiled. "Of course, I didn't tell him that, and he didn't get paid for it. I just let him go on making suggestions. They were always good ones, and they always worked." Atkins became a major star in the country-music field, but also, as he became more and more important to Victor for his skill in putting records together, he began to take on a true executive role. In 1957 he was made manager of all RCA Victor's operations in Nashville. He still holds the post—which has become a much bigger one now than it was then.

"We started in a jingle studio that once contained Andrew Jackson's law office," Atkins recalled, adding with a slow, slight smile: "We used to be in a garage for a while." Victor's Nashville facilities today are a far cry from such improvisational setups. The first company to build its own studio there, it now has three of them. They are of astonishing proportions to anyone used to the small, tight studios of New York, where space is at a premium and real estate costs astronomical. The control room of Victor's Nashville Studio A is bigger than some New York City studios, and Atkins' office, which is liberally scattered with sofas, armchairs, and expensive bibelots, is more luxurious than that of any of his bosses in New York.

But in a sense, Atkins has no boss. It has—thus far, at least—been his company's policy to keep New York's hands off the Nashville operation. This independence, Sholes thinks, has a lot to do with the natural, relaxed, spontaneous quality of recordings coming out of Nashville. Perhaps the general atmosphere has something to do with it too.

There is a cordial, cooperative, and amicable relationship among most of the music-business professionals in Nashville, which is in distinct contrast to the cutthroat competitiveness, the corridor conspiracies, the murderous politicking of the New York music business. As one New York man put it, "Here in New York, you spend ninety per cent of your time trying to keep the other guy's knife out of your back, or else trying to stick one into his, and ten per cent of your time making records. Down in Nashville they're away from all that, they think about the records they're making."

Chet Atkins is perhaps the best symbol of and spokesman for the Nashville attitude. Soft-spoken, a gentleman, he has a taste for tweed jackets rather than the garish costumes outsiders expect of country-music people. Tall and thin, he has the slight stoop of shoulders that so many guitarists seem to get from hunching over their instruments. He never appears to be in a hurry. Chatting in his office, he may pick up his guitar, which he plays astonishingly well and not only in country-music style, and do a little pickin', as it's called here. Asked how old he is, Atkins said, "Forty-two," "Ah Chet," groaned one of the executives from New York, "I thought we agreed you were thirty-nine." Atkins shrugged. He couldn't care less. He has none of the mannerisms of a star, which of course is what he is in his field. His one concession to his status is the Cadillac he drives, and he recently drawled, "I think I'd better get something else. This way, I look like one of the sidemen."

The sidemen—the studio musicians of Nashville—do indeed drive Cadillacs. The best of them earn as much as $100,000 a year, and some of them, such as pianist Floyd Cramer and Boots Randolph, an erstwhile jazz tenor saxophonist who elected to settle in Nashville rather than hazard the life of the New York musician, not only play on the record dates of other artists but have recording contracts of their own. With such financial rewards, it is hardly surprising that a great many first-rate musicians have drifted to Nashville including, oddly enough, a number of Negroes. "We'd use more of 'em if we had 'em," Atkins said of the Negro players.

What Nashville really needs is a good string section. With the tendency of country music to take on more of the manners of "class" popular music, this shortcoming is becoming glaringly apparent. The strings on records coming out of Nashville usually have a thin, weak, scratchy, amateur sound. "It's true," Atkins said. "We could use some good string players. I've had to import them on occasion. I think about all the fine young violinists coming out of music schools who go to the big cities to starve, when we could really use 'em here."

Nashville's musical year reaches its height each October when the annual country-and-western disc jockey convention is held. Its purpose is promotion, and the atmosphere becomes shrill with the twanging of amplified guitars as loudspeakers blare into streets suddenly dense with traffic. Prostitutes converge on the city to take advantage of the concentrated business opportunities, and everywhere there are disc jockeys and camp followers. These are the people who wear the gaudiest clothes—fringed shirts, silver belt buckles, hand-tooled high-heeled boots, and, for the ladies, cowgirl skirts or gold lamé pants. Broad-brimmed hats, usually white, are a commonplace. Not all the conventioneers dress this way, of course, but enough of them do to give the place the air of an unusually flamboyant carnival. Everyone seems to be bidding for attention, and some find it. At last fall's convention, would-be country star Hank Williams, Jr., held court in a trailer on a downtown parking lot; on exhibit next to the trailer was the Cadillac in which his father died.

One thing most of the visitors have in common is a taste for whiskey, which flows freely in the hotel suites of record companies and publishers, whose purpose is to push their artists.

"In three days they try to drink up all the booze in sight, because it's free," said one Nashville music professional. "A year or two ago one of them got so drunk he fell out of a hotel window, stark naked. All he got was a broken wrist."

There are huge dinners (from which most of the visitors come away complaining about the quality of the food) and there are speeches. Some of the speeches are a little defensive about country music, some are a little aggressive, as if the speakers are determined to make everyone recognize their music's new importance as a major force in the music business. Awards are given—for the best country singer of the year, the best single record, the best album, the best song. It is a little like the Academy Awards presentation, or the NARAS awards —an industry is patting itself on the back. Each night when the dinners and speeches are over, the hotel lobbies are crowded with milling conventioneers, and up in the rooms a good deal of whoopee gets under way.

Then, suddenly, it's all over. The disc jockeys are gone, the outgoing planes are crowded with homebound New York City music-business executives, the ladies of the evening pack their cosmetic kits and depart in search of richer pickings. Nashville goes back to the insurance business and the manufacture of shoes, which are two of its economic mainstays. It also goes back to a third and new industry—the business of being the second recording capital of the United States.

HANK BALLARD REVISITED

●

JAMES PAYNE

In Daytona Beach it rains every afternoon for half an hour or so. When Hank Ballard arrived it was raining. It's hard to make a dignified entrance in the rain.

Arriving in a Cadillac helped. The Midnighters' rather formal traveling duds helped too—for example, a cranberry Banlon knit shirt, lemon metallic slacks, contrasting see-through socks and patent leathers. The people standing around were impressed. Hank Ballard and the Midnighters have sold over five million records so I guess the people should have been impressed ("Annie Had a Baby," "Thrill Up On the Hill," "Work With Me Annie," "The Twist" [he wrote and sang the original version] and "Finger Poppin' Time").

The group had come a long way from somewhere. They were tired, and they weren't too enthusiastic about rehearsing. We were the house band at the club and we were going to back them up for the show that night.

The rehearsal was short and quick. Hank gave the directions. He didn't have any sheet music. "This one's a pretty fast shuffle in B flat, you know, with a break as you come down from the fifth to the fourth and a little intro like this . . ." We knew.

That night they did two shows. Hank sang his million-sellers, those uptempo shuffles with the break we knew about. They all had a happy, alive feeling you don't hear too much today. Everything's getting so down and serious. The crowd recognized most of them after a lick or two, but to keep things current and moving the Midnighters took turns singing tunes like "Mustang Sally" and "Hold On I'm Coming." They also went through a showtime comedy routine, although Henry, the comic of the original Midnighters who used to come on like Mr. Clean, is no longer there.

Both shows were the same.

The people clapped and stomped and pointed and drank beer. Mostly Southern college kids from Georgia and Tennessee come down to Daytona Beach to "raise a little hell." Football jerseys, 69 sweatshirts, loafers (no socks), short blond hair.

A good part of the time Hank stood off to the side in his black-and-white checked, skimpy-vent sport coat, slightly worn around the edges, and let his boys take care of the entertaining chores.

"Shout" was the finale. The crowd loved it and went home satisfied or drunk or something.

I went home with fixed feelings. I was happy because Hank had been able to put over this basically sham routine on the yahooing, pseudo-soul set who had bugged us all summer with requests for "Ninety-six Tears," or "Little Bit O' Soul," or "any of that wild nigger soul music, you know . . ." I was sad because Hank had to go through this in order to make a living.

Six or seven years ago Hank Ballard and the Midnighters were a top act—polished and clean. They were famous for their comedy routine along with the Coasters and the Vibrations, the great live comedy groups. To a great extent their act was entertainment and largely nonmusical, and of course many people today would say that's terrible. But then again, light shows and Indian beads aren't too musical either, and I'm rapidly getting tired of the anti-entertainment, screw-the-audience attitude—tuning up on stage, taking five minutes between songs, etc.

The music of the Midnighters is only important in historical context, but it is important. A commercial extension of the blues which was much happier and which moved faster in that easy, shuffle groove. It was back near the beginning of rock. And back near the beginning of rock is where a lot of people are going today. The purist blues groups are moving through changes in a matter of months that parallel the changes of the fifties when r and b developed out of the blues. Witness Spencer Davis's rather thin remake of the pre-Spector-Righteous Brothers' "My Babe," and Clapton doing Freddy King's "Hideaway" with the Blues Breakers, both shuffles. And Mike Bloomfield's added horns! I knew it would come.

Hank Ballard hasn't gone *back* to the fifties. He's been forced to stay there because he hasn't had a hit in six or seven years.

"I got a new one coming out though. Should be out next week. It's got that thing, that new sound."

Me: "That solid, Memphis thing?"

"Yea, that's it, that Memphis sound. That's what's happening today you know. I think this one's going to make it. I haven't had one in quite a while—I'm due. And a lot of the older cats are coming back—Lee Dorsey, Aaron Neville, King Curtis, a lot of 'em."

We were listening to a record called "I'm a Practical Guy" by Lee Rogers.

"Now that tune you got on there, that tune's a stone hit—got everything. But it never got anywhere cause it didn't have the money behind it. You gotta have the money you know. (I knew.) King—King Records out of Cincinnati—they haven't been giving me the promotion backing they should have. I'm due though. I'll hit again one of these days."

Without a hit, Hank has been forced to do the same routine for almost ten years now. In 1961 he came to Daytona for twenty straight nights at over $1,000 a night. He was doing basically the same thing but with a little more polish. This time he was booked for one night at about $400 and the Midnighters (none of whom were in the original group) were not very polished.

After a few years of constant one-nighters—playing to half-drunk kids in front of a long-hair band who doesn't understand you or your music, and with a PA that cuts off periodically and isn't loud enough—the artist gets lost and creativity dries up. The environment is just too hostile. It would happen with any artist. After a few drinks the crowd can recognize the old licks, so after a few drinks, or whatever, Hank can still sing them, but it's no longer the real thing. He knows it's not the real thing. He's just going through the motions.

THE FIRST TYCOON OF TEEN

TOM WOLFE

Phil Spector is sitting in a little cream room in his office suite at 440 East 62nd Street with his back to a window that is practically on top of the East Side Drive. Twenty-four years old, he has a complex of corporations known as Phil Spector Productions. One of them is Mother Bertha Productions, named after his mother, Bertha. She works for his office in Los Angeles, but only because she wants to. The main organization is Philles Records. Spector has produced twenty-one "single" Philles records since October, 1962, and sold more than 13,000,000 copies. All rock-'n'-roll. His big hit, "Walking in the Rain," by the Ronettes, went as high Number 20 on the cashbox chart and sold more than 250,000 copies. His latest record, "You've Lost That Lovin' Feelin'," by the Righteous Brothers, rose from the twenties to Number 37 with a "bullet" beside it, meaning "going up fast." He has produced seven albums. The first teen-age tycoon! He is leaning back in the chair. He has on a suede jerkin, Italian pants, a pair of pointy British boots with Cuban heels. His hair hangs down to his shoulders in back. The beard is shaved off, however.

Danny Davis, his promotion man, is talking on the phone in the inner office. A fellow sits across from Spector with his legs crossed and a huge chocolate brown Borsalino hat over his bent knee, as if he were just trying it on. He says, "Phil, why do you do—"

"I'm moving the whole thing to California," says Phil Spector. "I can't stand flying any more."

"Why do you do these things?"

Spector—without his beard, Spector has a small chin, a small head; his face looks at first like all those little kids with bad hair and reedy voices from the Bronx, where he was born. But—an *ordinary* Phil Spector? Phil Spector has the only pure American voice. He was brought up not in the Bronx, but in California. His voice meanders, quietly, shaking, through his doldrum fury out to somewhere beyond cynical, beyond cool, beyond teen-age world-weary. It is thin, broken, and soft. He is only twenty-three years old, the first millionaire businessman to rise up out of the teen-age netherworld, king of the rock-'n'-roll record producers.

Spector jumps out of the chair. "Wait a minute," he says. "Just a minute. They're making deals in here."

Spector walks into the inner office gingerly, like a cowboy, because of the way the English boots lift him up off the floor. He is slight, five-feet-seven, 130 pounds. His hair shakes faintly behind. It is a big room, like a living room, all beige except for eight gold-plated rock-'n'-roll records on the wall—some of Phil Spector's "goldies," 1,000,000 sales each. "He's a Rebel," by the Crystals. "Zip-a-dee-doo-dah," by Bob B. Soxx and the Blue Jeans. "Be My Baby," by the Ronettes. "Da Do Ron Ron," "Then He Kissed Me," "Uptown," "He's Sure the Boy I Love," all by the Crystals. "Wait Till My Baby Gets Home," by Darlene Love. And beige walls, beige telephones all over the place, a beige upright piano, beige paintings, beige tables, with Danny Davis crowding over a beige desk, talking on the telephone.

"Sure, Sal," says Danny, "I'll ask Phil. Maybe we can work something out on that."

Spector starts motioning thumbs down.

"Just a minute, Sal." Danny puts his hand over the mouthpiece and says, "We *need* this guy, Phil. He's the biggest distributor out there. He wants the 1,000 guarantee."

Phil's hands go up as if he were lifting a slaughtered lamb up on top of an icebox. "I don't care. I'm not interested in the money, I've got millions, I don't care who needs this animal. I'm interested in selling records, OK? Why should I give him a guarantee? He orders the records, I guarantee I'll buy 1,000 back from him if he can't sell them; he sells them, then after the record dies he buys up five hundred cut-rate from somebody, sends them back, and cries for his money. Why should we have to be eating his singles later?"

Danny takes his hand away and says into the mouthpiece, "Look, Sal, there's one thing I forgot. Phil says this record he can't give the guarantee. But you don't have anything to worry about . . . I know what I said, but Phil says . . . Look, Sal, don't worry, 'Walking in the Rain,' this is a tremendous record—tremendous, a very big record . . . What? . . . I'm not reading off a paper, Sal . . . Wait a minute, Sal—"

"Who needs these animals?" Spector tells Danny.

"Look, Sal," Danny says, "this man never made a bad record in his life. You tell me one. Nothing but hits."

"Tell him I'm not in," says Spector.

"Sal—"

"Who needs these animals!" says Spector, so loud this time that Danny cups his hand around the receiver and puts his mouth down close.

"Nothing, Sal," says Danny, "that was somebody came in."

"Joan," says Phil, and a girl, Joan Berg, comes in out of another room. "Will you turn the lights off?" he says.

She turns the lights off, and now in the middle of the day the offices of Philles Records and Mother Bertha Productions are all dark except for the light from Danny Davis' lamp. Danny crowds into the pool of light, hunched over the phone, talking to Sal.

Phil puts his fingers between his eyes and wraps his eyebrows around them.

"Phil, it's dark in here," says the fellow with the large hat. "Why do you do these things?"

"I'm paying a doctor six hundred dollars a week to find out," says Phil, without looking up.

He sits there in the dark, his fingers buried between his eyes. Just over his head one can make out a painting. The painting is kind of came-with-the-frame surrealist. It shows a single musical note, a half note, suspended over what looks like the desert outside Las Vegas. Danny has to sit there huddled in his own pool of light talking to this "animal" on the telephone.

"This is primitive country," says Phil Spector. "I was at Shepheard's, the discothèque, and these guys start saying these things. It's unbelievable. These people are animals."

"What kind of things, Phil?"

"I don't know. They look at, you know, my hair. My wife and I are dancing, and—I mean it's unbelievable—I feel somebody yanking on my hair in the back. I turn around, and here's this guy, a grown man, and he is saying these unbelievable things to me. So I tell him, like this, 'I'm going to tell you this one time, that's all: don't ever try that again.' And the guy it's unbelievable—he shoved me with the heel of his hand and I go sprawling back into a table—"

Spector pauses.

"I mean, I've studied karate for years. I could literally kill a guy like that. You know? Size means nothing. A couple of these"—he cocks his elbow in the gloom and brings up the flat of his forearm—"but what am I going to do, start a fight every time I go out? Why should I even have to listen to anything from these animals? I find this country very condemning. I don't have this kind of trouble in Europe. The people of America are just not born with culture."

Not born with culture! If only David Susskind and William B. Williams could hear that. Susskind invited Phil Spector to the "Open End" television program one evening to talk about the record business. Suddenly Susskind and William B., station WNEW's old-nostalgia disc jockey, were condemning Spector as one kind of sharpie poisoning American culture, rotting the minds of youth, and so forth. That was how it all hit Spector. It was as if he were some kind of old short-armed fatty in the Brill Building, the music center on Broadway, with a spread-collar shirt and a bald olive skull with strands of black hair pulled up over it from above one ear. There was something very ironic about that. Spector is the one record producer who wouldn't go near Broadway. His setup is practically out in the East River, up by the Rockefeller Institute.

Susskind and Williams kept throwing Spector's songs at him—"He's a Rebel," "Da Do Ron Ron," "Be My Baby," "Fine Fine Boy," "Breakin' Up"— as if he were astutely conning millions of the cretins out there with this stuff. Spector didn't know exactly what to tell them. He *likes* the music he produces. He writes it himself. He is something new: the first teen-age millionaire, the first boy to become a millionaire within America's teen-age netherworld. It was never a simple question of his taking a look at the rock-'n'-roll universe from the outside and exploiting it. He stayed within it himself. He *liked* the music.

Spector, while still in his teens, seemed to comprehend the prole vitality of rock-'n'-roll that has made it the kind of darling holy beast of intellectuals in the United States, England, and France. Intellectuals, generally, no longer take jazz seriously. Monk, Mingus, Ferguson—it has all been left to little executive trainees with their first apartment and a mahogany African mask from the free-port shop in Haiti and a hi-fi. But rock-'n'-roll! Poor old arteriosclerotic lawyers with pocky layers of fat over their ribs are out there right now twisting clumsily to rock-'n'-roll. Their wives wear stretch pants to the seafood shop. A style of life!

There have been teen-agers who have made a million dollars before, but invariably they are entertainers; they are steered by older people, such as the good Colonel Tom Parker who steers Elvis Presley. But Phil Spector is the bona-fide genius of teen. Every baroque period has a flowering genius who rises up as the most glorious expression of its style of life —in latterday Rome, the Emperor Commodus; in Renaissance Italy, Benvenuto Cellini; in late Augustan England, the Earl of Chesterfield; in the sad, volatile Victorian age, Dante Gabriel Rossetti; in late-fancy, neo-Greek federal America, Thomas Jefferson; and in teen America, Phil Spector.

In point of fact, he had turned twenty-one when he made his first clear million. But it was as a teen-ager, working within the teen-age milieu, starting at the age of seventeen, that Phil Spector developed into a great American businessman, the greatest of the independent rock-'n'-roll record producers. Spector's mother, Bertha, took him from the Bronx to California when he was nine. California! Teen heaven! By the time he was sixteen he was playing jazz guitar with some group. Then he got interested in rock-'n'-roll, which he does not call "rock-'n'-roll" but "pop blues." That is because—well, that's a complicated subject. Anyway, Phil Spector likes this music. He genuinely likes it. He is not a short-armed fatty hustling nutball fads.

"I get a little angry when people say it's bad music," Spector tells the man with the brown hat. "This music has a spontaneity that doesn't exist in any other kind of music, and it's what is here now. It's unfair to classify it as rock-'n'-roll and condemn it. It has limited chord changes, and people are always saying the words are banal and why doesn't anybody write lyrics like Cole Porter any more, but we don't have any Presidents like Lincoln any more, either. You know? Actually, it's more like the blues. It's pop blues. I feel it's very American. It's very *today*. It's what people respond to today. It's not just the kids. I hear cabdrivers, everybody, listening to it."

And Susskind sits there on his show reading one of Spector's songs out loud—no music, just reading the words, from the "Top Sixty" or whatever it is—"Fine Fine Boy," to show how banal rock-'n'-roll is. The song just keeps repeating "He's a fine fine boy." So Spector starts drumming on the big coffee table there with the flat of his hands in time to Susskind's voice and says, "What you're missing is the beat." Blam blam.

Everybody is getting a little sore, with Susskind reading these simple lyrics and Spector blamming away on the coffee table. Finally Spector starts asking Williams how many times he plays Verdi on his show?—Monteverdi?—D. Scarlatti?—A. Scarletti? "That's good music, why don't you play that? You keep saying you play only good music. I don't hear you playing that." Williams doesn't know what to say. Spector tells Susskind he didn't come on the show to listen to somebody tell him he was corrupting the youth of America—he could be home making money. Susskind: "Well, ah, all right, Phil." Everybody is testy.

Making money. Yes! At the age of seventeen Spector wrote a rock-'n'-roll song called "To Know Him Is to Love Him." He took the title off his father's tombstone. That was what his mother had had engraved on his father's tombstone out in Beth David Cemetery in Elmont, Long Island. He doesn't say much about his father, just that he was "average lower-middle class." Spector wrote the song, sang it, and played the guitar in the recording with a group called the Teddy Bears. He made $20,000 on that record, but somebody ran off with $17,000 of it, and . . . well, no use going into that. Then he was going to UCLA, but he couldn't afford it and became a court reporter —one of the people who sit at the shorthand machine taking down testimony. He decided to come to New York and get a job as interpreter at the UN. His mother had taught him French. But he got to New York, and the night before the interview he fell in with some musicians and never got there. Instead he wrote another hit that year, "Spanish Harlem." And then—only nineteen—he became head of A & R, Artists and Repertoire, for Atlantic Records. By 1961 he was a free-lance producer, producing records for the companies, working with Connie Francis, Elvis Presley, Ray Peterson, the Paris Sisters.

All this time Spector would write a song and run all phases of making records, get the artists, direct the recording sessions —everything. Spector would work with these kids who make these records because he was a kid himself, in one sense. God knows what the music-business biggies thought of Phil Spector —he already wore his hair like Salvador Dali did at that age, or like an old mezzotint of Mozart or something. And he was somehow *one of them*—the natives, the kids who sang and responded to this . . . music. Phil Spector could get in one of those studios with the heron microphones, a representative of the adult world that makes money from records, and it became all one thing: the kids comprehended him.

Spector had an ideal: Archie Bleyer. Bleyer was a band leader who founded a record company, Cadence Records. Spector formed a partnership with two other people in 1961, then bought them out and went on his own as Philles Records in October of 1962. His first big hit was "He's a Rebel," by the Crystals. Spector had a system. The big record companies put out records like buckshot—ten, maybe fifteen rock-'n'-roll records a month—and if one of them catches on, they can make money. Spector's system is to put them out one at a time, and pour everything into each one. Spector does the whole thing. He writes the words and the music, scouts and signs up the talent. He takes them out to a recording studio in Los Angeles and runs the recording session himself. He puts them through hours and days of recording to get the two or three minutes he wants. Two or three minutes out of the whole struggle. He handles the control dials like an electronic maestro, tuning various instruments or sounds up, down, out, every which way, using things like two pianos, a harpsichord, and three guitars on one record; then rerecording the whole thing with esoteric dubbing and overdubbing effects—reinforcing instruments or voices—coming out with what is known through the industry as "the Spector sound." The only thing he doesn't keep control of is the actual manufacture, the pressing of the records and the distribution.

The only people around to give him any trouble all this time are the distributors, cigar-chewing fatties, and . . . well, to be honest, there is a lot that gives Phil Spector trouble, and it's not so much any kind of or any group of people as much as his status. A teen-age tycoon! He is betwixt and between. He identifies with the teen-age netherworld, he defends it, but he is already too mature for it. As a millionaire, a business genius, living in a penthouse twenty-two stories up over the East River, with his wife, Annette, who is twenty, a student at Hunter College, and with a four-room suite downstairs on the ground floor as his office, and a limousine, and a chauffeur, and a bodyguard, and a staff—Danny and Joan Berg and everybody—and a doorman who directs people to Mr. Spector's office . . . well, that makes Phil Spector one of *them,* the universe of arteriosclerotic, hypocritical, cigar-chewing, hopeless, larded adults, infracted vultures one meets in the music business. And so here in the dark is a twenty-four-year-old man with a Shelley visage, a suede shirt, a kind of page-boy bob and winkle-picker boots

—the symbol of the teen world—sitting in the dark in this great beige office—the symbol of the tycoon world—in the middle of the day, in the dark, tamping his frontal lobes with his fingers in the gloom.

One of the beige phones rings and Danny answers. Then he presses the "hold" button and tells Phil Spector, "It's the Rolling Stones. They just got in."

Spector comes alive with that. He gets up on his ginger toes and goes to the telephone. He is lively, and he spins on the balls of his feet a little as he stands by the phone.

"Hello, Andrew," he says. He is talking with Andrew Oldham, the manager of the Rolling Stones. And then he puts on a Cockney accent, "Are you all in?" he says.

The Rolling Stones—all right. The Rolling Stones, English group, and Andrew Oldham, are like him. They grew up in the teen-age netherworld and made it, and they all want to have it all too, the kids' style of life and the adults'—money—and not cop out on one side or the other, larded and arteriosclerotic. Phil Spector's British trip! That was where suddenly he had it all.

Phil Spector is here! The British had the ability to look at all sorts of rebel baddies and alienated thin young fellows and say coo and absorb them like a great soggy, lukewarm, mother's poultice. The Beatles, Beatlemania, rock-'n'-roll—suddenly it is all absorbed into the center of things as if it could have been there all along if it only asked. Phil Spector arrives at London Airport and, Santa Barranza, there are photographers all over the place, for him, Phil Spector, and the next morning he is all over the center fold of the *London Daily Mirror*, the biggest newspaper in the Western World, 5,000,000 circulation: "The twenty-three-year-old American rock-'n'-roll magnate." He is in the magazines as the "U. S. Recording Tycoon." Invitations go out to come to the receptions to meet "America's outstanding hit-maker, Phil Spector." And then he lands back at Idlewild and waiting are, yes, the same bunch of cheese-breath cabbies, and he takes a cab on back to 440 East 62nd Street and goes into his beige world—the phones are ringing and it is all the same, the same . . . .

"Cigar-smoking sharpies," says Phil Spector. He is in a livelier mood after the talk with Andrew Oldham. "They're a bunch of cigar-smoking sharpies in record distribution. They've all been in the business for years, and they resent you if you're young. That's one reason so many kids go broke in this business. They're always starting new record companies—or they used to, the business is very soft right now. They start a company and pour all their money into a record, and it can be successful and they're still broke, because these characters don't even pay you until you've had three or four hit records in a row. They order the records and sell them and don't pay you. They don't pay you because they know they don't have to. You start yelling for the money and they tell you, 'What-ya mean, I have all these records coming back from the retailers, and what about my right to return records and blah-blah!' What are you going to do? Sue twenty guys in twenty different courts in the United States?

"They look at everything as a product. They don't care about the work and sweat you put into a record. They respect me now because I keep turning out hits, and after that they become sort of honest . . . in their own decayed way."

Where does a man find friends, comrades, anything, in a world like that? They resent his youth. They resent his success. But it is no better with the kids. He is so much more mature and more . . . eminent . . . they all want to form "the father thing" with him. Or else they want to fawn over him, cozen him, cajole, fall down before him, whistle, shout, stomp, bang him on the head—anything to get his attention and get "the break," just one chance. Or one more chance. Spector can't go near the Brill Building, the center of the music business, because the place is crawling with kids with winkle-picker shoes cracking in the folds who made one hit record five years ago and still can't realize that they are now, forever, in oblivion. They crawl all over the place, the way the small-time balding fatty promoters and managers used to in the days when A. J. Liebling wrote about the place as the Jollity Building.

Phil Spector steps onto an elevator in the Brill Building. The elevator is packed, and suddenly he feels this arm hooking through his in the most hideously cozy way and a mouth is closing in on his ear and saying, "Phil, baby, wait'll you hear this one: 'Ooh-oom-bah-ay,' " and Phil Spector is imprisoned there with the elevator inching up, " 'vah ump nooby poon fan ooh-ooh ayub bah-ay'—you dig that, Phil? You dig that, don't you, Phil? Phil, babes!" He walks down the hall and kids sneak up behind him and slip songs, music, lyrics into his coat pocket. He finds the stuff in there, all this ratty paper, when he gets home. Or he is leaving the Brill Building and he feels a great whack on the back of his head and wheels around, and there are four kids in the singing stance, their heads angled in together, saying, "Just one bar, Phil: 'Say wohna love boo-uh-ay-yay-bubby' "—while the guy on the end sings bass with his chin mashed into a pulpy squash down over his collarbone—". . . 'beh-ungggh, beh-ungggh.' "

Status! What is his status? He produces rock-'n'-roll, and therefore he is not a serious person and he won't join the Young Presidents or whatever kind of organization jaycee geniuses would join for their own good.

"Phil," says the man with the hat, "why don't you hire a press agent, a P.R. man?"

Phil is tamping his frontal lobes in the gloom. Danny Davis is hunched up in the little pool of light on his desk. Danny is doing his level best for Phil.

"Jack? Danny Davis . . . Yeah . . . No, I'm with Phil Spector now . . . Right! It's the best move I ever made. You know Phil . . . I'm in the best shape of my career . . . Jack, I just want to tell you we've got—"

"A press agent?" Phil says to the man in the hat. "In the first place, I couldn't stand to hear what he'd say about me."

"Got two tremendous records going, Jack, 'Walking in the Rain,' the Ronettes, and—"

"In the second place," Phil says, "there's no way my image can be bought."

"And 'You've Lost That Lovin' Feelin' ' by the Righteous Brothers," says Danny. ". . . Right, Jack . . . I appreciate that Jack . . ."

"The only thing I could do—you know what I'd like to do? I'd like to do a recording session in the office of *Life* or *Esquire* or *Time*, and then they could see it. That's the only chance I've got. Because I'm dealing in rock-'n'-roll, it's like I'm not a bona-fide human being."

". . . Absolutely! . . . If there's anything we can do for you on this end, Jack, let us know. OK? Great, Jack . . . "

"And I even have trouble with people who should never say *any*thing. I go over to Gristede's to get a quart of milk or something, and the woman at the cash register has to start in. So I tell her, 'There's a war in Viet Nam, they've fired Khrushchev, the Republican party is falling to pieces, the Ku Klux Klan is running around loose, and you're worrying about my hair!' "

America's first teen-age tycoon—a business genius, a musical genius—and it is as if he were still on the corner of Hoffman Street in the Bronx when the big kids come by in hideous fraternity, the way these people act. What is he now? Who is he in this weird country? Danny talks in the phone in the little pool of light; Joan is typing up whatever it is; Phil is tamping his frontal lobes.

UNDERGROUND RADIO

●

TOM NOLAN

"Aaawright, bay-aay-he-baay!"

What?

Wait a minute! no no no no no, turn the dial back to that, what is that, tune that in there . . . what—but what—what *is* that?

"Heah's a record's gonna knock ya *right-on-de-flowa, bay-aay-he-baay!"*

The record starts out, something by the Marvelettes, and the voice manages to control itself, sort of, throwing in only an occasional *"Aaawright! Aaawright!"* or a *"Have moicy, baay-baay!"* But then the record starts building and the voice can't hold itself back any longer. It starts singing along, "Yeah, yeah! . . . *gonna miss me! . . . uuunnh-huuunnh . . . aaawright!"* and it becomes a very physical thing, like a pressure cooker about to sputter and explode all the hell over the place, some kind of cacophonous symphony. The voice is growing, it almost overpowers the record—*"AAAWRIGHT! AAAWRIGHT! HAVE MOICY! BAA-HAAY-BAA-HAA!"* It's incredible, this shouting-grunting-grating-moaning-hoarse-rasping voice, this lead-pipe-dragging-on-asphalt cement-mixer of a voice! And you figure it must be some kind of joke, some kind of elaborate put-on—right?—because here is this . . . *guy,* this . . . *insane man . . . screaming* at me from my radio!

Now he's *shrieking, "CAA-CAA-REE!! CAA-CAA-REE!!"* What the—what the—who the—

"You listenin' ta de *Woofman Jack Show, baay-he-baay!* Fum X-E-R-B! Fum *Holly-wood,* Cali-*phone*-ya! Fifty thousan' watts a' *soul power,* man! *CAA-CAA-REE!!!"*

Then the capper: echoing back from who-knows-how-many radio kilowatt-canyons comes the super hyped-up guaranteed-ta-blow-yah-mind gen-u-wine patented Wolfman Jack super lobo wolf call! AAA-WOOOOH!

"CAA-CAA-REE!! CAN YA DIG IT, BAAY-HAY-BAAY? YA GONNA LOVE IT TA DEATH!!"

The *Wolfman Jack Show*?

The new *Wolfman Jack Show*, new, that is, in the sense that the Wolfman has changed somewhat since coming up from the underground. The old Wolfman could be picked up late at night for a period of several hours before some kind of awful Mexican mariachi rock took over XERB at about one in the morning; and it was a thrill and a delight to stumble across this madman because the Wolfman was, perhaps, the quintessence of all that was great about underground radio.

Underground radio has a great deal to do with the hour: it is on late at night, generally, because the reception is better, and there are all of these freaky people up at that hour, trying to tune in on *some*thing, *any*thing, a little bit wiggier than AM in the a.m.

It's also kind of a snobbish thing too: You'll be sitting there, crouched in the darkness, threading your way slowly through the band and dialing the skinny red tuning finger across all the luminescent numbers glowing out at you from the yellow rectangle, the only light in the room. And you're hunched over this little box there and suddenly, through the early morning hours and all the miles and miles of air waves and fading voices and signals and static, your ear snags on this weaving, faint, cultured French BBC voice saying: "*Ici Raa-di-o Ca-na-da*"—and it's like you've tuned into something incredibly special that nobody else in the whole world is hearing, and how lucky you are! You're pulling in this NBC station from San Francisco, and that gospel show from Chicago, and hunting for that phone show from Salt Lake City which people call from all over the country, mostly just to talk about the other people who call—*strange!* And it's ultimately more than just a snobbish thing, it's a kick because—if one wants to theorize verbally about what is mainly a nonmental reaction—you're getting, depending on what signals you're lucky enough to find, an aural sniff of the way things are, day by day, in a world or three which most of us will never—all things considered—really know.

BEGINNING OF A MAJOR DIGRESSION

Underground radio is something like underground television, if you can give that name to a certain kind of voyeuristic practice which is highly unorganized, random, uneven in results, and a very personal kind of pleasure—sort of an acquired taste, if you're lucky enough to get the opportunity to acquire it. Since they have a lot in common, as a roundabout way of showing the special pleasures of underground radio I might say a few words about its visual counterpart.

Have you ever turned on TV about four in the morning, and found what a wonderland it can sometimes be? Maybe you'll pick up an educational show taped at the University of Great Neck which the station is running as a "public service," telling the history of refrigerated freight cars on the Union Pacific Railroad (with visual aids). Or maybe by some freaky mistake the engineer or whoever's in charge (who would have to be either totally ignorant or the possessor of an insane sense of fun) has slipped on a reel of *Captain Video.* There is the old fellow in his funny little Captain Video space-suit with the big V on it in lightning, and by his side at the control panel of the good ship Galaxy is the Space Ranger, or whatever the teen-age kid with him was called, and suddenly—omygodno! —a *meteor* is headed straight for the ship and *pow! pow!* and again *POW!* The cameraman is giving all this great pinball machine body-english to his camera so it jiggles around and up and down violently. The Captain is jiggling the control panel and his chair with both hands. Wow, what a collision! Wow, Cap'n Video, wow, were we hit? Yes, I'm afraid so, Space Ranger, or whatever you're called, you wait here, take the controls—and crazy ol' Cap'n Video heads for the door, and opens it, and steps out there into all that galactic dust and everything, and closes the door behind him, and the kid is yelling at him, anything wrong out there? and the Cap'n yells back, no, no, looks okay, pretty cold out here though, and then he steps back into the ship and closes the door behind him and the whole spaceship wall shakes and trembles and threatens to fall down on top of him . . . and the sound of galactic carpenters running to hold it up. . . .

Or another real treat is watching the old movies, not the Bogart or Frank Capra or Cooper flicks—everyone *knows* how great *they* are—but the films they show once in a while about five in the morning that look like they were made for three hundred dollars in somebody's backyard in New Jersey in 1938.

Like this great Buster Crabbe movie that's on pretty often. It isn't really a Buster Crabbe movie, he's just in it, playing the part of a Great White Hunter. Mainly it's about this girl who was lost as a child when her father's plane crashed in the jungle of what looks to be Asbury Park; she's been raised by this giant gorilla, see, or anyway, this huge guy in a ratty gorilla suit; and the girl—by now a somewhat less-than-stunning dumb blonde in her twenties—flounces around in a supposedly hand-tailored flowered jungle sari, and this big gorilla, her friend, is real protective toward her, and he tries to get Buster Crabbe when Crabbe finds the girl; but she calls him off, *"Tonga! Tonga!"* And then she and Buster sit and talk in her little cave-den, there; and she says, "Well, you can sleep here in the cave with me," and he sort of . . . uuuh . . . ah . . . uu . . . hu . . . mmph . . . uhs . . . and chokes out a laugh: Ha, ha! No! Can't do that! Ho, ho! Silly, naïve little jungle girl, you!

That's one of the great things about these movies: they're dirty. That is to say, even if they don't show much, it's meant in a prurient way. For instance, there's one particular film, an English mystery, probably shot in the 'thirties to fulfill an interesting U.S.-English trade agreement which allowed the British to bring in as many American films as they wanted, the only requirement being that they make an equal number of their own films to send to America in return, the result being an incredible number of horrible English films, mostly mysteries, "quickies" done at breakneck speed, like one a week. Anyway, this mystery takes place in some old English mansion (probably somewhere in the English equivalent of south New Jersey) and the plot turns upon the fact that somebody is trying to kill the heroine. But the fascinating thing is that this heroine, in the course of being stalked, takes every opportunity to jump out of her clothes—like when some old lady brings her a corsage, and this big old hairy tarantula crawls out of it on his twenty-seven ookly-hairy legs just when the girl is pinning it on her dress, and it slips down her back. So she shrieks for help, naturally, and then j-u-m-p-s out of her dress and stands there in some kind of cast-iron-looking underwear which covers her from mid-chest to knee and which one supposes was pretty daring for those days—and she manages to do this about half a dozen times throughout the picture, which is called something like *The Curse of the Old Castle.*

Well, fair enough; that's certainly an equitable share of illicit sex for one early-morning's movie watching. But it is as nothing compared to one strange movie which, as far as I know, was shown once and never has been seen again in the L.A. area. It was a documentary, sort of, about cave people and the discovery of fire and all that stuff, and a stentorian announcer describing everything to you as you watched it: the guy kills a lion with his ax—*"Zar-gel kills the lion with his ax!"* Lots of stuff like that, making up for there being no other sound track except *strange* music. And it all was like an *Encyclopaedia Britannica* educational film (or a movie for grammar school kids) with some stupid plot about this tribe of women trying to capture Zar-gel to—well, *you* know—and everything went along pretty dull, except for general *strange*ness, and then suddenly—it's night and for no continuity-of-plot reason, they cut to all these women who are swimming around in a pool of water and one of them is standing on a rock up above, and—*none of them have any clothes on! None! Nothing! At all! No clothes! Or anything! At all! Nothing! Of any kind! Nothing-atall!* And as the girl up on top smiles and arcs into the water, this March-of-Time voice booms out, "*The swan dive is invented!*" It's moments like *these* that make it all worthwhile.

But the best movies are not these, great fun as they are; no, the best underground TV movies are the ones that give you a chance to see what life must be like for a group of people who aren't like you and me, they're *different*. And even though it may not be what you consider a *good* difference (like being poor which is not a good difference, John Steinbeck and his salt-of-the-earth to the contrary, even though poverty is the father of so many underground worlds: Negro, country, hip), the difference exists, and these people haven't been homogenized. They have their own distinctive *styles*, and it may not be such a bad thing these days to revel in novelty, or at least atypicality, as its own reward.

Perhaps the greatest film of this type is not about a subculture *per se* (though, depending upon your definition, it is a kind of psychological subculture, an underground of the mind), it is *The Girl Hunters*, wherein, as the title proclaims, Mickey Spillane *is* Mike Hammer; and this funny little man is doing kinky things which make his life so much fun, like beating up guys and killing broads and hammering some guy's hand to the floor with a giant spike. It's like picking up a rock and finding some ugly creepy-crawly thing under there, acting out its slimy little dreams ("So long, baby, he says to the chick, knowing full well that she'll blast her own brains out when she pulls the shotgun trigger to shoot him)—as if Shirley Eaton would be making love to this ugly runty little diseased fellow! But here it is, this guy's golden opportunity to *live out* his fantasies, and he's really making the most of it! It's the same kind of thrill you used to get from watching the geek in a side-show—I mean, yeah, sure it's ugly and all, but—wow!—he really did bite that chicken's head off, didn't he? And, in the sense of defining the psyche of a whole segment of postwar America, it comes close to being a perfect film.

AT LONG LAST, BACK TO THE SUBJECT (SORT OF)

So that is the kind of thing that makes for great underground TV, and the same kind of thing brightens up the radio dial in odd, out-of-the-way places; the same sort of thing allows you to see (and listen) into places you would otherwise never get to know. For instance:

The Bible Belt, where radio—at least the small country-gospel station—is a reflection of poor-white rural existence, the modern product of a subculture which half a century ago centered socially around the church and the farm (or cabin), and to a great extent still does. In the late 'thirties (underground radio being a fine American tradition), country people and mountain people in the South gathered 'round the old Sears Roebuck mail-order-catalogue battery-powered radio every day to hear the famous Carter family, Sara, Maybelle, and old A. P., on radio station XERA from Del Rio, Texas, singing their own songs like:

> Thar's a wonderful invention, it's
> called the radio,
> You can hear it every-whar you
> chance to go.
> But the static in th'air
> Sometimes makes it hard to hey-air,
> But it is not so with Heaven's Radio.
> Heaven's Radi-ooo
> On th'other shore,
> For my Precious Savior always lis-
> tens in (lis-sens in).

Today this particular subculture as represented by radio has vulgarized into something like: "Waaaaal, fray-ends un nay-bers, this hay-er's ol's Fray-ed Jenkins, broadcastin' ta you an' *all* a' our fray-ends *live* an' *di*-rect from the back room hey-er at yer ol' Cousin Fray-ed's Appliance Shop an' Record Store hay-er, ri-chere in th' cenner a' town hay-er, an' weyer 'bout ta play a good ol' good one fer ya hay-er. This one hay-er this one's called, 'Thank You Dear Lord fer Vic-t'ry in Korea

—Thank You Dear God fer What You Done'—but first we-yud lahk ta tell ya 'bout the fan-*tas*-ti-cal offer bein' made ta you, our fray-ends, *this week onlay:* When you git our wunnerful gospel song book, featurin' over fifty famous gospel songs made famous by sech as Cowboy Copas, th' Wilburn Brothers an' comparable others—fer ev-rah song book you buy fer the most nom-i-nal sum a' one dollar an' fifty cents plus a small charge fer postage an' handlin' an' ol' Uncle Sam, you git ab-so-*lute*-ly free one a' our Miracle Pic-tures a' Jee-sus, which glows in th' dark, an' is a constant companion an' con-so-lation to ya. So fray-ends, thet address agay-un—"

Or you can take a quick side-trip into the palmy jungles of political extremism: residents of Malibu can spend their breakfast hour listening to tiny stations in the hinterlands broadcasting their "public service" shows—various commentators of sorts warning about Communist conspiracies, United Nations conspiracies, civil rights conspiracies, mongrelizing-the-white-race conspiracies; spend an enthralling thirty minutes listening to a man trying to prove by the coroner's report and some elementary pathology a previously unexamined part of the controversy: that the man killed in the basement of the Dallas jail was not *really* ol' Lee Oswald at *all!* Son-of-a-gun! (A lot of this is mixed with a very serviceable kind of religion, like Dr. Carl McIntire's "Save us, Dear Lord, from th' comm-a-nist sympathahzers in th' gov-ern-ment, whom Ah will now name, Lord. . . .")

And a great thing about many of the most interesting radio stations in the country (the underground stations) is that they are great grab bags of different "minority" cultures, not being confined to Negro gospel or white Appalachian gospel or political paranoia, and often you can pick up several varieties of underground on the same station. So that at three in the afternoon on KTYM from Inglewood, California, right before the retired Marine colonel who plugs his newsletter telling how America was sold out in 1789 to a cartel of "foreign bankers," is a remarkable show by someone called Godfrey.

Godfrey comes on like gangbusters, a rhythmic piledriver: "Gettin' it *on!* Goin' *way* back, brothers and sisters! Rhythm and blues, the 1950's, the Checkers, *White Cliffs of Dover*—

> (There'll be blue—ha-birds ovah
> The white cliffs of Do-vah
> Hup de diddy diddy boom . . .)

—A Godfrey *Golden Oldie!* Hypno*tize* and crystal*lize!* We're blastin' ta you live and *di-rect* from the front window of *blasting*-ville, the *Flash Music Studio!*

R&b radio is still underground in a way, even though the big cities have it, and even though many stations have their own newspapers, like the KGFJ World of Soul. The thing is that not that many people outside of Negoes *know* about it, and even though the stations play all the Motown stuff that makes Top 40 radio, the great bulk of their programing is *real* r&b, meant solely (no pun) for a Negro audience.

This r&b underground is similar to the whole country-and-western *Gestalt:* the c&w DJ's playing records about truck-drivers and cops and how-we-got-to-*win*-that-war-boah! Right in the middle of all the big cities lives this group, a subculture contained within itself, at which the c&w station is aimed.

Now, most of these country and r&b artists remain in relative obscurity, never gaining attention outside their particular markets, but it may be rather a profitable obscurity: Buck Owens, for instance, is a very wealthy man, as was James Brown before he ever hit Top 40. But whereas the artists make hit records to break out of, say, the exclusively Negro market, the only way for an underground radio man to be noticed outside of his specific fiefdom would seem to be either to think of a way to make himself valuable to a larger audience—or to do something totally outrageous.

A good example of the former is Peter Bergman, a young guy who had a show on KPFK-Pacifica, listener-sponsored FM in L.A. He was putting on something called *Radio Free Oz,* playing the Wizard himself. It was a hippie-nirvana-oasis, a bit pretentious, perhaps, but it became so popular that KRLA, one of the two top AM rock stations in town, asked Bergman to put on the same kind of show Sunday nights.

(One of the greatest underground radio people, who has not as yet come aboveground, is a guy who used to put on shows for KPFK—Marshall Efron. Efron's *Club* 86 was a linear ancestor of *Radio Free Oz,* and was replete with such oddities as Efron improvising, at one a.m., an opera in three acts, or doing a routine about a karate butcher who carved his chops with his hands; or—culmination!—going out in the rain at midnight onto Cahuenga Boulevard to do a sports car broadcast which consisted of—*weird!*—identifying every passing car by model, year, body style, color, and speed.)

As for the totally outrageous, one thinks immediately of the Magnificent Montague. By mid-1965 he was probably the number one r&b DJ in all of Los Angeles, but of course only r&b listeners knew about him. Then, in the middle of the Watts riots, someone noticed that there was this guy, Montague something, on the radio yelling "*Burn, baby, burn!*" It was a slogan he had been using for some months, but no one had thought to take him literally before. After that, well, *every*body knew about Montague. (Later, in an attempt to live it all down, he changed his cry to "*Learn, baby, learn.*")

Now, what the Wolfman had when he began about a year ago on XERB was basically an r&b show, except that he was even more underground for two reasons: he was broadcasting from a tiny station with a weaving frequency, not an established r&b outlet; and he was playing mostly records obscure even by r&b standards: Slim Harpo and Big Mama Lee Thornton and other real nitty-gritty-type people—so that one would think that the Wolfman would perhaps forever remain in the netherworld of underground obscurity; fine, except that old Wolfman did have this outrageous thing going for him: he was the Original Wild Man of Night-time Radio. He was *terrible!*

And the word began to spread that there was this insane wild man on the radio, Wolfman Jack, yeah! You can pick him up about ten or eleven at night, just before they start playing some terrible kind of Mexican rock-and-roll or something, anyway this guy is screaming about all these things you can *buy:* "Yah, dis heah's de *Woofman's album, bay-aay-he-baay!* an' you gonna *love* dis rec-uhd ta *death, baay-aay-he-baay!* an' you send *faahv dollahs* in *cash, check,* or *monay owh-dah! no c.o.d., bay-buh!* an' send it ta *Uncle Geawge's Recuhd Shop, Chu-uuu-la Vis-ta, Ca-li-faaawn-ya, baay-ay-baaay!*"

And pretty soon a lot of hip people were clued to what was happening on this weird station, XERB. For instance, the first LP by Frank Zappa and the Mothers of Invention came out, and Frank had made a semi-comic list of "people who have influenced our music," and there, right between Roland Kirk (a jazz musician) and Snuffy Garrett (a record producer), is the name of Wolfman Jack! And pretty soon people are writing to the Wolfman, not just money orders and things, but fan letters (and not just ordinary fan letters, at that; some of them were getting pretty rasty, reminiscent of the ones Clark Gable used to get at MGM from some woman signing herself as White Bunny Mother).

So XERB, which had been broadcasting a lot of strange things (like those white gospel shows mentioned and mariachi rock) with Wolfman sandwiched somewhere in between them all, must have decided that the time was right, and changed to 24-hour r&b (with some early-morning Negro gospel for good measure).

And it began to be noticed that all the shoeshine stands in L.A. were switching from KGFJ to XERB. The pinch was felt. The Magnificent Montague was moved up opposite Wolfman at nine in the evenings, and even though all the kids from all the high schools in L.A. (it seemed) would call up the old MM —"This is Darlene an' I go ta Lincoln High an' I jus' wanna say *have mercy, Montague, have mercy!*"—still the Wolfman's popularity grew and grew.

And it wasn't just more and more Negroes who were finding XERB's fading signal, even though the station is of course aimed primarily at that market. Because of his freakiness, even straight people like *dentists* were coming into their offices on Wilshire in Beverly *Hills,* for godsake! and asking their nurses, say, have you heard this guy on the radio, Wolfman? Wow, ain't he somethin'? Wow! Yes, Judy, his name is *Woof-man* . . . And the Wolfman began taking calls, and most of the people phoning were *white:* "Yah, I'm up here in Palmdale, Wolfman! How *are* ya?"

And the show began to change in subtle and not-so-subtle ways—Wolfman stopped playing all those obscure records, coming over to the Motown side, and now he even plays people like Procol Harum, and the Rolling Stones. And the commercials on the Wolfman's show are more and more establishment-oriented: Wallich's Music City at Sunset and Vine, Schlitz Malt Liquor, Dr. Ross's Dog Food ("De Woofman eat it all de time, bay-bub"). And Wolfman's own tie-ins with enterprises are more professionally presented, sort of: no more shoddy records, etc., or "drawings of the Wolfman" (cartoon of a zoot-suited wolf with shades!); now it is the "gen-u-wine, guaranteed-ta-blow-yah-mind Woofman roach-holder!"

The Wolfman (who seems to be a genial enough fellow, Southern-born, of Spanish-Negro descent, claiming to be 34) came to XERB from a station in New York, and his bosses seem to be somewhat mystified as to what to do about all this publicity. Maybe they never expected him to break out of the underground. They seem to be in the unique position of wanting the popularity for obvious commercial reasons, and yet wanting to avoid being noticed too much, for other, not-so-obvious reasons.

Now, I have never seen the Wolfman. He has steadfastly refused to meet with any reporter or magazine writer. And while it might be expected that some people—Adam Clayton Powell, Judge Creater, Che Guevara—might not want to meet reporters, why Wolfman Jack?

When I first tried to get in touch with the Wolfman maybe six months ago, XERB referred me to a man named Marshall Berle, "Wolfman's manager," head of Marshall Berle Productions. He waxed eloquent: "Well, that's the thing, ya know, that's the big mystery, it's the secret of the year, ha-ha! Nobody knows who is the Wolfman, I mean. *Time* magazine wants to do a piece on him, *they* can't find out who he is! And we're keeping it that way . . .

"I must see the Wolfman," I say. I beg; I plead. Letters are written; calls are made. And, after a lot of *well—phone-me-back-tomorrow-I'll-see-what-I-can-do:* "Well, he comes into town about once a week to tape the shows. Probably on Thursday or Friday. You can speak to him on the phone. Just for a few minutes."

Swell. We chat. He tells me he has a house in Beverly Hills, a fascinating fact (because your ordinary DJ doesn't make quite that much money). He says I am the first writer he has talked to. Then I ask him why all the secrecy, and at first he says it is his gimmick; then he lowers his voice, confiding: "Mah people, you know, mah . . . *managers,* they tell me, uh, Ah . . . keep to m'self, Ah don't talk ta nobody, an,' uh . . . Ah don't get in no . . . *trouble,* ya know what Ah mean?"

"Well, uh, no, Wolfman, not really."

"Whasat?"

"I don't really know what you mean."

"Well, uh . . . It's kinda . . . *difficult* ta talk about, man . . ."

He says he'll try and arrange for me to see him, if I'll say some nice things about him. Don't mention about the transmitter being in Mexico. (Trying to clean up their image, he says.)

Hang up and try to puzzle out that bit of cryptic information: I don't talk to nobody and I don't get into trouble. Wow, is this guy some sort of arch-fiend or something, that they have to keep him away from people? Strange! Somethinggoingonheresomethinggoingonhere! somethingdontknowhatbutsomethingfunnygoingon. Maybe.

I phone Marshall Berle, and phone him again, and again. (Needless to say, he never calls me back.) I phone the p.r. firm. "Listen," they say, "we won't be handling the Wolfman for a little while; they're making a lot of, uh, changes, they're changing his show around, and so on. You phone Bob Smith, he's sort of the Wolfman's, uh, right-hand man. Okay?"

"Well," says Bob Smith, "can you write the thing without seeing the Wolfman?"

"Well, not really. I mean, I hate that sort of thing, you know?"

"Well, what exactly do you want to do?"

"Well, just to see him, maybe at the station there, doing the show or something. Just anything. Just for a few minutes. Just so I could *see* him."

"Well—I'd just as soon you wrote the thing without seeing him. You know, you might come down here and then you'd be all disappointed when you saw him doing the show."

After a couple of days of this, he tells me to come down to the office; I expect to see the Wolfman, of course.

Smith looks like no one you would ever expect to see—or have ever seen—in Hollywood or show biz or radio or anything like that. He looks like a fight promoter, big, beefy. One assumes the diamond rings on his fingers are real, and the gold wristwatch. He is on the phone, so I look around the walls of his office. On one of them is a map of the United States and parts of Canada, with three big swooping arcs drawn in magic markers showing where the Wolfman can be heard, for his voice is being broadcast from three stations: XERB, 50,000 watts, transmitter located in Tiajuana, Mexico, broadcasting to the western United States and Alaska, cutting halfway into Arizona, Utah, and Wyoming; XEG, 100,000 watts, transmitter in Monterrey, Mexico, broadcasting to the eastern states and parts of Canada; and XERF, 250,000 watts, transmitter in some tiny town in Mexico, covering the central states and overlapping into some of the eastern and western ones. There are only a very few states like Montana and North Dakota which cannot pick up the Wolfman.

He gets off the phone. "Well, what can I tell you about the Wolfman?"

"Well, uh, not a whole lot, you know. I just sort of . . . wanted to see him."

"Well, he's just too busy, you know? That's the thing, the fella is just too doggone busy, I mean. That's why I had you come down here, because it's hard to explain over the phone. You know, it's not as if we're trying to *hide* this guy or anything, you know; he's gonna be on the Joe Pyne Show, and next month he's doing the Joey Bishop Show, and the Tonight Show, with Johnny Carson—the *Johnny Carson* Show!" (*Oh, by-the-by department:* those last two shows have no listing of the Wolfman as a future guest.) "It's just that the guy is just so *doggone busy,* you just *can't pin him down!*

"Listen, the guy is just running around all the time, he's just never in one place long enough, that's all. He doesn't do the show here every night, you know. He tapes like a whole week's shows in some studio, whatever he can find, wherever he happens to be. He goes all around the country, you know. Like maybe he'll come in here and take phone calls, and he'll tape the phone calls for a whole week's shows in one evening. And right now he's setting up a whole string of tours. You know John Richardson? 'John R'? WLCA, Nashville? Well, he's a very famous deejay down South. Anyway, he and the Wolfman are setting up these tours, and they're going all over the South, they're gonna go to every little fart-blown town—look, I'd *like* to help you . . ."

But there might be a last chance . . . if I could get to see him doing one of those shows . . . and the Joe Pyne Show is the only one that checks out. The Joe Pyne Radio Show. The man there at first tells me, yes, of course I could watch them do the show. Then he phones me back and says he's been informed that Joe doesn't like anybody around who isn't supposed to be there—makes him nervous. But do I know of anyone who might make an interesting radio guest, since they have an interview time open the morning the Wolfman is set to tape. Then I could come and watch as the friend of someone to be interviewed (Joe wouldn't be nervous about me then) and they would have their guest, and everybody would be happy. I suggest a friend of mine, 19, who claims he can predict the stock market successfully through all kinds of bizarre methods like the number of sunspots at a given time of the year. The

Pyne man phones him, and they set it up; it looks like my friend is going to be on. Wonderful. Then a few days later he phones me back.

"You can't come in and watch," he says, "because we have an agreement with the Wolfman that no one can come in while he's on. Nobody can be there except Joe and the announcer. I don't know if he knows about the engineers, but they *have* to be there. Anyway, even our *producer* doesn't get to see him."

Well, that's beautiful. Here my friend is going to be on the Pyne Show talking about all these terrific ways to predict the market by getting the amount of solar radiation, dividing the score of the Army-Navy game by three, and so on, but that's not going to do *me* any good.

Except that I know when the Wolfman is supposed to tape. And no one can stop me from—my last chance!—bringing a photographer.

The Payne Show is recorded at the RCA Victor Studios on Sunset, in Studio C. There is only one entrance to Studio C and that is around the corner on Ivar. The taping is to start at 10:30, with Wolfman the first guest. The photographer and I are waiting at the door at 10:00. At 10:15 a car with lettering saying KLAC News pulls up, and a few seconds later Pyne gets out, wearing shades, looking surly, and limps past us and into the studio. A truck arrives and two men unload a large harp case and wheel it into the building. Wait a minute—naw, that's a little *too* baroque! At 10:25 a car with out-of-state tags drives by and the teen-age daughters peer at me to see if I'm a Monkee or a Rolling Stone, who record in these studios. I shake my long hair and wave casually.

It's 10:30 . . . no Wolfman. The Wolfman phoned at a quarter of ten and cancelled out, says one of Pyne's men. "He said he was very sick."

He is rescheduled, but phones the next week and cancels altogether. He hints that perhaps Pyne might ask him some embarrassing questions; he thinks he'd better take off for Las Vegas, just for a little while.

After all, you can't be too careful. There is a rumor floating around that the heat has been nosing around the Wolfman, but perhaps that's how it goes when you face the dangers of coming up out of the underground world.

When you're down there, you only have to contend with people desiring, and getting strangely excited about, small scraps of information. Once you surface, however, you're up against all of the machinery of the press—which assumes that its public wants to know *every*thing there is to know.

So the Wolfman goes on, howling, grunting, moaning—living on the double—screaming, shouting, rasping—don't make no trouble—moaning, grunting, howling—stick to m'self—flipped out crazy *weird*—who *was* that in that car?

"CAA-CAA-REE!! CAN YA DIG IT, BAAY-HAY-BAAY? YA GONNA LOVE IT TA DEATH!!"

A NON-INTERVIEW WITH A POP PRO

●

SALLY KEMPTON

I spent most of last week trying to get an interview with Albert Grossman. Grossman is Bob Dylan's manager and a major power in pop music, and he has always treated the press the way Queen Victoria treated Gladstone. One expects, when dealing with him, to be filtered through secretaries and relegated to anterooms, but on this occasion, after he failed to respond to my 17th phone call, something told me to forget it. Last year I spent three months researching a piece on pop music, and in the course of it I learned just how to tell when they are not going to talk to you. There is something peculiarly galling about being put off by music business people; perhaps because so many of them remind me of boys I could never talk to in high school. I always feel when they don't call me back that I am being spurned by the basketball player who tried to kiss me on Saturday night and then failed to recognize me in Study Hall on Monday.

When it comes to the put-off, hip, New Style, Today's Sound producers and managers are virtually unsurpassed. Performers are pretty nice, either because they think they need the publicity or because they just like to talk. Old-style producers, managers who have been in the business since 1952, record company executives, and r&b producers are almost courtly. Smokey Robinson will talk to you anytime. Jerry Leiber always calls back. Not Grossman. He has his sales charts, his acolytes, his record contracts, his movie contracts, his shrine in Woodstock, and all those cocktail party invitations. Most of all he has his Creativity Certificate. Bob Dylan is an Artist, the producers of Today's Sound are Artists, and Grossman, because he is Dylan's manager, is an Artist too. Reporters are no big thing to Albert Grossman. I don't really blame him; if I were as certain as he is of the intrinsic value of my task in life I wouldn't want to be interviewed either. I just wish he would return my phone calls. He makes me long for the good old days when pop merchants suspected themselves of hawking schlock. For the delusion of creative significance is finally so universal in pop music that even people like Neil Diamond will give you exegeses on the composition of their latest hit. Songwriters who have run out of inspiration talk about their blocks like so many failed novelists. And Janis Ian is Emily Dickinson.

I had my quintessential experience with the New Style music producers when I went last winter to look over Kama Sutra Records for a Life piece on pop. It is worth reporting in detail.

Kama Sutra handles the Lovin' Spoonful, as well as a number of more obscure artists and they are, or were at that time, trying to build an Empire. The company occupies two suites of offices at 1650 Broadway, and is run, as they put it themselves, by a triumvirate. I expected, when I went up there, to see a lot of teenage millionaires in leather vests and had dressed in a style calculated to inspire confidence in them. In fact, I had on my teenybopper costume, and when I gave my name and errand to the secretary she went rigid with suspicion. She was wearing her own teenybopper costume but I think she regarded herself as a special case. She waved me to a seat in the anteroom and went back to reading Cashbox.

The anteroom at Kama Sutra is designed to provide a foretaste of the splendors which will be revealed inside. It is carpeted in dark green, with a Dancing Shiva medallion set in, and its walls are golden. On the wall above the couch is a giant plaque which details the many services purveyed by the company and its subsidiaries. The secretary and others of her kind sit behind a glass wall doing their thing, which consists of taking phone calls and greeting with glad cries the messengers who come bearing manila envelopes and packets of sandwiches. Eight of these messengers arrived while I was waiting. At last the inner door buzzed open (it locks from the inside and can only be opened by an electronic device) and Phil Steinberg, the member of the triumvirate with whom I had my appointment, came out. He said "How do you do?", extended his hand graciously, and led me into what I can describe only as the sanctum.

It was an extraordinary room. The walls and floor were covered with green velvet. The windows were also carpeted in green; the room was lit from sconces, made in the shape of Dancing Shivas and coiled snakes, set here and there along the walls. Three enormous green velvet couches sat in one corner while in the other, on a green velvet platform, stood a clear plastic table, round, with three chairs around it. Three little plastic mushrooms grew out of the carpet next to each chair. On each mushroom was a telephone.

"This is an extraordinary room," I said.

"Yes, isn't it," said Phil Steinberg, beaming. "We hadda make it comfortable because we spend a lot of time here. Dig that no daylight gets in?"

Steinberg was about 30. He had close-cropped curly hair and a broad red face. He was dressed impeccably in a shiny gray suit, a shiny gray tie, and shiny black wingtips. On his right pinky finger he wore a ring in the shape of a coiled snake, its head forming a P. On his right wrist he wore a gold identification bracelet. On his left he wore a thin gold watch, slightly smaller than a butterplate. He waved me to a seat, and eyed me critically. "You say you're working for Life?" he said.

"Yes," I said.

"Have a drink," he said.

"No thanks," I said, "I don't like to drink before lunch."

"Oh come on, have a drink," he said. He pressed a Dancing Shiva on the opposite wall and an enormous bar swung out.

"I generally have a Pernod at this time of day," said Steinberg. "You ought to try some. It's good stuff." He poured himself a drink and sat down beside me.

"This business is like the oil business used to be," he said, "but we're the only company who's really taking advantage of the opportunities. We're not just a record company. We're an organization. We have five companies."

"Advertisers come to record companies for advice on the youth market," he went on. "Tv, we're doing teeny commercials for tv, there's big money in residuals, you have no idea. It's all in the promotion. When you record a group you create an image. We try to figure out that image and promote it. It's very rare that a business can give the opportunity to youth that this one can. Movie companies are hip to that. They come to us for movie scores. We're the only company that does that. The entertainment concept here goes way beyond the record business.

"But the backbone of our organization is our creative talent. You probably don't understand how sensitive creative people are, how difficult it is to work with them. We've made this into an art. Very few people can do it. We aren't so much a record company as a training center for young talent. We groom young producers. We train young writers. We try to build groups rather than simply put out hit records. We have," he said, "the groups of tomorrow. Gene Pitney, the Critters, Tommy Kaye, the Innocents—all groups of tomorrow.

"We're free thinkers," he added. "When you're fresh to a field you feel no restrictions. People keep telling us 'That's never been done before' but we go ahead and do it anyway."

"Where," I asked, "are your artists?"

"Oh, we keep them downstairs," he said. "We have a special suite for them. This is the executive office. You want to see them?"

"Yes," I said.

"So you're writing for Life?"

I followed him through the electronic door, out of the suite, and into the elevator. The elevator carried us to another floor, where we traversed a long corridor until we came to an unmarked door. Steinberg opened it. We entered a large, bare room with concrete walls. It contained a beat-up upright piano, a portable phonograph, and five Italian boys in black paints. "This is Vinny, and Tony, and Frank, and Sal and Vito," said Steinberg, wiping the dust off a folding chair and offering it to me. "What are you boys doing?" he asked the room at large.

"I'm waiting for Artie," Frank volunteered at last. "Vinnie's gonna record this afternoon."

"Is this a group?" I asked.

"No, no, producers," said Steinberg. "Maybe Tony would play his new record for you. It's fabulous."

Tony, who had a pretty face and a red shirt, followed us into a small room on the side of the main one, and put a record on the phonograph which was its only piece of furniture. It was a shing-a-ling number; the shing-a-ling was very big that year.

"I'd like to talk to them," I said, when the record was over.

"I don't think you should do that now, they've got a lot of work to do," said Steinberg. "Come back tomorrow and Artie" (Artie Ripp, the Artistic Director) "will take you around."

"OK," I said, and we left. I took one look backward before Steinberg closed the door. Vinny and Frank were practicing a dance step by the window, Tony was stacking records in the corner.

The next day I spoke to Artie Ripp and arranged to meet him at 3. I arrived at the office at 2.55 and was told by the secretary that Artie was over at MGM and would not be back this afternoon.

"I'll wait," I said.

"He won't be back," she said, "and if you think I'll let you in without an appointment you're crazy."

I sat down on the couch under the plaque and read Cashbox for half an hour. Twenty-two messengers came and went. At last I rose, full of purpose, and rapped on the secretary's glass wall. "Yes," she said.

"I am trying to write a piece for Life magazine," I said. "My time is limited, I have a deadline. Will you please give Mr. Ripp this phone number and tell him that if he hasn't called by tomorrow morning I will be unable to use Kama Sutra in the piece."

The secretary examined the paper I had given her.

"This isn't Life magazine's number," she said at last.

"No, it's my home number," I said.

"Hmph," said the secretary.

Three hours later Artie Ripp called, full of cheer.

"Sorry you had to wait, darling," he said. "If you come at 12 tomorrow I'll be there."

"Are you sure?" I said.

"Absolutely positive, sweetie," said Ripp.

I got to the office at 12.15 the next day. The secretary, in a tone bristling with what I interpreted as malevolent triumph, informed me that he hadn't been in and was not expected.

"If you want I'll give your name to our publicity director," she said.

"No, thank you," I said. I booted their copy of Record World and walked out. There is a point at which you figure they're not going to talk to you.

CAPTAIN PIMPLE CREAM'S FIENDISH PLOT

●

HARRY SHEARER

Lay-dies-and-gentlemen-YOU'RE-lissning-to-the-SOL-LID-GOLD-SOUND-of-a-*MIL-YON-DOL-LAR-WEEK*-end-featuring-the-GREATEST-HITS-of-*ALL-TIME*-pre-*sented-by*. . . .

The punctuation is wrong, if you think those dots indicate a pause. The high, urgent, insistent, *demanding* voice does not pause after telling you that. The last diphthong of his last word blends immediately into a chorus, and whether the chorus is singing "Kay-Aitch Jaayy Losss Ann Gel Lessss" or "See Kay Ell DUB bul yewwwww The Motor-Citeeeeee," it doesn't make much difference. Before the singers have finished milking that final vowel or consonant, another urgent, insistent voice comes through: this time, though, the voice may be tinged with just the suggestion that its owner is a crazy man:

Its-three-o-clock-in-*BAWWS*-SAN jew-luss-on-the reeyul-don-steeyul SHOW-im holdin-goldens-in-the-spirit-dont-try-to-*STOP*-me-Hiii!

This has all consumed, maybe, eight seconds—consumed them, that is, the way a napalm fire consumes oxygen. Noise, sound, words have over-used those seconds, obliterated them without a trace and are sucking in all the surrounding time. Now, before you have a chance to think about what's happening to you, you are sucked in too, you are halfway through listening to some record, probably some rot-rock record by the Buckinghams, or the Royal Guardsmen, or—since it is, after all, a mil-yon dollar weekend—maybe even by the Rivingtons, for God's sake.

And long before the record is really over, old napalm lungs will be back at it, incinerating those precious seconds with oh-so-incredibly fast words about what time it is and what record that was and whose show it is and *boffo* into a commercial while you still think the Rivingtons are going to do a little coda of Papa Oo Mau Mau.

This, of course, is a sound as familiar to the publicity-kissed under-25 generation as—but no, there is no sound so familiar. Rock radio probably constitutes *the* aural environment of this generation. We all grew up with the sound of frantic men, their voices dreadfully treble-ized by two-bit Japanese loudspeakers, yelling about the time and the weather and the Rivingtons and the pimple cream, as if it were tremendously important—life-and-death important—to us. And we were such silly little twerps that we didn't even have the smarts to pay attention unless these men screamed their lower jaws off at us.

But *this* particular sound, this specific kind of fast-paced, clean-cut rock radio, is the property of Bill Drake. What William Randolph Hearst was to a generation of newspaper readers, Bill Drake is to an age-group aurally swathed from birth in Top 40: he is the most powerful man in rock radio, though he likes to pretend otherwise ("If I had that power, I couldn't sleep at night for fear somebody would bump me off"), and he is perhaps the most powerful person in the popular music business.

When the folks in Donaldsville, Ga., tuned in to the local radio station to hear him and his high-school girlfriend playing Hank Snow records for an hour each week, he was plain old Phil Yarborough. But now that he relaxes on a deep, soft, blue velveteen-covered couch planted firmly at the top of Los Angeles's most exclusive residential district, Bel-Air, now that rumors cluster about his 6′5″ frame the way mosquitoes head for a warm human body on a Midwestern summer night, now that competitors and half the people in the record business and "rock-as-art" groups and fans reserve for him a daily ritual curse—now he is sleek, streamlined Bill Drake.

Up there in Bel-Air sits Rock Central. From this nerve center Drake monitors and supervisors the 11 rock stations he currently controls. Last year at this time, he controlled only four, but that was before the RKO General chain put all its stations in his hands, hoping for a wholesale application of the magic that had already turned their Los Angeles and San Francisco properties into "number one" stations.

Rock Central is really just Drake's current home, an unostentatious one-story house at the end of a private road entered from Bel-Air's east—old(er) money—gate, overlooking a thin strand of similar modest palaces strung atop a canyon ridge; surrounding these bastions of moneyed civilization, of course, is the famous Bell-Air burnable brush. Between the unfinished wood wall of this house and the visitor is a façade of five Spanish-style stucco archways, and inspection locates a set of double mahogany doors with foot-long handles behind one of those arches.

You walk through the doors across a section of terrazzo tile flooring and suddenly you almost fall down into a wine-red rug, a pudding-soft carpet that sinks you slowly towards that over-stuffed couch where Drake lounges, sipping his Seven and Seven. Once you sit down, the couch immediately begins absorbing you and your descent into decadent plush is braked only by your sudden, stunned realization that this is no ordinary rich man's house because right there, sitting on a small table beside your left hand, is the Batphone. This is obviously not Wayne Manor, but, just as obviously, that white Call Director telephone setup has the Batsign on the center of its dial instead of a number. What really jars you into curiosity about the man who lives here is the fact that the voice filtering through the Batphone line is that of Elvis Presley singing "Don't Be Cruel," piped in from Drake's newly acquired New York station. On this phone, Drake can listen in on any of the stations he controls, any time he likes, just by dialing a code number.

He can wander across the pudding into the dining room and shoot a leisurely game of billiards on the felt-covered table that nearly fills the room, while the Batphone pours out Boss Radio from San Diego or Cincinnati. He can stroll into the bedroom, glancing proudly at the backlit DRAKE coat of arms (bearing, besides the name, a two-handed, four-footed yellow lion above the motto, "Sic Parvis Magna" *), listening all the while to a Boss Jock from Memphis or one of the Six-Ten Men from San Francisco.

It is very important for Bill Drake or one of his partners to listen to these 11 rock stations constantly. It is the reason station owners turn their little treasures over to Drake and pay him a fee which is rumored to reach $100,000 a year per station to be their programming consultant. For money like

* "Great Things from Small Things."

that Drake first re-designs a station into his now-familiar Machine; then he winds it up and lets it go under the control of an on-the-spot custodian, a program director who takes care of the day-to-day problems of running a goldmine. But Drake keeps listening in on the Batphone, keeps traveling around to these stations, keeps making fine adjustments in the relationships of the precision parts of the Machine.

Back in 1955, a disc jockey named Alan Freed was beginning to become famous as the first person to play, on a major radio station, music he called "rock-and-roll." A New York station had carved a time spot out for Freed and his rock, carved it out of a broadcast day filled with what was then considered popular music—Rosemary Clooney, Joni James, Les Baxter's "Poor People of Paris," Kitty Kallen, Frankie Laine.

Tod Storz, who owned several radio stations around the country, was the first entrepreneur to see that the Kitty Kallen brand of slush had played itself out and that survival for radio in the television-obsessed year of 1955 lay in following Freed. So Storz's Kansas City station, WHB, became the first radio station to play nothing but rock-and-roll, rather than isolating it like a raucous island in a becalmed sea of Jo Stafford. The experiment was spectacularly successful, and, in a medium where imitation is the sincerest form of reflex, everyone who owned a radio station was at least thinking about going Top 40.

Storz, along with the owners of two other stations—a Memphis patent-drug company, and a publishing house which had just realized that all its magazines were failures—defined and refined the Top 40 routine into a formula so nauseatingly simple and so breathtakingly successful that literally anyone could do it. Or so literally anyone thought.

And so, in almost every major city, there was one station that went Top 40 early and has stayed that way ever since, somehow managing to remain a magnet for teen-age loyalties from the time when "teen-ager" had just become a Concept to the present period when adolescence has turned into a social movement. And, like pigs trying to nudge the largest hog away from the trough virtually every other station in town has tried Top 40 at one time or another, most giving it up in dismay or disgust.

In Los Angeles, KFWB attacked the air with Color Radio

in 1956, and immediately became the most imitated rock station on the West Coast. Time and styles have changed. KFWB has even retired its Fabulous Forty, but old Channel 98 still plays rock. Meanwhile, Pasadena's country-music station KXLA metamorphosed to Top 40 KRLA, heralding its transformation with a $50,000 Golden Key contest, find the key and win the money. Unfortunately for everyone concerned, the key existed only in the station manager's mind, and the FCC turned the station over to a non-profit trust that now runs rock radio for the fiscal benefit of educational TV. Half a dozen other local stations tried doing some sort of *records-cum-echo-chamber-cum-screaming* formula and failed dismally. One of the city's oldest stations, KHJ, probably tried a different style of radio each month for years, including three separate attempts at rock. Then, just about the time when even the engineers had stopped listening to it, KHJ went back to the drawing board one more time: this time they called Bill Drake.

That call was the most lucrative event in the lives of Drake and KHJ. Coming off his earlier successes in Fresno and San Diego, the spectacular recovery of KHJ and its current domination of the city's pop mind and ear have given Drake the reputation of The Great Resurrector. Station owners all over the West Coast and even through the Midwest have decided that if they can't afford to hire him, they can at least afford to imitate him.

And yet no one quite knows the intricacies of running the Machine as well as the man who has now built and maintained 11 of them. "The problem," he says, "with most of the stations, Top 40-wise, around the country, is that they create a product without paying much attention to *detail,* and they hope the public accepts it. Whereas we work a little in reverse, trying to find out what the public wants and then trying to create that. For instance, by finding why people tune out a station. It's actually even a subliminal area we try to go into, and precise attention is paid to the placement of everything. Everything has a particular place and is done in a particular way. There's a *great* amount of emphasis put on detail and streamlining the sound and keeping it CLEAN."

Clean—for God's sake, if there's one word that describes the way rock radio has traditionally *not* sounded, the word is clean. Drake has indeed streamlined the sound of Top 40, the same way he streamlined his name. His stations now have that same direct, CLEAN, one-syllable simplicity.

Station jingles, for example, have existed from the beginning of Top 40, supposedly to take care of the routine function of identifying the station in a mildly pleasant way. But they quickly became mammoth production numbers, grandiose and stunningly superfluous compositions obviously written to accompany a June Taylor Dancers routine on the Gleason show, with stupefying, silly lyrics and with melodies composed from the leftover scraps of Winston cigarette jingles: "There's always some-thing HAP-pen-ning at num-ber ONE-der-ful RAY-DEE-YO, so stay-in-tune and don't miss a se-cond, the go-*go* sta-shun for *go*-GO people, where the hits keep HAP-pen-ning, where the AC-shun is, you're a pussy-cat, you're where it's at, with the INNNNN SOUNNNND . . ." A huge orchestra was usually vamping wildly in the background while all of this went on, and sometimes one even heard that machine that made the electric guitar sound as if it were singing the lyrics.

Drake changed all this. He dispensed with the orchestra altogether. Instead, he simply hired a good singing group, the Johnny Mann Singers, and had them sing incredibly short little *a cappella* messages: "The Big Six-Ten, Goldennn," "Los Angeles Weatherrr," or "KHJ, Boss Hitbound." Still nothing very profound, but very short, and very, very CLEAN.

When Drake talks back there about getting *subliminal*, he simply means—among other things—that one of these mini-jingles, always a variation of the simple and easily identifiable F-C-G-F-high C leitmotiv of his stations, is played at the beginning of every record. From this experience, the listener is supposed to gain the subliminal notion that a Drake jingle is always followed by music, and draw the subliminal conclusion that a Drake station must therefore be true to its oft-repeated motto: MUCH more *MU*SIC.

There are still contests, and Drake hasn't raised their intelligence level much, either. But they are very simple, streamlined, CLEAN-sounding contests. One archetype goes like this: the first person to call the Bossline at the sound of the funny noise wins the prize. This theme has enjoyed infinite variations: the funny noise has been the crowing of the Big Kahuna's cockatoo, the gobble of a Thanksgiving turkey, the honking of the pair-of-Camaro horns, and the rasping of a New Year's noisemaker; the prize has been an invitation to the Big Kahuna's luau, a free turkey, a chance at a car, the top 93 records of the year, or a ride with Sitar the Pirate to search for loot on an island. The other contest pattern has a listener call in to guess which year, or which time of day, out of a group of dozens, will come up next on a rotating recording. The funny noise, or five to ten seconds of the listener's voice are the only interruptions in the flow of music-commercials-time-weather.

Now, of course, these are hokey give-away gimmicks and Drake has even retained the old trick of sneaking in a plug for the current contest with each time-signal that compulsively follows a record ("It's three-fifteen, KHJ Kahuna Cockatoo Time"). "Contests, promotions, the 'big sound'—the feeling of a successful Top 40 station is the feeling of being put on, and the audience is in on the joke," says Tom Rounds, for 12 years a Top 40 program director, the last two for Drake in San Francisco; like McGeorge Bundy, Rounds knows the System intimately, and can, now that he has quit, enjoy the luxury of sitting outside it and thinking about it critically. "It's easy to attack Drake on an intellectual level. The turning point in rock came when people started to take it seriously, which is not to understand Top 40 for what it is: a put-on that the audience is aware of. Kids have the insight to know that you can't be believable and sincere and authentic when you're introducing a record by the Monkees. But when you're talking about Top 40, Drake really knows the difference between good radio and bad radio."

But Drake takes himself much more seriously than Rounds does. "Our job," Drake says with solemn earnestness, "is to play the records and not put the people on." Yet his stations abound with minor put-ons of which the audience, Rounds notwithstanding, is not aware: listeners are urged to call the request lines, with a promise of "You say it, we'll play it." But if a listener's request doesn't correspond with the sharply limited list of records which can be played, he is told the station is merely conducting a survey, and that he can't really count on hearing his record. And Drake can't really explain why his stations remain "the home of the nonstop contests": "I can't say how much it means. We've found that when we have run constant promotions, we are very successful. We have also been very successful without running them at all."

"Drake," says one of the few people who have worked for him and quit, "may still not know that you don't have to buy or bribe an audience."

Can you find five mistakes in this picture? an ad used to

ask when I was a kid, and some kids could only spot three errors. Similarly, Drake suffers from a certain failure of vision—he was able to see only a limited number of the hundreds of things that were going wrong with Top 40. This fact is at once his prime weakness and, at the moment, the source of his fabulous monetary success. He chuckles, sort of an inhaling chuckle with a folksy breathiness about it, as he talks about how fabulous that success has really been in this, his 30th year: "It's been very good . . . very, ve-ry good." He strokes his oiled dark brown hair, combed the way Ronald Reagan would comb *his* hair if he let it grow longer: a quasi-pompadour rolling up off his forehead, rolling back across the crown, rolling right straight down onto just the top of the collar of his dark blue denim-style shirt. "Everything has been based on the stations' making it. And they've made it because they have a sound of consistent excitement without getting ridiculous—they have a consistently moving, involved, believable sound, eliminating as many of the irritants as possible." Failure of Vision Number One: A station would sound far saner, and even CLEANER, if it didn't have to sound consistently exciting. "It's very difficult to do this format and not sound phony," recalls Ed Mitchell, who quit Drake's San Francisco station late last year, having spent almost 18 months being one of the Six-Ten Men. "You have to really believe it, really mean it, really feel excited about what's happening at the Big Six-Ten, or else it comes out sounding phony. But if it's just another tired contest that's been done a million times before, you can't do it."

How many of those irritants is it really possible to eliminate? In addition to shortening the jingles and the contests, Drake disposed of Top 40's security blanket, the echo chamber which used to drown the music and the disc jockeys and everything else into a generalized, murky audio soup. In place of the standard screaming announcements proclaiming contests or rattling off a list of the weekend record hops to be hosted by the station's disc jockeys, Drake substituted his own urgent and compelling but reasonably modulated voice, identifying the station and dramatizing the current giveaway. The insane cacophony of electronic beeps, staccato musical notes, messages in Morse code, and canned teletype noise that accompanied the typical ten-sentence Top 40 newscast is gone, and so is the hourly newscast itself, replaced by longer, less repetitive news interludes.

And then there are the commercials. Typically, on Top 40, pimple-cream ads and hysterical pleas to come see the drag races proliferate like algae on a stagnant pond. But Drake proudly points to his limit of ten "sets" of commercials each hour. A set means two commercials totaling not more than 70 seconds, so Drake's stations are below the usual commercial load by about one-third. The reason, of course, is that bunching and limiting hypes and hucks is vital to maintaining the "MUCH more MUSIC" image his stations prize as much as their licenses.

Absent, too, is most of the sound of the disc jockey's voice. "There's a vast difference between talking a lot and saying something. I know guys who can talk all day and say absolutely nothing. I know guys who can talk for three seconds and actually say more and get more of a reaction than guys that babble on for two-three minutes." Drake's star three-second talker is old napalm lungs, the Real Don Steele, who each afternoon in Los Angeles, while being buffeted by records and commercials and jingles, is in the three-hour throes of some indefinable, unutterable lunacy, a lunacy that drives him charging up and down his limited vocal scale like a man who has just swallowed a siren, sometimes repeating in frenzy phrases from commercials that hang him up ("Drainage trouble in your home" he yells through clenched teeth at random intervals, mimicking a Roto-Rooter commercial). Drake's conversational tone is a far cry from Steele, and at least an octave lower than the Bill Drake voice that proclaims a mil-yon dol-lar weekend. His voice is low and pleasant and somewhat nasal, and there are slight hints of Donaldsville in the way he strings words together, in the rolling inflections, in the sibilants that come out half-whistling.

"Our theory is that the jock should feel free to talk if he has anything to say—anything as far as content or anything else. But if you're going to say nothing, say it in as few words as possible."

"The format," according to Tom Rounds, who used to have to push, mold and shape his disc jockeys into it, "is a bitch. You have to completely concentrate—every word and every second is important. Mistakes aren't tolerated. But, if you have seven flawless gods on the air, your sound is no longer believable. The hangup is to be flawless and still get out compressed, concentrated warmth." *That's* what The Real Don Steele's psychotomimetic afternoons have—intensely concentrated warmth.

"They'd just tell you not to talk too much," ex-Drakeman Ed Mitchell remembers, "and after a while you were afraid to talk, you'd just say the time and your name."

"Drake felt a jock should be a cool, hip, sauve older cat who knew where it's at." This from a collegiate-looking fellow who was a KHJ Boss Jock for all of two months, and was too young to be an older cat anyway. And who doesn't want his name mentioned. "Everything you said had to be said over the top of a record, everything was written, it was all one-liners"—he doesn't mean Henny Youngman jokes, he means one-sentence self-congratulations like "Boss Radio, thanking you for making us the sound of the Southland"—"And you kept worrying whether you were going to say those 12 words right."

The reason to worry is because, back up in Bel-Air, someone is probably listening to the Batphone. And that someone, either Drake or one of his several partners and assistants, will place a call on *The Red Phone* if anything sounds wrong, if the Machine seems to need just the merest drop of oil. This particular "inverse morale factor" has survived from Top 40's earliest days, its purpose then as now to keep people ON THEIR TOES. "A guy on the air becomes a lump of shit, he becomes absolutely paralyzed by that kind of thing," says a veteran of Top 40, "because when that phone rings, you know it's death time, man."

On the other hand, as longtime Top 40 listeners know, your average run-of-the-Machine rock jock is a certifiable cretin anyway, so Drake's decision to shut them up might well be his greatest benefaction. Instead of, "Well, it's about 26 minutes before the big hour of three o'clock this beautiful Tuesday-type afternoon here in the city," Drake has his minions offer a crisp "two-thirty-four." Instead of "Make the mark of the merc at the tip-top of the time-and-temperature tower at 80 big degrees," the Drakemen blurt out a curt weather bulletin.

So far, so good; lots of irritants eliminated. Now Drake takes the next step, and seeks to eliminate what he thinks are musical irritants, and now people start getting angry.

"We think Bill Drake does more to retard popular music in America than any other single individual." The "we" are John Hartmann and Skip Taylor, managers of Chad and Jeremy and the Canned Heat Blues Band. "Drake has no esthetic interest in the music; he sees it only as a commercial machine. If he were in the music business instead of the radio business, he would be aware of the cultural difference between the Buffalo Springfield, or any of these young and beautiful groups that need to be supported during their early stages, and, on the other hand, somebody like Tommy James and the Shondells, people doing thirteen-year-old records with a beat, a gimmick and a teenybopper message. He can't hear that difference because he's *lame* esthetically."

Tom Rounds is not "lame esthetically." While he was Drake's program director in San Francisco, he played local groups' records and thought their sound was so "honest" that it "corroded" the Top 40 format within which they were exposed. He, too, looks like a college student—short-cropped light brown hair, white-and-striped shirt open slightly at the neck, letting his conservatively striped necktie hang slackly. "Our approach was more conservative than on stations where they have less to lose. We had to look to the smaller stations to break [music-industry jargon for premiere] records; quite often, the Drake stations were the last to get on a record. You were listening for certain success-proven factors. When I heard Simon and Garfunkel's 'Sounds of Silence,' for instance, I was flipped out. But we didn't play the record at first because it was too high-level, not in our mainstream. The business is full of such inertia."

Rounds is sitting behind a desk whose clutter argues with the cavernous space around the desk in this nearly unfurnished wood-paneled office in Hollywood's unglamorous underbelly. Today, he is in the relatively uncynical business of making films that accompany hit records on TV rock and variety shows, and it is easy to recall the cynicism that was part of his approach as a Drake executive. "The general listener doesn't have enough patience to listen to something unfamiliar or strange. If he wants to do that, he'll go listen to the record player where he can get better sound quality. He won't listen to a new record until he's heard it enough that it's familiar. When it's familiar, there's no tuneout."

TUNEOUT!!! Bill Drake *hates* tuneout—hates it the way Katy Winters hates sweat, the way President Johnson hates Nervous Nellies. Tuneout is that dreaded situation in which a listener decides that the radio station he's tuned to is not giving him, at the moment, what he wants, . . . and . . . he . . .

(it's even painful to talk about it) moves . . . the . . . dial. Now, you and I and Tom Donahue know that "most people are button pushers. Man, I hear my old lady or my kids create a whole show of their own; when a record ends, they start pushing those buttons till they find something else they like, and they never hear a jock or a commercial." Donahue is another ex-top 40 jock who, we shall see, puts his criticisms of Drake into practice.

But Bill Drake is determined to wipe out TUNEOUT, to rivet people to his stations for as long as possible. So, given his penchant for the trappings of science, the first thing he did was take a survey. "We've done extensive surveying, comprehensive research. We asked kids what would make them tune out a station the most—commercials, a bad jock, what? Forty-seven percent of them," Drake is at his most earnest now, resting his elbow on his right knee, holding his cigarette aloft *à la* Ed Murrow, flaring his nostrils to emphasize his points, "for-ty-sev-en percent of them said a *bad record* makes them tune out the most." The sample turns out to be 6,000 L.A. kids, but, in the same tedious way that A. C. Neilsen can explain how 1,200 Audimeter families can serve as a reliable guide to the nation's television habits, Drake can explain why his surveys mean more than flipping coins or consulting one's horoscope. The point, as it is with all such probings of the public psyche, is that a vast gulf may exist between what people say they do when they're listening to radio (or, for that matter, voting for President) and what they actually end up doing.

But Drake's response to that survey about *bad records* was: play fewer records. If people don't like unfamiliar records, then play very few records, and play them very often. Things will get familiar quite fast that way. This approach is known as the tight playlist, and Tom Rounds affirms that "the whole idea of a tight playlist is to make it as familiar as possible."

You may have had an evening like this once, when you just left the radio on, tuned to a Top 40 station pouring out the hits while you studied, or wrote, or whatever. One night I was studying for finals in Boston and the only station available for background was WABC in New York, a typical non-CLEAN Top 40 station so crammed with overlong jingles that it could go on Broadway as an original musical. Here I was, studying non-stop through the night, letting WABC play about the margins of my consciousness, until a depressing thought broke through:

I was hearing exactly the same records, in exactly the same order, as I had heard about 90 minutes earlier. Sure enough, the pattern continued throughout the night, repeating a cycle about an hour and a half long. If I heard "Downtown" by Petula Clark at 2:30, I knew with a dread certainty that I would hear "Downtown" again at 4. If it was followed, at 2:33, by "Love Potion Number Nine," so it would be again at 4:03.

But what I was doing was cheating. The tight playlist is based on the premise that people don't listen to radio for long periods at a time. "Drake told me, the ex-KHJ jock recalls, "that the average listener only listened for 20 minutes at a time—and this is where it's at for 20 minutes."

Top 40 radio has always had a relatively tight playlist—hence the name. Drake cut the list down to the Boss 30, plus between three and six "hitbounds," new records not yet on the sales charts. When your Machine is grinding out so few different pieces of music, deciding what records to play becomes extremely important—to the station, to the musicians, to the record companies. It is the very scarcity of spaces for records on Drake's stations that makes him so influential.

"It stands to reason: If you're playing the 35th worst record in town, and somebody else is playing the 87th worst record in town, you're better off than they are. This is as bad as you can get, but look how bad they can get. That's all it boils down to. The tight list is merely one aspect of the concept"—Drake thinks a great deal in terms of "concepts": placing newscasts at 20 minutes before the hour is the 20–20 News Concept, having "golden" records appear at certain fixed spots in each hour is the Timing Concept—"but it's just that we don't want to bore our audience with losing records. We want to be as right as possible."

Though Drake makes those coy disavowals of his power, he indirectly acknowledges it in this context. "When you go and do this in a town, you see pretty fast that everybody else begins tightening up just a little. If they don't, it gets ridiculous, because they don't have a chance. The problem is that with a tight list you can wind up in worse shape if you don't know what you're doing, because of the number of times a record would get played."

"I would rather have a groovy new Righteous Brothers record played once every two hours than once every eight hours," Drake told me some time ago. "I think the public wants to hear that record. So why play that once in eight hours and play seven other garbage records? They don't care about those others. We want the groovy new records on im-MED-diately. But the thing is that if you have to play 97 bad records in order to come up with two that please your audience, you've done 'em a great disservice. Now, on the other hand, you can play three and come up with one, and I think you're a whole lot better off. That's where it is, it's all percentages."

But beneath the percentages are a well-aged supply of unarticulated assumptions; they are the accumulated heritage of the race of Top 40 concept-makers, and they deserve examination. First, of course, is that fascinating leap of faith Drake makes when he identifies the 35th record in sales with the 35th worst record: sales equal quality. By this very American illogic, "I Am the Walrus" was a much better record the week it was the best-selling single in Los Angeles than the week it was only the eighth-best-selling record in town. Sure enough, as a matter of policy, the top 15 records on the week's list receive more frequent play than the bottom 15. And actually, Drake is not equating sales with quality so much as equating sales with what he presumes his audience, the mass audience, wants to hear. Whoever it was that invented "Your Hit Parade" numberless years ago can see that his simple conceit, presenting the nation's 10 best-selling songs on a weekly program, has blossomed into hundreds of stations which assume that their audiences only *really* want to hear the 30 best-selling records in town.

Second unspoken assumption: that single records are the main barometer of the rock audience's taste. The complex mathematical formula that is superimposed on reports from a rotating group of record stores only tabulates single-record sales; yet singles are to the music business what Moxie is to the soft-drink business—the one-time sales leader that has lost its position.

"We knew at the beginning"—Tom Rounds means the beginning of Drake's reign at KFRC, San Francisco, in the spring of 1966—"that singles were dying out pretty well. Everyone had the feeling that the same audience was buying albums, so we devised a tabulation of album sales. The thing got more and more complicated as time went on, and we kept trying to compensate. Some record stores decided it wasn't worth the trouble to keep track, some of them were bought, we started tabulating requests, and, by the time I left, you practically had to get a goddam computer to run the thing. Top Forty is a complete product of the singles market, and finally now singles are fading."

This is borne out by the indisputable fact that, in some weeks, the singles at the bottom of the Boss 30 are selling very few copies, fewer, in fact, than the number one album may be selling in that period of time.

"Any store's top-selling records would be at least half LP's," says another renegade Top 40 disc jockey. "Then comes the taste factor, which is where they blow it. They say, let's just ignore all that music that people are buying on albums."

"How the hell does Drake know what's commercial?" Skip Taylor explodes, "he's looking at the past, at bygone years. Every record company is in business to sell albums, not singles. Besides, you don't expose an artist with just one piece of work in a gallery—and that's what a single on the radio is like. Albums are a giant part of the scene, and when Drake realizes this, everybody will be better off—not just the people in the industry, but even those people who sit at home and listen to Boss Radio. Drake knows radio and cities front, back, upside down and sideways, but he doesn't know a damn thing about the music." From Taylor's tone, you might gather he has something more than interest in the arts to feed his pique at Drake. He does, and that comes later.

Now Drake, as befits his position and wealth, is far calmer about the whole thing. He's pacing that spongey red carpet, still flaring those nostrils for emphasis, perhaps as compensation for the fact that his upper lip hardly every moves as he talks. His eyes are set wide apart and serve as some sort of benchmark for his face: from the eyes down, the face slowly recedes, ultimately ending up in the slight suggestion of a double chin being born. Those eyes and his rounded cheeks give Drake almost a baby-faced appearance when you look at him straight on, unless he's laughing—in which case he more closely resembles nearly everybody on Cliffie Stone's Hometown Jamboree: his smile is pure Southern country. From a profile, his long hair, the way his heavy lids hood his eyes, and that receding line from the eyes down remind one of the elder statesman of a motorcycle club. Drake paces, hands thrust into the slit front pockets of his beltless blue twill slacks, and he talks about singles and albums, while an assistant murmurs into The Red Phone.

"When you get into a situation of analyzing the thing, there are a lot of artists most of whose album sales are reflected by single hits they've had. There are still so many groups who have so much trouble getting *one more* good cut that's a hit, let alone fill an album. A lot of albums sell without airplay"—this is an answer to the argument that the audience is ahead of the stations, when artists like Country Joe, the Mothers and the Vanilla Fudge have healthy album sales without benefit of a hit single—"talk and comedy albums, how do they sell? But they appeal to a very specific category of people. My design is to play what *most* people want to hear *most* of the time."

Drake interrupts his Benthamite discourse to take the call on The Red Phone. It's from one of his partners, reporting on Drake's Memphis station. "How's the Christmas Wish response?" Drake runs this promotion on every station, write in your Christmas Wish and we'll grant as many as possible; most of them turn out to be the cheapest wishes imaginable, a book or a new record album. Tough luck to all those people who took him at his word and wished for a new car.

"What's the general opinion about the Top 300?" Like the Big 93 and the Mil-yon Dol-lar Weekend, this is one way Drake eases the strain of that tight playlist: he has people vote for their five favorite records, and from the votes he compiles a composite list of 300 favorites, which are played—IN ORDER, he urgently reminds you each half hour—for several days, and given away each hour. With such periodic heavy doses of old records, Drake can take some of the sting out of listening to those same 35 or 36 songs. "How's disc jockey depth?" Drake prides himself on the way he trains new Boss Jocks: into the booth for a month or two, before the station goes on the air, to do a daily three-hour dummy show. Only Drake and his assistants hear these shows; the men are being drilled in the Machine's own manual of arms, with the incentive that this year's job in Fresno can, Drake willing, turn into next year's job in New York or L.A.

He is off The Red Phone and back on albums. "We threw more album cuts in on KFRC in San Francisco, but it hurt us more than it helped us, so we deleted it. It was an honest attempt to find out what people want," and now Drake raises his voice somewhat, and it becomes apparent that all the criticism from people in the record business, all the name-calling from the L.A. *Free Press*, all the barbs from competitors have penetrated that alternatingly serious-and-folksy Georgia façade a bit, "and we don't get credit for that. I'm amazed at how we can do so many things wrong and still do so well."

Third unspoken assumption: Drake's belief that most of the music being recorded and released today is unworthy of airplay because it's bad. When he talks about the eight records out of 300 or 400 a week that "people will care about," he is talking the same language radio people spoke five or six years ago. It may well be that as many rotten singles are being turned out now as then—but then there are all those album cuts; are they hitting that poor a percentage?

Naturally, people connected with performing groups and record companies think not. And obviously Drake thinks that they are indeed, although he is perfectly willing to be forced into playing something rotten (e.g., "Boogaloo Down Broadway," which Drake admits is an "unbelievable piece of garbage") if he sees evidence that the record will sell. But Tom Donahue, who is over there in the basement of the Pasadena Presbyterian Church, waiting to be introduced as the Top 40 refugee who now provides the ultimate antidote to Boss Radio, doesn't buy this theory, nor does Tom Rounds. "The record business," says Rounds, "is much more creative than Top 40 radio is. The record business is opening up all kinds of music, while Top 40 winnows out and selects what *it* thinks is commercial. As a result, there is pressure on groups to get in shape, clean up, get less far out, so they can get played on Top 40 stations. All Drake asks about a record is: Is it commercial? Is it minimal bad taste? Is it minimal tuneout?"

And one more set of assumptions: the twin beliefs that a good record will always get the necessary exposure *somewhere,* if not on Drake's stations, and that no matter how often you play a "stiff" record you can't turn it into a hit. These are really specific applications of proverbial American wisdom: "You can't keep a good man down," and "You can't make a silk purse out of a sow's ear." More to the point, these positions are relentlessly self-justifying. With the jaunty confidence that a good record will always make it to the top somehow, and equipped with the circular argument that you can't bludgeon people into liking a non-hit (circular because, if people are being bludgeoned into liking a non-hit, they buy it, and it is redefined), Drake can bolster his position as a man who knows how to pick records people will like. Because hundreds of craven little program directors follow Drake's every move, hoping to share in his success, a record he ignores they will ignore. Such a record can then safely be defined as a non-hit, for it will probably disappear.

And yet now, just as Drake is tentacling out over the country, reaping the rewards of having taken Top 40 to its cleanest, most streamlined, least irritating level, here is that *huge* man from San Francisco in his black sports jacket, black slacks, black turtleneck, his black-and-gray hair combed back, without benefit of pompadour, curling in behind and under his ears, curling greasily in to hit his collar at almost precisely the same point where Drake's hair hits *his* collar, his black-gray spade-shaped beard bushily scurrying about his face, gnarling out from his ruddy skin. Here is that 39-year-old man, his deep resonant voice hitting a conversational tone two B-flats below middle C, the kind of range bass baritones used to sing, from somewhere inside his 320 pounds, recalling his days in San Francisco working *for* Bill Drake, now relishing the fact that in two cities he is competing against Bill Drake. Here, broadcasting from that Pasadena church basement, all Gothic and ivy-covered on the outside, all modern and soundproofed on the inside, right across the hall from a music room where blond, apple-cheeked young girls obviously on assignment from Norman Rockwell Central Casting are rehearsing religious songs, here is Tom Donahue, sending out raunchy stuff like "Cocaine Blues" that really might corrupt those beautiful little God-fearing 13-year-olds next door if it weren't for that soundproofing. Tom Donahue has a new idea.

"Hell, it's not my idea, man, thousands of people have had it. I'm just fortunate enough to be in a position to put it into practice."

True enough; it probably started out as the idea of Murray Kaufman, still another ex-Top 40 star (for years, Murray the K with his Swingin' Soirée), who wanted a station to reflect the changes in rock music and rock audiences. By October 1966, he had convinced the management of New York's WOR-FM that this was the wave of the future, and for nearly a year Murray and his crew of Top 40 renegades played album cuts, shook up WABC (New York's leading top 40 station), cut the station's expected loss from $300,000 to $50,000, and achieved some successes in the ratings—all this according to Murray.

But that particular wave of the future turned into a riptide when RKO General, owners of the station, made WOR part of the package of all their stations which they turned over to *Bill Drake* last September. "Aaaaarrrghh!" said Murray and his fans, as Drake went about converting WOR-FM into a variant version of the Machine, grinding out a few selected "middle rock" new records and a steady diet of 1950s rock hits, all held together by those CLEAN jingles and those voices bearing compressed warmth. Kaufman is outraged still ("He didn't understand what the hell we were doing. He's playing music that has no meaning to our audience, and these plastic voices with happiness time—New York's too hip, man, audiences don't want to be insulted. I've never seen people angrier; we related to their intelligence. Besides, we ran goldies into the ground in New York in 1963, you can no longer become involved with 'Blue Suede Shoes'"), but Drake keeps his cool even in the face of an unprecedented and virulent attack on him in the music business trade-paper, *Billboard*. "We changed the station to get it into a situation of a salable commodity for a larger audience, and I simply told them to play the greatest rock-and-roll records of all time. We just designed it to fill the void—the rock audience over 18 that Alan Freed created, that wasn't being served by anybody. The station was not making money, and I went in and did what I was supposed to do."

Drake's takeover of WOR-FM led to some authentic radio events: Murray and his fellow jocks quitting publicly, on the air, and giving the reasons why; Rosko, one of the WOR crew, being cheered wildly at a Donovan concert in New York; WNEW-FM abandoning its format of middle-of-the-road and hiring most of the WOR crew (excluding Murray, who has been on bad personal terms with the WNEW people for some time); Drake and WOR being named "Bummer of the Year" in a pop poll conducted by Richard Goldstein in *The Village Voice*.

Before WOR-FM traded the Mothers for the Penguins, Tom Donahue had found a longtime FM engineer in San Francisco who just happened to own an FM stereo station. This was after Donahue had spent two years running a moderately successful record company and a very successful record tip sheet (a publication that reviews records and reassures nervous, mindless program directors that a record they're afraid to be the first to play is already getting requests in Seattle and Denver—a strange but necessary middleman function in this business); and all that, in turn, was after Donahue had left his job as a top rock jock in San Francisco because "we were down to 35 records, and it got pretty damn monotonous."

The station-owner offered Donahue a deal: replace some of the evening foreign-language shows with Donahue's brand of rock. If it succeeded, Donahue could take over the whole schedule. If not, the station would go back to the Serbo-Croatian Top 40.

"I knew," says Donahue, "that FM stereo would be dominant in five years because of everybody's interest in improving sound. Rock record producers are the first people to realize the possibilities of stereo. And this guy had been eating baloney sandwiches for a long time because he believes in FM."

So the former Big Daddy of the Top 40 station on Nob Hill headed for San Francisco's waterfront factory district last April 3, to the studios of WMPX, to follow a Japanese-language program with his own. He was replacing a Chinese-language show, and in San Francisco that's alienating a hell of a lot of people.

But a few months later, Donahue had indeed taken over the station, and success took him and his owner-friend down to Pasadena where the Presbyterian Church was putting its FM station up for sale. Here again, after Donahue assumed the reins, there was stranger company on the air than Alan Freed had ever kept: a set by Bob Dylan would be followed by the voice that, in past years, was speedy Alka-Seltzer, now doing a high-school football play-by-play; Ravi Shankar would come in with the closing theme for the Pasadena Junior Chamber of Commerce's talk show; and people speaking German and French and Swedish hung around for weeks.

This makes it hard on a convert to Donahue's Pasadena station (he was going to change it to KHIP, then decided that "it wasn't hip. It would be like living in the thirties and naming your daughter Trixie—a cute name, but it becomes dated very quickly"). When Drake takes over a station, he cleans out all the cobwebs, and old listeners, by playing two solid months of old records, the Cavalcade of Hits. Then, on one appointed D-Day, the New Boss Jocks, all fitted in their station blazers, appear, the Machine is plugged in, and—as Drake insists each hour—"THE HITS . . . JUST KEEP ON COMIN'!" Aside from the fact that the Cavalcade of Hits often turns out to be more popular than the Machine, Drake makes it easy on his new listeners. A Donahue fan, though, has to make his way past all sorts of strange programs, like navigating around huge schools of weird creatures from the ocean floor to arrive at the promised rock.

Yet this massive father of four, straining all the capacity of a wooden swivel chair to contain his black-garbed bulk, seems happy doing "real underground radio" one story below the rest of the little old lady city, gathering about him a growing number of Top 40 deserters and building his second critical success. He hopes that his stations do moderately well in the occult sweepstakes of the ratings, sufficiently well to allow survival, and he doesn't see that goal as unrealistic. "I'm not trying to do cult radio. I'm not playing music for hippies, especially since I don't know what they are, aside from a creation of the media. We play to a lot of hip people who are still existing and working in a fundamentally straight community. We just think the mass audience has far better taste than most stations do.

"All I hear from broadcasters now is, 'Well, San Francisco is a freak scene, you know, all those hippies, that's why you're making it up there.' We'll click here in Los Angeles, then they'll say, 'Yeah, well, that's the goddam West Coast for you, Aimee Semple McPherson and the Kooks.' But hell, this thing will work in Buffalo and Cleveland as well as in San Francisco."

San Francisco, though, really does define the difference between Drake and Donahue. Donahue's style, and that of his stations, comes from that city, even though he instructs his broadcasters to avoid "pseudo-hippie talk—that's as bad as calling yourself Boss, which went out of the language in 1961." His studio walls are decorated in Late Turned-On Art Student Dormitory Wall style, the air in the control rooms is fragrant with incense, and occasionally Alan Watts's philosophy weaves its way through the music from his Sausalito houseboat. Donahue's Bay Area station became a part of the local music scene, breaking records that the AM stations were afraid to play until requests forced them on ("That's when I stopped playing singles for a while, to avoid the whole series of ego trips, 'Hey, we're breaking records!' ").

But what Donhaue saw as the "most explosive rock scene

in the country," Drake saw as a "myth," built up by publicity, and "magnifying itself basically on fumes." When Drake talks about the money he thinks record companies wasted on San Francisco groups, his voice takes on a serious, indignant tone, protesting the companies' gullibility in a way that suggests he hates to see any part of the music business be less commercially acute than he is. "As far as, you know, a music bag or a movement or anything else, let's face it, there were more hit records cut in Houston, Texas. This thing has been going on up there for a year and a half, and we're getting more and more away from that type of sound, because the mass audience is not ready for it. It may well one day be acceptable to the masses, at which time that's what you want to be doing. But not now."

Drake's complaint against the San Francisco sound is that his station was forced to jump on the bandwagon quite late; now he claims that the music was so far-out that it reduced the total San Francisco rock audience. Ed Mitchell, who was Drake's music director in San Francisco at the time, says the real problem was that Drake "was just no hip to what was happening there, although it was affecting everybody in the city." Mitchell frequented the dance ballrooms, and even when non-Top 40 groups—like the Butterfield Blues Band and John Lee Hooker—were performing, "I kept seeing our audience there. These weren't hippies, these were three or four thousand people from the East Bay, the people we were trying to reach." But Drake, in Bel-Air, was hardly feeling those vibrations: "What if Billy Graham fills the Cow Palace with 15,000 people, does that mean we should all of a sudden program a lot of George Beverly Shea records?"

Drake claims the San Francisco music received plenty of nationwide exposure, enough to allow the records to become hits if they really "had it." Despite the tight playlists on each of his stations, Drake claims that three or four new records a week on each of 11 stations adds up to more "new product" than anybody else is exposing. But Country Joe and the Fish hit #1 on Drake's station in San Francisco with "Sweet Lorraine," yet it was never played on KHJ in Los Angeles. Drake explains:

"This music is pretty much like jazz was: it's groovy, and you have a fantastic hard-core following for it, and it's getting a lot of publicity, and it can be considered a this or a that or an art form or whatever, but there just has not been anywhere near the end results that would justify all that's been said about that particular thing. As far as what *we* want to do, which is to reach the most people—and we don't care what it is, whether it's gospel music, or sitars, or psychedelic, or Patti *Page*—the moment that we do away with some of these irritants, some of the stuff that is, shall we say, a little too, quote, progressive, rock music in general has a bigger share of the total audience. People are going anywhere to avoid this stuff, and yet stations are just trying to be hip and quick and alert and carry the banner, jump up and down and make a lot of noise and get a lot of yeas at just about any street corner, because it's a crusade. People are saying, yeah, well, this is the thing, man. But this becomes an *ego thing*, and if you have the responsibility of trying to please the most people you can't afford yourself that luxury."

When Drake puts down many of the rock-as-art performers as imitators of the Beatles, he may be right; when he says that "99 percent of them don't do it as well," he may be wrong. But when he'd rather play Jay and the Techniques imitating the second-line Motown groups as a ballyhooed World Exclusive, rather than a Beatles imitator, because it's more probable that the mass audience will like that Jay and the Techniques record and therefore like his station for playing it constantly, you have to agree with Donahue and Skip Taylor that Drake is seriously retarding the country's popular music. Especially since Taylor feels he was a witness to a particular act of retardation.

Taylor, and his partner Hartmann, don't like Bill Drake because he's not "really aware of what's happening in the world." Now Taylor and Hartmann had this single record, made by their charges, Chad and Jeremy, and they wanted to get this single record played on the radio so they could all become wealthier and we could enjoy a reasonably good piece of pop music. So they began playing the record for an elaborate chain of people who have closer and closer contacts with Drake, which is presumably the way you gradually expose him to a record, unless you are one of the people who are rumored to be "tight" with him (a substantial number of Drake's ex-employes swear to his honesty, supporting his claim that he won't play a "stiff" record for friends out of concern for the harm an oft-played loser would inflict on his stations; but some people formerly in his operation swear he does it anyway).

"Everybody in Drake's office flipped; they dug the record,"

Hartmann recalls, sitting in his sub-Hollywood apartment-turned-office. "When Drake finally heard it, he said it was a Top 15 record. We offered it to him as an exclusive, but he said it wasn't *good* enough to be an exclusive." Taylor and Hartmann, undaunted, gave it to Drake's major Top 40 rival in Los Angeles, which duly played the record.

"The next day when Drake hears it on KRLA, he goes through the roof," Hartmann reports, relaying the story as he claims to have heard it from Drake's personal secretary, "and he says I will never again play *that* or *any* Chad and Jeremy record."

Well! That's just one of the many stories about records and Bill Drake that flit about Hollywood, sinful little gossip center that it is. Bill Drake won't play the Byrds . . . Bill Drake wouldn't play the Spoonful or the Beach Boys for a while because someone else was offered first crack at the records . . . Bill Drake played "Yes, We Have No Bananas," a little exploitation quickie cashing in on the banana-skin rumors, because its producers provided him with a pirated version of "A Day in the Life" for use as a "KHJ World Exclusive" (exclusives are another holdover irritant: no one but Drake thinks listeners give a damn about them, especially since they are layered with frequent whispered announcements to prevent other stations from taping the record and stealing the glory). Like the smog that hangs over Hollywood, these rumors are pervasive and unavoidable—and impossible either to turn into something tangible or to dissipate. Drake denies them all, bitter record promoters spread them all, and the temptation is to assume that the truth can be found somewhere in between.

Almost everyone except Drake acknowledges some sort of closeness between his stations and Sonny and Cher, the equine-looking epitomes of teeny-togethernessbopping. What isn't clear is how much of this tie-in is make-a-hit-for-personal-friends, and how much is the more traditional Top 40 game, "Please like us for playing your teen idols a lot on our station."

But it is clear that linking his stations with Sonny and Cher is Drake's own choice of symbolism regarding where he wants to be in the world of rock music: on the conservative side of the middle. It represents a hedging of even his own musical taste, since his album collection includes every Jackie Wilson record ever made, as well as the patently commercial performances of the Supremes, Nancy Sinatra, and Johnny Rivers. The kinds of records which get into his periodic broadcast festivals of oldies, like the hit singles included in the special oldie albums his stations heavily promote, are largely the worthless dross of the one-hit groups, works like "Snoopy vs. the Red Baron" and "Yellow Balloon." Yet Drake makes that ever-cautious attempt to strike a balance, to offer a slight appeal to everyone—the cover of that special album containing those hopeless songs is festooned with "hippie" symbols, peace trademarks dancing around a psychedelically distorted girl's face, her mouth cavity replaced by the word "LOVE" in shimmering letters. And Drake's San Francisco and Los Angeles stations at one time broadcasted the most radical religious program ever put on radio, "The Transcendental, Ever-Changing, Multi-Lingual Two-Ton Mustard Seed"; the program blended sound collages, rock music, and essentially Oriental religious insights into a Sunday half-hour that was widely listened to, until complaints against a Fugs record that began a "Mustard Seed" program resulted in cancellation of the experiment.

Politically, Drake tries to play an equally balanced game with his stations. Though LA Provos sometimes picket the local station for being owned by a company that does defense work, Drake's stations have been scrupulously fair in news coverage. He claims to have received more listener heat for playing "Universal Soldier" and "There But for Fortune" back in 1965 when rock folked, than for playing "Letter to My Teen-Aged Son" every two hours last fall. Personally, he hesitates even to say where he stands, only allowing as how he agrees with parts of "Letter to My Teen-Aged Son" and disagrees with parts. And since the record assumes three different political positions in the course of three minutes, Drake characteristically admits to a point of view almost everyone can agree with.

He likes to talk a lot about his objectivity in picking records for his stations (officially, Drake merely recommends records; and officially, Vietnam is not a war). But objectivity in picking records just isn't that appropriate or desirable. "If every program director were totally objective," says Tom Rounds who isn't, "there'd be a lot more Monkee crap on the air."

What Drake really means by objectivity is compulsive personal caution combined with the opinions of assistants trained to be as cautious as he is. "If you listen, really listen, you can tell generally if a record has it, particularly if you have the proper people involved and everybody has a feel for a *sound,* and you're also watching very carefully for trends and this and that and the other, and you watch the trades and the tip sheets." And, like a man who thinks there must be something wrong with a club that would accept him for membership, each person on this committee is expected to compensate *against* his own musical taste. "I'm more critical of, say, a record in the Phil Spector or Righteous Brothers bag," Drake will explain, "because I personally *freak out* for that sort of stuff. So when a record comes in with this style and I immediately say 'Yeah!', then I overcompensate by trying to be as objective as possible about it, because you kid yourself a lot."

But now, as Los Angeles, already the pop Vatican, becomes the battleground for the two contending ideologies of rock radio, the appropriate question might well be, "Who's kidding whom?"

"The believability of Top 40 depends on its exclusivity with its audience." Tom Rounds is now explaining the potential decline and fall of Bill Drake. "If KHJ plays a record, there's no doubt that it's a hit, *because they're playing it.* This is the image that Top 40 constantly seeks. But the flaws start appearing when another commodity, like Donahue, appears and says this is all bullshit."

And Donahue, having appeared and having survived for a year, is on his way out of that church, a location that added inaudibility and inconvenience to incongruity. The station is juicing up to its full 50,000 watts and will broadcast in stereo, and then the battle for men's ears begins in earnest.

Donahue's side will benefit from some locally prominent disc jockeys who have taken substantial salary cuts to leave Top 40. He's got to gain some listeners, for example, who are curious to hear how B. Mitchell Reed, one of radio's original forty-words-a-second freaks, sounds when he talks like a real person. On the other hand, Donahue's people have been accused of sounding asleep—or stoned—on the air. The Real Don Steele, who talks as fast off the air as on, only in a lower key and punctuating with chop-the-air hand gestures, calls this relaxed approach the "nod-out, roach-holder bullshit. Ten years ago it was called 'Be adult,' now it's called 'Be hip.' "

"Hell, man," chimes in another Drake jock, Bobby Tripp,

"they're all goddam HEADS, they're all so stoned they don't know what's goin' on anyway. They don't give the time on that station because goddam HEADS don't make appointments *any*way, so they don't need to know what time it is, and even if they *do* make appointments, they're always late, so what the HELL's the difference?" But at least Donahue's men don't sound like displaced speed freaks, and Donahue claims that his stations are free of the "veiled allusions to narcotics that are rampant down here, usually some dip doing psychedelic babble."

Top 40 has survived as long as it has on a dual manipulation, of the music and of the audience. As long as singing groups appeared with the speed and surprise of an overnight acne attack, and disappeared just as quickly, the stations were in control: they were the authoritative arbiters of tastes and trends, and the audiences followed where they led. This was when, in the words of Tom Rounds, Top 40 was "a definitive source of material, really a cultural statement, like a television documentary in the sense that it defined what you were. It provided canned insight, canned identity, better than a kid could answer for himself. It was the most tangible way of relating to the scene; it could tune one in all over the country, always there, like a big blanket. The overwhelming truth, of course, is that Top 40 is shallow and plastic, one huge promotion. American culture has now gotten so that you can't channel a particular audience in a particular direction any more."

For one thing, the Beatles and Bob Dylan and the Rolling Stones and Van Dyke Parks have shown how creative musicians can lead the audience miles past the point where the men in Top 40 feel comfortably in control. That Donahue feels comfortable operating at that new point, without being in control, is a healthy sign.

"I think Drake is on a McLuhan trip," Donahue muses. "He wants to build background radio." God knows whether Drake has ever read McLuhan; even if he hasn't, he may well continue to manipulate the mass audience in the CLEANEST style Top 40 has ever known, maintaining all the while that the amorphous mass manipulates *him:* "I'd say to a program director who runs around to all the clubs or around on the Strip and says the hippies are taking over, 'Sober up, go to a hot dog joint, look at the people there and think about it. How many of them go to stupid movies, how many of them go to church, how many of them watch Beverly Hillbillies?' There are so damn many different kinds of people, and the only reason they should give a damn about you is if you do something they like."

But while Drake is deciding what the percentages indicate they like, the hard-to-ignore figure of Donahue will always be lurking, on the other side of the radio, on the other side of town, casting an ironic glance towards Bel-Air from Pasadena, re-doing commercials to resemble "posters on radio" instead of broadcasting Top 40's strident hymns to blemish removal. "We will be," says Ed Mitchell, who dropped out of Drake radio to drop into Donahue's style, "hipping people to the subtleties of rock, and not giving a damn whether people can buy it or not, just whether it's *good music.*"

WAITING FOR MORRISON

●

JOAN DIDION

It is six, seven o'clock of an early spring evening, and I'm sitting on the cold vinyl-tile floor of a sound studio on Sunset Boulevard, watching a rock group called The Doors record a rhythm track. On the whole my attention is less than entirely engaged by the preoccupations of rock groups (I have already heard about acid as a transitional stage and also about the Maharishi and even about universal love, and after a while it all sounds like marmalade skies to me), but The Doors are different, The Doors interest me. They have nothing in common with the gentle Beatles. They lack the contemporary conviction that love is brotherhood and the *Kama Sutra*. Their music insists that love is sex and sex is death and therein lies salvation. The Doors are the Norman Mailers of the Top 40, missionaries of apocalyptic sex. "Break On Through," their lyrics urge, and "Light My Fire," and—

> *Come on baby, gonna take a little ride*
> *Goin' down by the ocean side*
> *Gonna get real close*
> *Get real tight*
> *Baby gonna drown tonight—*
> *Goin' down, down, down.**

This is an odd neo-Wagnerian premise for a rock group, yes, but it has given The Doors three gold records in less than a year, and it makes them $10,000 to $12,000 a concert against a percentage of the gross, and right now they are gathered together in uneasy symbiosis to make their third album, and the studio is cold and the lights are too bright and there are masses of wires and banks of the ominous blinking electronic circuitry with which the new musicians live so casually. There are three of the four Doors. There is a bass player borrowed from a group called Clear Light. There are the producer and the engineer and the road manager and a couple of girls and a Siberian Husky named Nikki with one gray eye and one gold. There are paper bags half filled with hard-boiled eggs and chicken livers and cheeseburgers and empty bottles of apple juice and California *rosé*. There is everything and everybody The Doors need to cut the rest of this third album except one thing, the fourth Door, the lead singer, Jim Morrison, a twenty-four-year-old graduate of U.C.L.A., who wears black vinyl pants and no underwear and tends to suggest some range of the possible just beyond a suicide pact. It is Morrison who describes The Doors as "erotic politicians." It is Morrison who defines the group's interests as "anything about revolt, disorder, chaos about activity that appears to have no meaning." It is Morrison who got arrested in New Haven in December for giving an "indecent" performance. It is Morrison who writes most of The Doors' lyrics, the peculiar character of which is to reflect either an ambiguous paranoia or a quite unambiguous insistence upon love-death as the ultimate high. And it is Morrison who is missing. It is Ray Manzarek and Robby Krieger and John Densmore who make The Doors sound the way they do, and maybe it is Manzarek and Krieger and Densmore who make seventeen out of twenty interviewees on *American Bandstand* prefer The Doors over all other groups, but it is Morrison who gets up there in his black vinyl pants with no underwear and projects the idea, and it is Morrison they are waiting for now.

"Hey listen," the engineer says. "I was listening to an FM station on the way over here, they played three Doors songs, first they played 'Back Door Man' and then 'Love Me Two Times' and 'Light My Fire.'"

"I heard it," Densmore mutters. "I heard it."

"So what's wrong with somebody playing three of your songs?"

"This cat dedicates it to his family."

"Yeah? To his family?"

"To his family. Really crass. We're not a family outfit."

Ray Manzarek is hunched over a Gibson keyboard. "You think *Morrison's* gonna come back?" he says to no one in particular.

No one answers.

"So we can do some vocals?" Manzarek says.

The producer is working with the tape of the rhythm track they just recorded. "I hope so," he says without looking up.

"Yeh," Manzarek says. "So do I."

My leg has gone to sleep, but I do not stand up; unspecific tensions seem to be rendering everyone in the room catatonic. The producer plays back the rhythm track. The engineer says that he wants to do his deep-breathing exercises. Manzarek eats a hard-boiled egg. "Tennyson made a mantra out of his own name," he says to the engineer. "I don't know if he said 'Tennyson Tennyson Tennyson' or 'Alfred Alfred Alfred' or 'Alfred Lord Tennyson,' but anyway, he did it. Maybe he just said 'Lord Lord Lord.' "

"Groovy," the Clear Light bass player says. He is an amiable enthusiast, not at all a Door in spirit.

"I wonder what Blake said," Manzarek muses. "Too bad Morrison's not here. *Morrison* would know."

It is a long while later. Morrison arrives. He has on his black vinyl pants, and he sits down on a leather couch in front of the four big blank speakers, and he closes his eyes. The curious aspect of Morrison's arrival is this: No one acknowledges it by so much as a flicker of an eye. Robby Krieger continues working out a guitar passage. John Densmore tunes his drums. Manzarek sits at the control console and twirls a corkscrew and lets a girl rub his shoulders. The girl does not look at Morrison, although he is in her direct line of sight. An hour or so passes, and still no one has spoken to Morrison. Then Morrison speaks to Manzarek. He speaks almost in a whisper, as if he were wresting the words from behind some disabling aphasia.

"It's an hour to West Covina," he says. "I was thinking, maybe we should spend the night out there after we play."

Manzarek puts down the corkscrew. "Why?" he says.

"Instead of coming back."

Manzarek shrugs. "We were planning to come back."

"Well, I was thinking, we could rehearse out there."

Manzarek says nothing.

"We could get in a rehearsal, there's a Holiday Inn next door."

"We could do that," Manzarek says. "Or we could rehearse Sunday, in town."

"I guess so." Morrison pauses. "Will the place be ready to rehearse Sunday?"

Manzarek looks at him for a while. "No," he says then.

I count the control knobs on the electronic console. There

are seventy-six. I am unsure in whose favor the dialogue was resolved, or if it was resolved at all. Robby Krieger picks at his guitar, and says that he needs a fuzz box. The producer suggests that he borrow one from the Buffalo Springfield in the next studio. Krieger shrugs. Morrison sits down on the leather couch again and leans back. He lights a match. He studies the flame a while and then very slowly, very deliberately, lowers it to the fly of his black vinyl pants. Manzarek watches him. The girl who is rubbing Manzarek's shoulders does not look at anyone. There is a sense that no one is going to leave the room, ever. It will be some weeks before the Doors finish recording this album. I do not see it through.

ABOUT THE EDITOR

JONATHAN EISEN is associate editor of *Commonweal* magazine. He was a founder of *The Activist* at Antioch College, and is co-editor, with Dennis Hale, of *The California Dream.* Mr. Eisen is a frequent contributor to magazines and periodicals.